Liberalization and its Consequences

Liberalization and its Consequences

A Comparative Perspective on Latin America and Eastern Europe

Edited by

Werner Baer and Joseph L. Love

University of Illinois, Urbana-Champaign, USA

Edward Elgar

Cheltenham, UK • Northampton, MA, USA

Published by
Edward Elgar Publishing Limited
Glensanda House
Montpellier Parade
Cheltenham
Glos GL50 1UA
UK

Edward Elgar Publishing, Inc.
136 West Street
Suite 202
Northampton
Massachusetts 01060
USA

A catalogue record for this book is available from the British Library

Library of Congress Cataloging in Publication Data

Liberalization and its consequences : a comparative perspective on Latin America and Eastern Europe / [edited by] Werner Baer and Joseph L. Love.
1. Europe, Eastern—Economic conditions—1989—Congresses. 2. Europe, Eastern—Economic policy—1989—Congresses. 3. Latin America—Economic conditions—1982—Congresses. 4. Latin America—Economic policy—Congresses. 5. Privatization—Latin America—Congresses. 6. Democratization—Europe, Eastern—Congresses. 7. Democratization—Latin America—Congresses. I. Baer, Werner, 1931– II. Love, Joseph LeRoy.

HC244 L469 2001
338.947—dc21

00–037622

ISBN 1 84064 436 2
Printed and bound in Great Britain by MPG Books Ltd, Bodmin, Cornwall

Contents

Figures

Tables

Participants

The following people participated in the conference that resulted in this volume:

Lee Alston, University of Illinois and National Bureau of Economic Research
Edmund Amann, Centre for Brazilian Studies, University of Oxford
Mary Arends-Kuenning, University of Illinois
Werner Baer, University of Illinois
Josef Brada, Arizona State University
Thomas Brockmeier, Philipps Universitaet, Marburg, Germany
Victor Bulmer-Thomas, Institute of Latin American Studies, University of London
Daniel Chirot, University of Washington, Seattle
Donald Coes, University of New Mexico
Jack Edwards, Cummins Engine Company
Hadi Esfahani, University of Illinois
Eduardo Fernández Delgado, former Deputy Finance Minister, Colombia
Albert Fishlow, Violy, Byorum & Partners Holding, and Yale University
Marshall Goldman, Wellesley College and Harvard Univesity
David Good, University of Minnesota
Lawrence Graham, University of Texas at Austin
Béla Greskovits, Central European University, Budapest, Hungary
Anthony Hall, London School of Economics and Political Science
Geoffrey Hewings, University of Illinois
Marcos Holanda, Federal University of Ceará, Brazil
Nils Jacobsen, University of Illinois
Jacek Kochanowicz, University of Warsaw
Diane Koenker, University of Illinois
Alexander Kozhemiakin, Putnam Investments, Boston, MA
John Lampe, University of Maryland
Carol Leff, University of Illinois
Joseph Love, University of Illinois
William Maloney, The World Bank
Alessandro Merli, Il Sole-24 Ore, London and Milan
Geraldo Munck, University of Illinois
Larry Neal, University of Illinois

Rachel Schurman, University of Illinois
Richard Snyder, University of Illinois
John Welch, Barclays Capital, New York
Laurence Whitehead, Nuffield College, University of Oxford

1. Introduction

Joseph L. Love and Werner Baer

During the last decade of the 20th century profound winds of change have swept through Eastern Europe and Latin America. The dramatic political and economic reforms instituted in these regions, including multi-party elections, privatization, dismantling of protective barriers, and openness to foreign capital and ideas, have been transforming everyday life. Democracies have replaced authoritarian regimes, and market-driven open economies have replaced closed and state-dominated ones.

The failures of communism in the former Soviet bloc as an economic and political system, and the economic failures of both authoritarian military and populist regimes in Latin America, combined with pressures from Western governments, banks and international lending agencies, prompted deep structural reforms of a political and economic nature. In Eastern Europe (including Russia), the adoption of market-oriented policies, privatization, democracy, and the de-emphasis on social safety nets has created new societies with widely varying degrees of success in producing growth and efficiency, while simultaneously introducing striking new inequalities.

In Latin America, the limits of import-substitution industrialization, an exaggerated presence of the state in the economy, and the failure of macro-populism, were accompanied by a fiscal impasse resulting from a dissensus about who would pay for the massive investments in infrastructure needed to cope with rapid industrialization and urbanization. These intersecting problems resulted in inefficiency, waste, and in many cases runaway inflation.

In both Eastern Europe and Latin America, one of the goals of the new market-oriented policies in the 1990s was to reduce inefficiency and thereby spur long-term economic growth. Although there have been some successes and many failures from the efficiency/growth point of view in both regions, it is still far from clear whether the new institutional arrangements and policies will redress or worsen social inequities in the long run.

The events of the 1990s have raised important questions for social scientists working in both geographical areas. In the case of Latin America, these include:

1. Why did the market paradigm prevail over populism?

2. Populism and the large presence of the state in Latin American economies were supposed to redress many of the inequities inherited from a previous era, when the private sector and foreign capital were given many freedoms and privileges. Why did this not occur? To what extent does market-oriented neo-liberalism in the 1990s differ from the liberalism of previous eras? Can a privatized market economy result in both growth and greater social equity?
3. What lessons from previous periods of market-oriented policies might be useful in the present era?
4. Do such phenomena as the Chiapas revolt in 1994, the rise of the Movement of the Landless (MST) in Brazil in the second half of the 1990s, the widespread use of armed retainers in Colombia, and the appearance of a populist authoritarian leader (President Hugo Chávez) in Venezuela in 1999 augur a bleak future for neo-liberalism?
5. Are there any serious efforts at developing viable alternatives to market-oriented systems on the horizon?

A similar set of questions arise when considering East European countries:

1. With the collapse of communism, the adoption of a system of market economies, privatization, the decline of traditional socialist safety nets, and the establishment of democracy, what sort of economic and political systems are emerging?
2. How much inequality can the new systems arising in Eastern Europe tolerate?
3. Are there significant differences between the older generations (without skills or time to adapt to the new system) and the younger generations? In other words, is the problem primarily one of generations?
4. Are former communist *apparatchiki* on their way to becoming well-connected business tycoons, similar to the tycoons of Latin America, who often accumulated large fortunes through special political connections?
5. To what extent does political instability or insecurity affect the short and long-term decisions of firms?

There are additional questions which relate to both geographical regions. How do the institutions and practices preceding the advent of neo-liberalism determine the process of economic reform? What is the relationship between political and economic reforms? Why were neo-liberalizers being re-elected in some parts of Latin America (in spite of the high social costs of their actions), while in Eastern European countries they have often been voted out of office?

But the issues are not explicable only in terms of post-1989 or even post-1945 processes. The fact that, in broad terms, the relative rank of national per-capita incomes within both world regions was roughly the same on the eve of World War II as in 1999, implies that longer-term historical processes need to be considered. Such issues as state intervention vs *laissez-faire* and the ideologies that support such positions have deep historical roots relevant to current problems. Despite some striking similarities between the two regions on these matters, rarely have they been studied comparatively.[1]

The transformation of the economic systems of Eastern Europe after 1989 is obviously a more drastic process than the contemporaneous liberalization of the Latin American economies, but the processes are related, because prescriptions prepared for Latin America were applied in Eastern Europe. The Soviet regime and its satellites failed because they could not solve three fundamental problems: The first – and most important – was the long-term effect of poor material incentives for high-quality work, owing in part to limits on wage differentials, and in part to an economic system that assigned low penalties to sloppy work, rent-seeking behavior, and shirking. The second was the inability of the command economy to establish an efficient and dynamic system of relative prices; in fact 'shadow' prices of analogous Western goods were often employed. A third underlying factor in the crisis of the 1980s was the secrecy characteristic of the Soviet political system. This policy impeded the diffusion of new techniques across the economy, relative to the technologically-induced efficiency gains of the post-1945 economies of Western Europe, the United States, and Japan.

Latin America's problems were grave enough, but of a different order. There government bureaucracies were often bloated, transparency was minimal, and the state was viewed as a patrimonial entity by politicians and citizens. In the more economically advanced countries, such as Juan Perón's Argentina and Getúlio Vargas's Brazil, macroeconomic populism in the 1950s and later had swollen the size of the state, and had discriminated against traditional export industries to benefit industrialists and workers. Such policies extended into the 1970s, if we classify the Socialist Salvador Allende (President of Chile, 1970–73) as a populist.

Furthermore, external debt was accumulated at low interest rates in the 1970s, owing to the recycling of 'petrodollars' after 1973. With the drastic increase in US interest rates in 1979–80 resulting in a similar increase in world interest rates, there was a sharp spike in the cost of borrowing by Latin American countries and in the servicing of their external debt. The decade-long stagnation of the region in the 1980s, accompanied by the collapse of the Soviet Union and the consequent monopolar power of the United States, gave a hitherto unprecedented authority to the coordinated action of the Treasury Department, the IMF, and the World Bank. At the end of the decade, Chile's impressive performance under the free-enterprise regime of General Augusto Pinochet gave a new prestige to liberalization policies within Latin America and elsewhere.

The 'Washington Consensus,' a term coined in 1990 by the economist John Williamson, summed up the views of economists and officials at the IMF, the World Bank, the US government, and Williamson's Institute for International Economics. This ten-point program emphasized privatization, fiscal discipline, tax reform, freeing the market from constraints in trade policy and interest and exchange rates, and strengthening property rights for domestic and foreign investors. These were the marching orders for Latin American policymakers throughout the 1990s.

But these remedies were also formulated at the time of the collapse of the Warsaw Pact economies, and were applied as *prêt-à-porter* solutions for the 'transition economies' of Eastern Europe. According to a Polish expert, Grzegorz Kolodko, such recommendations did not include all the crucial elements for the proper reordering of the East European economies. These essentials were 'institution-building, improvement of corporate governance of the state sector prior to privatization, and [redesigning] the role of the state,' rather than simply shrinking its presence in the economy. Partly as a result of the insufficiency of the one-size-fits-all reform program, the former Comecon countries lost a quarter of their combined GDPs between 1990 and 1998. In Kolodko's opinion, 'A lack of institutional development turned out to be the missing element in transition policies based on the Washington consensus. Instead of sustained growth, liberalization, and privatization without a well-organized market structure led to extended contraction.'[2]

To grapple with some of these questions, the editors, with the support of the University of Illinois,[3] commissioned twelve papers from internationally-known experts on Latin America and Eastern Europe. They represented five disciplines – economics, political economy, history, sociology, and political science. Their essays were presented at a conference at the University of Illinois, Urbana-Champaign, on April 23–24, 1999. In addition, other specialists on Eastern Europe and Latin America from a variety of institutions were invited to comment.[4] This volume contains the revised versions of the papers presented, as well as some of the commentators' remarks.

Two of the chapters offer a historical perspective on the neo-liberal policies of the 1990s. Victor Bulmer-Thomas finds that in the twentieth century, the performance of most Latin American economies was generally poor, when defined in terms of closing the gap in GDP per capita between them and the United States. He argues that over the century the oligarchic state gave way to the bureaucratic state, which was often the captive of its employees, resulting in an inefficient allocation of resources; moreover, the rule of law in the economic sphere was often weak. Although in most countries the state did not contribute to equity through land reform, its actions accelerated the transition to modern capitalist agriculture. The state also did little to improve labor productivity and real wages. Its policies of protection resulted in an absence of competitive markets, reducing pressure on firms to innovate.

Bulmer-Thomas notes that despite Latin America's unequal income distribution, it has traditionally experienced low savings rates, but this situation was partially offset by the state's role in maintaining overall investment. Thus, with the retreat of the state in the 1990s, the reliance on the private sector to carry most of the burden of investment implies the need for access to international capital markets through bond issues, and points up the crucial role of bank borrowing and equity investment in future growth. This also means that the state should seek to implement policies which minimize the foreign perception of risk in the country at issue. In the new era of neo-liberalism, globalization has placed constraints on the state's freedom to maneuver.

In the second historical chapter, David Good calls attention to the century-old lag of Russia and Eastern Europe behind the West, and shows how this has preoccupied successive generations in the region. His statistical analysis leads him to conclude that the slow growth in the two decades prior to 1989 cannot be wholly attributed to the nature of the institutions which prevailed under communism. Nor does he find that a center-periphery type of analysis accounts for historically slow growth rates. The region grew rapidly as an exporter of primary goods prior to World War I, while a poorer growth performance occurred with the closing of the economy in the inter-war period. This trend continued into the period of state socialism. The basic reason for the relatively poor growth performance over most of the 20th century, Good holds, was the relative isolation of Central and Eastern Europe from the full force of the commercial revolution centuries ago, so that '... the region entered the modern era not only at low levels of socioeconomic development, but also . . . with relatively weak state structures . . . [And the latter] . . . proved to be highly vulnerable to the shocks of war and depression that characterized the twentieth century.'

Josef Brada's chapter follows, concentrating on the economics and politics of the transition in Eastern Europe. In his view, part of the initial decline in output after 1989 may owe to the stabilization programs which accompanied the transition, while part may have been due to the 'premature abandonment of central planning' and what he sees as the unsuccessful efforts to replace it with market mechanisms. The latter did not function well in the absence of adequate institutional and legal underpinnings.

Brada notes that during the early transition years in many East European countries the decline in consumption was less than the fall in investments, which may account for the relative social tranquility during this period. In addition, he points to the stagnation which preceded the decade prior to the transition, making the initial low growth rates in the new market economies more acceptable to the population. He further explains the lack of social unrest by the fact that, by the second half of the 1990s, consumption was higher than earlier in the decade for a number of countries.

Brada considers the political process involved in the transition to be as important, if not more so, than the economic transformation. The yearning for new political systems and human freedoms, and for new links to Western societies were such as to more than counterbalance significant economic sacrifices in the eyes of the respective populations. However, Brada also calls attention to those former communist counties where so-called reforms ('pseudo-liberalization') were designed to generate rents for various types of political, ethnic or economic élites. He calls these 'kleptocratic states' which are dominated by single parties or individual politicians. He concludes that transition strategies are determined by a number of variables, including economic, cultural and historical backgrounds.

Laurence Whitehead's chapter concentrates on the privatization aspects of neo-liberal policies in Latin America. He points out the complexity of issues surrounding the privatization of public utilities, such as the telecommunications companies. He shows how difficult it is to introduce competition and to obtain optimum market results through regulation, how concessions can be manipulated for political purposes, and how the judiciary can get involved in quasi-regulatory matters even though its members do not have the training to specify how an economy can be made to function more efficiently.

Whitehead also points out that privatization programs were far from uniform in Latin America. He illustrates this by contrasting the 'root-and-branch' approach of Chile, the incrementalist approach of Brazil and the opportunist approach of Venezuela. He then considers various alternative theories which could explain the upsurge in Latin America's privatization process, ranging from the power of those who share the Washington consensus to alternating cycles of statism and liberalism, and 'catch-up' theories. He concludes on a speculative note, considering that reversals from the neo-liberal trend might occur if the legal system is not strong enough to support the demands of a market economy, or if rising social inequalities were to remain unaddressed.

Marshall Goldman's chapter deals with the phenomenon of the post-communist Russian oligarchs. The fact that a communist system was implanted when a market economy was still embryonic at the time of the 1917 revolution and endured for 70 years was bound to result in a transition process which would be quite different from that taking place in countries '... with a market infrastructure already in place, partly in place, or in place at one time but now dormant.' Therefore, when the communist system collapsed and privatization was introduced, there were '... no meaningful or operational price system, wholesalers, marketers, labor markets, commercial codes, or civil court procedures.' As a result, Russian privatization perhaps uniquely made it possible for a small number of oligarchs to buy state properties at a fraction of their true worth.

Goldman identifies three categories of oligarchs which emerged: the factory directors, former members of the communist *nomenklatura*, and outsiders. The last-named were considered outside the law under the communist system, many belonging to ethnic minorities. Goldman provides a number of examples of each group. He makes it clear that the oligarchs of the first two groups were not like the US robber barons of the late nineteenth century. The latter constructed their empires by building steel mills, railroads and refineries, while the Russian oligarchs '... simply purloined what previously belonged to the state.' Goldman concludes from the Russian experience that private ownership is not necessarily preferable to state ownership, especially when it takes place in a society where no market and regulatory infrastructure exists.

The chapter by sociologist Anthony Hall concentrates on another aspect of neo-liberalism in Latin America, namely the privatization of nature, or '... the gradual appropriation or indirect privatization and enclosure of rural common property,' which has occurred especially in the Andean highlands and the Amazon basin. In most of the area of the Amazon he surveys, private property ownership had been relatively rare, while over generations collective resource governance had been developed by the users as a way of managing fragile ecosystems. Hall takes as a main theme the indirect privatization of land and natural resources in the Brazilian Amazon region, where since the 1960s governments have encouraged settlement for economic, social and strategic reasons. Through various types of incentives, investments by large groups has been encouraged, especially in cattle ranching. Such holdings encroached on small farmers, as well as native Americans, causing violent conflicts over the control of land and an acceleration of the deforestation of the region. In the cases of Ecuador and Peru, Hall shows how the exploitation of oil and gas production in the respective Amazon region of these countries has also contributed to environmental degradation and has threatened the livelihood of indigenous peoples. The author notes that after decades of passive acceptance of these trends, new social movements arose in the 1990s to resist encroachment by outsiders. He presents three case studies, indicating how countervailing forces, in the form of grassroots organizations, have counteracted unchecked privatization and its negative environmental impact.

In a case study of Brazil, political scientist Lawrence Graham considers the recent experience of that country in the context of an ensemble of Latin American nations undergoing economic and political reform, showing the dilemmas Brazil faces in attempting to combine democratic initiatives and orthodox structural adjustment policies. The first administration of Fernando Henrique Cardoso provides an instructive case study of successful 'reform-mongering' in the context of the globalization of the 1990s. Yet his second administration raises serious questions about the ability of democratically elected presidents without disciplined congressional majorities to sustain reform into a second term. Devaluation in early 1999, the President's diminishing control of the government coalition in Congress, and the reliance on markets to produce further economic restructuring have severely limited Cardoso's capacity to make coherent policy. Although there is a danger that protests by those hurt by market reforms will bring social policy issues to the fore, current trends suggest that a strategy combining decentralization, international support, and commitment to engaging groups in civil society may create sufficient space within the Brazilian system to head off a revolt by voters. If so, Brazil may avoid the fate of Peru and Venezuela, nations where the populace rejected established parties and supported broad presidential powers to thwart market-determined outcomes.

In another case study – this one in Eastern Europe – Daniel Chirot offers a sociologist's perspective on the problems of Romania, a relatively backward East European nation. Chirot argues how little we can understand the problems of economic and social backwardness without an appreciation of local history. He seeks to identify the roots of Romania's underdevelopment, pointing to Orthodox religious tradition, persistent or recurring land tenure patterns in an overwhelmingly peasant society, and a historically truncated experience with capitalist industrialization before 1945. Chirot is 'guardedly pessimistic' about Romanian development, for at least the next generation. Worse yet, for those who seek the rapid transformation of Eastern Europe, is the realization that Romania had a less negative growth experience for 1990–97 than the majority of the countries in the region composed of East Central Europe and the former USSR.[5]

The political scientist Béla Greskovits examines the post-1989 performance of his native Hungary in another country study. Hungary offers a story of relative success, in part because of the fact that the transition to capitalism began well before 1989, in the country's experiment with 'market socialism'. Hungary also had the 'negative' advantage of not having to build a new nation or even a new state (unlike many CIS nations and those of ex-Yugoslavia), since the old state underwent a sweeping transformation. Nonetheless, as measured in GDP per capita (at purchasing power parity), Hungary was well behind Chile, Argentina, and even trailed Mexico in 1997.

Politically, too, Hungary's story was one of qualified success. The post-1989 governments took advantage of the demobilizing policies of the old regime, and this fact, combined with a relatively egalitarian distribution of income, tended to hold collective action in check for the first decade after communism. In the process, the new capitalist democracy had the additional advantage of a relatively good performance of state-operated enterprises. The government and the dominant political parties, together with other strategic élites, managed to create winners in the new system while neutralizing losers. But the political process still excluded the majority of the population, and the informal economy became the social safety net of the poor: as much as one-third of the Hungarian population retreated into, or remained in, the informal sector.

In his chapter, economist Jacek Kochanowicz offers a broad synthesis of the first decade of the Eastern European transition. He characterizes the economic experience in Eastern Europe between 1945 and 1989, not as underdevelopment, as in Latin America, but 'misdevelopment': Economies were overindustrialized, based on outmoded and static technologies. In surveying the contemporary scene, the writer sees a pattern of increasing differentiation, with three broad trends – political and economic convergence with the West, divergence, and drift. East Central Europe, plus Estonia, constitutes the first group; Russia, Belarus, and Ukraine, the second; and Bulgaria, Moldova, and Romania the third. While expressing some optimism about the chances of the first group, Kochanowicz points out that the road leading to Western prosperity is still a rocky one, and points to sharpened disparities in income and wealth across the whole region. Institution-building is still needed everywhere, including a broad acceptance of capitalist 'rules of the game.'

The differentiation of the three groups of countries leads the author to ask: why is the first group apparently on the road to high per capita incomes and integration with the West? Was it just because of good policies? Good policies, plus strong and skillful leaders? Blind luck? Like Chirot, Kochanowicz argues that the ultimate causes lie deep in the past, that 'history matters.' Exposure to Western ideologies, religion, and outlooks was much more extensive in Poland, Hungary, and the Czech Republic, and this centuries-long experience gave those nations advantages in playing what is still a Western game. Nevertheless, following the development theorist Alexander Gerschenkron, Kochanowicz allows for the possibility of successful adaptations of local practices and the development of new institutions to shorten the path to modernity.

Like Kochanowicz on Eastern Europe, economist Albert Fishlow considers the present and possible future of his area of expertise, Latin America. Fishlow finds that for the neo-liberal economic model to be effective, Latin American countries will have to retain as their centerpiece: a low rate of inflation, the state as a regulator rather than as manager, and openness to trade. His message is to hold steady to the course already begun. Fishlow notes that the new model may make it easier for the region to increase its rate of savings, which has been traditionally low because of the governments' propensity to dissave.

His discussion of the Latin American privatization process dwells especially on the opportunities and possible pitfalls in regulating the recently privatized public utilities, and he concludes that the '… test of the new capitalism will be the ability to combine the initiative of investors with the constraint of public regulation.' Furthermore, Fishlow points to the link between the opening of

Latin America to international trade and the achievement of a permanently stabilized economy. He points to the fact that it was easier at first to increase imports which were financed to a large extent by capital inflow, while exports have grown at a modest rate. The coming challenge is for the region to achieve a substantial increase in its non-traditional exports.

In a chapter rich in wide-ranging comparisons and imaginative speculations, Fishlow points out that beyond implementing the painful short- and middle-term measures resulting from a shrunken public sector and adjustments to the international economy, an essential feature in a successful reform program is institutional change, a problem for the medium and long term for both the state and private economic actors.

The final chapter, by economist Lee Alston attempts to integrate the chapters, showing the centrality of successful political economy in achieving reform. He emphasizes that the perceptions of, and expectations about, economic performance are as important as the performance itself in keeping reform on track. Alston sees the issue of legitimacy at the fore of the political process, until such time as broad consensus is achieved on social and economic goals, and requisite institutions have been reconfigured or created *ex nihilo*. Meanwhile ethnic, religious, and national fragmentation may impede, block, or reverse reforms in Eastern Europe, the successor states to the former Soviet Union, and Latin America.

A successful reform process, Alston argues, is less an issue of the 'big bang' vs. the gradualist approach, than how the reforms are arrived at and carried out. But in general Alston favors the gradualist path, if it results from consensus-building that will prevent a reversal of policy at a later date. Both process and institution-building are important, and institutions must become flexible, efficient, and transparent. The writer also considers how Western countries, trading blocs, and international agencies may influence the reform process, but points out the limitations on their power. He also considers the lessons we might draw from the first decade of privatization in East Europe and Latin America.

NOTES

1. Two recent comparative projects dealing with contemporary economic reforms in Latin America and Eastern Europe are those directed by Carol Graham of the Brookings Institution and Joan Nelson of the Overseas Development Council. Both deal with the extension of market reforms into the area of public goods (for example, education, health care, pensions) through the creation of 'stakeholder' constituencies to sell and consolidate these reforms. See: Graham (1998) and Nelson (1997).
2. See Kolodko (1999), pp. 5, 8. Williamson himself revised his 1990 views seven years later, taking into account experiences in both Latin America and Eastern Europe, adding an emphasis on institution-building, primary and secondary education, and fiscal inducements for protection of the environment.

3. The following units at the University of Illinois sponsored the conference: The Center for Latin American and Caribbean Studies, International Programs and Studies, The Center for International Business Education and Research (CIBER), and the Russian and East European Center. A generous contribution was also made by Cummins Engine Company.
4. See list of participants at the beginning of this volume.
5. This is true even if the Muslim-majority states of the CIS are omitted. See Kolodko (1999), p. 4 (Table 1).

REFERENCES

Graham, Carol (1998), *Private Markets for Public Goods*, Washington, DC: The Brookings Institution.

Kolodko, Grzegorz W. (1999), 'Ten years of postsocialist transition: the lessons for policy reforms', Paper for The World Bank: Development Economics Research Group, Washington, DC, March 1999.

Nelson, Joan (1997), 'Equity and security in a globalizing world: a proposal for research on the politics of pension and health care reforms in Eastern Europe and Latin America', Washington, DC: Overseas Development Council, May 1997.

2. Economic performance and the state in Latin America

Victor Bulmer-Thomas

This chapter begins with an examination of economic performance in Latin America with an emphasis on the 20th century. This is a long enough period to establish which countries have been successes or failures according to well-established criteria. The data set used also allows for determination of the sub-periods in which success or failure has been most marked. The regional variations in Latin America's economic performance have many possible explanations. One of these is the role of the state. In the second part of the chapter I outline the theory of the state with reference to economic development, drawing attention to the different ways the state can influence the allocation of resources and affect the rate of economic growth. The state will have an impact on both the supply- and demand-side of the economy. In the third part of the chapter I look at the supply-side, focusing in particular on the markets for factors of production (land, labor and capital) and on technical progress. In the next part of the chapter I explore the impact of the state on the demand-side and I focus on both macro- and microeconomic policies. In the final section of the chapter, I draw out the main conclusions on the role of the state in Latin America using a chronological approach. This starts with export-led growth up to the 1920s, then moves to the inward-looking phase of development that began in the 1930s and ends with the neo-liberal experiment currently in progress.

ECONOMIC PERFORMANCE IN LATIN AMERICA SINCE 1900

At the beginning of the 20th century, after nearly a century of independence, few Latin American countries had achieved sustainable long-run economic development and none had achieved the high expectations vested in the region at the birth of the republics. Although cross-country statistics are woefully inadequate, a clear picture emerges for 1900 in which Argentina and Uruguay can be classified as 'successful', Chile and Cuba as 'moderately successful' and Mexico as a special case. The other Latin American countries were all failures as far as economic development was concerned.

There are several reasons for this judgment. First, of the nine countries for which we have figures on Gross Domestic Product (GDP) per head in 1900 (see Table 2.1), only four – Argentina, Chile, Cuba and Mexico – had achieved even ten percent of the comparable figure for the United States. There are no figures for Uruguay, but when GDP per head was calculated for the first time in 1940 it was the highest in Latin America, making it highly probable that Uruguay was among the leaders in 1900.[1] Secondly, illiteracy rates, for which we have data for all countries except the Dominican Republic and Nicaragua, confirm the superior status of Argentina, Chile, Cuba and Uruguay (see Table 2.1). Mexico, however, lags behind in 13th place, suggesting that the social development in the Porfiriato[2] fell far behind the economic achievements; that is why I have labeled Mexico in 1900 a special case.

The third statistic we can use is exports per head. During a period of export-led growth, such as Latin America experienced before World War I, exports per head are highly correlated with GDP per head. While the figures for 1900 are incomplete, we do have figures for c. 1912 (see Table 2.1) and the ranking of countries is unlikely to have changed by much in the intervening years. Once again, Argentina, Chile, Cuba, Mexico and Uruguay emerge as the success stories. The fourth statistic is bank deposits per head. Financial intermediation is a good proxy for the level of development and its depth can be measured by this indicator. As Table 2.1 shows, Argentina stands out, with Chile and Uruguay following at some distance. The other countries for which data exist (for example Venezuela) appear to have had very shallow finance at the beginning of the century.

Argentina is the most straightforward case of a successful country if judged by the statistics in Table 2.1. It ranks first in GDP and bank deposits per head, second in exports per head and literacy. Uruguay ranks first in literacy, second in bank deposits and third in exports per head (there are no figures for GDP per head), but already by 1900 Uruguay had shifted from an export-led growth model to one in which the internal market was probably growing as fast as exports.[3] Chile and Cuba (still not fully independent in 1900)[4] perform well in relation to the rest of Latin America, but lag some way behind Argentina on all four criteria. Mexico remains a special case, in which economic development had effectively been postponed by 50 years after independence in the 1820s as a result of the cycle of civil wars and foreign intervention.

The Latin America panorama is, therefore, a gloomy one at the start of the 20th century. Of the 15 failures,[5] some were quite spectacular. Brazil in 1900 had a GDP per head only 4.8 percent of the US level despite the advances in industrialization since 1870. Many republics had exports per head valued at less than ten dollars while bank deposits per head outside of the southern cone were uniformly low. Comparisons of GDP per head require the use of exchange rates and it might be argued that these bias the results against Latin America.

Table 2.1 Economic and social indicators for Latin America: c. 1900

Country	GDP per head as % of US	Illiteracy rate (%)[a]	Exports per head ($)[b]	Bank deposits per head($)[b]
Argentina[c]	29.7	48.7	62.0	75.7
Bolivia		81.5	18.6	3.3
Brazil	4.8	65.3	14.2	9.4
Chile[d]	19.1	56.5	44.7	26.0
Colombia	8.0	66.0	6.4	
Costa Rica		64.4	27.1	
Cuba[d]	18.4	54.0	64.7	
Dom. Rep.			15.5	
Ecuador	6.0	66.9	7.9	1.6
El Salvador		73.7	8.3	2.3
Guatemala		88.1	7.2	0.9
Haiti		92.0	6.1	
Honduras		71.7	4.7	
Mexico[e]	17.7	75.6	10.7	
Nicaragua			10.8	
Panama		82.7		
Paraguay		68.6	8.6	
Peru	7.0	75.7	9.4	0.9
Uruguay[c]		40.6	50.3	29.5
Venezuela	7.2	72.2	10.5	1.2
Latin America	12.5[f]	66.1[f]	20.4	

Notes:

a Percent of population over 15.
b c. 1912.
c 'Success' story.
d 'Moderate success' story.
e Special case.
f Six countries only (Argentina, Brazil, Chile, Colombia, Mexico, and Venezuela).

Sources: Bulmer-Thomas (1995); Thorp (1998).

However, the exchange rates used in Table 2.1 for GDP per head are purchasing-power parity exchange rates and not official exchange rates. Using the latter, Brazil's GDP per head would have been only four percent of the US figure in 1900 – not 4.8 percent.[6]

Throughout the 20th century (see Table 2.2), GDP per head for Latin America as a whole has remained the same proportion of US GDP per head. This suggests a simple definition of success or failure for 20th century economic performance. Those countries that closed the gap on the United States can be defined as successes; where the gap widened, the country can be classified as a failure. This analysis can be applied both across the whole century and to different sub-periods. It has the additional advantage that 'success' in this context means that the country outperformed the Latin American average while 'failure' means that it underperformed.

Looking at the century as a whole, only three countries can be clearly classified as success stories: Brazil, Colombia and Venezuela (see Table 2.2). Of these three countries, Brazil is the clearest case; its GDP per head reached a higher proportion of the US figure in every decade until the 1980s. Indeed, without the successful economic performance in Brazil, the Latin American performance relative to the United States would have looked truly dismal for most of the 20th century.

Table 2.2 GDP per head as percentage of US GDP per head: 1900–95

	1900	1910	1920	1930	1940	1950	1960	1970	1980	1990	1995
Argentina	29.7	32.4	27.0	26.0	26.0	23.4	22.2	23.1	21.9	15.5	18.1
Bolivia						7.9	5.6	5.7	5.6	3.9	4.0
Brazil	4.8	4.8	5.1	5.9	6.4	6.5	8.4	8.7	12.3	10.7	10.4
Chile	19.1	19.8	16.6	23.3	19.4	17.5	17.7	16.5	15.2	14.9	18.0
Colombia	8.0	8.5	9.0	10.7	11.7	10.9	10.9	10.4	10.7	10.2	11.1
Costa Rica			14.6	12.9	13.1	11.2	12.2	12.7	14.0	10.9	11.4
Cuba	18.4	24.0	21.1	17.0	15.1	11.5	10.1	7.2	10.3	9.3	6.2
Dom. Rep.						7.4	7.8	7.4	8.6	6.9	7.0
Ecuador	6.0	6.3	6.9	7.2	6.4	7.0	7.4	6.9	8.6	7.0	7.1
El Salvador			8.6	8.3	7.6	8.3	8.6	7.9	6.5	4.8	5.5
Guatemala			12.4	11.4	15.4	9.4	8.8	8.1	8.2	6.1	6.1
Haiti						3.9	3.1	2.3	2.5	1.6	1.1
Honduras			11.4	12.3	7.9	6.9	6.2	5.4	4.9	3.7	3.8
Mexico	17.7	18.4	18.2	14.6	14.4	13.9	15.9	17.1	18.5	15.0	14.1
Nicaragua			9.1	9.3	7.4	6.6	7.5	8.3	5.0	2.6	2.3
Panama						13.9	14.6	17.3	17.4	12.8	14.2
Paraguay					12.8	8.9	7.9	7.0	9.8	7.6	7.2
Peru	7.0	8.7	10.1	12.6	12.4	11.2	12.6	11.9	11.1	6.7	7.3
Uruguay					26.7	26.2	23.8	18.8	18.3	15.7	17.5
Venezuela	7.2	6.7	7.5	19.0	20.2	29.5	29.3	25.8	24.3	16.9	16.1
Latin America[a]	12.5	13.3	12.4	12.9	12.9	12.5	13.6	13.7	15.4	12.7	12.8
Latin America[b]						11.9	12.7	12.6	14.0	11.3	11.4

Notes:
a Six countries only (Argentina, Brazil, Chile, Colombia, Mexico and Venezuela).
b All 20 countries.

Source: Derived from Thorp (1998).

The Colombian and Venezuelan stories are somewhat different. Both countries did indeed close the gap, but in the case of Colombia the gap ceased to narrow after 1940 and in the case of Venezuela the watershed year is 1960 (from 1950 to 1980 Venezuela was the richest country in Latin America). Ecuador and Panama narrowly closed the gap on the United States, but the narrowing is not statistically significant in the case of Ecuador and in the case of Panama is limited to the period from 1950 to 1980. Peru, virtually unchanged over the century, is also worthy of mention here as the Peruvian data show a strong improvement up to 1960 and a sharp deterioration subsequently. Elsewhere, the differential either widened or was unchanged. Furthermore, in the case of the five success stories in 1900 (Argentina, Chile, Cuba, Mexico and Uruguay), all suffered severe losses. This was almost continuous after 1910 in the cases of Argentina and Cuba, and after 1930 in the cases of Chile and Uruguay. Mexico succeeded in narrowing the gap with the United States between 1950 and 1980, but for the rest of the century suffered a widening of the differential, ending substantially below its position at the beginning.

Some of the losses are truly tragic. Haiti, with a GDP per head in 1950 only 3.9 percent of the US figure, experienced an almost continuous decline and ended the period with a GDP per head of 1.1 percent of the US figure. Bolivia also suffered a continuous decline until a very modest reversal began in the 1990s. Even Costa Rica, a model democracy and one of Latin America's best-governed countries, failed to narrow the differential on the United States. Elsewhere in Central America the ratio fell severely throughout the century and not just during the turbulent decade of the 1980s.

When sub-periods are analyzed, starting with the phase of export-led growth up to 1930, the performance of Venezuela stands out (see Table 2.2). The exploitation of oil under the dictatorship of President Juan Vicente Gómez helped GDP per head jump to almost 20 percent of the US figure. In Peru foreign investment and the mining boom almost doubled the ratio, while Chile – despite the dislocation of World War I – managed to narrow the gap between them and the United States and Argentina. The latter's performance was disappointing, but still gave no hint of the horrors to come.

The inward-looking development phase, based on import substitution, is conventionally placed from 1930 to 1980. It brought some successes, notably in Brazil and in Mexico. Argentina and Uruguay held their own from 1930 to 1940 before experiencing a steady decline subsequently. Chile performed poorly and Cuba disastrously; in both cases decline set in long before socialist economics took hold.

Economic performance since 1980 must be divided into two phases despite the short length of the period. The first is the 'lost decade' of the debt crisis, during which all countries lost ground on the United States. Since 1990 no fewer than 12 republics have narrowed the differential, albeit by a very small amount in many cases, but too much should not be read into this.[7] In most cases the catching-up can be attributed to a short phase of non-sustainable economic growth based on recovery after severe recession. Examples are El Salvador, Panama and Peru. A few countries, however, appear to have moved towards a new and sustainable growth model capable of narrowing the differential with the United States. Argentina and Chile are the most obvious cases, but Bolivia may also be in this category. Sadly, neither Brazil nor Mexico can yet be placed in this group with any confidence.

THE STATE AND ECONOMIC DEVELOPMENT IN LATIN AMERICA

There is a vast literature on the role of the state in Latin America. However, much of this literature explores those parts of the state's activities that do not impinge directly on economic performance. Examples are the relations between the state and civil society, the transformation of subjects into citizens and the establishment of electoral and political rights. These non-economic functions of the state are very important and will undoubtedly have indirect implications for the economy. Nevertheless, they are not central to the argument in this chapter and will not be pursued further.

The starting point for an analysis of the state's role in Latin America has to be an examination of the dominant economic system. With minor exceptions the dominant system in Latin America in the last century has been capitalism. The exceptions (Cuba since 1959 and Chile from 1970 to 1973) are well known and need not detain us further. It should, however, be clear that the role of the state in a socialist system – such as in Cuba – is quite different from the role of the state in capitalism. It is not possible to develop a theory of the state for the two cases except at the most superficial level.

The state under capitalism has many functions. In order to carry out these functions, several preconditions must be met. These preconditions are usually taken for granted in analysis of the state in developed market economies, but they need to be specified clearly in the case of Latin America. The first precondition is the consolidation of the nation state and the establishment of territorial control. This has now been largely achieved in all Latin American countries, but it was not the case at the start of the 20th century. The large Indian populations in countries such as Bolivia, Guatemala and Paraguay were treated as second-class citizens by the ruling élite and did not in many cases see themselves as part of the nation; and the territorial integration of many large republics was not assured before the advent of civil aviation and the widespread use of roads for travel. Civil war, a condition now found only in Colombia, has disrupted the nation state in many Latin American countries this century and has undermined the ability of the state to fulfill its functions within capitalism.

Second, the state must exhibit a certain autonomy from the private sector élites that dominate the economy under capitalism. At the beginning of this century, when the state was usually under oligarchic control, there was often little or no autonomy in state action. Indeed, in the smaller states the state oligarchy and the private sector élite were often the same people. Where the state is too close to private sector interests, it can generate rapid growth – as in Nicaragua under the Somoza dynasty – but it is not sustainable; the inability of the state to mediate between conflicting interests eventually leads the losers to resort to force. As the oligarchic state in Latin America has given way to the bureaucratic state, marked by high levels of public sector employment, the state's capacity to act independently of private sector interests has increased. However, this is no guarantee of rational behaviour as the state may become captive to the interests of its own employees. This inertial state has been particularly problematic in three of the region's longest-standing democracies – Costa Rica, Uruguay and Venezuela – where the link between political parties and the state bureaucracy has been particularly damaging.

The third precondition is the establishment of the rule of the law. This is in many ways the most important precondition and yet it is the furthest from being universally achieved. The establishment of institutions capable of enforcing and upholding the legal system is a goal to which many republics in Latin America can only aspire. Far too often wrong-doing is not punished and there are no satisfactory mechanisms in place for resolving disputes. To these traditional problems in the application of the rule of the law, a new one – personal security – has now been added. Fear of robbery, kidnapping or murder is a serious obstacle to rational economic decision-making.

The preconditions outlined above must be met if the state is to carry out its functions effectively. Of course, the state must still attempt to meet the demands placed upon it even when the preconditions are not met, but its capability to do so is likely to be highly constrained. In what follows I shall therefore assume that the preconditions have been satisfied.

The first function of the state is the provision of public goods, i.e. those that are non-rival and non-exclusionary.[8] The most obvious example of a public good is defence and this has indeed occupied the attention of all Latin American states. However, servicing the external public debt is another public good that has absorbed a high proportion of public expenditure in Latin America. There are two other public goods that deserve special mention in the Latin American context. One is macroeconomic stability, which is correctly defined as a public good as its consumption by one citizen does not reduce the supply available for others and users cannot be prevented from consuming the good. The other is measures to protect or improve the environment, although some such measures could possibly be excludable. Defence, external debt servicing, macro-economic stability and environmental protection are not the only public goods of interest to Latin America. However, they do absorb a high proportion of government expenditure and administrative effort. Latin America's record in the provision of public goods has been mixed with only defence consistently receiving a high priority. Yet in many cases defence expenditure has been used for internal repression rather than the protection of territorial integrity, distorting its definition as a public good.

The second function of the state is the provision of semi-public goods. These are goods that are either non-rival and excludable (club goods) or rival and non-excludable (common property goods). The most important are education, health, social security provision and physical infrastructure. Expenditure on semi-public goods now accounts for a very high proportion of total public expenditure in Latin America (see Table 2.3) – as in developed countries – with serious problems in the quality of the output obtained from this level of spending.

The third function of the state is the provision of private goods – usually through state-owned enterprises (SOEs). This function has now fallen out of favor, as in developed countries, but a residue remains in all republics. It was not important in the first half of the 20th century and it was originally seen as a response to market failure, i.e. the state provision of private goods and services was seen as the appropriate response to some perceived failure of the private sector.

The fourth function of the state is a concern with equity. The state has always been responsible for the alleviation of extreme poverty (including famine and disaster relief). However, it is also widely accepted that the distribution of income emerging from a private market system may be sub-optimal. Thus, all states use a system of transfers and subsidies to redistribute income. While this secondary distribution of income is supposed to be more equitable than the primary distribution of income, this may not be so if either the state has been unduly influenced by strong pressure groups or if the state bureaucracy is able to thwart the intentions of governments in this area. This has been a serious problem in Latin America for most of this century.

These functions can only be satisfied with public revenue and the capture of resources to fulfill state functions is the final state activity to be discussed here. Ideally, the state would acquire its resources in a non-distortionary way; however, there are almost no taxes that do not alter relative prices and therefore affect the allocation of resources. Thus, the impact of public taxation on the private sector needs to be taken into account in any discussion of the state under capitalism.

At the beginning of the 20th century, all Latin American states relied heavily on income from trade taxes (import tariffs and export duties). It has been estimated[9] that the average for Latin America was 64 percent, that is, nearly

Table 2.3 Structure of central government expenditure[a], 1991–95 (%)

	Public Goods			Semi-public Goods		Other
	Defence	Interest payments[b]	Health	Education	Social security & welfare	
Argentina	6.8	10.2	2.2	7.0	47.5	26.2
Bolivia	9.5	8.3	6.3	18.0	15.3	42.5
Brazil	2.8	44.5	5.9	3.5	30.6	12.8
Chile	9.2	6.3	11.4	13.5	33.5	26.0
Colombia	8.0	10.0	5.4	18.3	8.3	50.1
Costa Rica	–	15.2	26.7	21.0	14.4	22.8
Dom. Rep.	4.9	6.1	11.0	10.1	3.7	64.3
Ecuador[c]	12.2	17.8	9.0	24.9	1.4	34.8
El Salvador	14.0	13.2	8.0	13.4	4.5	46.9
Guatemala	13.9	11.4	10.1	16.8	4.4	46.8
Haiti[c]	–	3.4	–	–	–	–
Honduras	–	–	–	–	–	–
Mexico	3.8	22.7	3.0	23.7	21.0	25.9
Nicaragua	7.6	10.7	13.4	15.4	16.3	36.6
Panama	5.2	9.7	20.5	18.4	22.4	23.8
Paraguay	12.1	7.0	6.3	17.6	15.6	41.5
Peru[c]	20.1	21.6	5.7	16.9	–	35.6
Uruguay	6.5	5.9	5.4	6.7	58.4	17.1
Venezuela[c]	6.3	12.4	8.6	18.3	6.7	47.8

Notes:
– = not available.
a Excludes expenditure by provinces (states) and municipalities (this helps to explain low figure for education in Brazil).
b Includes payment on internal debt (not a public good).
c 1981–90.

Source: Derived from World Bank (1997).

two-thirds of all revenue came from trade taxes. This ratio was still around 40 percent in 1930 and 20 percent as late as 1950. This dependence on trade taxes was a reflection both of the importance of foreign trade and of the ease of collection. However, trade taxes are never neutral and the impact on the allocation of resources – not to mention rent-seeking – has been considerable. The distortions associated with trade taxes eventually became excessive and were one of the reasons for the abrupt shift to trade liberalisation after the 1980s. The state supplemented taxes on trade with taxes on domestic goods and services (sales taxes). Since these were typically levied at a non-uniform rate or were subject to exceptions as well as partial evasion, they also had a major impact on the allocation of resources. They were also not applied to the informal sector, which is one reason why the latter has grown so rapidly in many Latin American countries.

From the 1930s onwards the state came to rely increasingly on social security contributions. Since these were collected on a pay-as-you-go basis, they should be viewed as a tax on labor in the formal sector. Demographic changes, coupled with populist legislation, have made the social security system technically bankrupt in many countries and have forced a reconsideration of pension provision in particular. Income taxes, including taxes on profit and capital gains, also became important from the 1930s onwards. Although they have never represented the same proportion of revenue as in developed countries, at their peak in 1970 they accounted for 36.5 percent of the total. Most of this was attributable to large-scale enterprises where the tax burden could be reduced through capital expenditure. Thus, income tax has also been non-neutral in its impact on the allocation of resources.

Table 2.4 Structure of central government revenue[a]*, 1991–95 (%)*

	Income, profit and capital gains	Social security contributions	Domestic goods and services	Foreign trade	Other taxes	Non-tax revenue
Argentina	2.6	45.9	26.6	7.9	4.6	9.1
Bolivia	4.3	7.5	38.5	6.6	0.5	33.9
Brazil	16.3	30.1	19.2	1.9	5.2	27.2
Chile	18.1	6.7	45.2	9.6	3.7	16.7
Colombia	39.3		37.2	9.7	0.7	13.2
Costa Rica	9.8	27.7	32.2	16.1	0.7	13.1
Dom. Rep.	17.1	4.1	25.1	44.2	0.3	8.6
Ecuador	56.0		24.9	11.6	1.0	5.5
El Salvador	22.2	–	49.8	17.0	0.2	7.1
Guatemala	19.4	–	42.4	20.1	3.5	13.7
Haiti[b]	14.9	0.3	30.7	23.8	6.2	11.5
Honduras[b]	24.2	–	25.9	42.4	1.0	5.7
Mexico	34.2	17.9	50.2	7.1	2.4	9.0
Nicaragua	11.2	11.8	45.1	19.4	5.3	6.6
Panama	18.0	20.5	16.8	10.5	1.7	31.1
Paraguay	9.8	–	27.7	14.8	11.9	30.0
Peru	12.5	12.3	49.3	9.8	7.3	8.6
Uruguay	7.3	30.1	32.4	5.6	8.4	5.9
Venezuela	50.6	5.5	10.4	9.1	1.3	22.3

Notes:
– = not available.
a Excludes provincial (state) and municipal revenues.
b 1981–90.

Source: World Bank (1997), Table A.1, p. 196.

The overall structure of state revenue in the 1990s is shown in Table 2.4, where it can be seen that trade taxes are now of negligible importance while indirect taxes (including value added taxes) are dominant. What the data do not show is the impact of the inflation tax, which was used by the state in many countries after 1940 to transfer resources from the private to the public sector. As is well known, the 'inflation tax' is paid primarily by those who rely on cash rather than interest-bearing deposits and is therefore a tax on the poor. The reduction in inflation in Latin America has substantially reduced the importance of this inequitable and regressive tax.

ECONOMIC PERFORMANCE AND THE STATE – THE SUPPLY-SIDE

The growth of the economy can be seen from either the supply-side or the demand-side. To analyze the supply-side, a technique known as growth accounting has been developed. This disaggregates growth in any period into a contribution from the growth of factor inputs (land, labor and capital) and the growth of total factor productivity (TFP), that is the growth in output per unit of factor input with all factors of production aggregated together. A few attempts have been made to apply growth accounting to Latin America.[10] The results are not very reliable in view of the quality of the data, although they do suggest the limited importance of TFP growth and the greater importance of the increase in factor inputs. What can be done, however, is to apply the growth accounting approach to economic performance in Latin America to see what light it sheds on the role of the state. In order to do this, it is necessary to resolve how to treat the change in the quality – and not just the quantity – of factor inputs. In the simplest versions of growth accounting, this qualitative change is treated as part of TFP. However, it is also possible to treat the change in quality as a separate variable in the explanation of growth. Thus, for the three factor inputs we have to consider both the change in quantity and the change in quality, while continuing to include TFP as the residual in the growth accounting equation.

By the beginning of the 20th century, the state had already distributed a large proportion of the public land it had inherited from the Spanish or Portuguese crown. This had vastly increased the land in private ownership and led to an accumulation of productive land inputs. This process continued after 1900, with many governments offering land on very favorable terms to new immigrants. Deforestation played only a small role in the growth of land devoted to agriculture in the first half of the century. However, it became increasingly important after 1950 as demographic pressure combined with the tax system to provide incentives for the encroachment of agricultural land on the primary and secondary forests. By the 1980s it had become apparent that the tax system was producing major distortions in the choice of land use, particularly between forests and pasture, but deforestation has not yet ceased because the private rate of return to non-forest use remains higher.

The final way in which the state has affected the accumulation of land inputs is through land reform. Although much of this involves a redistribution of land, the theory behind it assumes that a larger proportion of land held in large units is idle than in small units. Thus, land reform should lead to an increase in land inputs. However, land reform in Latin America has been a big disappointment for those who hoped that it would improve equity. However, it did accelerate the transition to modern capitalist agriculture, leading to a big increase in agricultural output and labor productivity.[11] Indeed, agricultural labor productivity growth (see Table 2.5) seems to have peaked during the years in which land reform was being implemented.

Table 2.5 Agricultural labor productivity: average annual growth rate (%)

	Argentina	Brazil	Chile	Colombia	Mexico	Venezuela
1st Period	1.7	0.8	0.6		1.3	
	(1903–52)	(1921–48)	(1909–26)		(1901–10)	
2nd Period		2.6	0.8	2.1	0.9	1.2
		(1947–70)	(1927–41)	(1926–66)	(1922–47)	(1926–50)
3rd Period	3.9	5.9	3.3		3.3	6.0
	(1953–79)	(1971–81)	(1942–71)		(1944–70)	(1951–80)
4th Period	–0.7	1.1	1.8	3.0	0.6	–1.1
	(1980–90)	(1982–90)	(1973–90)	(1967–93)	(1971–90)	(1981–90)
Overall	2.1	2.2	1.9	2.4	1.6	3.1

Source: Thorp (1998), Appendix Table IV.1, pp. 328–9.

The state has therefore played a key role in the growth in the quantity of land inputs. What about its contribution to the quality of land inputs? Here the picture is more mixed. State-sponsored irrigation schemes have been the most important source of an increase in quality, but these have not been very widespread.[12] Meanwhile, the tax system has encouraged the spread of agriculture to lands that are not well-equipped for this purpose – the Brazilian Amazon being the main, but not the only, example.

The fiscal system has also had a strong urban bias for much of the 20th century as a result of the policy of import-substituting industrialization. The agricultural sector often received zero tariff protection, but paid high tariffs on its inputs. At the same time, price control on foodstuffs lowered its relative price and encouraged a shift of resources out of rural areas. The worst distortions in the tax system had been corrected by the 1980s and trade liberalization has now led to a tax system which is more neutral between agriculture and other activities. With a few exceptions, such as El Salvador and Haiti, there is no evidence that the growth of aggregate output was constrained by a shortage of land. Thus, the state must be judged to have fulfilled its functions in this area. The same is not true of labor inputs, where shortages were endemic until the fall in the crude death rate after 1930 turned Latin America's labor shortage into a labor surplus. The state's preferred response to labor shortages was legislation to encourage immigration, preferably from Europe. Only a handful of republics – Argentina, Brazil, Chile, Cuba and Uruguay – had much success in attracting immigrants and only in Argentina, Cuba and Uruguay did it amount to a significant share of the labor force. Where voluntary migration from Europe failed, the state resorted to indentured labor from Asia or coercion of domestic labor. The latter was achieved primarily by denying part of the rural population access to land, thereby forcing them to work for wages. These short-sighted policies help to explain the stagnation of real wages in Latin America at a time when labor productivity was rising. The stagnation of real wages in turn undermined the growth of the internal market, making it difficult for the export sector to stimulate the growth of the non-export sector.

From the 1940s onwards there has been no labor shortage in Latin America. Thus, the growth of output in the second half of the century has not been constrained by labor supply. The quality of labor inputs, however, is another story. Studies of contemporary Latin America have emphasized the educational deficit among Latin American workers compared with other developing regions.[13] Since mass educational spending was not until recently a priority in most Latin American countries (the main exception is Costa Rica – see Table 2.3), it is not unreasonable to assume that the educational deficit existed in earlier years. Much the same is true with regard to health spending, which has an important bearing on the quality of labor inputs.

If the state can be accused of negligence with respect to the quality and quantity of labor inputs, the same is not true of capital inputs. On the contrary, it can be argued that the state has at times encouraged excessive accumulation of capital at the expense of employment and with insufficient attention to the social rate of return on investment. At the beginning of the century, the main instrument used by the state to promote capital inputs was legislation in favor of foreign investment. This included generous – often excessively generous – concessions to foreign companies through guaranteed minimum rates of return or tax holidays. These policies were supplemented after the Great Depression in two ways. First, the tariff system favored the import of capital goods where no capital goods industry existed; second, development banks were established to channel long-term finance to projects that failed to find favor with private commercial banks. The result was a substantial increase in the accumulation of capital inputs – not all of which was economically rational.

The state's role in promoting the growth of capital inputs was further advanced with the explosive growth of SOEs after 1950. Originally justified by reference to market failure, SOEs were located above all in the capital-intensive branches of the economy where they were responsible for up to half of all gross fixed capital formation. In the larger countries (Argentina, Brazil and Mexico) they were also mainly responsible for the growth in the public external debt after the first oil crisis in 1973.[14] The state has therefore played a major part in promoting the accumulation of capital inputs. However, the quality of this increase has left much to be desired. The tax system gave a capital-intensive bias to much private sector investment, while the financing of capital inputs in SOEs became a vehicle for capital flight in the 1970s and 1980s.[15] The quality of capital inputs in Latin America has been disappointing for much of this century.

The growth of TFP in Latin America, particularly when stripped of the change in the quality of factor inputs, has almost certainly been modest, although empirical data are not strong enough to confirm this. TFP, until recently, was treated as exogenous, although the new growth theory now views it – probably correctly – as largely endogenous.[16] TFP is influenced by many things. First is the legal framework to encourage innovation, where it is widely assumed that a strong patent law is important. The legal system in much of Latin America has been deficient with respect to patent protection in general and intellectual property in particular, although this is now changing under pressure from the World Trade Organization. Innovation has been far less important than imitation in Latin America, but – unlike in post-war Japan – imitation did not lead on to innovation. One reason is the absence of competitive markets. Shielded from imports by high nominal tariffs and unable to export because of anti-export bias, industrial firms in Latin America have operated in oligopolistic markets where innovation was not necessary to sustain profitability. Even Brazil, with its vast internal market, suffered from this problem, although the Brazilian state did at least benefit from research and development expenditure by foreign companies that required some response from local firms.

The third stimulus to TFP growth is economies of scale. As the market expands, the unit cost of production falls and total factor productivity rises. Economies of scale are primarily found in the manufacturing sector, which is related in turn to the size of the internal market under import substituting industrialization (ISI). It is no accident, therefore, that Brazil has been the biggest beneficiary of TFP growth induced by economies of scale, although it is by no means clear that this has anything to do with the role of the state.

The state in Latin America has therefore been successful in preventing land from constraining growth, but less so in the case of labor during the period of labor shortages. The state has contributed to the rapid growth of capital inputs, particularly after World War II, but the quality of these inputs has left much to be desired. Finally, the state has played little or no role in the growth of TFP; this is in marked contrast to developed countries throughout this century or a number of countries of Southeast Asia since the 1950s. The most important exception has been the state in Brazil. Although the growth of capital inputs – at least in the formal sector – may have been excessive, the Brazilian state has played a key role in facilitating the growth of all factor inputs throughout this century and has even played a modest role in promoting the growth of TFP. In this respect it has benefitted from the size of the internal market – a key determinant of growth in an inward-looking model of development. Although the tax system has created many distortions in Brazil, the autonomy of the state allowed bureaucrats to design policies that partially compensated many of the losers. This was far from ideal, but it did help Brazil to close the gap on the United States.

ECONOMIC PERFORMANCE AND THE STATE – THE DEMAND-SIDE

Growth accounting can be applied to the demand-side as well as the supply-side. Using techniques pioneered by Hollis Chenery in the 1960s, it is possible to calculate the contribution to growth in real GDP of import substitution on the one hand and on the other the components of final demand (private consumption and investment, public consumption and investment, and exports) on the assumption of no change in the import coefficient.[17] Let us start with import substitution. It is often assumed that import substitution refers only to manufacturing or perhaps industry (that is, including mining), but it can include any tradeable sector where imports are significant. Thus, in some countries in Latin America import substituting agriculture (ISA) has been important and in the region today there is negative import substitution in services (ISS) as a result of the replacement of previously non-traded activities (for example, financial services) by imports.

With this proviso the main focus this century in Latin America has been import substituting industrialization (ISI). However, much ISI is 'natural' and takes place without state intervention. As the market widens, firms with increasing returns to scale (common in manufacturing) are able to lower costs of production and replace part of the import supply. This natural process was well under way in the larger Latin American republics before the 1930s. The state, however, plays a key role in import substitution by selecting the rate for tariffs and many non-tariff barriers (for example, quotas). Raising these barriers creates new 'artificial' opportunities for import substitution even if the state increased tariffs and quotas for other (that is, revenue) reasons. It was only in the 1950s that most Latin American states embraced a tariff and non-tariff barrier (NTB) structure that was overtly protectionist.

As a device for accelerating industrialization, state-sponsored ISI was highly successful. The share of industry (or more precisely manufacturing) in Latin America rose sharply from the 1930s to the debt crisis in the early 1980s and the contribution of import substitution to the growth of manufacturing was almost 50 percent. However, the protection offered was excessive and generated several distortions. First, it turned the internal terms of trade against the agricultural sector and, second, it created a strong anti-export bias making it difficult for even successful firms to sell their production outside the national market. Finally, by limiting imports it reduced competition in the home market and contributed to the problem of chronic inflation in the larger countries. The state-sponsored regional integration schemes adopted in the 1960s were too timid to make much of a difference, and the problems were only addressed with the adoption of trade liberalization and bolder integration schemes in the wake of the 1980s debt crisis.

Private consumption in Latin America is the largest component of final expenditure and absorbs a very high proportion of private incomes. It is a function not only of the level of income, but also its distribution. Thus, the high degree of income inequality in all Latin American republics is, and has been, reflected in the pattern of consumption. The state has rarely tried to fine-tune private consumption – a very difficult task in view of the modest impact of interest rates on household spending until recently in Latin America. However, the state's reliance on net indirect taxes (that is, net of subsidies) has substantially affected household expenditure. Subsidized items, such as tortillas in Mexico, usually form a substantial part of the expenditure of low-income families, while the impact of tax rates depends on the price elasticity of demand; where it is high, contraband is often the consequence and this is one of the reasons why governments in the region have adopted more modest rates of indirect tax (including tariffs).

The income of households is either consumed or saved. Thus, the level of private consumption also depends on the incentives for private savers. These have been very unsatisfactory for much of this century as a result of a lack of financial instruments for private savers and frequently negative real rates of interest. Thus, despite the unequal distribution of income, Latin America has had low savings rates – the worst of both worlds.[18] The most important impact of the state on private consumption has probably been through the tariff on imports of consumer goods. Before 1930 a high proportion of imports consisted of consumer goods; by 1980 this was close to zero in the larger republics so that almost all private consumption was met through domestic supply. With trade liberalization in the 1980s and regional integration in the 1990s, the proportion of imports consisting of consumer goods has risen sharply; this negative import substitution has lowered *ceteris paribus* the contribution of private consumption to GDP growth. Recently, with the increase in the importance of durable goods consumption, credit cards and personal credit, the state has begun to refine its approach to the management of private consumption. This has been most apparent in Brazil since the launch of the Real Plan in 1994, where measures have been taken at regular intervals to curb private consumption. Brazil is not alone in this, however, and many Latin American states are now closer to the European or North American model in which household consumption is sensitive to the rate of interest as well as to the level of disposable income.

The role of the state in the promotion of private and public investment has already been discussed (see previous section); and the accumulation of capital inputs on the supply-side has its mirror image in investment expenditure on the demand-side. It is worth stressing, however, the role of SOEs in sustaining high rates of investment during the final two decades of the import substitution phase. The private sector almost never achieved a rate of investment in excess of 20 percent of GDP and in some cases it was less than 10 percent. State companies, with their privileged access to the domestic and international capital markets, were responsible for between one-third and one-half of gross fixed capital formation in the larger republics before the debt crisis. Today, however, public investment, both by government and by SOEs, is now much lower as a proportion of GDP. The private sector is being asked to carry the main burden of investment, but domestic real interest rates remain high. Thus, access to foreign capital markets through bond issues, bank borrowing or international equity issues has become much more important. The state has an important role to play here since the terms on which private firms access the international market are affected by the foreign perception of country risk. A low rating imposes additional costs on all investments, not just those carried out by state agencies. In terms of growth accounting, what matters is the domestic component of investment expenditure, that is, after excluding imported capital goods. The capital goods share of imports is high in all republics and in most countries – Brazil is the main exception – the domestic component of investment in machinery and equipment is low. This, however, is nothing new and is a reasonably accurate description of Latin America throughout this century.

Public consumption is an important component of final expenditure and its import content is low because it is dominated by wages and salaries. It has grown faster than GDP this century, as in almost all countries in the world, both because the demand for public services increases with urbanization and the rise in GDP and because the state now has duties (for example the maintenance of an airforce) that did not exist at the beginning of the century. Indeed, it is probable that public consumption's share of GDP has doubled or even trebled in the last 100 years. Unfortunately, it is not possible to compare public consumption over time for all Latin American countries. We do know, however, that in general the proportion devoted to health, education and social security has risen and that the proportion spent on defense and debt servicing has fallen. The fall in debt service costs may seem surprising, until one remembers the small size of total public consumption at the start of the century in absolute terms.

Growth accounting can show the direct impact of public consumption on GDP growth, but how effective has the growth of public consumption been in the promotion of GDP growth? The indirect effects come in several forms – positive and negative. The positive impact comes from the increase in private sector factor productivity made possible by greater public expenditure. Before World War II, it was widely assumed that spending on infrastructure had the greatest impact; in more recent years, with the private sector playing a greater part in the provision of physical infrastructure, attention has shifted to health and education. There is no doubt that, with a few exceptions, state spending on health and education has not brought the expected benefits for much of the post-war period. There have also been indirect costs. In developed countries the problem has often been seen as one of 'crowding out' private spending through the impact of public borrowing on interest rates. In Latin America this has been much less serious because the economies are less sensitive to interest rates. However, the state has relied on indirect rather than direct taxes to pay for public spending and this has often distorted relative prices and incentives. This has been the most serious negative effect of increased public spending in Latin America and examples have been given above. Furthermore, the growth of public spending has also led to a huge increase in the size of the state bureaucracy. It has been estimated[19] that public employment as a proportion of total employment rose sharply between 1950 and 1986 at a time when total employment was itself rising rapidly. In Costa Rica, for example, it rose from 2.5 to 19.8 percent, in Uruguay from about 9 to 20.7 percent and in Venezuela from 6.7 to 19.3 percent. These public sector bureaucracies have become an interest group in their own right, often thwarting the implementation of government policies and resisting administrative reform.

The final contribution to GDP growth on the demand-side comes from exports. At the beginning of this century public policies laid great stress on the promotion of exports. Those countries that out-performed the United States before 1930 (see Table 2.2) did so in most cases as a result of a fast growth of exports. Foreign direct investment played a major part in this export expansion (for example, Venezuela after 1917), but it would be wrong to underestimate the part played by the state through the legal framework, infrastructure spending, the tax and subsidy system as well as other incentives. In Colombia, for example, the outperformance of the United States before 1930 was clearly linked to the rapid growth of exports of coffee and bananas where, in different ways, the state's role was very important. After the 1929 depression the state struggled to support the export sector in the face of the decline in world trade and the collapse of commodity prices. Public policies were not unsuccessful and the volume of exports (if not the value) recovered quickly after 1932 in most countries. However, the move to a fully-fledged model of inward-looking development after 1950 crippled the export sector in most countries. As the anti-export bias inherent in the structure of protection began to take effect, Latin America saw its share of world trade decline sharply.

The new growth model, based on market-friendly policies and low trade barriers, has created new opportunities for the export sector.[20] Latin America, however, has not returned to export-led growth. With the exception of Mexico, where NAFTA provides unrivalled opportunities for export expansion, the new growth model has eliminated the worst distortions faced by the export sector, but has not produced a consistent policy of export promotion. Policy is now more neutral between exportables, importables and the non-traded sectors with the allocation of resources determined primarily by relative prices set in free markets. This is a far cry from state-directed development, as occurred in many parts of Southeast Asia, but it is a big improvement on the anti-export bias found before the debt crisis and may be the best that can be achieved with Latin America's badly trained and poorly motivated public sector bureaucracies.

ECONOMIC PERFORMANCE AND THE ROLE OF THE STATE: CONCLUSIONS

The 20th century in Latin America divides relatively easily into three periods. In the first, up to the end of the 1920s, Latin America continued to pursue the model of export-led growth developed in the second half of the previous century. In the next period, up to the first oil crisis in 1973, Latin America followed an inward-looking model of development with a heavy emphasis on industrialization. In the final period, which began in the southern cone after 1973 and in the rest of the region after the 1982 debt crisis, Latin America adopted a neo-liberal model in response to globalization, external shocks and the perceived exhaustion of the inward-looking model.

The role of the state in Latin America has evolved as the economic paradigm has changed. The secular increase in resources at the disposal of the state has helped to resolve some problems, but at times the state has been unable to respond adequately to the new challenges it has faced. The state has also become more effective in meeting some of its functions and less effective at addressing others.

In the first period, marked almost everywhere by an oligarchic state commanding few resources, the preconditions for an effective state were often absent. Territorial integrity was not assured in many countries, the state lacked autonomy from the private sector élites and the rule of law left much to be desired. The main exceptions (Argentina, Chile and Uruguay) were all in the southern cone. In Mexico the state was too closely identified with private sector interests and in Brazil the control of the federal government over the provinces was minimal, leaving the authorities unable to implement an effective state policy. In many of the smaller states of the Caribbean basin, the 'state' consisted of representatives of the US government, as dollar diplomacy was applied to resolve the vacuum created by weak domestic rule. During this period the priority for the state was the promotion of the export sector, where oligarchic interests were concentrated. These efforts were highly successful in the period until World War I as the state cooperated closely with the private sector. However, the war served as a reminder of the vulnerability of Latin American economies to external shock and this fact was driven home further by the collapse of commodity prices in the 1920–21 global depression.

While the export sector boomed, macroeconomic stability was assured and the public debt was serviced without difficulty. Before the war this was underpinned in many countries by the gold standard, the silver standard or even the dollar standard. However, monetary arrangements were disrupted by the war and macroeconomic stability suffered accordingly. The state in this period devoted a high proportion of its scarce resources to defense and a modest amount to semi-public goods such as health and education. Only Uruguay, the pioneer of the welfare state, devoted resources to social security and the provision of private goods through SOEs was minimal. Neither protection of the environment nor promotion of equity were taken into account at this time. Even if they had been, the tiny share of GDP captured by the state would have ruled out any major initiatives. The state in this period was effective in promoting export-led growth, but suffered from two main weaknesses. First, it had no response to external shock, which could easily overwhelm its best efforts to encourage international trade; only Brazil, with the adoption of a valorization scheme for coffee, made a serious effort to address this problem and even in this case the initiative did not initially involve the federal government. Second, the close ties between business and government prevented the state from making a serious attempt to diversify the economy away from excessive dependence on a small number of export products. The region paid a heavy price for such dependency during the Great Depression.

In the second period, the paradigm shifted to an inward-looking model of development. The state, with a few tragic exceptions such as the Chaco War between Bolivia and Paraguay in the 1930s, was no longer troubled by an absence of territorial integrity. The federal government in Brazil, particularly after Getúlio Vargas instituted his Estado Novo (New State) dictatorship in 1937, gained greater control over public policy; meanwhile, President

Roosevelt's Good Neighbor Policy encouraged dictators in the Caribbean basin to fill the gap left by the withdrawal of US troops. All these states began to distance themselves from the traditional élites that had dominated decision-making before the 1930s and this process was carried further with the enfranchisement of a greater proportion of the population.

Autonomy did not necessarily bring accountability, but the growth of state resources strengthened the rule of law. Banditry declined, the judiciary was strengthened and the state acquired the ability to negotiate on more equal terms with foreign investors. These encouraging trends reached a peak in the 1950s, after which the rise of guerrilla movements, the spread of military regimes and a growing hostility to foreign companies once again raised doubts about the rule of law in many countries. The preconditions for an effective state were therefore closer to being met during the second period than ever before. In addition, the prevailing global ideology – heavily influenced by experience in World War II – favored a strong state and the new international agencies were able to support many government activities. The most important was investment in infrastructure, where the state set about constructing the transport, energy and finance systems needed to support industrialization.

The shift to an inward-looking model of development, with its inevitable anti-export bias, placed a strain on the balance of payments and led to chronic inflation in the larger countries. Smaller countries, where the export sector was not so neglected, suffered much less. Almost all countries wasted resources on defense and not a single state put in place a system of protection for the environment despite the mounting evidence of rural degradation and urban pollution. The growth in revenue allowed the state to address the shortcomings in public health and education. Spending on social security also rose, although the beneficiaries were usually restricted to public sector employees and a small number of private sector workers. However, it was in the area of private goods provision through SOEs that state intervention differed most clearly from the period before 1930.

The case of Brazil can be used by way of illustration. From President Vargas onwards, the state in Brazil was distinguished by its commitment to developmentalism. While many things changed with military rule in 1964, this commitment remained the same. The state used public investment to promote those sectors that were considered crucial to development, particularly transport equipment, and an alliance was forged with labor and capital (both domestic and foreign) to secure public goals. The first oil crisis in 1973 exposed the vulnerable side of developmentalism in Brazil and the state was unable to find a suitable response. Elsewhere in Latin America disillusionment with state-led development was already apparent by the end of the 1960s. All countries looked for an exit from the constraints of inward-looking development: some promoted non-traditional exports, others emphasized structural reforms and almost all experimented with regional integration. None of these policies achieved much success and most policymakers were at a loss to respond to the rapid growth of the East Asian tigers.

The question has often been asked if Latin American countries could have replicated the role of the state in East Asia during this phase of its development. The answer is almost certainly in the negative. The East Asian state (for example, in South Korea and Taiwan) was very authoritarian and the presence of an external aggressor gave the state a legitimacy that would have been difficult to repeat in Latin America. In addition, the civil service in the East Asian countries had a different tradition and ethos, being much less politicized and more subject to executive authority. Finally, the state in East Asia was seeking to promote exports while in Latin America ISI was the goal. Thus, the state in the two regions did not even share the same objectives.[21]

From the 1950s onwards, the issue of equity came onto the agenda for the first time. Survey data confirmed what had been long suspected: Latin America had the most unequal distribution of income and wealth of any region in the world. A few countries, notably Colombia and Costa Rica, made a serious effort to tackle inequality through the tax and subsidy system, but most governments took refuge behind the Kuznets curve, which purported to show that inequality will at first worsen with development before eventually improving.

The rise of the developmentalist state during this second period was not without its successes. Between 1930 and 1970, as Table 2.2 shows, Brazil, Mexico and Venezuela were able to reduce the gap in living standards with the United States. Yet it is surely significant that no other country for which we have data in these years was able to do so and in some cases the relative decline was very severe. Honduras and Cuba (first under capitalism and then under socialism) suffered the most, but the southern cone countries were also very badly hit.

The final period, since 1973, marks the long transition over a quarter of a century to neo-liberalism. While there are similarities between this period and the one at the beginning of the century, it would be an error to identify the new paradigm as export-led growth. The reason is that the state now sees its role as one of liberalizing markets so that domestic prices can move closer into line with international prices. Resources are then allocated according to these free market prices; the outcome may favor the export sector, but this is not necessarily so. The state is now supposed to be indifferent between different outcomes provided that they do not threaten macroeconomic stability.

This period has been marked by the increase in the mobility of domestic capital and the rise of globalization. The private sector, in the striking phrase of Albert Hirschman, can now threaten the state with 'exit' and has done so on numerous occasions since 1973 through capital flight.[22] At the same time globalization has put new constraints on the state's freedom of maneuver. The result is a decline in the autonomy of the state, which must increasingly take into account the interests of domestic and foreign capital. This decline in autonomy has gone hand in hand with a serious deterioration in the rule of law. The reasons are complex even if the result is not in doubt. Recession in the 1980s led to a rise in the underclass, which has been swollen by private sector restructuring in the 1990s. Far from absorbing a portion of these displaced workers, the state has been forced to add to their numbers through administrative and SOE reform (including privatization). The result has been an increase in violence and insecurity to which the judicial system has been unable to respond. The preconditions for effective state action have therefore largely been absent in this final period. As a result, there are only modest successes attributable to the public sector. The most significant so far has been macroeconomic stability with a sharp decline in inflation rates in almost all countries. The control of inflation has benefitted from the greater autonomy given to the monetary authorities in each country and the price competition forced on domestic firms by the rise in imports following trade liberalization.

In the provision of other public goods, the role of the state has been very patchy. Defense spending has been cut and the armed forces of many countries are moving towards a new and more relevant concept of national security. The protection of the environment has been pushed up the agenda at the rhetorical level, but state action falls far short of the required response. The external public debt, following restructuring under the Brady Plan, has been serviced in full, but Latin American states still face a hefty risk premium as a result of the failure of governments to establish credibility. The problem of credibility was much less serious in previous periods, but has become a major burden for the modern Latin American state. Credibility should therefore be added to the list of public goods to be provided by an efficient state. To achieve it, a Latin American state must not only carry out coherent and consistent economic policies, but must also differentiate itself in the eyes of (mainly foreign) investors from other countries both inside and outside the region. Even Chile, the most effective of the states in the neoliberal period, has found this to be a difficult task. The reduction of defense spending and subsidies to SOEs, coupled with a greater role for the private sector in the provision of infrastructure, has released resources that the state has been able to devote to semi-public goods – particularly health and education. The state, however, still faces a grave problem; first, the backlog in social spending is enormous and cannot be completed quickly; second, the state is entering new territory in which there is much learning by doing. The optimal balance between the private and public sectors in the provision of semi-public goods has yet to be found. This helps to explain the disappointing impact of neo-liberalism on equity. While poverty has in general fallen in those countries where real GDP per head is growing, the distribution of income has failed to improve. Education is widely seen as the key to greater equity through its impact on the distribution of human capital and it will take many years for the new emphasis by the state to bear fruit.

In conclusion, the state's contribution to Latin America's economic performance has been disappointing in the 20th century. The state must share much of the blame for the failure of the region to close the gap on the United States and for the failure to improve income distribution and management of environmental resources. Yet the new context gives some grounds for optimism – not so much because of the choice of a new economic paradigm (neo-liberalism), but because of the deepening of the democratic process. The empowerment of individual citizens, the emergence of a free press and the spread of non-governmental organizations is making new demands on the Latin American state. In the short-run, the inability of traditional political parties to respond to these demands has made the problem of state failure appear greater, but in the long-term democratization is the best possible assurance of an improvement in state performance.

NOTES

1. Uruguay's GDP per head in 1940 is estimated at $662 (1970 PPP prices) compared with $645 for Argentina. See Thorp (1998), Appendix Table IX.1, p. 353.
2. The Porfiriato is the name given to the period in Mexico's history (1876–1910) dominated by Porfirio Díaz. It was a period of substantial economic achievement, but social and political development lagged far behind.
3. See Bulmer-Thomas (1995), Chapter 3.
4. Cuba ceased to be a Cuban colony at the end of 1898, but it was still under US occupation in 1900 following US intervention in 1898.
5. I here follow the conventional definition of Latin America that excludes Puerto Rico. The latter's level of development was similar to Cuba in 1900 and its peformance would allow it to be classified as a moderate success.
6. PPP exchange rates take into account the difference in the price of non-traded goods and services. These are generally much lower in Latin America (compared with the United States) than is implied by the use of official exchange rates.
7. The Asian financial crisis, which began in 1997, the fall in commodity prices in 1998 and the Brazilian devaluation in 1999 have combined to lower the growth rate of GDP per head below that in the United States since 1996.
8. See World Bank (1997), p. 26.
9. See Thorp (1998), Appendix Table VII.1, p. 346.
10. One example is Elias (1992). The main problem in all these studies is measurement of the capital stock; this has complicated use of the methodology in all regions, but in Latin America the problem is exacerbated by high rates of inflation in many of the larger countries during the years to which growth accounting is applied.
11. See De Janvry (1990). For a good survey on land reform in the region, see Thiesenhusen (1989).
12. The main problem has been the high cost and the difficulty of ensuring that all beneficiaries contribute to the costs.
13. The Inter-American Development Bank (IDB) has carried out numerous studies in this area. See, for example, IDB (1996), Chapter 4.
14. See Bulmer-Thomas (1995), Chapter 10.

15. There is a clear correlation between lending to SOEs and capital flight, although the mechanics under which this occurred is shrouded in mystery.
16. On the new growth theory, see Barro (1998).
17. On growth accounting applied to the demand-side, see Chenery (1960).
18. On savings in Latin America, see Grosse (1998).
19. See Whitehead (1994), p. 398.
20. On trade liberalization in the new growth model, see the chapter by FitzGerald in Bulmer-Thomas (1996).
21. The World Bank has devoted one of its more controversial publications to an analysis of the East Asian state, which contains many interesting comparisons with Latin America. See World Bank (1993).
22. On the concept of 'exit', see Hirschman (1981).

REFERENCES

Barro, R. (1997), *Determinants of Economic Growth: a Cross-Country Empirical Study*, Cambridge, MA: MIT Press.

Bulmer-Thomas, V. (1995), *The Economic History of Latin America since Independence*, Cambridge: Cambridge University Press.

Bulmer-Thomas, V. (ed.) (1996), *The New Economic Model in Latin America and its Impact on Income Distribution and Poverty*, Basingstoke: Macmillan; New York: St. Martin's Press.

Chenery, H. (1960), 'Patterns of industrial growth', *American Economic Review*, **50** (3).

Colclough, C. and J. Manor (eds) (1991), *States or Markets? Neo-liberalism and the Development Policy Debate*, Oxford: Clarendon Press.

De Janvry, A. (1990), *The Agrarian Question and Reformism in Latin America*, Baltimore: Johns Hopkins University Press.

Elias, V. (1992), *Sources of Growth: A Study of Seven Latin American Economies*, San Francisco: International Center for Economic Growth.

Emmerij, L. (ed.) (1997), *Economic and Social Development in the XXI Century*, Washington, DC: Inter-American Development Bank.

Evans, P., D. Rueschemeyer and T. Skocpol (eds) (1985), *Bringing the State Back In*, Cambridge: Cambridge University Press.

Geddes, B. (1994), *Politician's Dilemma: Building State Capacity in Latin America*, Berkeley: University of California Press.

Grosse, R. (ed.) (1998), *Generating Savings for Latin American Development*, Miami: University of Miami, North-South Center Press.

Hirschman, A. (1981), *Essays in Trespassing:Economics to Politics and Beyond*, Cambridge: Cambridge University Press.

Inter-American Development Bank (1996), *Economic and Social Progress in Latin America*, Washington, DC: Inter-American Development Bank.

Klitgaard, R. (1991), *Adjusting to Reality: Beyond 'State versus Market' in Economic Development*, San Francisco: ICS Press.

Maxfield, S. and B.R. Schneider (eds) (1997), *Business and the State in Developing Countries*, Ithaca: Cornell University Press.

Thiesenhusen, W. (1989), *Searching for Agrarian Reform in Latin America*, Boston: Unwin Hyman.

Thorp, R. (1998), *Progress, Poverty and Exclusion: An Economic History of Latin America in the 20th Century*, Washington, DC: Inter-American Development Bank.

Whitehead, L. (1994), 'State organization in Latin America since 1930', in L. Bethell (ed.), *The Cambridge History of Latin America*, Vol. 6, Part 2, Cambridge: Cambridge University Press.
World Bank (1993), *The East Asian Miracle: Economic Growth and Public Policy*, Washington, DC: World Bank.
World Bank (1995), *Bureaucrats in Business: The Economics and Politics of Government Ownership*, Washington, DC: World Bank.
World Bank (1997), *World Development Report*, Washington, DC: World Bank.

COMMENTS ON VICTOR BULMER-THOMAS, 'ECONOMIC PERFORMANCE AND THE STATE IN LATIN AMERICA'

Rachel Schurman

As a sociologist, I very much like Victor Bulmer-Thomas's use of an historical approach, and his emphasis on long-run trends. His chapter gives us the big picture of Latin America's economic performance, and of the changing role that the state has played in this process since the turn of the century. Far too often we find social scientists taking a very short-term perspective, and interpreting contemporary trends as if they could give us a complete view of what is happening. In many cases, adopting a short-term perspective leads us to conclusions that are profoundly misleading. I often see this in the case of Chile, which has had tremendous economic ups and downs over the last 30 years, and for which it matters very much how one periodizes economic trends.

Another strength of Bulmer-Thomas's chapter is his consideration of the varied ways in which the state has influenced Latin America's economic performance over the present century. In an age when neo-liberal thought has become such a powerful influence on development theories and thinking, and such an important purveyor of anti-state sentiments, it is gratifying to hear a discussion that takes a thoughtful and exacting look at the state, asking what it has done to foster economic growth in Latin America, and what it has failed to do, though not necessarily for lack of trying. To paraphrase Peter Evans's latest book (Evans 1995), the fact of state involvement is a given. The relevant question is not about *how much* states should intervene, but what kind of interventions are helpful in achieving specific economic and social objectives. This is clearly the spirit in which Bulmer-Thomas is writing.

I would also like to offer a couple of critical comments, and mention several questions I would like to see more fully addressed. One observation has to do with the problem of breadth vs. depth, which I suppose is inevitable in any paper that is about something as big as Latin America's economic performance over the last century. On the one hand I very much admire Bulmer-Thomas's mastery of Latin American history, and ability to even write such a paper, but on the other, I worry about what is lost by engaging in such an encompassing endeavor. The problem, of course, is that in seeking to identify broad trends, we lose much of the sense of historical specificity that makes such an investigation appealing to begin with. This is particularly the case in the second half of the chapter, which discusses the state's historical role in the growth process. By necessity, this discussion remains very general and abstract, and doesn't give us a sense of texture, variation, and difference in state interventions and their effects, both over time and across space. For example, we all know that similar state policies (such as land reform) did not always produce identical effects in different countries, but that outcomes depended on national contexts, the constellation of class forces, the ways in which policies were implemented, resisted, and so on. Similarly, we know that different states took different actions on the supply and demand side, and that this too, had an impact on outcomes. However, this variation is not explored, and probably cannot be in a chapter that has such a broad scope (beyond the act of identifying the most significant exceptions, which he was able to do). I won't harp on this more, except to add that I would like to see more specific examples and a description of state interventions that succeeded or failed to improve economic performance in a particular country at a given moment in time.

My second critical observation concerns the way the international context and transnational processes are implicated in the successes and failures of the Latin American state. While he certainly does not ignore these relationships, much could be gained by thinking more profoundly about the ways in which the international context shaped state actions, and influenced their effectiveness in stimulating Latin America's economic development. While I think critics were right to challenge the many problematic assumptions of dependency, unequal exchange, and world systems theories, what these theories *did* bring to the fore was the reminder that no country's economic development can be studied in isolation. I think this point also applies to an examination of the role and effectiveness of the state in Latin America.

This brings me to some important questions that I wish the chapter had addressed more directly. One is, What does all that we have learned from this brief historical review, as well as from other studies of the state and economic performance in developing countries, suggest in terms of the future? That is, what kinds of state policies and roles show the most promise of being effective? Bulmer-Thomas partially answers this question in his discussion of policies aimed at achieving macroeconomic stability, but I believe there is more to it than this. In this regard, I would like to mention Peter Evans's recent book, *Embedded Autonomy: States and Industrial Transformation* (Evans 1995). Evans points us toward a much more positive conceptualization of what states can do (and have in some cases, have done) to stimulate the process of economic development. Based on his study of the informatics sector in Brazil, India, and South Korea, respectively, Evans argues that it *is* possible for states to promote economic growth, and to help change their countries' positions in the international division of labor. This is most likely to happen, he says, when the state is both autonomous from the ruling class, yet is firmly embedded in society. By state 'autonomy,' Evans is referring to something similar to that which Bulmer-Thomas emphasizes in this chapter, although Evans makes an important qualification about the character of this autonomy, which is that state agencies need to maintain close ties to the private sector. These ties can help foster the latter's cooperation in the project of domestic economic development, and can serve as two-way channels of information and communication about investment opportunities, state and non-state incentives and disincentives to particular kinds of investment, and so on. Evans also identifies key facilitating roles that the state can play in ushering in or furthering industrial development, namely, the role of midwife, and that of husbandry.

This brings us to my second question, namely, whether specific Latin American states are likely to take on the kinds of policies and fulfill the roles which Evans identifies as key facilitators of industrial development? Stated somewhat differently, we might inquire about the ways in which the last 25 years of neo-liberal thinking and policies have affected states' capacities and proclivities to be proactive in the economic realm, and what kinds of actions are even possible. This chapter certainly begins to address this issue, when Bulmer-Thomas points out the constraints that Latin American states are under because of the increase in capital mobility and direct foreign investment, the threat of domestic capital flight, and the deterioration in the 'rule of law' in many countries. Other constraints he doesn't mention but that would also be important are the de-funding of certain parts of the state bureaucracy, which has reduced the state's capacity for effective action; and the increased economic power of the Latin American bourgeoisie. By attributing the loss of the state's autonomy to globalization, the author draws our attention away from this very important phenomenon, which I think has been a direct outcome of neo-liberal-inspired privatization, 'flexible' labor market policies, regressive tax systems, and other policy changes. The Latin American state does indeed have less 'freedom of maneuver', as he puts it, but part of its loss of autonomy has to do with the private sector's increased economic and hence political power. A third way in which neo-liberalism has affected the state's capacity and proclivity to be proactive in the economic sphere is through the profound ideological effect that this discourse has had on the state's perceived *legitimacy* as a social actor. While I don't mean to suggest that the state should return to playing the role of *demiurge* or direct investor, there *is* a leadership role states can play by the creative use of various forms of industrial policy. The likelihood that the state will be permitted to try out this role, though, is very slim, for the reasons that both Bulmer-Thomas and I have enumerated. It is both ironic and depressing that just at the moment when Latin American countries so much need to build strong, competent, and proactive states to deal with the mounting challenges of globalization, on the one hand, and the problems of economic exclusion, social unrest, and increased violence, on the other, they are in a very weak position to do this. Given this state of affairs, there is important work to be done to help restore the state's legitimacy and capacity for progressive economic and social action, and to think creatively about what forms such action might take.

Reference

Evans, Peter B. (1995), *Embedded Autonomy: States and Industrial Transformation*, Princeton, NJ: Princeton University Press.

3. Rethinking economic performance in Central and Eastern Europe, 1870–1989: old narratives and new evidence[1]

David F. Good

Conditioned by 40 years of cold-war rhetoric, even well-informed observers viewed the economic lag of the former East bloc chiefly as a legacy of communism. Not surprisingly, the initial euphoria in the wake of '1989' quickly gave way to pessimism as the reality of lengthy economic restructuring set in. In long-term historical perspective, both the lag under communism and the shaky path of the Central and Eastern European economies since its demise have a familiar ring. From the middle of the 18th century, political and economic élites in the region have been preoccupied with its low levels of income and wealth compared to the rest of Europe and have advocated strategies of modernization to raise them. Since the mid-19th century, successive shocks on the scale of the collapse of the Soviet Union have led to dramatic, sometimes revolutionary shifts in these strategies. Taken together, these initiatives have led to a profound economic and social transformation that resembles the rest of Europe, but the region remains at best a junior member of the European growth league.

The story of this persisting lag has not been told systemically because the very shocks that had such far-reaching effects in 'the lands between' Germany and Russia make it difficult to measure and interpret the region's long-term economic performance. As a result, the literature on the region's modern economic history is sizable but highly fragmented in its coverage.[2] My current project seeks to provide the synthesis of the region's modern economic history that is missing. In the first phase, I worked with Tongshu Ma to develop the quantitative foundations for the analysis (Good and Ma 1998, 1999). Here I construct four grand narratives of the region's political economy that shape discussions of its long-term economic development and evaluate them in the light of the Good and Ma evidence, which we have expanded to include Latin America.[3]

NARRATIVES OF POLITICAL ECONOMY IN CENTRAL AND EASTERN EUROPE

The periodic refashioning of the region's ideological formations, political boundaries, and institutional arrangements over the past century makes it difficult to conceptualize an overarching framework for interpreting its economic history. Political scientists and economists have articulated the most explicit and well thought-out narrative in focusing on the economic consequences of communism within the overall debate on the economic performance of capitalism and socialism (Ofer 1987). Most assessments are overwhelmingly negative and regard the communist era as a kind of 'missed opportunity' for Central and Eastern Europe. The sources of the missed opportunity were both internal and external. Internal problems were rooted in the institutional mechanisms of state socialism even in its reformed versions – the system's striking inability to provide incentives for 'positive-sum' productivity-raising behavior and its rigidity in the face of changing external circumstances. External problems arose from the region's fundamental isolation from the more dynamic western economies, which persisted despite some opening up in the 1980s. With only limited access to western markets and capital, the region could not tap the sources of economic growth that continued to fuel the catching-up of Western Europe to the United States. Obviously the internal and external factors are related. In the early years, the closed nature of the economic system and the self-sufficiency of the East bloc were mutually reinforcing. The internationalization of the socialist economies in the 1970s aimed at restarting sputtering growth engines; ultimately it may have undermined the system itself.

Recognizing that the economic lag of the region pre-dates the communist era, historians are much less comfortable with a narrative based strictly on the failures of socialism in the post-1945 period. Historians from the states of the former East bloc and Turkey have followed Immanuel Wallerstein (1974) in regarding Eastern Europe as a dependent area within the early modern world system.[4] According to this view, Eastern Europe's trade relationships with Western Europe relegated it to the periphery where it stagnated as a supplier of primary products to the more dynamic states of the core. More recently, Ivan Berend (1996) used the overall vision of core/periphery analysis, if not the model itself, in arguing that state socialism was 'part of a twentieth century rebellion of the unsuccessful peripheries, which were humiliated by economic backwardness and the increasing gap which separated them from the advanced Western core' (p. x). Unable to cope with the structural crisis of the 1970s, the regimes collapsed, which left the region still languishing on the periphery as the 21st century dawns.

Other historians focus on the character of state building in the region rather than its position within the European-wide economic division of labor (Janos 1982; Sugar 1984). According to this view, state structures in Western Europe gradually grew out of and reinforced a self-generating social transformation. By contrast, the political sphere in Eastern Europe played a revolutionary function in the context of highly rigid social and economic relations, which led to top-heavy state structures, and to hierarchical modes of resource allocation and income distribution in the modern period. State socialism represented only the most recent incarnation of this long-standing pattern of state-dominated, hierarchical institutional forms. This literature has not examined the economic consequences of the region's 'abnormal' modernization, but a major implication is that the 'primacy of politics' acted as a drag on economic growth throughout history, not just in the era of state socialism.

The end of the cold war gave a new lease on life to an older narrative based on the prevalence of empire in the region. With the collapse of the Soviet Union, historians and social scientists labeled the former superpower the Soviet 'empire' and included it in formal analyses of the other large, land-based, multinational empires – the Russian, the Habsburg, and the Ottoman – that preceded it in the region (Rudolph and Good 1992; Barkey and von Hagen 1997). These comparative discussions gave little attention to economic issues, but the basic narrative could be extended in this direction using the standard literature on the economies of empires in decline (Cipolla 1970) and the work of nationalist-minded historians who argued that the lesser-developed imperial successor states of the region were systematically exploited by the core areas of the fallen empires.

THE ECONOMIC GROWTH OF CENTRAL AND EASTERN EUROPE IN COMPARATIVE PERSPECTIVE

The Data

All international comparisons of income involving historical data confront two main problems – how to convert data from national currencies to a common base to ensure comparability and how to assure reliability in earlier time periods. Angus Maddison's (1995) handling of these problems has made his country-level estimates of GDP per capita a staple in such international comparisons, and accordingly provide the basis for the data set used here. Following the approach of the International Comparison Project,[5] Maddison (1995) starts with estimates of GDP per capita in 1990 Geary-Khamis dollars, which rely on purchasing power parities rather than exchange rates to convert GDP in different national currencies into a single currency. To develop a time series for each country, he projects back these 1990 levels of GDP with indexes that he derives from the work of country specialists, and uses population estimates to convert these to GDP per capita for the states in their present-day boundaries. Over the years he has modified these indexes as country specialists improve their long-term estimates of GDP.

The periodic 'reinventing' of Central and Eastern Europe in geographical, ideological, and institutional terms over the last century not only hampers interpretations of its long-term economic development; it also compounds the normal problems of making international income comparisons that include the present-day states of the region. Generating long-term data on national income and other economic indicators is especially difficult for the pre-World War I era, when most of the region was under imperial (largely Habsburg) rule. Maddison, for example, has had to rely on fragmentary data for the territories of its post-1919 states. For example, his benchmark estimates for Austria, Czechoslovakia, and Hungary rely on crude 'back-of-the-envelope' calculations based on assumptions about sectoral growth rates in the two quasi-states of the Habsburg empire – Cisleithania (imperial Austria) and Transleithania (imperial Hungary) (1995). He also has very rough estimates for Bulgaria and Yugoslavia for 1913, but no estimates for Poland and Romania.

To provide firmer foundations, Tongshu Ma and I expanded on my earlier adaptation (1994) of a technique that is widely used when national-income type data are poor but a wide range of other socioeconomic data are available.[6] Along the lines of N.F.R. Crafts (1983), we used data for seven benchmark years – 1850, 1860, 1870, 1880, 1890, 1900, and 1910 – and for twelve European countries with reasonably good national income data, Belgium, Denmark, Finland, France, Germany, Italy, Norway, Russia, Sweden, United Kingdom, Netherlands, and Switzerland, to estimate a regression equation where GDP per capita is a function of several proxy variables.[7] Assuming that this structural equation holds for Central and Eastern Europe, we used its coefficients to estimate incomes from proxy data for the Habsburg regions and successor states, and for the independent Balkan states for key benchmark years.[8]

The post-1945 communist era poses an even more basic problem for international comparisons of income that include Central and Eastern Europe. Western specialists agree that the methods used by central planners to calculate the value of national output in socialist economies grossly overstates actual rates of growth. This occurs because output measures involve double counting, exaggerate quality improvements, and reflect political influences to a greater degree than was true in the West (Pryor 1985, pp. 204–6; Marer 1992, pp. 35–8; Maddison 1995, p. 139). In the case of Eastern Europe, the most thorough reworking of the official data using standard national income methodology is by Thad Alton and his associates (Alton 1974, 1985; Alton *et al.* 1985).[9] For this reason, we prefer Maddison's time series data, which rely on Alton's work, instead of the main alternative, the series of the Penn World Tables, which uses growth rates based on the official national accounts of the East bloc countries to project back 1990 levels of income.[10]

The growth rates generated by Maddison's data are also preferred to those produced by the method of physical indicators, which was pioneered in the late 1950s by Ferenc Jánossy and developed further by Eva Ehrlich (1990/1991, 1991), and is a far more complex variant of standard proxy approaches like the one we used for the pre-World War I era. For our purposes, the method has limitations because it generates growth rates between only two benchmark years (1937 and 1960) rather than annual estimates of GDP per capita. More importantly, its growth rate estimates between these two years lead to differences between the former East bloc and the rest of Europe that are very similar to Maddison's. Also, Harrison's (1994) estimate of GDP levels in 1937 for the Soviet Union and Eastern Europe using a modified version of the physical indicators approach and contemporary evidence yields relative income levels in Eastern Europe that are also very close to Maddison's.[11]

Patterns of Long-term Economic Growth

It is not known how rapidly the economies of Central and Eastern Europe grew in the early modern period, and especially in the decades prior to the late 19th century, but the Good and Ma data show unequivocally that the region's lag was well entrenched by 1870. According to the country rankings of Table 3.1 (see Table A3.1 for the underlying data), GDP per capita in the region approached levels in Northwestern Europe only on the territory of present-day Austria and, to a lesser extent, former Czechoslovakia. Moving south and east along the economic gradient, income levels were lower in Hungary, and significantly lower in the Yugoslav lands and in the former Habsburg portions of present-day Poland, Ukraine, and Romania, and in Bulgaria. In addition, based on the data for 1910, income levels were generally higher in Central and Eastern Europe than in Latin America, except for Argentina, whose income level was exceeded in Europe only by the United Kingdom, Switzerland, and Belgium.

How rapidly did the region grow after 1870 and how does this performance compare with the rest of Europe and the economies of Latin America? To answer this question, we estimate the growth rates over the entire period 1870–1989 and within three sub-periods set off by the two world wars of this century: 1870–1914, 1920–1938, and 1950–1989, the standard periodization scheme in modern European economic history.[12] The pre-1914 decades were a period of internationalization and rapid economic growth. Within a liberal international economic order underwritten by British leadership (Brawley 1993), flows of trade, capital, and labor accelerated (Williamson 1996), and fueled

Table 3.1 Rank order of economies in Europe and Latin America according to GDP per capita: 1870, 1910, 1938, 1989

1870	1910	1938	1989
United Kingdom	United Kingdom	Switzerland	Switzerland
Belgium	Switzerland	United Kingdom	Germany
Netherlands	Belgium	Denmark	Sweden
Switzerland	*Argentina*	Germany	Denmark
Denmark	Netherlands	Netherlands	France
Germany	Denmark	Belgium	Finland
Austria	Germany	Sweden	Norway
France	**Austria**	France	**Austria**
Sweden	Sweden	*Venezuela*	Belgium
Czechoslovakia	France	*Argentina*	United Kingdom
Italy	**Czechoslovakia**	Norway	Netherlands
Spain	*Chile*	**Austria**	Italy
Argentina	Italy	Finland	**East Germany**
Norway	**Hungary**	Italy	Spain
Hungary	Spain	*Chile*	Portugal
Bulgaria	Norway	**Czechoslovakia**	Greece
Finland	Finland	Greece	**Czechoslovakia**
Portugal	**Poland**	**Hungary**	*Venezuela*
Poland	**Romania**	**Poland**	**Hungary**
Romania	**Yugoslavia**	*Colombia*	*Argentina*
Yugoslavia	**Bulgaria**	*Peru*	*Chile*
Brazil	*Mexico*	Portugal	**Bulgaria**
Mexico	Portugal	**Bulgaria**	**Yugoslavia**
	Peru	*Mexico*	**Poland**
	Venezuela	**Yugoslavia**	*Brazil*
	Brazil	*Brazil*	*Mexico*
		Romania	*Colombia*
			Romania
			Peru

Notes: Rankings based on the data in Table A3.1. Central and Eastern European countries in bold; Latin American countries in italics.

industrialization over much of continental Europe and in the lands of overseas settlement. In the two decades between the world wars, international flows of trade, capital, and labor shrank drastically (Williamson 1996) as the international economic order collapsed (Eichengreen 1992), class conflict severely hampered the formation of economic policy (Maier 1975), and economic growth slowed, especially under the weight of the great depression. In the post-World War II era, flows of trade, capital, and labor surged within a liberal international economic order that was underwritten this time by American economic leadership and by domestic institutional arrangements in Western Europe that fueled rapid productivity growth (Van der Wee 1986). In the East, the institutions of Soviet-style central planning promoted aggressive policies of modernization within a highly regulated and self-contained international economic order (Berend 1996).

Based on the regional growth rates of Table 3.2, Central and Eastern Europe grew rapidly from 1870 to World War I at a rate that was exceeded only by Latin America[13] and matched only in Europe by the Nordic economies. Between the two world wars, the region grew at the European average; slower than the Nordic, about the same as the Mediterranean, but faster than both the Northwest and Latin America. The region also grew at the European average in the post-1945 era (slightly above it before 1973 and well below it after 1973); slower than the Mediterranean, somewhat faster than the Nordic and the Northwest, and considerably faster than Latin America. Over the entire period 1870–1989, the region grew very close to the European average; somewhat slower than the Mediterranean and the Nordic, but faster than the Northwest and Latin America, which grew more slowly than all the regions of Europe.

The finding that growth was substantially lower in the former East bloc than in the rest of Europe after 1973 is consistent with the view of most specialists who disagree on its sources, but agree that the slowdown in economic growth after the golden age was more pronounced than in the West (Bergson 1978; Ofer 1987; Brada 1989; Banerjee and Spagat 1991; Pryor 1994). Ma and I have used Maddison's data on GDP per capita to calculate more precise measures of the growth slowdown. Two of them build on the notion of a trend break that divides two phases of growth in GDP. The first is measured as the percentage point difference between the growth rates before and after the trend break in 1973, the year of the oil-price shock, which follows standard interpretations of the post-1945 'golden age.' The second measure is like the first except that the year of the trend break is estimated separately for each country based on the behavior of its time series.[14] The third measure starts from the notion that GDP gradually slowed down over the entire period with no clear break in trend. The deceleration in growth is estimated for each time series as the annual percentage point drop in the growth rate from the initial rate in 1950.

The evidence in Table 3.2 on all three measures largely confirms the conventional wisdom about the growth slowdown in the former East bloc. The data show that except for the Mediterranean the growth slowdown was more pronounced in the state socialist economies of Eastern Europe than in the rest of Europe and Latin America. The percentage point difference in growth rates before and after 1973 (the first measure) averaged 2.9 in Eastern Europe, which

Table 3.2 Long-term economic growth in Latin America and in four regions of Europe

	Annual rate of growth in GDP per capita						Post-WWII slowdown		
	1870–1910	1920–38	1950–73	1973–89	1950–89	1870–1989	TB73	TBE	GS
Europe	1.23	2.00	4.06	1.68	3.23	1.92	–2.38	–2.37	–0.05
Northwest	1.19	1.51	3.45	1.61	2.75	1.64	–1.84	–1.87	–0.04
Nordic	1.32	2.76	3.41	2.38	3.04	2.12	–1.04	–0.08	–0.02
Mediterranean	0.89	1.97	5.41	1.87	4.24	2.09	–3.55	–3.37	–0.07
Central/East (A)	1.37	1.99	4.17	1.29	3.18	1.99	–2.88	–3.40	–0.07
Central/East (B)	1.40	2.22	4.10	1.17	3.10	1.94	–2.92	–3.51	–0.07
Latin America I	1.55	1.89	2.24	0.18	1.70	1.76	–2.06	–2.08	–0.04
Latin America II	1.55	0.22	2.78	0.39	2.40	1.76	–2.39	–3.28	–0.04

Notes: Central/Eastern Europe (A) includes Austria. Central and Eastern Europe (B) excludes Austria. Latin America I includes Argentina, Brazil, and Mexico only. Latin America II includes all countries for which data are available. The regional growth rates and measures of the growth slowdown are calculated from Table A3.2 as the simple averages of the individual countries in each region.

was less than the Mediterranean (3.6), but larger than Latin America (2.1), the Northwest (1.84), and the Nordic (1.04). The percentage point difference in growth rates before and after the year of the trend break as estimated for each country (the second measure) averaged 3.5 for Eastern Europe and 3.4 for the Mediterranean, compared to 2.1 for Latin America, 1.87 for the Northwest, and 0.08 for the Nordic. The annual percentage point decline in the growth rate of GDP per capita after 1950 (the third measure) was 0.07 for Eastern Europe and the Mediterranean compared to 0.04 for Northwest Europe and Latin America, and 0.02 for the Nordic.

ASSESSING THE REGION'S ECONOMIC PERFORMANCE

Taken alone, these data on levels and rates of growth in GDP per capita are not sufficient for drawing conclusions about the long-run economic performance of Central and Eastern Europe. Growth at the European average from 1870 to 1989 implies that the region's relative position within Europe remained essentially unchanged over the long run, which is confirmed by a comparison of country rankings (Table 3.1) and of income levels (Table A3.1) for 1870 and 1989.[15] More importantly, both economic theory and economic history suggest that the region's economies had the potential for growth well above the European average within the subperiods between 1870 and 1989 and over the period as a whole. By this standard, the region's economies performed rather poorly.

A sizable literature has debated the notion that low income economies may, by their very nature, grow faster than high income economies in a temporary period of catch-up. In the 1950s, neo-classical growth models (Solow 1956) led to predictions of income convergence across nations and regions, while models of uneven regional development (Myrdal 1957; Hirschman 1958) allowed for income disparities to persist and even widen.[16] Similarly, among economic historians Gerschenkron (1962) argued that certain advantages of backwardness may have permitted low income economies in 19th-century Europe to engineer a 'great spurt' of industrial growth, but that a sustained catching-up was in no way inevitable. Working within the framework of the new growth theory, macroeconomists have recently revived the debate. Cross-country empirical analyses based on neo-classical models, including those augmented by measures of human capital, technological diffusion, and political institutions, have confirmed the predictions of convergence (Baumol 1986; Dowrick and Nguyen 1989; Mankiw et al. 1992; Barro 1997), while models of endogenous growth contain no necessary convergence properties (Romer 1990; Rebelo 1991; Lucas 1993).

A large literature also surrounds the idea that an economy may temporarily experience unusually rapid growth after a period of slower growth or a sharp downturn in economic activity. Short-term business cycles normally display this pattern, but some scholars have argued that secular trends also follow a regular cyclical pattern (Kondratieff 1935; Schumpeter 1935; Kuznets 1965, pp. 1–81 and 328–78). Maddison (1991) agrees that major turning points and changes in momentum can signal changes in the secular trend of economic activity, but he sees their sources in system shocks that are exogenous rather than in long swings or long waves that are endogenous to the economic system. Maddison's view is consistent with the vast literature on 20th-century economic history, which sees the two world wars of this century as major watersheds in European economic development. In the now standard view, the slow growth in the inter-war period, which was associated with incomplete recovery from World War I and the great depression contrasts sharply with the more rapid growth in the decades before World War I and in the unprecedented golden age of growth that followed World War II. Finally, the recent debate among new growth theorists about the nature of time series data (Nelson and Plosser 1982) supports the notion that shocks may lead to temporary changes in the secular trend of output. Econometric tests on a time series like GDP that allow for breaks in trend as a result of exogenous shocks like the two world wars, support the idea that output moves over time in a trend stationary rather than random walk fashion, which means that deviations will only be temporary and that the series will eventually return to its trend (Perron 1989; Rappoport and Reichlin 1989). The Good and Ma analysis follows in the tradition of Crafts and Mills (1996) who applied the new growth theory in analyses of post-1945 growth in Western Europe after World War II, and especially of Dumke (1990) who demonstrated econometrically that the size of shocks induced by World War II and the subsequent recoveries from them account for much of the differences in growth rates among 16 OECD countries in the post-1945 era.

In summary, the literature suggests that two key factors should be taken into account in assessing long-term economic performance in a comparative context. In a given time period, a country's measured rate of economic growth may be judged fast or slow depending on its relative income level and the relative severity of its economic downturns in the wake of major shocks. All things being equal, those economies that start at lower income levels and experience greater shock-induced declines in output have the potential for growing faster than those economies that have higher income levels and experience smaller shock-induced output declines.

Table 3.3 shows the potential significance of this for the particular case of Central and Eastern Europe. As a group, the economies of the region had consistently low income levels (the lowest of all regions in 1938, and the lowest except for Latin America in 1870 and 1910) and experienced greater shock-induced output declines (the worst as a result of the two world wars, and the worst except for Latin America in the case of the great depression). To test whether measured rates of growth in the region fell short of the potential inherent in its relatively low income and more severe shocks, Ma and I specify a formal model in which the rate of growth in GDP per capita in a given time period is a function of three variables – the relative economic lag, the severity of shocks, and a variable that tests for regional effects – and use regression analysis to estimate it for economies in both Europe and Latin America.

The ratio of each country's GDP per capita to GDP per capita in the United States measures the growth potential inherent in the size of a country's economic lag; the bigger the lag, the greater the potential for rapid growth in a catch-up phase. The lag is measured in 1870 for the pre-World War I period, in 1910 for the period between the wars, and in 1938 for the post-World War II period. The ratio of the post-shock to the pre-shock level of GDP per capita measures the severity of shocks. The more severe the shock, the greater the potential for rapid growth during a post-shock phase of recovery. For the pre-World War I era, there were no universal shocks on the scale of the two world wars and the great depression of the 1930s. For the inter-war period, the severity of the shock of World War I is measured as the ratio of GDP per capita in 1920 to 1910. The severity of the shock of the great depression is measured for each country as the ratio of GDP per capita in the trough of the depression to the peak of the previous boom. For the post-1945 period, the severity of the shock of World War II is measured as the ratio of GDP per capita in 1950 to 1938. The regional effects are captured by a third variable that is composed of three separate 'dummies,' one each for the three low-income regions in the group – Central and Eastern Europe, Mediterranean Europe, and Latin America. In each case, the dummy variable for a region equals 1 for all countries in the region and 0 for those outside it. The sign and significance level of the coefficients on each regional dummy indicate whether the region's rate of economic growth differed significantly from that of the countries in Northwestern and Nordic Europe given its relative income levels and the relative severity of shocks.

For the pre-World War I era, the estimated regression coefficient for the regional dummy variable shows that the higher than average measured growth (Table 3.2) meant that the region grew at 0.2 percentage points above the rate that was consistent with its relatively low income level in 1870.[17] The same conclusion holds for Latin America, which grew at 0.4 percentage points above the potential inherent in its low income, but not for the Mediterranean, which grew at 0.3 percentage points below its potential. These results are not statistically significant, but at least they indicate that after accounting for differences in income levels, growth rates were no different in Central and Eastern Europe than elsewhere.

In the inter-war period, the estimated coefficient on the regional dummy variable shows that the measured rate of growth in Central and Eastern Europe at the European average actually may be considered as a kind of missed

Table 3.3 *Levels of GDP per capita and the severity of shocks in four regions of Europe and in Latin America 1870–1989*

	GDP per capita (1990 Geary-Khamis Dollars)							Shock variables		
	1870	1910	1920	1938	1950	1973	1989	WWI	GD	WWII
Europe	1643	2657	2466	3586	4026	9725	13096	0.89	0.88	1.10
Northwest	2414	3819	3847	5281	6081	13451	17577	1.01	0.86	1.14
Nordic	1500	2612	2741	4366	5630	11977	17141	1.05	0.94	1.29
Mediterranean	1309	1914	1914	2324	2477	8629	12005	0.96	0.95	1.05
Central/East (A)	1207	2005	1363	2227	2458	6354	8258	0.65	0.83	1.00
Central/East (B)	1093	1837	1185	2001	2277	5646	7108	0.63	0.84	0.99
Latin America I	920	1732	1817	2518	3478	5617	5571	1.14	0.79	1.35
Latin America II	920	2017	1988	2248	2915	5357	5562	1.06	0.80	1.34

Notes: Central/Eastern Europe (A) includes Austria. Central and Eastern Europe (B) excludes Austria. Latin America I includes Argentina, Brazil, and Mexico only. Latin America II includes all countries for which data are available. The regional levels of GDP per capita are calculated from Table A3.1 as the simple averages of the individual countries in each region. The severity of the shocks are calculated as the simple averages of the individual countries from time-series data in the sources described in Table A3.1. The measures are defined as follows:

WWI: The ratio of GDP per capita in 1920 to 1910.
GD: The ratio of GDP per capita in the trough of the great depression to the peak of the previous boom.
WWII: The ratio of GDP per capita in 1950 to 1938.

opportunity for the region. The region grew at 2.0 percentage points below its potential, that is, the rate that was consistent with its income level in 1910 and the output declines associated with both the World War I and the great depression. In this period, all three low-income regions performed relatively poorly. Latin America also grew at 2.0 percentage points below potential while the Mediterranean grew at 1.4 percentage points below potential.[18]

In the post-1945 era, the states of the former East bloc grew very rapidly during the post-1945 era at or near the European average, but this period, too, clearly represents a decisive missed opportunity than was true to the inter-war era. Growth in the former East bloc was 1.4 percentage points below the rate that was consistent with its low income levels in 1938 and the large declines in output associated with World War II.[19] The shortfall was even greater for Latin America where growth was 2.1 percentage points below potential.[20] By contrast, the high rate of growth of the Mediterranean after World War II was very close to the rate that was consistent with its income levels in 1938 and its decline in output associated with World War II. These results for the era of the cold war conform to the pattern for the entire period 1870–1989. Over the long run, both Central and Eastern Europe and Latin America grew below the potential inherent in their initially low incomes (the former by 0.5 percentage points and the latter by 0.9 percentage points) while the Mediterranean grew more or less at its potential.[21]

The same factors that may lead to temporary periods of unusually rapid growth (catching up by low income economies and rapid recovery from shocks like war) imply that if growth is above normal for a period of time, it will eventually slow down and give way to more normal rates. For this reason, we need to test more formally the evidence reported earlier, which confirmed conventional wisdom that the former East bloc suffered an unusually sharp slowdown in economic growth at the end of the golden age. Regression estimates of the full model that includes the three measures of slowdown as the dependent variables, and relative income levels in 1938, the ratio of income in 1950 to 1938, and the three regional dummies as independent variables, suggest that the substantial slowdown in the former East bloc (and the Mediterranean as well) represented a return to a more normal growth path after a vigorous phase of catch-up after World War II. Only for the third measure (the annual percentage point decline in the rate after 1950), did the dummy variable come close to being statistically significant. These findings differ from Pryor (1994) who, as noted above, uses a different sample of western countries and does not include a shock variable for World War II, but they are consistent with Harrison (1998) who found that the exhaustion of post-war recovery possibilities accounts for a good portion of the slowdown in labor productivity in the Soviet Union from the late 1940s through the 1960s.

THE NARRATIVES IN THE LIGHT OF THE EVIDENCE

How do the four narratives of the economic lag in Central and Eastern Europe on the eve of '1989' stack up against the evidence presented above? The finding that the former East bloc, unlike the Mediterranean, did not grow at its potential after 1945 is certainly consistent with the failures-of-socialism approach, but the evidence that the shortfall of actual growth below potential was even greater in Latin America is not. In addition, the results do not support the conventional wisdom that the growth slowdown in the former East bloc during the two decades before 1989 was more severe than in the rest of Europe, which supports the view that the sources of the slowdown may transcend the system's peculiar institutional features (Maier 1997). Finally, the evidence confirms what most specialists already know: that state socialism cannot bear the full burden of the region's lag in 1989 because the communists took over economies with a long history of relatively low income levels.

Nor does the bulk of recent scholarship give much support for a core/periphery narrative of Central and Eastern European economic history. Lampe (1989), for example, argues that the region had too little contact with the rest of Europe, not too much. The region became systematically integrated into the higher-income economies in Western Europe only in the era of internationalization before World War I, which may explain its ability to grow at a rate that was consistent with its low income levels. By contrast, the states of the region tended to grow below their potential when the international economic order collapsed between the wars, and when their isolation from the West became especially acute during the cold war. Long-term growth in Latin America shows a similar pattern that is also not consistent with a core/periphery narrative – growth at potential in the pre-1914 era of internationalizaton, and growth below potential in the inter-war years when the international economy disintegrated and in its era of inward-looking development during much of the post-1945 period.

The relatively poor performance of Central and Eastern Europe between the wars and in the post-1945 periods seems to support a narrative of the economic lag based on the primacy of politics inherent in its allegedly abnormal modernization. Against it, however, is the finding that the region grew at a rate that was consistent with its relatively low income levels before 1914. Moreover, historians of the pre-World War I era agree that its modernization was unique, but challenge the idea that it was abnormal (Mishkova 1995; Cohen 1998) and political scientists have cast doubt on the basic premise that autocratic, bureaucratic political regimes necessarily choke off economic growth, while democratic regimes foster it (Przeworski and Limongi 1993). Many of these points seem relevant for evaluating the quite similar long-run economic performance of Latin America as well.

The relatively poor performance of Central and Eastern Europe under Soviet rule also seems to support the burden-of-empire view. But against this view is the evidence that rates of economic growth before 1914 may have been more rapid in the territories under Habsburg and Ottoman rule than in the independent Balkan states (Okyar 1987; Palairet 1997), and also our findings that the region did not grow up to potential in the inter-war period when no imperial yoke was in place. Also, within the Soviet imperial system, trade between the Soviet 'core' and the Eastern European 'periphery' did not conform to the standard model of exploitation: Soviet primary products were exchanged for East European manufactured goods at terms of exchange that favored East Europe rather than the other way around (Gati 1990). Finally, economic performance in Latin America, as has been noted, largely mirrored that in Central and Eastern Europe, yet its countries achieved political independence in the early 19th century, and their relationship with the United States never involved the degree of subordination to imperial power that characterized the socialist states within the Soviet orbit.

AN ALTERNATIVE NARRATIVE

Taken alone, none of these narratives is very useful in providing a framework for understanding patterns of long-term economic growth in Central and Eastern Europe. They do, however, offer insights into the key elements of a plausible story. The narratives of failed socialism and of the region's unique path to modernization point to the importance of institutional differences between West and East, while the narratives of core/periphery and of imperial burden point to the importance of the region's position within the division of labor both Europe-wide and within the region itself. In contrast to existing narratives, I favor one that puts greater weight on discontinuities rather than continuities in the region's institutional arrangements and on the benefits of contact rather than isolation within the international division of labor.

At this point, I can only sketch out the basic outlines of an alternative framework. Consistent with the perspective above, it would draw on the recent work of political economists and economic historians who stress the key role of institutions and incentive structures in determining rates of investment, human capital formation, and technological change – the proximate, narrowly economic sources of long-term growth in per capita income (Hayami and Ruttan 1985; North 1990). The striking thing about the character of institutional arrangements in Central and Eastern Europe over the last one hundred years or so is not their stability, but their instability in the wake of major shocks. The source of this institutional instability may lie in the pattern of state building and economic development in the region, which differed from the West in its timing, but not necessarily in its underlying character. Due to the relative isolation of Central and Eastern Europe from the full force of the commercial revolution in the late medieval and early modern periods, the peoples of the region entered the modern era not only at low levels of socioeconomic development, but also, contrary to the primacy-of-politics narrative, with relatively weak state structures (Mishkova 1995). Accordingly, in face of competition from abroad, ruling élites promoted state-building agendas and strategies of economic development much later in Central and Eastern Europe and with a greater sense of urgency than elsewhere. These emerging state structures and their underlying economies proved to be highly vulnerable to the shocks of war and depression that characterized the 20th century.

The shocks of the two world wars had an impact that went far beyond the destruction of human life, capital equipment, and infrastructure that typically follows military clashes. They led to large-scale efforts by élites to reinvent institutions and ideology that were far more profound in Central and Eastern Europe than elsewhere. Prior to World War I, local élites in the region used ethnic symbols and appeals to mobilize local populations in the context of uneven economic development but, at least in the lands under Habsburg rule, political mobilization occurred within a largely stable set of institutional arrangements. After World War I, the Paris peace treaties fundamentally redrew the map of the region, which brought disruptions in financial and labor markets, and in legal structures, as new states came into existence. Elites spent the next two decades adapting existing institutions to the new set of international realities.

World War II initiated institutional discontinuities of a different kind. As in the case of World War I, institutional arrangements were disrupted by some territorial realignments, but this occurred on a relatively modest scale. The major shock to institutions was an indirect result of the war – occupation by the Soviet Union. By 1950, modernizing élites were promoting state socialism on the Soviet model as an answer to the discredited models of development in inter-war Europe – fascism and liberal capitalism. They spent the next three decades implementing and fine-tuning this systemic transformation in the context of the cold war. After 1989, the erosion and sudden collapse of the Soviet Union launched a new era of institutional change whose scale and scope has matched the previous post-1945 systemic transformation to communism.

A growing literature in political science and economics (Sierman 1998) argues that the transactions costs of this kind of institutional instability are large. The uncertainty surrounding these frequent large-scale, ongoing transformations in Central and Eastern Europe would have created disincentives for individuals and economic élites to undertake productivity-raising investments in physical and human capital and to respond flexibly to rapid change. Over time, the sheer task of reinventing new institutional arrangements every few decades would have made it difficult for the region to grow at its potential and begin catching up with the rest of Europe. Considering that no existing narrative adequately accounts for the persisting economic lag of the region over the last century, this narrative merits careful examination.[22]

Two important issues must be resolved before applying the framework outlined above in a synthesis of long-term economic development in Central and Eastern Europe. First, my description of an alternative narrative based on the notion of institutional instability has been quite abstract. How should institutional instability be measured? What features of the institutional landscape that shapes economic decision-making should be included? Land tenure arrangements? Capital markets? Fiscal systems of taxation and spending?

Second, in focusing on cross-regional comparisons, my chapter has treated Central and Eastern Europe as a homogeneous entity and ignored the substantial variation in economic performance and underlying institutions within it. It seems reasonable to expect that explanations for why the region's lag within Europe persists would also account for the persistence of economic disparities within the region.

The Good and Ma analysis does reveal considerable variation in economic performance within the region. For example, the territory of present-day Austria grew relatively slowly before World War I and in the inter-war period, and relatively fast after 1945. The performance of the present-day territory of Hungary was the opposite; it grew relatively fast before World War I and in the inter-war period, and relatively slowly after 1945.

In addition, the region shows substantial variation in its institutional landscape. Despite being a part of Central and Eastern Europe in some broad historical and cultural sense, for example, the territories of present-day Austria, Bulgaria, Croatia, the Czech Republic, Hungary, and Serbia represent quite different patterns of institution change in politics and economics since the middle of the 19th century. Some (Austria, the Czech Republic, Hungary, and Croatia) had histories under Habsburg rule through World War I; while others (Bulgaria and Serbia) fell under Ottoman rule but gained independence before 1914. Within the Habsburg Monarchy, the territories of present-day Austria and the Czech Republic were administered from Vienna in the Austrian lands, the territory of present-day Hungary was administered from Budapest in the Hungarian lands, and the territory of present-day Croatia fell under administrative control of both Vienna and Budapest. After 1919, Austria, Bulgaria, and Hungary functioned as states in more or less their current boundaries, while the other three were territories in two newly-formed multinational states, which dissolved after 1989: Croatia and Serbia in Yugoslavia, and the Czech Republic in Czechoslovakia. In the cold war, Austria was the only state in the region to avoid communist rule. Finally, during the cold war communism evolved quite differently in Hungary, in the Czech republic within Czechoslovakia, in Bulgaria, and in Croatia and Serbia within Yugoslavia. Do these differences in patterns of institutional change help to explain differences among these states in economic performance in the three sub-periods since 1870?[23]

This rethinking of economic performance has important implications for the post-communist transformation currently underway. As noted above, the region is currently in the midst of fundamentally reinventing institutional arrangements for the third time this century. If the story of institutional stability makes sense, then for the states of Central and Eastern Europe to begin catching-up, new arrangements must be adaptable in face of changing circumstances yet stable enough to withstand the impact of major shocks, a characteristic that has eluded the region in the 20th century. The findings also have implications for the big debates among economic historians about 'why the West grew rich,' which tend to focus on continents rather than states as units of analysis. It is true that in a cultural sense individual European states resemble each other and other European offshoots more than the states of Africa and Asia. Yet, long-standing economic disparities within Europe persist and continue to be very large, so lumping together the states of Europe in explanations of when and why Europe and the non-European world diverged should be avoided. Finally, the comparison of long-term economic growth in Central Eastern Europe that includes Latin America suggests the value of a deeper, more substantive historical comparison of economic development in the two regions. In particular, because the long-term pattern of economic growth in the periods set off by the world wars in Latin America resembled that in Central and Eastern Europe, it would be worthwhile examining whether Latin America also had a broadly similar pattern of institutional instability.

NOTES

1. The quantitative analysis of growth in Central and Eastern Europe was carried out under a German Marshall Fund of the United States Research Fellowship and with the aid of a grant from the Graduate School of the University of Minnesota. I wish to thank Tongshu Ma for extending the quantitative work underlying our co-authored articles to include Latin America, and Carol Skalnik Leff for her detailed and valuable comments on the initial draft.
2. Lampe and Jackson (1982) focus on the Balkans in the four centuries ending in 1950 while Palairet (1997) deals with the 19th century only. Good (1984) and Komlos (1983) cover the lands under Habsburg rule in the century and a half before World War I. Aldcroft and Morehead (1995) and Kaser and Radice (1985) focus on the post-1919 era and exclude Austria. In an earlier work, Berend and Ranki (1974) include Austria but devote little attention to the communist era, while in his more recent work Berend (1996) focuses on the communist era and excludes Austria. Finally, the contributions in Chirot (1989) cover a large chronological span, but ignore Austria and the communist experience.
3. For a recent survey of Latin American economic history see Bulmer-Thomas (1994). For an analysis of economic performance in the era of inward-looking development from 1930 to the 1980s, see Taylor (1998).
4. Cited in Lampe (1989).
5. For a useful summary of this approach see Kravis et al. (1978), Kravis (1986) and Summers and Heston (1988).

6. The remainder of this section relied on Good and Ma (1998; 1999). See these sources for details.
7. The data for GDP per capita are from Angus Maddison (1989, 1990) and the independent variables were calculated from data in B.R. Mitchell (1975). Taking account of criticisms and comments, especially Pammer (1997), we refined the estimating procedure and the underlying data. We used the maximum likelihood method to deal with the panel data problem that is inherent in using ordinary least squares to estimate the structural equation from pooled time series and cross-sectional data, and Maddison's (1995) most recent estimates of GDP per capita as the dependent variable. Estimates using several combinations of independent variables yielded an equation with the best fit, which included a constant term, mailed letters per capita, the crude death rate, and the share of the non-agricultural labor force in the total labor force.
8. The resulting estimates of income in the region are more reliable than earlier ones (Good 1994) and there is less uncertainty surrounding the 95 percent confidence intervals. The pattern of the residuals indicates that the structural relationship in the equation is stable over time and comparisons of these proxy-based estimates with national income-based estimates for the two imperial 'halves' of the post-1867 Habsburg empire, and for the territory of present-day Austria indicate that it is reasonably stable as we move from the European countries with good data to Central and Eastern Europe. They also reinforce the view of John Hanson (1986, 1991) who argues from export data that existing studies greatly underestimate pre-1914 levels of GDP in both the Third World and in Eastern Europe.
9. See Maddison (1995, pp. 139–41) and Pryor (1985, p. 206, n. 4).
10. Formal statistical tests on the ratio of the Penn Tables series and the Maddison series using annual data for the socialist and non-socialist countries of post-1945 Europe show that there is no significant difference between the two series in the case of the non-socialist countries, but compared to the Maddison series the Penn Tables series leads to systematically higher rates of growth in the socialist countries.
11. Harrison's main conclusion is that Maddison's estimate of GDP per capita (1980 international dollars, based on Phase IV of the International Comparisons Project) for the Soviet Union is too high because it stands at 50 percent of the British level. But Maddison's most recent estimate of Soviet GDP per capita (1990 Geary-Khamis dollars) for 1937 is only 36 percent of the British level, which exactly matches the income relative implicit in Harrison's estimate using his preferred Model B. Also, Harrison's income relatives for the Eastern European countries in 1937 compared to Britain are actually somewhat *higher* than Maddison's for Hungary, Poland, Bulgaria, and Czechoslovakia, and quite a bit higher for Romania and Yugoslavia (calculated from data in his Table 5).
12. Austria clearly belonged to Central and Eastern Europe under Habsburg rule before World War I and in the inter-war era. It was not part of the East bloc in the era of state socialism, which means that in institutional terms its economic, social, and political development diverged significantly from its neighbors in the region. Accordingly, we provide two sets of estimates for income levels and growth rates in Central and Eastern Europe (Tables 3.2 and 3.3) – one that includes and one that excludes Austria in the three periods. In the formal analysis of growth rates that we discuss later, we include Austria in Central and Eastern Europe in the pre-World War I and inter-war periods, but not after 1945. Austria's Anschluss with Germany between 1938 and 1945 and its evolution outside the East bloc until 1989 in no small measure overwhelmed the long-standing cultural, political, and economic ties that bound it inextricably to the region prior to World War II.
13. Based on data available for three countries only, two of which – Argentina and Mexico – experienced exceptionally high growth.
14. The estimated trend-break year for individual countries ranges from 1961 (East Germany) to 1985 (Norway), although they do tend to cluster in the early 1970s. The growth slowdown for each country is measured as the percentage point difference between the growth rates in the two periods before and after the year of each country's trend break.
15. The rest of this section draws on Good and Ma (1999). See original source for details.
16. For a survey and analysis of this earlier literature see Williamson (1965).

17. The estimates described in the following paragraphs follow the same procedure as Good and Ma (1999).
18. Although the standard errors of the estimated coefficients are much smaller than was the case for the estimates using pre-1914 data, only the result for Central and Eastern Europe is close to being statistically significant even at the 0.10 level.
19. The Good and Ma results differ from Pryor's (1985) who found that after accounting for differences in initial levels of income, growth rates in post-1945 Eastern European economies were not slower. Apart from differences in underlying data, his results are not strictly comparable with ours. His sample of western countries included all OECD countries, not just European members, and his sample of Eastern European countries included the Soviet Union. Also, he did not include a war shock variable in his regressions.
20. For both regions, the statistical significance of these results is very high – at the 0.001 level.
21. The result is significant for Central and Eastern Europe at the 0.05 level and for Latin America at the 0.01 level.
22. The argument might be weakened somewhat if the Soviet Union were brought into the analysis. It could be argued that the Soviet Union experienced less institutional stability than the rest of Central and Eastern Europe, which was reinvented after both world wars, not just the first. But the reality may have been quite different. The dramatic policy shifts in the inter-war years associated with War Communism, the New Economic Policy and the Five-Year Plan, and the purges, plus the effects of World War II, suggest that the institutions of state socialism in the Soviet Union did not stabilize until well after 1945. Our data for Central and Eastern Europe and Maddison's data for the Soviet Union (Maddison 1995) show that the two had very similar growth experiences. In 1910, GDP per capita in Russia stood at 90 percent of the average for Central and Eastern Europe. Subsequently, the Soviet Union did grow faster, but only marginally. By 1989 its level of GDP per capita stood at the average of the states in the former East bloc, which is consistent with its slightly lower income level in 1910.
23. The published results in Good and Ma (1999) include analyses of growth rate estimates for the Habsburg successor state territories for the period 1870–1910 and 1950–89, but not for the period 1920–38.

REFERENCES

Aldcroft, D.H. and S. Morehead (1995), *Economic Change in Eastern Europe since 1918*, Aldershot, UK and Brookfield, US: Edward Elgar.

Alton, T.P. (1974), 'Economic growth and resource allocation in Eastern Europe', *Reorientation and Commercial Relations of the Economies of Eastern Europe*, USC Joint Economic Committee, Washington, DC: Government Printing Office, 251–98.

Alton, T.P. (1985), 'East European GNPs: origins of product, final uses, rates of growth, and international comparisons', *East European Economies: Slow Growth in the 1980s*, USC Joint Economic Committee, Washington, DC: Government Printing Office, 81–132.

Alton, T.P. (1985), 'East European GNP by origin and domestic final uses of gross product, 1965–1984', New York: Research Project on National Income in East Central Europe.

Banerjee, A.V. and M. Spagat (1991), 'Productivity paralysis and the complexity problem: Why do centrally planned economies become prematurely gray', *Journal of Comparative Economics*, **15**, 646–60.

Barkey, K. and M. von Hagen (eds) (1997), *After Empire: Multiethnic Societies and Nation Building: The Soviet Union and the Russian, Ottoman, and Habsburg Empires*, Boulder and Oxford: Westview Press.

Barro, R.J. (1997), *Determinants of Growth: A Cross-Country Empirical Study*, Cambridge, MA: MIT Press.

Baumol, W. (1986), 'Productivity growth, convergence, and welfare: what the long-run data show', *American Economic Review*, 1072–85.

Berend, I.T. (1996), *Central and Eastern Europe 1944–1993: Detour from the Periphery to the Periphery*, Cambridge and New York: Cambridge University Press.

Berend, I.T. and G. Ránki (1974), *Economic Development in East-Central Europe in the 19th and 20th Centuries*, New York and London: Columbia University Press.

Bergson, A. (1978), *Productivity and the Social System: The USSR and the West*, Cambridge, MA: Harvard University Press.

Brada, J.A. (1989). 'Technological progress and factor utilization in Eastern European economic growth', *Economica*, **56**, 433–48.

Brawley, M.R. (1993), *Liberal Leadership: Great Powers and Their Challengers in Peace and War*, Ithaca and London: Cornell University Press.

Bulmer-Thomas, V. (1994), *The Economic History of Latin America since Independence*, Cambridge and New York: Cambridge University Press.

Chirot, D. (ed.) (1989), *The Origins of Backwardness in Eastern Europe*, Berkeley: University of California Press.

Cipolla, C.M. (ed.) (1970), *The Economic Decline of Empires*, London: Methuen.

Cohen, G.B. (1998), 'Neither absolutism nor anarchy: new narratives on society and government in late imperial Austria', *Austrian History Yearbook*, **29** (1), 37–61.

Crafts, N. and T.C. Mills (1996), 'Europe's golden age: an econometric investigation of changing trend rates of growth', in B. van Ark and N. Crafts (eds), *Quantitative Aspects of Post-War European Economic Growth*, Cambridge: Cambridge University Press, 415–31.

Crafts, N.F.R. (1983). 'Gross national product in Europe 1870–1910: some new estimates', *Explorations in Economic History*, **20**, 387–401.

Dowrick, S. and D.-T. Nguyen (1989), 'OECD comparative growth 1950–85: catch-up and convergence', *American Economic Review*, **79** (5), 1010–1030.

Dumke, R.H. (1990), 'Reassessing the Wirtschaftswunder: reconstruction and postwar growth in an international context', *Bulletin of Economics and Statistics*, **52**, 451–90.

Ehrlich, E. (1990/1991), 'The competition among countries', *Eastern European Economies*, **29** (2), 67–100.

Ehrlich, E. (1991), 'Contest between countries: 1937–1986', *Soviet Studies*, **43** (5), 875–96.

Eichengreen, B. (1992), *Golden Fetters: The Gold Standard and the Great Depression, 1919–1939*, Oxford and New York: Oxford University Press.

Gati, C. (1990), *The Bloc That Failed: Soviet-East European Relations in Transition*, Bloomington and Indianapolis: Indiana University Press.

Gerschenkron, A. (1962), *Economic Backwardness in Historical Perspective: A Book of Essays*, New York: Frederick A. Praeger.

Good, D. F. (1984). *The Economic Rise of the Habsburg Empire, 1750–1914*. Berkeley: University of California Press.

Good, D.F. (1994), 'The economic lag of Central and Eastern Europe: income estimates for the Habsburg successor states', 1870–1910', *Journal of Economic History* **54**, 869–91.

Good, D.F. and T. Ma (1998), 'New estimates of income levels in Central and Eastern Europe, 1870–1910', in F. Baltzarek, F. Butschek and G. Tichy (eds), *Von der Theorie zur Wirtschaftspolitik – ein Oesterreichischer Weg. Festschrift zum 65. Geburtstag von Erich Streissler*, Stuttgart: Lucius.

Good, D.F. and T. Ma (1999), 'The economic growth of Central and Eastern Europe in comparative perspective, 1870–1989', *European Review of Economic History*, **3** (2).

Hanson, J.R., II (1986), 'Export shares in the European periphery and the Third World before World War I: questionable data, facile analogies', *Explorations in Economic History*, **23**, 85–99.

Hanson, J.R., II (1991), 'Third world incomes before World War I: further evidence', *Explorations in Economic History*, **28**, 367–79.

Harrison, M. (1994), 'GDPs of the USSR and Eastern Europe: towards an interwar comparison', *Europe-Asia Studies*, **46** (2), 243–59.

Harrison, M. (1998), 'Trends in Soviet labour productivity, 1928–85, postwar recovery, and slowdown', *European Review of Economic History*, **2**, 171–200.

Hayami, Y. and V.W. Ruttan (1985), *Agricultural Development: An International Perspective*, Baltimore and London: Johns Hopkins University Press.

Hirschman, A.O. (1958). *The Strategy of Economic Development*, New Haven, CT: Yale University Press.

Janos, A.C. (1982), *The Politics of Backwardness in Hungary 1825–1945*, Princeton: Princeton University Press.

Kaser, M.C. and E.A. Radice (eds) (1985), *The Economic History of Eastern Europe 1919–1975*, Oxford: Clarendon Press.

Komlos, J. (ed.) (1983), *Economic Development in the Habsburg Monarchy in the Nineteenth Century*, Boulder, CO: East European Monographs.

Kondratieff, N.D. (1935), 'The Long Waves in Economic Life', *Review of Economics and Statistics*, **XVII** (6), 105–15.

Kravis, I. (1986), 'The three faces of the international comparison project', *Research Observer* **1**, 1–26.

Kravis, I., A. Heston and R. Summers (1978), 'Real GNP per capita for more than one hundred countries', *Economic Journal*, **88**, 215–42.

Kuznets, S. (1965), *Economic Growth and Structure: Selected Essays*, New York: W.W. Norton.

Lampe, J. (1989), 'Imperial borderlands or capitalist periphery? Redefining Balkan backwardness, 1520–1914', in D. Chirot (ed.), *The Origins of Backwardness in Eastern Europe: Economics and Politics from the Middle Ages until the Early Twentieth Century*, Berkeley and London, pp. 177–209.

Lampe, J. and M. Jackson (1982), *Balkan Economic History 1550–1950: From Imperial Borderlands to Developing Nations*, Bloomington, IN: Indiana University Press.

Lucas, R.E. (1993), 'Making a Miracle', *Econometrica*, **61**, 251–72.

Maddison, A. (1989), *The World Economy in the 20th Century*, Paris: Organisation for Economic Cooperation and Development.

Maddison, A. (1990), 'Measuring European growth: the core and the periphery', in Erik Aerts and Nuno Valério (eds), *Growth and Stagnation in the Mediterranean World in the 19th and 20th Centuries*, Leuven: Leuven University Press.

Maddison, A. (1991), *Dynamic Forces in Capitalist Development*, London and New York: Oxford University Press.

Maddison, A. (1995), *Monitoring the World Economy 1820–1992*, Paris: OECD.

Maier, C.S. (1975), *Recasting Bourgeois Europe. Stabilization in France, Germany, and Italy in the Decade After World War I*, Princeton: Princeton University Press.

Maier, C.S. (1997), *Dissolution: The Crisis of Communism and the End of East Germany*, Princeton: Princeton University Press.

Mankiw, G.N., D. Romer and D. Weil (1992), 'A contribution to the empirics of growth', *Quarterly Journal of Economics*, **107** (2), 407–37.

Marer, P., et al. (1992), *Historically Planned Economies, A Guide to the Data*, Washington, DC: The World Bank.
Mishkova, D. (1995), 'Modernization and political elites in the Balkans before the First Wolrd War', *East European Politics and Societies*, **9** (1), 63–89.
Mitchell, B.R. (1975), *European Historical Statistics 1750–1970*, London: Macmillan.
Myrdal, G. (1957), *Economic Theory and Underdeveloped Areas*, London: Methuen.
Nelson, C.R. and C.I. Plosser (1982), 'Trends and random walks in macroeconomic times series: some evidence and implications', *Journal of Monetary Economics*, **10**, 139–62.
North, D.C. (1990), *Institutions, Institutional Change and Economic Performance*, Cambridge: Cambridge University Press.
Ofer, G. (1987), 'Soviet economic growth: 1928–1985', *Journal of Economic Literature*, **XXV** (4), 1767–833.
Okyar, O. (1987), 'A New look at the problem of economic growth in the Ottoman Empire (1800–1914)', *Journal of European Economic History*, **16** (Spring), 649–69.
Palairet, M. (1997), *The Balkan Economies c. 1800–1914: Evolution without Development*, Cambridge and New York: Cambridge University Press.
Pammer, M. (1997), 'Proxy data and income estimates: the economic lag of Central and Eastern Europe', *Journal of Economic History*, **57** (1), 456–63.
Perron, P. (1989), 'The great crash, the oil price shock, and the unit root hypothesis', *Econometrica* **57**, 1361–401.
Pryor, F.L. (1985), 'Growth and fluctuations of production in OECD and East European Countries', *World Politics*, **37**, 204–37.
Pryor, F.L. (1994), 'Growth deceleration and transactions costs: a note', *Journal of Economic Behavior and Organization*, **25** (1), 121–33.
Przeworski, A. and F. Limongi (1993), 'Political regimes and economic growth', *Journal of Economic Perspectives*, **7**, 51–69.
Rappoport, P. and L. Reichlin (1989), 'Segmented trends and nonstationary time series', *Economic Journal*, **99** (supplement), 168–77.
Rebelo, S. (1991), 'Long-run policy analysis and long-run growth', *Journal of Political Economy*, **99** (3), 500–521.
Romer, P. (1990), 'Endogenous technological change', *Journal of Political Economy*, **98** (5, Pt. II), S71–102.
Rudolph, R.L. and D.F. Good (eds) (1992), *Nationalism and Empire: The Habsburg Monarchy and the Soviet Union*, New York: St. Martin's Press.
Schumpeter, J.A. (1935), 'The analysis of economic change', *Review of Economics and Statistics*, **XVII** (4), 2–10.
Sierman, C.L.J. (1998), *Politics, Institutions, and the Economic Performance of Nations*, Cheltenham , UK and Lyme, US: Edward Elgar.
Solow, R. (1956), 'A contribution to the theory of growth', *Quarterly Journal of Economics*, **70** (1), 65–94.
Sugar, P. (1984), 'Continuity and change in Eastern European authoritarianism: autocracy, fascism, and communism', *East European Quarterly*, **XVIII** (1), 1–23.
Summers, R. and A. Heston (1988), 'A new set of international comparisons of real product and price levels: estimates for 130 countries, 1950–1985', *The Review of Income and Wealth*, **34**, 1–25.
Taylor, A.M. (1998), 'On the costs of inward-looking economic development: price distortions, growth, and divergence in Latin America', *Journal of Economic History*, **58** (1), 1–28.

Van der Wee, H. (1986), *Prosperity and Upheaval: The World Economy 1945–1980*, Berkeley and Los Angeles: University of California Press.

Wallerstein, I. (1974), *The Modern World-System. Capitalist Agriculture and the Origins of the European World-Economy in the Sixteenth Century*, New York: Academic Press.

Williamson, J. (1965), 'Regional inequality and the process of national development: a description of the patterns', *Economic Development and Cultural Change*, **XIII** (4), 3–47.

Williamson, J.G. (1996). 'Globalization, convergence, and history', *Journal of Economic History*, **56** (2), 277–306.

APPENDIX

Table A3.1 GDP per capita in Europe and Latin America 1870–1989

	GDP per capita (1990 Geary-Khamis Dollars)						
	1870	1910	1920	1938	1950	1973	1989
Northwest							
United Kingdom	3263	4715	4651	5983	6847	11992	16288
Belgium	2640	3978	3878	4730	5346	11905	16299
Netherlands	2640	3684	4117	5122	5850	12763	16024
France	1858	2937	3196	4424	5221	12940	17457
Germany	1913	3527	2986	5126	4281	13152	18015
Switzerland	2172	4070	4256	6302	8939	17953	21381
Nordic							
Denmark	1927	3564	3840	5453	6683	13416	17620
Finland	1107	1852	1792	3342	4131	10768	16676
Norway	1303	2052	2529	3945	4969	10229	16675
Sweden	1664	2980	2802	4725	6738	13494	17593
Mediterranean							
Italy	1467	2281	2530	3244	3426	10409	15650
Portugal	1085	1366	902	1707	2132	7568	10355
Spain	1376	2096	2309	2022	2397	8739	11752
Greece	NA	NA	NA	2727	1951	7800	10262
Central/East							
Austria	1891	3016	2428	3583	3731	11308	16305
Czechoslovakia	1508	2497	1933	2971	3502	7036	8729
Hungary	1180	2194	1709	2655	2480	5596	6787
Poland	946	1690	676	2182	2447	5334	5685
Romania	930	1661	831	1242	1182	3477	3890
Yugoslavia	864	1524	1054	1360	1546	4237	5917
Bulgaria	1132	1455	909	1595	1651	5284	6217
East Germany	NA	NA	NA	5364	3128	8559	12530
Latin America							
Argentina	1311	3822	3473	4072	4987	7970	6655
Brazil	740	795	937	1291	1673	3913	5139
Mexico	710	1435	1555	1380	2085	4189	4893
Chile	NA	2472	2430	3139	3827	5028	6347
Peru	NA	981	1331	1757	2263	3953	3228
Venezuela	NA	886	1173	4144	7424	10717	7928
Colombia	NA	NA	NA	1843	2089	3549	4804

Notes: NA: No data available or not applicable. The GDP per capita data are for the states in their post-1945 boundaries with the following exceptions for the period 1870–1910 only: the data for Bulgaria are for the state in its pre-World War I boundary; the data for Poland and Romania are for the territories of the present-day states that were in the Habsburg empire.

Sources: The data are from the following sources (see text for a summary of the methodology and the original sources for details): For Western, Nordic and Mediterranean Europe in all periods, and Central and Eastern Europe (including Austria) for the period 1920–1938 and the periods after World War II, the data are from Maddison (1995 #1637 Table D-1a). For Central and Eastern Europe, including Austria, for the period 1870–1910 only, the data are revised estimates by Good and Ma (1998 #1636 Table 3) of earlier estimates by Good (1994 #344 Table 3). For Latin America, the data in periods are from Maddison, (1995 Table D-1d).

Table A3.2 Long-term economic growth in Europe and Latin America 1870–1989

	Annual rate of growth in GDP per capita (1990 Geary-Khamis Dollars)						Post-WW II slowdown		
	1870–1910	1920–38	1950–73	1973–89	1950–89	1870–1989	TB= 1973	TBE	GS
Northwest									
United Kingdom	0.98	1.55	2.32	1.94	2.13	1.22	–0.38	–0.33	–0.01
Belgium	1.00	0.78	3.43	1.75	3.07	1.38	–1.68	–1.46	–0.02
Netherlands	0.80	1.48	3.43	1.11	2.68	1.45	–2.32	–2.36	–0.05
France	1.22	1.32	3.99	1.74	3.22	1.81	–2.25	–2.26	–0.05
Germany	1.54	2.02	4.57	1.96	3.35	1.80	–2.61	–3.39	–0.07
Switzerland	1.59	1.89	2.97	1.18	2.07	2.19	–1.79	–1.41	–0.04
Nordic									
Denmark	1.59	2.10	3.33	1.98	2.70	1.89	–1.36	–1.27	–0.03
Finland	1.37	3.23	3.98	2.72	3.57	2.32	–1.26	–0.96	–0.02
Norway	0.96	2.84	3.14	3.20	3.34	2.19	0.06	3.26	0.01
Sweden	1.37	2.87	3.20	1.62	2.56	2.09	–1.58	–1.37	–0.03
Mediterranean									
Greece	NA	NA	5.89	1.64	4.57	NA.	–4.25	–3.98	–0.08
Italy	0.96	1.17	4.87	2.45	3.82	2.00	–2.43	–2.53	–0.06
Portugal	0.65	3.54	5.41	2.05	4.32	2.36	–3.36	–3.08	–0.06
Spain	1.07	1.19	5.49	1.33	4.23	1.90	–4.16	–3.88	–0.07
Central/East									
Austria	1.22	0.62	4.68	2.10	3.77	2.26	–2.58	–2.63	–0.06.
Czechoslovakia	1.30	1.59	3.24	1.25	2.49	1.79	–1.99	–2.02	–0.05
Hungary	1.53	1.87	3.60	1.27	2.69	1.68	–2.33	–2.32	–0.06
Poland	1.53	4.69	3.24	–0.02	2.53	1.80	–3.26	–3.17	–0.06
Romania	1.42	1.09	4.66	0.62	3.14	1.59	–4.04	–4.70	–0.09
Yugoslavia	1.35	0.86	4.79	2.08	4.10	2.10	–2.71	–4.44	–0.06
Bulgaria	1.26	3.20	5.14	0.92	3.62	2.69	–4.22	–4.38	–0.10
East Germany	NA	NA	4.01	2.08	3.11	NA	–1.93	–3.51	–0.05

Table A3.2 (continued)

	Annual rate of growth in GDP per capita (1990 Geary-Khamis Dollars)						Post-WW II slowdown		
	1870–1910	1920–38	1950–73	1973–89	1950–89	1870–1989	TB=1973	TBE	GS
Latin America									
Argentina	2.71	0.38	2.08	−1.15	1.30	1.23	−3.23	−3.36	−0.06
Brazil	0.13	1.59	3.26	1.35	3.33	2.28	−1.90	−1.75	−0.02,
Mexico	1.81	−1.31	3.00	0.96	2.57	1.79.	−2.04	−4.73	−0.04
Chile	NA	1.40	1.55	1.38	0.94	NA	−0.18	1.90	−0.01
Peru	NA	2.74	2.46	−0.94	1.31	NA	−3.40	−3.66	−0.08
Venezuela	NA	6.53	1.33	−2.08	0.19	NA	−3.40	−2.92	−0.08
Colombia	NA	NA	2.03	1.73	2.26	NA	−0.30	−0.04	0.00

Notes: NA: No data available or not applicable. The growth rates for the individual countries are estimated from a regression of the log of GDP per capita on time that relies on all available data points in the time series rather than the two end points. See Table A1 for data sources. The three measures of the growth slowdown are defined as follows:

TB=1973: The percentage-point difference between the growth rates before and after the trend-break year 1973.

TBE: The percentage-point difference between the growth rates before and after the trend-break year as estimated separately from the time series of GDP per capita for each country.

GS: Based on the idea that GDP gradually slowed down over the entire post-1945 period with no break in trend, GS is estimated from the time series for each country as the annual percentage point drop in the growth rate from the initial rate in 1950.

Source: See Table A3.I for data sources.

COMMENTS ON DAVID F. GOOD, 'RETHINKING ECONOMIC PERFORMANCE IN CENTRAL AND EASTERN EUROPE, 1870–1989: OLD NARRATIVES AND NEW EVIDENCE'

Carol Leff

Theoretically, scholarship builds systematically on previous work –but in practice that isn't always true. Just as often it circles back on itself, without establishing a consensual base for moving forward, or slides over the absence of that very important base. The current intensive interest in market transitions in post-communist Eastern Europe has tended to fall into the latter category, with scholars forced to build, if they build at all, from a very short time line of analysis of the economies of the recent communist period. In that context, David Good's chapter, which extends the historical purview of East European economic development, and incorporates the communist period into a framework highly relevant to present marketization efforts, is of exceptional value in focusing on fundamental questions of chronic economic lag, and in offering a more solid platform for assessing post-communist economic transition than we have previously had.

Tracing the reconstructed record of economic growth in the 19th and 20th centuries, he offers a provocative and productive challenge both to approaches that overemphasize the specificities of the communist economic project, and to certain broader approaches that argue for the explanatory power of geopolitical patterns of external exploitation (under 19th-century empire as well as under Soviet control). He hypothesizes that substandard rebound from systemic shocks in the inter-war period and under communism points derived from institutional disruption, which hence figures as the key element contributing to continued regional economic lags in the 20th century.

This argument is stimulating because it opens multiple avenues of investigation for further refinements and tests of some of the key propositions. A major issue would appear to be how institutional disruption is to be understood as an impediment to rebound growth after systemic shock. To give a sense of the directions in which further research might go, consider first of all the problem of systemic shock itself. Its severity can be measured, as Good notes, in terms of the ratio of the post-shock to the pre-shock level of GDP per capita, with shocks of greater severity offering greater potential for rapid growth during a post-shock phase of recovery. However, to measure the magnitude of the shock isn't the only relevant way to think about the challenges posed by such exogenous traumas, or about an economy's rebound potential. Shocks varied in type as well as intensity; even a common event like World War I did not produce a generic shock factor that acted uniformly on all European states.

The shocks experienced by Eastern Europe following World War I – a period identified as critical in this research – differ significantly from the 'simple' shock imposed on the economy of an established state that enjoys territorial and institutional continuity before and after the war. The post-war period was one of multiple shocks for Eastern Europe: war damage to productive facilities and infrastructure, and wartime disruption of production and markets, gave way to the institutional shocks Good has emphasized, and these are themselves multiple. To regime change – defined as a basic alteration in political rules and institutions by which political actors are selected and decisions taken – must be added the change in territorial boundaries, thus further disrupting previous labor and capital markets, transportation and distribution systems, and a range of policies associated with new state-building projects (such as strategies designed to 'nationalize' financial institutions, or to harmonize diverse legal frameworks in states that had to assimilate territory from several former empires). These adaptations represent high transaction costs indeed for both winners and losers of the territorial sweepstakes after World War I. It is quite reasonable to suppose that rebound potential from 'simple' trauma is greater than that which is impeded by multiple institutional dislocations.

The tax imposed by institutional disruption is patently a continuing problem for later periods. The ongoing interlinkage of exogenous shocks, regime change and territorial realignment in 20th century East Europe – all portending high transaction costs in post-shock readjustment – is very striking. Although the wave of new state creation in Eastern Europe after World War I was perhaps the most dramatic, territorial realignment continued to be a factor in East European regime change and hence putatively implicated in laggard growth suffered by new regimes in subsequent periods. World War II introduced a new set of territorial realignments, most notably Soviet land grabs on its western borders, and Poland's territorial shift westward. Territorial discontinuities also accompanied the collapse of communism, in the dissolution of the two ethnofederal states of Yugoslavia and Czechoslovakia, compelling renewed state building projects on those territories. War and geopolitical realignments were of course central to the introduction of communism to the region, but also to its collapse – given the demise of Soviet imperium and the Yugoslav succession wars. Even if war was not the engine of post-communist East European regime change outside of Yugoslavia, the demise of Cold War bipolarity did impose a severe economic shock in the form of the collapse of Eastern bloc trade. Thus, throughout the 20th century, we see the pattern of exogenous shocks inflicted on the region accompanied both by important changes in political and economic institutions, and territorial discontinuities.

On the one hand, this briefly sketched historical pattern lends weight to Good's hypothesis of the implication of institutional instability in substandard rebound growth in the region. To follow up on that insight, however, is quite a challenge – we will first need to define, disentangle, and measure the variant types of institutional instability, and subsequently to attempt to weigh their impact. Being able to 'unpack' the sources and dimensions of different sorts of institutional disruption is important to the ability to 'read' the record of economic development. How much weight should be attached to variant components of institutional instability such as the loss of knowledge capital needed to replace bureaucrats, politicians and technocrats of previous eras?[1] How large is the penalty paid as a result of the necessary adjustments following territorial revisions and new state creation? Are there economic penalties, either chronic or episodic, associated with the maintenance of multi-ethnic states with substantial variation in the development levels of the component national groupings? Is the *type* of institutional change as important as the fact of institutional change *per se*? Finally, it is also necessary to distinguish East European problems from cases, like that of Germany, which also experienced very substantial institutional and territorial discontinuities, and yet were apparently able to sustain rebound growth in the wake of systemic shock.

These are vexed questions. Some of them can only be answered to the extent that we are able to disaggregate the portrait of the region as a whole – and data limitations present a serious problem here – and to begin to examine how variance in economic outcomes tallies with variable strength of institutional impediments in individual cases. Eastern Europe is not a seamless economic whole in any period, varying as it does in everything from literacy to urbanization to sectoral development, and it might be desirable to probe more deeply into variations in regional growth patterns as a means of gauging the impact of some of the factors mentioned above that collectively define the range of institutional disruptions. This stricture applies not only to the inter-war period, but also to the communist era, for socialism was not the same experience country to country, despite the widespread imposition of the Soviet model at the outset.[2]

Data limitations are critical here. Indeed, some of the most interesting puzzles – the questions of variable substate development in multi-ethnic states, for example – may be beyond the reach of the existing data. Where substate regional economies within a single political unit become a set of new state economies in the next historical period, we have not only a statistical nightmare, but also a major source of institutional disruption and instability. Given the unavailability of relevant economic data, however, what would have been a major test of the impact of institutional volatility is thus obscured by the very institutional instability we seek to evaluate.[3]

On the other hand, institutional stability is not only a complex and somewhat elusive concept to parse, but it also need not be inherently beneficial economically. The drawbacks of instability don't automatically demonstrate that long-term institutional continuity is a panacea. The Soviet case, at least, raises some real issues in this regard.[4] Probably the reigning argument in political science in interpreting the collapse of Soviet communism is that put forward by Philip Roeder (1993), that the stability of the 'Bolshevik constitution,' as consolidated in the 1930s, created a rigid institutional 'lock-in' that profoundly inhibited subsequent growth and adaptation.

Even without further exploring the multi-dimensionality of institutional stability, however, Good's analysis carries some potentially optimistic implications for the post-communist period. He identifies the periods of laggard rebound growth as periods of greater isolation from neighboring western states, in contrast with the more 'normal' growth patterns of the previous century. The message here is rather hopeful; the current period is one of intensified contact with the global market, and one might therefore derive from past record the expectation, or hope, that intensified contact will be a valuable palliative for a chronic ailment. It is true that the euphoria of opening to Western economies (and hopefully to western prosperity) that obtained in the early 1990s has given way to greater caution registered in opinion surveys as accession to EU membership looms closer at the decade's end; post-communist publics have registered that conformity with the *acquis communitaire* of the European Union requires of post-communist countries a substantial and very detailed adjustment of economic policy to European norms – particularly for economic sectors such as agriculture that face the EU's most contentious and contested policy area. It can thus be heartening to conclude that greater market openness points in the direction of growth rather than peripheral subordination, and will have a long-range pay-off.

A second promising implication of the analysis lies directly in the prospects for institutional stability afforded by a much more benign international environment for the East European economic and political projects than that which obtained earlier in the century. If the exogenous shocks that triggered institutional upheaval were driven in no small part by war, the post-war history of close cooperation among erstwhile West European rivals, coupled with the fact that this cooperative economic and security framework is now on offer to the East, would augur a more stable external climate to nurture greater internal stability.

Notes

1. Elite turnover can obviously impose penalties on economic performance, and élite transformation was a rather pronounced concomitant of the systemic shocks of the 20th century, whether through the loss of imperial bureaucratic corps as in Austro-Hungarian successor states; through emigration/flight; through ethnic or class disqualification, etc.

2. Over time, there were clear deviations in the organization of production (Yugoslavia), the openness of contact with the West, and even in the amount of officially sanctioned private sector activity.
3. Substate economic development is particularly problematic and theoretically interesting in multinational states. One of the economic subnarratives of the communist period was the conviction of wealthier republics of the three ethnofederations – Slovenia and Croatia in Yugoslavia, Czechs in Czechoslovakia and the Baltic republics in the USSR – that they were underwriting, as one Slovenian put it, the 'equal distribution of poverty' that transferred resources to the poorer states in a conscious program of economic equalization. In addition to the contentious political impact of this redistributive policy, what is the economic effect on growth? The result may well have been suboptimal economic outcomes precisely because of the political fall-out. Very clearly, in Yugoslavia, this dispute eventually generated a nasty tendency toward economic autarky at the republic level, made possible by decentralized political institutions. This situation was evident in the final days of the Soviet Union as well. And in all three cases, suspicions of economic disadvantage rose as state disintegration progressed. The interaction of institutional change and ethnic diversity thus raises some interesting questions for the economic growth curve.
4. In this context, it is important to remember that one can dispute the point at which the Soviet Union finally did enjoy institutional stability – in light of World War I, the revolution and Civil War, the massive industrialization and collectivization campaigns, the purges and famines, World War II ... it is quite possible to argue that there *is* no institutional stability in the Soviet model until the 1950s.

Reference

Roeder, Philip (1993) *Red Sunset: The Failure of Soviet Politics*, Princeton, NJ: Princeton University Press.

4. Economic transition in Eastern Europe: how successful is the project and how much political support does it have?

Josef C. Brada

HOW SHOULD WE JUDGE THE TRANSITION?

The question above is of course the wrong question to ask. The opinions of outsiders are largely irrelevant to how the populations of East Europe judge how their economies have performed, just as they are irrelevant to the political support that these populations will provide for these efforts at transformation. I nevertheless ask this question, precisely to caution the reader against attempting to answer it, or at least to answer it in the way that it has generally been approached. Many intellectuals and policymakers have, of course, sought to answer it, but in ways that strike me as problematic and unlikely to lead to satisfactory answers.

The Economic Consequences of Transition

Evaluations of economic performance fall into two categories. In one of these we find analyses that point to the decline in output in the transition economies and view this as evidence that transition strategies were wrong, largely because they called for excessively aggressive stabilization policies, and because they relied on market mechanisms too soon and too extensively. These policies are often seen as the result of a liberal economic ideology that was imposed on the region by western advisors and especially by the International Monetary Fund (IMF) and the World Bank, which, by virtue of their command over resources and expertise, came to dominate policy making in the region. Moreover, those economies that have been able to recover are seen as having done so by abandoning the policies espoused by the Washington consensus in favor of policies that rely on fiscal stimulus and on greater government intervention in the economy (Haynes and Husan 1998).

In the other category are analyses that interpret the economic situation in East Europe more sanguinely. They view the initial fall in output as inevitable and perhaps overstated by faulty statistics. In those economies that have stayed the course of stabilization and reform, there is economic recovery and growth, expanding trade and slowing inflation. The poor performance of the transition economies is seen by these observers as a cautionary example of what happens to countries that fail to follow the kinds of policies suggested by liberal economics and proposed by the IMF and World Bank.

Such broad-brush approaches to the economic performance of a group of countries with different starting conditions, economic systems and policies is likely to prove unsatisfactory, precisely because almost any half-plausible hypothesis can be accepted or rejected on the basis of such a wide range of outcomes as are to be found among the transition economies. An explanation of the causes of economic decline or of relative prosperity during the transition is irrelevant if we believe that the population's political response to economic outcomes is dependent solely on the existing economic situation and independent of how these economic outcomes are brought about. However, an understanding of the determinants of economic outcomes, that is to say, an understanding of the effects of different approaches to stabilization and transition, does become relevant if political attitudes in the transition economies reflect expectations about the future, preferences about the economic and political means used to achieve economic outcomes, and an understanding of the constraints facing policymakers. Because I argue below that the latter view of how East European populations interpret the transition process is the more appropriate one to understanding political responses to the transition in the region, in the remainder of this section I will briefly review the evidence regarding the forces shaping economic performance in East Europe.

The fall in output

The facts of the output decline are captured in the data on real GDP reported in Table 4.1. Output fell sharply in the early years of the transition, to an extent that has led many observers to compare the decline to the Great Depression of the 1930s. At least on a statistical basis, this is perhaps the correct analogy, but care must be taken not to confuse similarities in output declines to similarities in causes, consequences or appropriate policy remedies.

There are three broad explanations for this output decline. One is that stabilization measures were too harsh and that they therefore caused excessive declines in output. Proponents of this view, as evidence for their argument, often point to the admission of the Polish reformers that the output decline was greater than they had expected.[1] That most East European countries adopted some form of stabilization package is incontrovertible, but how much this stabilization contributed to the fall in output is unclear. Moreover, given the repressed and open inflation that characterized the pre-transition economies and the external shocks to these economies that I discuss below, stabilization of some sort was necessary and it is difficult to see how it could be carried out in a gradual way.

Table 4.1a Macroeconomic indicators for East Central Europe (index)

Country	1980	1989	1993	1997
Real GDP				
Albania	89.4	100.0	65.9	82.1
Bulgaria	76.2	100.0	73.3	64.2
Croatia	99.0	100.0	59.5	78.7[a]
Czech Republic	91.3[b]	100.0	85.0	97.5
Hungary	86.3	100.0	81.9	95.1[a]
Poland	91.1	100.0	87.6	116.7[a]
Romania	88.5	100.0	76.2	82.3
Slovak Republic	91.0[b]	100.0	75.1	99.7[a]
Slovenia	98.9	100.0	81.4	99.6[a]
Real consumption				
Bulgaria	91.3[c]	100.0	86.2	64.0
Croatia	NA	100.0	85.3	109.2[d]
Czech Republic	NA	100.0	90.4	103.2
Hungary	92.2	100.0	97.9	90.7
Poland	108.0	100.0	103.0	131.5
Romania	83.9	100.0	91.8	106.6
Slovak Republic	81.8	100.0	74.3	88.5
Slovenia	NA	100.0	99.1	116.6
Real fixed capital formation				
Bulgaria	NA	100.0	61.2	44.1
Croatia	NA	100.0	94.5	108.2[b]
Czech Republic	93.4[c]	100.0	81.0	118.8
Hungary	114.7	100.0	82.6	112.0[d]
Poland	124.6	100.0	75.7	142.0
Romania	163.7	100.0	52.9	59.7
Slovak Republic	NA	100.0	68.5	103.3
Slovenia	NA	100.0	85.4	140.3[b]

Notes:
a 1998.
b 1995.
c 1987.
d 1996.

Sources: United Nations Economic Commission for Europe, *Economic Survey of Europe*, 1998, No. 2. New York and Geneva: United Nations, 1998 and updated from *PlanEcon Reports*, various issues.

Table 4.1b Macroeconomic indicators for East Central Europe

	Unemployment (%-end 1997)	Inflation (% change in CPI/year-1997)
Bulgaria	13.7	1082.6
Croatia	17.6	3.7
Czech Republic	5.2	8.4
Hungary	10.4	18.4
Poland	10.5	15.1
Romania	8.8	154.9
Slovak Republic	12.5	6.2
Slovenia	14.8	8.4

The evidence regarding the costs of stabilization is mixed. Halting inflation is costly in terms of the necessary decline in output, but failing to reduce inflation is also costly in terms of future output forgone due to the pernicious effects of inflation on resource allocation. Cottarelli and Doyle (1999) argues that some countries, such as Croatia, may have deflated too rapidly while countries such as Hungary, proceeded at a more appropriate speed, thus reducing the amount of forgone output due to stabilization. Christoffersen and Doyle (1998), on the other hand, find that the evidence from transition economies shows that rapid disinflation caused serious output loss only in countries with pegged exchange rates. Finally, a perusal of the GDP and inflation data presented in Table 4.1 suggests that those countries that have failed to reduce inflation to at least moderate levels have also suffered the largest and longest-lasting declines in output.[2]

A second cause of the output decline is the disruptions and dislocations caused by the premature abandonment of central planning and the unsuccessful effort to replace it with market mechanisms. In the absence of functioning markets and of the institutional and legal underpinnings for a market economy, the abandonment of state guidance of production led to a failure in coordination of production. Firms were unable to find, or effectively to contract to purchase, inputs or to sell their output without the help of the plan, thus leading to increased costs of production and to a fall in output due to the difficulties in coordinating productive activity. Murrell and Wang (1993) and Blanchard (1997), for example, have constructed theoretical models that demonstrate this possibility.

How much such discoordination hampered production in the early transition is unclear. Kornai (1971) stresses the role of routine in sustaining economic activity. He illustrates his point with the example of socialist firms that continued and even increased their production in the absence of both plan and market when final versions of central plans were delayed, and thus were unavailable to guide enterprise behavior. One wonders whether much the same following of past routines and relationships could, and did, sustain and coordinate production in the period following the outset of the transition. Moreover, case studies of enterprises in transition economies provide little support for the discoordination hypothesis (Estrin et al. 1995). Finally, it may well be that much output disappeared not because market coordination could not sustain production, but because the market functioned well enough to actively suppress uneconomic and unprofitable production. The work of Winiecki (1991), Hughes and Hare (1994) and of Gaddy and Ickes (1998, 1999) stresses the fact that a large part of the output of the planned economy was in fact value-destroying and that, therefore, eliminating such production should be an expected and welcome consequence of market-based transition.

The third source of output decline in East Europe was the exogenous shock caused by the collapse of trade with the Soviet Union and among the members of the Council for Mutual Economic Assistance (CMEA). This collapse, in the estimation of Rodrik (1992), accounted for about 40 percent of the output decline in East Europe.[3] Indeed, Finland and India also suffered output declines of a magnitude comparable to their trade with the Soviet Union at the same time as this shock hit East Europe (Brada, 1993). Some understanding of the impact of the trade shock can be gleaned from Figure 4.1. Poland, which began its stabilization program in 1990, suffered a sharp decline in output, followed by a lesser but large decline in 1991, the year that trade collapsed. The Czech

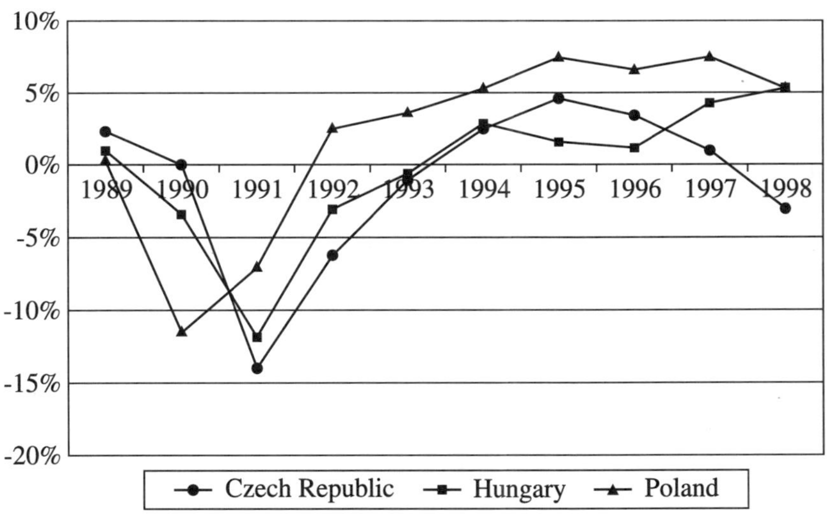

Figure 4.1 Growth of real GDP

Republic and Hungary, on the other hand, experienced both the stabilization shock and the trade shock in the same year, 1991. Note that their output decline on an annual basis exceeds that of Poland despite the fact that the Polish stabilization was considerably harsher.

Interpreting the consequences of the output decline

The foregoing discussion suggests that a large part of the decline in output in the transition economies was, at least in the first several years, the result of exogenous events and policy measures. Moreover, the collapse of trade with the CMEA was an exogenous shock whose causes and consequences the population could easily understand. The stabilization also reduced open inflation or, in the Polish case, near-hyperinflation, or eliminated the pervasive shortages, the queues and the informal rationing system of the pre-transition period. A more rational allocation of resources also meant that the utility that the population derived from the available output was greater than it had been in the socialist period, when the mix of consumer goods available had reflected planners' rather than consumers' preferences.

While the data on GDP growth between 1989 and 1993 reported in Table 4.1 do suggest a Great-Depression-like fall in aggregate output, the data on real consumption reveal a somewhat different picture. With the exception of the Slovak Republic, in every transition economy, the fall in consumption was much less than the fall in aggregate output. This is because consumption was cushioned by disproportional declines in investment, especially inventory investment, and in government consumption and by increases in imports of consumer goods from the West. Once we turn our focus from output to consumption, which is what directly affects the welfare of households, then the analogy between the Great Depression and the early period of transition loses much of its validity. It also helps to explain why the populations of East Europe were relatively quiescent during this period.

Another factor conditioning the popular response to the economic travails of the early transition period was the performance of the East European economies in the decade of the 1980s. As Table 4.1 shows, this decade was one of extremely slow growth in most of these countries; GDP growth was less than 1 percent per year as both technical progress and capacity utilization slumped (Brada 1989). Moreover, the East European economies experienced very little structural change during this decade, and they kept falling further behind the advanced industrial countries in the application of new technologies. These poor dynamics of the socialist economy affected popular perceptions of transition-era economic performance in two ways. First, both policymakers and ordinary people had been aware of this communist-era economic stagnation, and so they may have responded with less alarm to the post-transition downturn than they might have if the last decade under communism had been one characterized by buoyant growth of consumption and output. Second, it is likely that the growth of the post-1993 period that characterized most transition economies represented, in fact, a significant ray of hope. As Table 4.1 shows, the post-1993 period represented the highest levels of growth of output and of living standards that the populations of these countries had encountered in two decades. Indeed, in a number of East European countries, by 1997 real consumption was higher than it had been in 1993, and it had shown considerable growth from its nadir in 1993. Such a result may represent an important source of support for the transition strategies being followed by these countries.[4]

It should also be noted that the growth rates of real output and particularly of real consumption are biased downward, perhaps by a large amount (Dyba and Svejnar 1994; Filer and Hanousek 1998). This is because the consumer price index (CPI) has probably overstated inflation in transition economies. In part this is because the CPI in these countries has underestimated the magnitude of quality improvements and improvements in the variety of goods available to consumers; such underestimation of quality improvements overestimated the increase in prices, thus lowering the measured growth of real consumption. Moreover, there were major improvements in the quality and quantity of retail services and in convenience offered to consumers by the retail network during the transition. To the extent that these improvements were of value to consumers but added to retail mark-ups and thus to consumer prices, they too, served to overstate the rate of CPI increase and thus to understate the growth of consumption. There were also large changes in the relative prices of goods and in the mix of goods available on the market, in part due to the flood of imported consumer goods brought about by trade liberalization. Large changes in relative prices and in the mix of goods available suggest major shifts in consumer expenditure patterns. If these shifts were in favor of cheaper goods or of goods whose higher quality was not captured by the statistical agencies, as seems likely, then the use of a fixed market basket to construct the CPI would also overstate the increase in consumer prices and to understate the growth of real consumption.

Finally, not only did the period following 1993 represent a period of rising living standards, but it also represented a period when both GDP and investment grew very rapidly by historical standards in many transition economies. In many ways, for the populations of transition economies, 'lasting growth is,' in Kornai's (1997) words, 'top priority.'[5] Thus, the rapid rates of growth of output after 1993 and the surprisingly high rates of real fixed capital formation reported in Table 4.1 represent for the populations of most transition economies an important portent, if not a guarantee, of a better future.

The foregoing discussion and the evidence presented of course cannot resolve the 'half-empty, half-full' debate over the economic consequences of the transition in Eastern Europe. However, I believe that the evidence does suggest that the population of these countries may have seen the economic situation from a perspective that showed it to be less bleak than suggested by naïve references to the early output declines. At the same time, I do not wish to minimize either the short-term decline in economic welfare suffered in all transition economies nor the continuation of that decline in some of them.

The Political Consequences of Economic Outcomes

If the evaluation of the economic outcomes of the transition has tended to focus rather simplistically on the declines in output and its recovery, much the same criticism can be raised regarding the political evaluation of these economic developments. Policymakers (Balcerowicz 1995, 1997), economists (Aghion and Blanchard 1994; Dewatripont and Roland 1995; Rodrik 1995; Roland 1994) and political scientists (Przeworski 1991, 1993) have sought to interpret political support for, and, consequently, the appropriate design of, transition strategies from the standpoint of an economic model of voter behavior.[6] This model is based on the theories of the public choice school, and it sees voter support for transition measures as depending critically, if not exclusively, on current consumption, which is usually proxied by the level of output or by the level of unemployment that is brought about by stabilization and restructuring.

Models based on this assumption have been used to derive an optimal approach to restructuring and stabilization. The set-up of the models is relatively straightforward. Restructuring causes output declines and unemployment in the short run and improved economic performance only in the long run. With political support determined by the level of unemployment and its duration or by the decline in incomes, the necessity for either a rapid approach that takes advantage of a period of 'extraordinary politics' (Balcerwicz 1995) or a slow approach that does not overstep the electorate's toleration of economic hardship can be demonstrated. While such single-objective models can be instructive regarding the specific trade-off between speed of transition, unemployment or output, and political support for the regime, they are of little use in more realistic settings where the population has multiple economic and political objectives. Nevertheless, such models and the reasoning behind them have been a major component of the rhetoric regarding policy prescriptions for the region. On the one hand, proponents of fast liberalization such as Balcerowicz (1995) argued that shock therapy had to be applied so as to get as much of the transition completed as possible before the population began to suffer from 'reform fatigue.' Opponents of shock therapy used the same logic to argue for slow transition so as to avoid overstepping the population's tolerance for economic hardship and causing them to turn to other, less fruitful, reform strategies or abandoning reform altogether.

While I do not dispute the usefulness of political economy models based on the self-interested voter for analyzing policy choices in economies whose structure, political economy and production are all relatively stable, I do question their appropriateness for the period of the transition.[7] In part this is due to the fact that the transition, by its very nature, is, and was seen by voters as, a long-term project. Consequently, when evaluating public sentiments in transition economies, expectations regarding the future need to be considered to a much greater extent than these models imply. Moreover, the transition was an economic project that addressed not just current levels of output. It was also, and perhaps predominantly, directed toward system change: the construction of a new type of economy, the realignment of property relations and the redirection of foreign trade in a very fundamental way.[8]

A second, and perhaps even more critical, problem with the political economy approach is that it focuses exclusively on economic objectives. Yet the transition in East Europe is as much, if not more, a political process as an economic one. For many of those in East Europe, it was the desire to create new civil societies, political systems and human freedoms that aroused the social resistance that led to the collapse of Communist regimes. Thus, to try to understand political support for transition measure on the basis of short-term economic indicators while ignoring voters' long-term expectations and political objectives is likely to lead both to bad policy prescriptions and to a faulty understanding of political dynamics in transition economies.

Among the political objectives that accompanied the transition in East Europe were the creation of a functioning multi-party democracy to replace the false democracy of the communist state. Another important political goal was the rejoining of Europe. In many of the East European countries, the period of communist domination was seen as a time when these countries' ties to Europe (meaning Western Europe), and to European cultural, social and economic processes had been severed. Reestablishing those links was seen as a key objective of the transition process. This, of course, had an economic component, expressed in the desire to join the European Union (EU), but it also had important social, cultural, and security components as well. How strong these feelings were in individual transition economies varied considerably across East Europe. In some countries, the striving for democracy was attenuated and even submerged as a social objective by the replacement of the communist dictatorship by some other oligarchic or one-party regime. In other countries, democracy was not able to function effectively despite the absence of a strong one-party regime. But, in many countries, multi-party democracy has emerged, allowing the population to change the ruling regime several times during the course of the transition.

The political power of the idea of a move toward Europe also varies among these countries. In those countries such as Poland, Hungary, the Czech Republic and Slovenia whose chances of joining the EU are good and are seen by their populations as realizable in the foreseeable future and whose cultural and social ties to West Europe are strong, this is a powerful factor for shaping popular political attitudes as well as government policies. In countries that have historically occupied a place on the periphery of European processes and whose economic or political situation makes them less likely to join the EU in the near future, the power of the European ideal is correspondingly weaker in the political calculus.

These broader political objectives are important for an analysis of public support for East European transition policies and outcomes in two ways. First they need to be included in models of voter behavior alongside the level of unemployment or output in determining public support for reform programs. Indeed, in many transition economies, the 'European-ness' of policies, meaning their conformity to EU standards and practices, is a powerful legitimizing force, even if the short-term economic consequences of these policies may be unfavorable. Second, these broad political objectives have to be kept in mind in considering policy options because they serve as powerful constraints on the economic and social models that politicians can choose for the transition process.

THE EFFECT OF LIBERAL ECONOMIC POLICIES

Before considering what alternative models might have been chosen for the implementation of transition and stabilization and for the political process by which those choices were made, it is instructive to ask whether the decade or so of restructuring and stabilization in transition economies has thrown up any evidence that liberal policies did, indeed, yield superior economic results. If such evidence exists, it would not, of course, entirely explain why these policies were chosen and then sustained in many of the transition economies, but it would provide some understanding of why governments did not quickly shift to other policy regimes.

The Evidence for the Superiority of Liberal Policies

A number of studies has appeared that purport to show a clear relation between various measures of liberalization and economic performance, usually measured by the growth of aggregate output and by the decline in inflation for transition economies. Most notable of these studies are those of Aslund et al. (1996), deMelo and Gelb (1996, 1997) Fischer et al. (1996) and Sachs (1996). Although these studies differ from each other in the specific way in which they measure the dependent and explanatory variables, in the countries included in the sample, as well as in the precise specification of the regression equation, their general approach is much the same, and it is one that appears both robust and capable of yielding unambiguous results.

The authors take as their dependent variables output growth since the start of transition or from some base year or in some recent year, such as 1995. Several studies also consider inflation measured over a similar interval as another outcome of transition policies. Some studies also use other performance indicators including unemployment and the reorientation of trade toward world markets. The key explanatory variable is an index of liberalization that measures the liberalization of internal prices and markets, of the foreign trade and exchange rate regimes, and of privatization. Data for constructing these indexes are drawn from various sources or based on indexes compiled by the European Bank for Reconstruction and Development. Usually, the index is cumulated from the start of reforms – on the reasonable assumption that the beneficial effects of reform will increase over time, leading to the concept of a cumulative liberalization index (CLI).

The dependent variables, meaning the economic outcomes of the transition, are then determined by the CLI and by additional variables that capture unique exogenous forces, such as wars, of country-specific starting conditions such as the level of development, or the legacy of central planning, and of specific policy choices such as the use of a fixed exchange rate. Despite the differences in the specific variables and specifications used, all of these exercises yield quite similar results. The CLI variable is always statistically significant. For economic growth, it has a positive sign, meaning that faster and more extensive liberalization is associated with faster economic recovery and the earlier resumption of output growth. In the case of inflation, the CLI has a significant and negative sign, meaning that countries that quickly implemented extensive reforms experienced lower rates of inflation either during the entire period under review or were experiencing lower inflation at the end of the sample period. This conclusion suggests that the so-called Washington consensus, the approach of the World Bank and of the IMF, and, more generally, of neo-classical economics, to stabilization and reform is the correct one, and that the experience of the transition economies to date is the clearest possible proof of this lesson.

Why We Should Accept This Conclusion Cautiously

Like many purported lessons in economics, the lesson set out above is one that many would like to believe, but we should be careful in considering the evidence that supports it. There are two lines of objection to the conclusions urged by the research described in the foregoing section.

As already mentioned above, some transition economies instituted reforms that sought to introduce the workings of the market and private property in concert with democratic political institutions. It is also an incontrovertible fact that a number of transition economies have made economic changes that, while having some element of moving from central planning to market, had little intent to create, and little success in introducing, either an impersonal market economy based on clear property rights or a democratic political system. Instead, these so-called reforms were, in fact, measures designed to put into place mechanisms for generating and collecting economic rents and for distributing these rents to various political, ethnic or economic élites.

In such states, corruption, access to government favors and the regulated rights to undertake certain economic activities play a major role in the allocation of resources and of incomes. Such rent-seeking, or what I would call kleptocratic, states would find it hard to exist in the presence of a functioning democratic political system. A democracy enables groups to check each other's ability to generate and to capture such rents. This is why many of these kleptocratic states are dominated by single parties or by individual politicians, because a monopoly on political power enables the beneficiaries of kleptocratic behavior to maintain their hold over economic rents for a long time.

Evidence for this connection between kleptocratic behavior and the absence of democracy can be found in deMelo and Gelb (1997) who argue that 'political reforms have driven economic reforms – or at least have allowed space for them …' (p. 63). In their Table 2, they group the transition economies into four categories, from those with the highest levels of CLI to those with the lowest. They then compare the CLI scores for each country with the change between 1989 and 1995 in its Gastil index of political rights and civil liberties, as compiled by Freedom House. The Spearman rank correlation between the two indexes is 0.91. Thus, countries with greater political liberalization also have higher levels of CLI. However, what is even more striking and relevant to the argument here is that the increase in the Gastil index averages 9.5 for the most liberalized countries, the Czech Republic, Hungary, Poland, Slovak Republic, and Slovenia, but it is 0.3 for the least liberalized ones, Belarus, Turkmenistan, Ukraine and Uzbekistan.[9] Such low scores for the latter group of countries imply no improvement in democracy and political rights relative to the late Soviet period, and they suggest the current existence of either a dysfunctional democracy or some form of a dictatorship. In such a political system, it is not an impersonal market economy based on private property that is being created through the new economic laws and institutions reflected in the country's CLI. It is rather an economy designed to extract economic rents for those in power that is being created through these pseudo-liberalizations.

We have ample evidence that such kleptocratic economies fail to generate much economic progress, and that there are few incentives for politicians in such economies to weaken their grip on power by attempting painful stabilization measures. Thus, the regression results cited above may tell us more about the relative ability of market systems and kleptocratic systems to generate economic growth than they can tell us about the appropriate speed of introducing reforms within either system. Nevertheless, these results do demonstrate that economies that have not liberalized extensively, with whatever motives in mind, have not been able to achieve the output growth and decline in inflation achieved by those that reformed quickly and extensively. This evidence is to some extent weaker than would be evidence of a direct link between reform and economic performance, but it should not be entirely discounted on this account.

A second problem with the econometric evidence is that recent research suggests that a large proportion of the differences in the performance of transition economies can be explained by other explanatory variables. Krueger and Ciolko (1998) and Stuart and Panayotopoulos (1999) show that, once the differences in starting conditions of the transition economies are taken into account, the CLI loses its significance in explaining economic performance. Krueger and Ciolko, for example, show that the inclusion of dummy variables for regional tensions and for the successor states of the Soviet Union and measures of openness to international trade and the level of development prior to transition explain as much of the post-transition performance as does the CLI. Moreover, in the presence of their explanatory variables, the CLI is not a statistically significant determinant of economic performance. Accepting these starting conditions, however, can be taken to represent the readiness of these countries to join the EU. The higher their per capita incomes and the greater their trade with the West at the start of the transition, the more suitable are these countries for membership in the EU. Being more suitable for membership, however, was an important reason for these countries to adopt policies that would further increase their chances of being admitted to the EU. These policies quite clearly required economic liberalization, conformity to EU laws and regulations and the achievement of economic stability at levels that reflected the Maastricht criteria. There is also anecdotal evidence that a regression linking growth of output during transition to the distance between Berlin or Vienna and each transition economy's capital city would yield an explanation of economic growth at least as satisfactory as those obtained using CLI. This distance from West Europe can be viewed as a proxy for cultural and historical closeness between these countries and Western Europe and thus, to some extent, a proxy for their desire to rejoin Europe socially and culturally and to join the EU economy (Roland 1997).

The foregoing discussion suggests that the economic performance of the transition economies is over-determined, in that we can explain it using three different sets of explanatory variables, the CLI, starting conditions and social–historical connectedness to Europe. While this over-determination is something of an econometric embarrassment, it is a rather satisfying result. It indicates that transition strategies are jointly determined by economic, cultural, social and historical factors, with the last three being formed by expectations of, and the desire for, a link to Western Europe and the EU. If one accepts that such desires and expectations can play an important role in the political calculus of the populations of these countries, then the pattern of support for liberal economic policies in Eastern Europe becomes more understandable.

WHAT ABOUT OTHER MODELS?

Although the foregoing discussion has tried to make the case that there was more support for the liberal economic model than commonly thought, it is worth examining why it and the kleptocratic model have been the two predominant models adopted in transition economies. In the late 1980s and early 1990s, a number of other models of economic and political governance were seriously discussed and proposed as alternatives to the approach espoused by the Washington consensus. None of these models survived these discussions to get a very fair trial in East Europe, at least so far as stabilization or market and foreign trade liberalization were concerned. In contrast to the general adherence to either liberal orthodoxy or to kleptocracy in the design of stabilization and liberalization, in the case of privatization East European governments proved to be wildly innovative. They adopted a great variety of mechanisms for privatizing state-owned firms, and it can be argued that these approaches to privatization did, indeed, reflect a number of political philosophies that had been excluded from consideration in the design of stabilization and liberalization programs.

The Chinese Model

At the beginning of the transition, the complexity of the process and the exceptional growth exhibited by the Chinese economy combined to lead some observers to propose the Chinese model as an appropriate transition mechanism. The theoretical appeal for this approach was that rapid efforts to privatize state-owned firms would lead to chaos and that nascent markets would be unable to coordinate the activity of large firms with any efficiency. Thus chaos and an unacceptable fall in output would result. The Chinese model was seen as a way of avoiding this danger. In this model, newly founded private firms and agricultural units would emerge alongside the existing state-owned firms. Over time, the superior dynamism of the private sector, bolstered by emerging capitalist institutions and by an increasingly efficient market, would overtake and swallow up the inefficient state sector. In the interim, employment and output in the state-owned sector could be sustained by the state, and, thus, dangerous declines in employment and in living standards would be avoided.

This model was never seriously considered in East European countries because of the perceived differences in economic structure between them and China. The Chinese economy had a much larger agrarian sector and a large surplus of labor in the countryside. It was there that the emerging private sector in China flourished, both on farms and in the township-village enterprises. The European economies had a much smaller agrarian sector and no labor surplus to staff the new private sector. Beyond these practical considerations, there were also political objections to the Chinese model. One of these was that it implied an evolutionary approach toward the market, and such an evolutionary development of the market would unacceptably delay the entry into the EU. Even worse, the hallmark of the Chinese model is economic reform without political reform. In Europe, people wanted to get rid of communism as soon as possible. The Chinese model, however, was allegedly successful precisely because of the firm hand of the Communist Party on the process. Indeed, there is no 'withering away of the Party' in the Chinese model, and this alone may have been sufficient to make it politically unacceptable in East Europe.

The Asian Tigers as a Model

The economies of Southeast Asia represented to many in East Europe a much more attractive model that that offered by China, and support for the Asian model has even survived the meltdown of the Asian economies at the end of the 1990s. The Asian 'tigers' were attractive to East Europeans for a number of reasons: their level of development was closer to that of East Europe than was China's, so their experience seemed more relevant. They had achieved the fastest growth rates in the world, they were aggressively mastering advanced technologies, their exports were buoyant, and there was strong state involvement in setting the direction for industrial policy. This last feature of the Asian strategy appealed to those in East Europe who sought a 'third way' because the strong role of the state in directing economic activity implied a diminution of the role of the market. Moreover, export-led and technology-based development seemed a good way to set the stage for entry into the EU.

A closer examination of the experience of the Asian economies suggests that, however attractive the results may have appeared at first, the Asian model would be neither easy to duplicate nor as appealing as the Asian tigers' high rates of growth of GDP suggested. The high rates of growth in these countries were not necessarily based on growing productivity, rather they reflected the rapid mobilization and expansion of both captal and labor inputs (Krugman 1994). East Europe could not hope to duplicate such rapid factor growth, because it had little surplus labor and because it could not generate the rates of capital growth that were possible in Asia. Moreover, the Asian countries had first honed their skills at production and marketing by exporting goods that were competitive, owing to the low wages in the region. Wages, of course, grew somewhat over time, but wage costs were kept low by what Shin (1998) calls 'factory despotism,' a system that keeps wages and social benefits appallingly low and subjects workers to harsh working conditions and strict discipline. It is unlikely that East European workers, used to socialist indiscipline on the job and expecting to achieve West European living standards in the foreseeable future, could have been made subject to the rigors of such factory despotism.

The Asian miracle was also based on the specific role that these countries played in the global economy. On the one hand, they were critically dependent on the United States economy (Numazaki 1998). This dependence took two forms. First, they were almost entirely dependent on the United States for market access because the overwhelming share of their output was exported to America. Second, much of the ability to penetrate the United States market was due to the fact that Asian firms were able to produce goods extremely well suited to the needs of United States consumers. This was due to the outsourcing strategies of United States-based multinationals who quickly provided designs, technology and market intelligence to allow Asian firms to respond rapidly to market trends in the United States. Japan also played an important role in the emergence of the Asian economies. As wages rose in Japan, Japanese firms sought to maintain their global competitiveness in labor-intensive products by transferring their technology, capital and ability to access global markets to Southeast Asia, taking advantage of the region's low wages.

To some extent, East Europe has been able to replicate the Southeast Asian model in that it serves as a low cost source of manufactured goods for the EU, and this strategy has driven much of the foreign direct investment into the region.[10] Nevertheless, the fit is not ideal. On the one hand, there is considerable resistance in the EU to the loss of jobs to Eastern Europe through foreign direct investment. Also, the production capacities that West European firms are transferring to East Europe are more intended for re-export back to Western Europe rather than for export to third-country markets. Another barrier to emulating the Asian model for East Europe is that the EU market has been remarkably closed to Asian exports, even technologically sophisticated ones, and the EU's trade policies clearly preclude any efforts by East Europe to copy the textile and footwear factories of Asia or Korea's burgeoning steel industry. Because the EU is the focus of East Europe's economic strategy, even if the United States market could be tapped as an outlet for the products of an East European effort to imitate Asia, it is unlikely that this would be viewed as a positive impetus for East Europe's efforts to join the EU.

Populism

If, to paraphrase Marx, a specter is haunting the economies of East Europe, it is the specter of populism.[11] Liberal economists fear that popular dissatisfaction with the slow pace of transition will spill over into support for populist policies that will undo much of the market and macroeconomic discipline that has been achieved to date. Proponents of gradual transition fear that popular discontent with the harsh consequences of shock therapy will do the same. Yet, when viewed as an economic doctrine, populism clearly seems to have a number of economic and political liabilities for East Europe.

Although populism is not one of the 'isms' usually included in textbooks on comparative economic systems, it does represent a coherent economic system (Dornbusch and Edwards 1991). To some extent populism operates along corporatist lines. It seeks to promote the welfare of industrial workers (who are usually unionized), white-collar workers and government employees through a process of wage-setting that, unlike corporatism, aims less at the reconciliation of the interests of workers and employers and more at raising workers' incomes. Employment is maintained by means of neo-Keynesian fiscal policies and the easy money policies that are occasioned by the government's fiscal deficits.[12] Markets and the rights of property owners are both attenuated, and import restrictions are used to protect inefficient domestic production and to shore up what is often an overvalued exchange rate. In these ways, the volume of foreign trade is reduced, and foreign direct investment is discouraged.

These policies failed in Latin America, and to the extent that East European populists would adopt similar ones if they came to power, they seem to hold some appeal: this is suggested by the fact that elements of the populist model can now be found in several East European countries. A number of economies, including those of the Czech Republic and Hungary, have set wages through nation-wide negotiations between owners, unions and the government, and in Poland, Solidarity has been both a labor and a political movement, though with mixed success. However, national-level wage negotiations in East Europe have generally sought to restrain wage growth rather than to promote worker interests at the expense of employers. In East Europe there is also popular concern regarding the role of foreign capital in the national economy, and it is often expressed either in a reluctance to sell firms to foreign investors or in a tendency to criticize the behavior of foreign owners. Price controls over rents, municipal services and other consumer goods are also increasingly difficult to reduce.

Nevertheless, despite these developments, the rhetoric of populist politicians and the alleged restiveness of the working classes, there are serious constraints on the ability of populists to implement their programs in East Europe. First of all, the system that is being dismantled was one that already provided a wage structure and a system of extensive social benefits that favored those that populism proposes to help. The deleterious effects of past policies are still evident to voters, and it is also clear that the infrastructure for providing extensive social benefits has largely disappeared.

Even more problematic are the international implications of populism. The East European economies cannot expect to enter the EU on the basis of overvalued currencies and extensive restrictions on imports. Indeed, it is quite clear that they need just the opposite, undervalued exchange rates to stimulate exports and liberal import regimes both to prepare structurally for the time they join the EU and to gain acceptance in the larger international community. Despite populist complaints about foreign ownership, which are present in every country, foreign direct investment is for most of these countries a key source of capital and technology, and offers access to international markets. Finally, a populist state is a state whose citizens would find themselves increasingly closeted in a closed social and economic system, a prospect at odds with the agenda of joining European political, social and cultural processes.

Where Choice is Possible – Privatization

While policymakers in East Europe faced significant constraints in their choice of a model for stabilizing and liberalizing their economies, they encountered great freedom in determining how to privatize their economies. The goal, the more or less total privatization of state-owned enterprises in the most expeditious way, was in part given by the same considerations that impelled the liberal programs of stabilization and market liberalization. Yet even here, because the credible prospect of privatization could improve the performance of state-owned firms (Brada 1996), some delay in their actual privatization was possible. More important, there was no guidance from liberal economics on how to privatize on such a massive scale and with so little capital to pay for the assets being privatized.

Consequently, it is in the design of privatization programs that we should expect to see a greater variety of approaches. Indeed, the privatization programs of individual countries should, to a greater extent than stabilization programs, reflect the national tendencies toward populism, kleptocracy and liberalism. Czechoslovakia, for example, adopted the voucher privatization method. This was a rather imaginative effort at creating a broad share-holding class, although it may also be viewed as a populist gimmick pandering to the masses. Unfortunately, this program failed in its objectives because of the unanticipated emergence of bank-owned investment funds that gained about two-thirds of all coupons and thus control over the firms being privatized, leaving the Czech economy with poor corporate governance and a fragile and as yet unprivatized banking system. The Hungarian approach, which relied on foreign investors for the capital to buy, and the managerial skills to run, firms being privatized, proved somewhat more successful. Poland's situation was somewhat more complex in that workers' councils dominated most firms, limiting managerial freedom. In many cases, workers were induced by wage promises to cede their powers, allowing managers and outside owners to gain control. While formal privatization was delayed, this approach did give managers both the incentives and the power to manage the firms effectively.

In economies where the European option or liberal ideology were less strong, more kleptocratic approaches to privatization were adopted, or, as in Slovakia, privatization slowed appreciably over time. In these countries, privatizations often tended to favor workers and managers by reserving large portions of shares for workers in an enterprise being privatized or by giving workers and managers the right to buy a firm for some small down payment and then to allowing them to pay the rest of the purchase price out of future profits. To the extent that workers actually chose to purchase shares or were required to do so when their enterprise was privatized, such worker-centered privatizations can be seen as part of a populist program aimed at favoring industrial workers over those citizens, such as farmers, government employees, etc., who were not employed in factories. In the end, these workers' shares, and thus the control of the firms, actually ended up in the hands of the managers. Often, collusion between managers and government officials led to the underpricing of the firms being privatized, thus allowing managers to buy a controlling interest in the firms. In this way, a kleptocratic outcome emerged.

CONCLUSIONS

The argument in this chapter is relatively straightforward: To a greater or lesser extent, the populations of East Europe viewed transition as a complex economic, political, social and cultural process that at its core involved a reattachment to European social and political processes and eventual membership in the European Union. This set of objectives imposed on these countries a set of constraints that made it difficult for them to deviate from the liberal model of economic stabilization and market liberalization.

As a result of these long term and multifaceted objectives, the populations of the East European countries undergoing transition were likely to be less responsive in the political behavior to short-run fluctuations in income and unemployment. I have also argued that, even if East European voters were to react to transition strategies largely by reflecting on output declines and increases in unemployment, a more nuanced examination of the performance of the transition economies suggests that the economic outcomes were not as bad as often portrayed. Moreover, when viewed from a broader perspective, the performance of the liberal model seems to have been arguably better than that of the kleptocratic model, the only other system that seems to have been systematically implemented in transition economies. In part, this failure to adopt other models of economic management such as populism, or the so-called Asian model, is the result of a poor fit between these models' outcomes and the desire for European re-integration that shapes East Europe's efforts at transformation.

The process of transition is rapidly ending in many of the East European economies. In some it is ending because the institutions of a market economy are sufficiently in place to allow policymakers to grapple with economic problems using the kinds of instruments and approaches found in more advanced market economies. This is not to say that, in these post-transition economies, market institutions and processes are as well developed or effective as they are in advanced economies, but clearly policymakers are more concerned with the management of the economy than with its radical reconstruction. In other countries, transition may be ending either because a functioning market economy was not the initial objective, and the stagnant kleptocratic state that has emerged has sufficient power to fend off political challenges, or because there is no will for further reform. Thus we are likely to see a shift of the European Union's borders to the East, but not the total absorption of East Europe by the liberal political and economic ideal.

NOTES

1. See Gomulka (1995) for a discussion of the expectations of the framers of the Polish stabilization program.
2. Of course, some of these countries did attempt to implement a stabilization program.
3. Some have argued that the collapse of CMEA was itself part of the liberal agenda, but there was, in fact, no practical way in which this trade could be sustained (Brada 1993).
4. It is true that income inequality has increased along with rising levels of consumption. What the political implications of this are, however, is unclear. Any redistribution produces both winners and losers. Moreover, not all egalitarianism is seen as desirable. For example, were equal incomes between a medical doctor and a Party apparatchik viewed as a politically popular result?
5. It is instructive to cite at length Kornai's *cri de coeur* about the lack of growth in Hungary because it reflects the widespread despair of many East Europeans. He writes, 'It arouses especially bitter feelings to compare Hungary's stagnation and contraction of production with the performance of so many other countries. Hungary's GDP in 1993 was back at its level in 1976–77 ... So there has been zero average annual growth for a period of 17 years while many Asian countries have had annual average growth rates of 4–9 percent, so that their production has increased by two to three-and-a-half times'. (Kornai 1997, p. 70).
6. This is by no means an exhaustive set of citations, as the literature is quite voluminous.
7. See Rodrik (1996) for a survey of the political economy approach and its usefulness.
8. Balcerowicz (1997) also discusses these interactions between political and economic goals.
9. Only two of these countries are European, and I do not consider them in this chapter, as they are former Soviet Republics. However, other European countries can be found in the two intermediate groups of countries.
10. Among the most striking of these outsourcing investments are those in the automobile industry.

11. One indication of the feelings towards populism among its East European opponents is that, in describing populist politicians, the word 'populist' is almost invariably followed by the word 'demagogue'.
12. I use the label 'neo-Keynesian' rather reluctantly, as the current usage seems to imply a profligate tendency toward government spending with little thought for inflation. Neither Keynesians nor neo-Keynesians used to support such one-sided policies, but perhaps the general abandonment of Keynesian macroeconomics by economists has left the label to those who do espouse such policies.

REFERENCES

Aghion, Philipe and Olivier Blanchard (1994), 'On the speed of transition in Central Europe', *NBER Macroeconomics Annual.*

Aslund, Anders, Peter Boone and Simon Johnson (1996), 'How to stabilize: lessons from post-communist countries', *Brookings Papers on Economic Activity,* No. 1, pp. 217–91.

Balcerowicz, Leszek (1995), *Socialism, Capitalism, Transformation*, Budapest: Central European University.

Balcerowicz, Leszek (1997), 'The interplay between economic and political transition', in Salvatore Zecchini (ed.), *Lessons from the Economic Transition: Central and Eastern Europe in the 1990s*, Dordrecht: Kluwer.

Barro, Robert J. (1997), *Determinants of Economic Growth: a Cross-Country Empirical Study*, Cambridge: MIT Press.

Blanchard, Olivier (1997), *The Economics of Post-Communist Transition*, Oxford: Clarendon Press.

Brada, Josef C. (1996), 'Privatization is transition – or is it?', *Journal of Economic Perspectives*, **10** (2), 67–88.

Brada, Josef C. (1993), 'Regional integration in Eastern Europe: prospects for integration within the region and with the European Community', in J. deMelo and A. Panagariya (eds), *New Dimensions in Regional Integration*, Cambridge: Cambridge University Press.

Brada, Josef C. (1989), 'Technological progress and factor utilization in Eastern European economic growth', *Economica*, **56** (224), 433–48.

Christofferson, Peter and Peter Doyle (1998), 'From inflation to growth: eight years of transition', International Monetary Fund, Working Paper WP/98/100, July.

Cottarelli, Carlo and Peter Doyle (1999), 'Taming inflation in the transition economies', *Finance and Development*, **36** (2), June, 11–14.

deMelo, Martha and Alan Gelb (1996), 'A comparative analysis of twenty-eight transition economies in Europe and Asia', *Post-Soviet Geography and Economics*, **37** (5), 265–85.

deMelo, Martha and Alan Gelb (1997), 'Transition to date: a comparative view', in Salvatore Zecchini (ed.), *Lessons From the Economic Transition: Central and Eastern Europe in the 1990s*, Dordrecht: Kluwer.

Dewatripont, Matthias and Gerard Roland (1995), 'The design of reform packages under uncertainty', *American Economic Review*, **85** (5), 1207–23.

Dornbusch, Rudiger and Sebastian Edwards (eds), (1991), *The Macroeconomics of Populism in Latin America*, Chicago: University of Chicago Press.

Dyba, Karel, and Jan Svejnar (1994), 'Stabilization and transition in Czechoslovakia', in O.J. Blanchard, K.A. Froot and D.J. Sachs (eds), *The Transition in Eastern Europe. Vol. 1: Country Studies*, Chicago: The University of Chicago Press.

Estrin, Saul, Josef Brada, Alan Gelb and Inderjit Singh (eds), (1995) *Restructuring and Privatization in East Central Europe*, Armonk: M.E. Sharpe.

Filer, Randal and J. Hanousek (1998), 'Output changes and inflationary bias in transition', CERGE-EI Working Paper, Prague.

Fischer, Stanley, Ratna Sahay and Carlos A. Vegh (1996), 'Stabilization and growth in transition economies: the early experience', *Journal of Economic Perspectives*, **10** (2), 45–66.

Gaddy, Clifford G. and Barry W. Ickes (1999), 'An accounting model of the virtual economy in Russia', *Post-Soviet Geography and Economics*, **40** (2), 79–97.

Gaddy, Clifford G. and Barry W. Ickes (1998), 'Russia's "Virtual Economy"', *Foreign Affairs*, **70** (5), 53–67.

Gomulka, Stanislaw (1995), 'The IMF-supported programs of Poland and Russia: principles, errors, and results', *Journal of Comparative Economics*, **20** (3), 36–346.

Haggard, Stephan, Robert Kaufman and Matthew Shugard (1998), *Hungarian Fiscal Policy Making in Comparative Perspective,* Collegium Budapest, Discussion Paper 151.

Haynes, Michael and Rumy Husan (1998), 'The State and market in the transition economies: critical remarks in the light of past history and the current experience', *The Journal of European Economic History*, **27** (3), 609–44.

Hughes, Gordon A. and Paul Hare (1994), 'The international competitiveness of industries in Bulgaria, Czechoslovakia, Hungary and Poland', *Oxford Economic Papers*, **46** (2), 200–221.

Kornai, János (1997), 'Adjustment without recession: a case study of Hungarian stabilization', in Zecchini Salvatore (ed.), *Lessons from the Economic Transition*, Dordrecht: Kluwer.

Kornai, János (1971), *Anti-equilibrium*, Amsterdam: North Holland.

Kornai, János (1997), 'Lasting growth as top priority: macroeconomic tensions and government economic policy in Hungary', in J. Kornai, *Struggle and Hope: Essays on Stabilization and Reform in a Post-socialist Economy*, Cheltenham, UK and Lyme, US: Edward Elgar.

Krueger, Gary and Marek Ciolko (1998), 'A note on initial conditions and liberalization during transition', *Journal of Comparative Economics*, **26** (4), December, 718–34.

Krugman, Paul (1994), 'The myth of Asia's miracle', *Foreign Affairs*, **76** (6), 62–78.

Murrell, Peter and Yijiang Wang (1993), 'When privatization should be delayed: the effect of communist legacies on organization and institutional reforms', *Journal of Comparative Economics*, **17** (3), 385–417.

Numazaki, Ichiro (1998), 'The export-oriented industrialization of Pacific Rim nations and their presence in the global market', in Eun Mee Kim (ed.), *The Four Asian Tigers: Economic Development and the Global Political Economy*, San Diego: Academic Press.

Przeworski, Adam (1991), *Democracy and the Market: Political and Economic Reforms in Eastern Europe and Latin America*, Cambridge: Cambridge University Press.

Przeworski, Adam (1993), 'Economic reforms, public opinion and political institutions', in L.C. Bresser et al., (eds), *Economic Reforms in New Democracies*, Cambridge: Cambridge University Press.

Rodrik, Dani (1992), 'Making sense of the Soviet trade Shock in Eastern Europe: a framework and some estimates', CEPR Discussion Paper No. 705.

Rodrik, Dani (1995), 'The dynamics of political support for reform in economies in transition', *Journal of Japanese and International Economics*, **9** (4), 403–25.
Rodrik, Dani (1996), 'Understanding economic policy reform', *Journal of Economic Literature*, **34** (1), 9–41.
Roland, Gèrard (1994), 'The role of political constraints in transition strategies', *Economics of Transition*, **2** (1), 27–41.
Roland, Gèrard (1997), 'Political constraints and the transition experience', in Salvatore Zecchini (ed.), *Lessons from the Economic Transition: Central and Eastern Europe in the 1990s*, Norwell, MA and Dordrecht: Kluwer, pp. 169–87.
Sachs, Jeffrey D. (1996), 'The transition at mid-decade', *American Economic Review Papers and Proceedings*, **86** (2), May, 128–33.
Shen, Raphael (1997), *The Restructuring of Romania's Economy*, Westport: Greenwood.
Shin, Kwang Yeong (1998), 'The political economy of economic growth in East Asia: South Korea and Taiwan', in Eun Mee Kim (ed.), *The Four Asian Tigers: Economic Development and the Global Political Economy*, San Diego: Academic Press.
Stuart, Robert C. and Christina M. Panayotopoulos (1999), 'Decline and recovery in transition economies', *Post-Soviet Geography and Economics*, **40** (4), 267–80.
Wellisz, Stanislaw (1997), 'Inflation and stabilization in Poland, 1990–95', in Mario I. Blejer and Marko Skreb (eds), *Macroeconomic Stabilization in Transition Economies*, Cambridge: Cambridge University Press.
Winiecki, Jan (1991), 'The inevitability of a fall in output in the early stages of transition to the market: theoretical underpinnings', *Soviet Studies*, **43** (4), 171–92.

COMMENTS ON JOSEF C. BRADA, 'ECONOMIC TRANSITION IN EASTERN EUROPE: HOW SUCCESSFUL IS THE PROJECT AND HOW MUCH POLITICAL SUPPORT DOES IT HAVE?'

Donald V. Coes

Policymakers and academics who once focused rather narrowly on specific geographical regions have gradually awakened to how much there is to learn from international, or even intercontinental comparisons. For Latin Americanists, the lessons – both positive and negative – that may be learned from Eastern Europe are fine examples, as Brada's insightful chapter makes clear to those of us with a Latin American focus.

Surely one must begin by setting forth some explicit standards for judgments about economic success or failure. Yet reasonable observers can disagree with what those standards should be. As Brada rightly notes, perhaps the only valid judges are those citizens of the economies whose performance we outsiders would presume to evaluate. Such an intellectual *laissez-faire* attitude will not preclude external judgments, however, and, in any case, multilateral organizations like the IMF or the World Bank, or foreign governments, will sometimes be forced to define 'success' or 'failure.' Brada's chapter suggests several standards, and provides some guarded and well-qualified support for some of the standards that might be viewed as part of the 'neo-liberal' or 'Washington Consensus' view.

It is clear that even though Eastern Europeans and Latin Americans might differ with respect to emphasis and many significant details, judgments about their respective transitions to more open, market-oriented economies share a number of common elements. Because they are in principle measurable, recent trends in GDP and other aggregate product and income levels are a common starting point in both regions. Brada usefully extends this view to include judgments about likely future trends and the sustainability of reforms. He also notes that in the Eastern European case, greater political freedom and the rejection of communism have strongly influenced judgments about relative success or failure.

At the heart of much of the debate about economic performance in the two regions is the question of the path that an economy is likely to follow in a transition phase. Not only do we not know just what that path is, but we also have only vague ideas about how long that path might be traveled. The standard neo-classical model, even if it is something of a caricature, is nevertheless a useful point of reference from which to address this question.

Until the past decade, both Latin American and Eastern European economies were distorted by price controls, trade interventions, state planning or enterprises, and a myriad of other interventions. In this context, the neo-classical model suggests that output will be significantly lower than its potential, but may be relatively stable. In graphical terms, such a non-optimal equilibrium could be represented by a point well within the production possibility frontier. Privatization, greater trade openness, and other policy reforms may permit the economy to move toward a new equilibrium. But it should be clear from both Latin American and Eastern European experience that the transition paths may vary widely among economies with respect to duration, price changes, and the behavior of aggregate output. Given the recentness of major reform in both regions, moreover, it is unlikely that many, if any, of the economies are close to completing the transition.

The neo-classical model has never told us all we would like to know about the transition path, due to its focus on long-run equilibrium positions. But it certainly does not rule out the possibility that output may fall significantly, as factors become unemployed in sectors which were formerly supported by different forms of policy intervention. This scenario is entirely consistent with the experience of both regions. Nor does the neo-classical model rule out strong and even decisive institutional influences, as comparisons within Latin America and Eastern Europe or between them make clear.

Some of the observed fall in output, moreover, may be as much a problem of measurement as of underlying trends. Without doubt, a rise in unemployment of a number of factors reflects actual output loss, but other apparent loss may be due in part to the absorption of factors into less regulated or controlled and informal sectors of the economy. As centralized control of many economies, especially those of Eastern Europe, weakened, and as the suppression of many markets was reduced, some of the apparent lost output may have disappeared from the official statistics, but not necessarily from the economy.

Brada's attention to the political dimensions of the transition path is of particular interest. He cogently argues that political support cannot be naïvely linked to current GDP trends, but must reflect in part prospects for the future growth of products, as well as non-economic considerations such as greater personal freedom, and an expanded, more democratically determined agenda for the society. In this respect, there is an interesting contrast with Latin America, in which political support for reforms probably has been far too closely linked to current output trends than may be helpful for the sustainability of longer run reform. Brazil's experience during the post *Plano Real* period provides a good example of this problem, since support for the current government (and its re-election) hung largely on the favorable performance of output in the first several years of the period, and eroded sharply after output fell or stagnated subsequently.

Another contrast between the two regions highlighted by Brada is the simple fact that the majority of Eastern Europeans had determined to create whole new societies, decisively turning their backs on over four decades of communism. In Latin America, with the possible exception of Argentina, the feeling of rejection of the past is much less deep. Many Latin Americans would be content with incremental change, or in some cases, no change at all, as long as their relative position in society would not be adversely affected.

One of Brada's most interesting points, and one that easily generalizes to Latin America, is that geography matters. While distance from Berlin and Vienna might not be a plausible explanatory variable, there is clearly a difference between the Mexican reforms and embrace of NAFTA and the more inwardly focused rise of MERCOSUR in the Southern Cone of South America. If we extend geography to include strong local variations in historical and cultural tradition, then apparent differences in the success of reforms make even more sense. Chilean or Uruguayan progress, in contrast to Venezuela or Central America, may provide Latin American examples, parallel to Brada's distinction between Hungary, Poland, and Slovenia on the one hand, and economies like Romania, Slovakia, or Bulgaria, on the other.

COMMENTS ON JOSEF C. BRADA, 'ECONOMIC TRANSITION IN EASTERN EUROPE: HOW SUCCESSFUL IS THE PROJECT AND HOW MUCH POLITICAL SUPPORT DOES IT HAVE?'

William Maloney

Reading Josef Brada's chapter brought home how similar some dimensions of the transition process are in Eastern Europe and Latin America. This is true both in the problems of evaluating the success of the reform strategies to date, but also more broadly in the design of longer term development strategies for the region.

Brada makes a compelling case that the pure statistical evidence on the success of reform strategies is ambiguous, and that isolating the impact of economic policies versus other political or historical factors is extremely difficult. He breaks down Eastern Europe into the democracies (the west) and kleptocracies (in the east) and then raises the question of whether the superior performance of the former is due to better economic policy-making, or rather the greater accountability of policymakers in the west. More generally, it is virtually impossible not to attribute much of the success of the western countries to inherited cultural and historical capital: as he points out, the single most important determinant of success of the emerging eastern nations appears to be the distance from Berlin.

These same considerations arise in Latin America as well. Some serious research by Easterly, Loayza, and Montiel (1997) and Fernández-Arias and Monteil (1997) suggest that a decent econometric evaluation is possible and that, in fact, reforms broadly in the neo-liberal framework have led to better performance. That said, these studies may also suffer from some of the same omitted variable bias. As Gerardo Munck has frequently reminded me (see, for example, Munck 1998) it is virtually impossible to separate the neo-liberal reforms and particularly 'labor market reforms' from the radical demobilization of the popular sectors that occurred across the same period. The design of pre-reform policies in the region was in no small measure the result of political dynamics that were altered dramatically in the military periods. Chile's particular success may also be partially due to a strong legal tradition (despite the military dictatorship) and a different set of cultural habits not uniformly shared throughout the region.

Further, finding that the neo-liberal reforms had positive outcomes does not imply that these were the optimal policies. Despite being the poster-country for reform success, Chile's progress in the first 15 years of reform was unimpressive, largely due to errors, among them deficient regulation of the banking sector and capital account liberalization, leading to crisis half way through the process. This crisis was avoidable and perhaps the 'correct' set of policies and sequencing would have led to even better results.

Unfortunately, the problem of identifying optimal sequencing is theoretically difficult. Not only does policy need to be made when the underlying parameters of the economy are by definition changing, but some of these parameters are, in turn, dependent on how agents learn and adapt to the new structure. Policymakers need to learn, but they also need to know how their citizens are learning (Maloney 1997). It is no wonder that policy advice often seems to revert to clever, but perhaps unreliable analogies for example 'gradualism is like changing the side of the road traffic drives on, alternating cars today with trucks and buses tomorrow'. In the absence of reliable theoretical prescriptions, it is difficult to develop a standard against which to measure the success of policymaking.

Brada has observed that what really matters to the populace is integration with Western Europe – however achieved – and that discussions of reform strategy are of secondary importance. This is perhaps the overriding lesson to carry home, especially for those countries most proximate to Berlin. But I would have liked to see a deeper and more nuanced discussion of the eastern laggards. I sense that the development problems are probably more daunting there than in the Czech Republic or Hungary, and further, that there may be more fruitful comparisons with Latin America in a couple of dimensions.

First, as Joseph Love (1996) has noted, Manoilescu was developing a theory of development under dependency in Rumania and the other more 'peripheral' eastern European states before Prebisch, Furtado and their ilk in Latin America. These issues are still on the table in Latin America, either in their traditional form (Argentina's concern with exporting primary goods) or newer concerns about the havoc wreaked by capital flow volatility.

Second, entrepreneurship is weak. Concerns with stimulating industry led to development agencies like Chile's CORFO, which would eventually control most investment in the country. This seems to be a concern now in the peripheral countries of Eastern Europe. Here I wonder if we're not in danger of giving kleptocracy a bad name. As Daniel Chirot notes in his chapter on Romania, the entrepreneurs are in fact those working the gray areas, much as were the antecedents of some Chaebols in Korea. Creating and channeling existing entrepreneurial talent seems an ongoing challenge in both regions.

Third, whereas the level of education is very high in the Czech republic, Hungary and Poland, human capital accumulation lags farther east and in Latin America. The possible links from here to growth and distribution are manifold. There are certainly other parallel challenges, but my point is that neither region has converged on a development paradigm that provides convincing answers to the issues raised above (as well as others), and there may be benefits from exploring such problems comparatively.

References

Easterly, William, Norman Loayza and Peter Montiel (1997), 'Has Latin America's Post-reform growth been disappointing?', *Journal of International Economics*; **43** (3–4), 287–311.
Fernández-Arias, Eduardo and Peter Montiel (1997), 'Reform and growth in Latin America, all pain, no gain?', IDB Working Paper 351.
Love, Joseph L. (1996), *Crafting the Third World: Theorizing Underdevelopment in Rumania and Brazil*, Stanford, CA: Stanford University Press.
Maloney, William F. (1997), 'Chile', in Laura Randall (ed.), *The Political Economy of Latin America in the Post War Period*, Austin, Institute of Latin American Studies: University of Texas Press.
Munck, Gerardo L. (1998), *Authoritarianism and Democratization. Soldiers and Workers in Argentina, 1976–83*, University Park, PA: Pennsylvania State University Press, pp. 200–203.

5. How much does the past count? Interpreting the Romanian transition's political successes and economic failures

Daniel Chirot

Since the fall of communism in December, 1989, Romania has experienced some very significant successes and equally important failures. The main success has been that it has established a viable democracy and freely elected a genuinely liberal, reformist government.[1] Its main failure has been economic. By the late 1990s, the economy as a whole was performing no better than it had been in the late 1980s. Though the distribution of consumer goods and services was far better than it had been during the period of late communism, overall productivity was not, and much of the population remained in dire poverty. Why has it been so difficult to make economic improvements, and why have Romania's liberal reformers failed in their endeavor to improve economic performance?

No definitive answer to these questions exists, but some tentative ones can be proposed. Though they address Romania's problems, any such answers also may be useful guides to a better understanding of similar partial failures elsewhere in the former Soviet Union and the Balkans.

THE LIBERAL TRIUMPH OF 1996 AND THE NATO FIASCO

In 1996 Romania elected a committed, sincere, democratic, and market oriented president and parliament. They were, in the best and most general sense of that word, genuine liberals. The defeated included both the xenophobic far right as well as the more or less reformed communists who had been in power since the revolution of December 1989.

It is important to point out that the elections of 1996 marked the first time in Romania's history that a truly liberal government came to power in Romania.

The Liberals in the late nineteenth century and until World War II were actually economic protectionists, followers of List, and they believed that only a strong central government could modernize the economy.[2] By the late 1930s, what was left of traditional liberal sentiment backed an authoritarian monarchy against the rising fascist tide. Only the Peasant Party retained a sense that it was important to sustain some semblance of a free market economy.[3] In any case the central ideals of liberalism – democracy, tolerance, private property, markets – became historical anachronisms as first the Iron Guard fascists, then a military dictatorship, and finally the Communist Party, backed by Soviet power, seized control. Only after 1989 was there a revival of such ideas. But as long as the old (albeit reformed) communist apparatus held on to the power that it had seized in December, 1989, genuinely liberal sentiments had only limited influence.[4]

A brief examination of the presidential election results in 1996 show how dramatic a shift occurred, and the opportunity given to liberals in the form of the reconstituted Peasant Party led by Emil Constantinescu.

The Romanians follow the French model for electing their president, and as in France, the President is more powerful than the Prime Minister whom he appoints, subject to the approval of parliament. In the first round, no candidate in a divided field won a majority. The top two candidates were Ion Iliescu, the incumbent and leader of the Romanian Social Democrats (reformed communists), and Emil Constantinescu, the candidate of the liberal Romanian Christian Democratic and Peasantist opposition alliance.

In the runoff election, on November 17, 1996, Constantinescu gained the vote of those who wanted to push ahead faster with privatization, who wanted to be more open to Western European and American influence, and who were less chauvinistic in their nationalism. Iliescu won the vote of the more traditional, anti-Western nationalists, of those who were nostalgic about the social security once offered by socialism, and of those who feared the effects of further privatization. Constantinescu won 54 percent of the vote to Iliescu's 46 percent, and a liberal alliance took control of parliament.[5]

More than the general outcome of the election, however, it was the distribution of the vote that meaningfully revealed what was going on. Of Romania's 42 *judeţi* (counties) 20 went for Constantinescu, and 22 for Iliescu.

With one exception, every county of the 16 that were once part of the Habsburg Empire (Transylvania and the Banat) went for Constantinescu. In the single exception, Hunedoara, Iliescu won only 50.06 percent of the vote, the closest result in any county.

On the other hand, in the *Regat* (literally, Kingdom, meaning the pre-1918 Romanian Kingdom whose two principalities of Wallachia and Moldavia had been Ottoman dependencies for about four centuries before full independence in 1878) Iliescu won 21 of 26 counties. One of these was actually the southern half of Dobrogea, whose two counties were not part of any Romanian principality until 1878, and were turned over to the Kingdom to give it a seacoast. Of the remaining 24 counties of the Kingdom, 20 went for Iliescu. The exceptions were particularly interesting because they included the most urbanized and industrialized parts of the Kingdom. One was the county of Prahova, site of the oil industry which had contained independent Romania's only partly industrialized area before World War I. Another was Bucharest itself and Ilfov, which now surrounds the capital and consists of its suburbs. The other exception, Galaţi, the only Moldavian county voting for Constantinescu, contains what was before World War I Moldavia's only seaport. It is also very heavily industrialized.

What was interesting about the exceptions in the 'Old Kingdom' was that they were its most urbanized, least traditional, and historically most cosmopolitan regions. This applied to Dobrogea, too, because it is an area of more recent Romanian settlement, and the county that went for Constantinescu in this region contains Romania's main seaport, Constanţa, which was already a city before it was absorbed into Romania.

Part of the explanation lies with the ethnic composition of Romania's various regions. The Hungarians, who make up about 8 percent of the Romanian electorate, and are concentrated in Transylvania, voted for the Hungarian Party's candidate in the first round. According to exit polls, 97.2 percent of this candidate's voters moved to Constantinescu in the second round. Given Iliescu's on and off alliance with the most intransigently nationalist, and therefore anti-Magyar parties during his second term (1992–6), this is not surprising. Indeed, the two Transylvanian counties with large Magyar majorities, Covasna and Harghita, gave Constantinescu his biggest majorities, 86.81 percent and 91.59 percent, respectively. But the Hungarian vote cannot explain very much of Iliescu's weakness in most of Transylvania or in the Old Kingdom's and Dobrogea's least traditional, most urbanized, and most cosmopolitan counties.

It turns out that Transylvanian counties that used to have a significant ethnic German population went very heavily for Constantinescu, too, even though there are fewer than a hundred thousand, mostly older, Germans left in Romania. In no county were there enough to account for Constantinescu's overwhelming strength where there used to be major German cities. Brasov (former Kronstadt) county gave Constantinescu a 69.61 percent majority, Sibiu (formerly Hermannstadt) gave him 73.82 percent, and Timis, whose capital, Timişoara, was once the capital of the heavily German Catholic Banat, gave him 72.72 percent of its vote. There are simply not enough Germans, or even Hungarians in these counties to come close to accounting for Constantinescu's lopsided victories.

The presence of minorities might have inflamed nationalist passions, as it used to in Romania's pre-war elections, and caused ethnic Romanians to vote for a more nationalist candidate. That is one of the explanations given for the

'Funar' phenomenon, in which a xenophobic Romanian nationalist by that name held on to the elected position of mayor in Cluj, Transylvania's leading urban center. Yet in this election, the county of Cluj also gave Constantinescu an overwhelming victory, with 69.03 percent of the vote. In fact, Funar, who ran in the first round and garnered less than 5 percent of the national vote, saw 58 percent (according to exit polls) of his own former voters shift to Constantinescu in the second round, an outcome that makes one wonder what happened to their xenophobia and anti-liberalism.

The residual effect of the ethnic German presence was simply that in those regions where there used to be many Germans, the population remained on the whole more educated, more sophisticated, and therefore, politically more aware. This is true of Transylvania and the Banat as a whole, as these former Habsburg domains entered the Romanian Kingdom in 1918 already more literate and sophisticated than the Old Kingdom. Very few Germans are left there, but these formerly German cities remain the most westernized in Romania, and this was where Constantinescu did best (leaving aside the Hungarian counties of Covasna, Harghita, and Satu Mare, which is on the Hungarian border and also contains a large proportion of Magyars).

In the capital city of Bucharest, Iliescu won only 37.18 percent of the vote, an overwhelming defeat.

Iliescu's greatest strength was in the Old Kingdom counties that were traditionally the least urbanized. Table 5.1, grouping the counties by percentage of the population that was urban in 1974, shows this.

It was not just the voting by county which indicated how the majority of traditional, less sophisticated Romanian voters stuck with Iliescu. Exit polling by category of voter showed a similar pattern. IRSOP (Institutul Român Pentru Sondarea Opiniei Publice, the Romanian Institute for Public Opinion Polling), found the voting to be as shown in Table 5.2. These data were not collected by ethnic category and show unambiguously that the more educated, the more urban, the younger, and those generally more aware of the outside world voted more for Constantinescu. Even the gender gap confirms this, because in Romania women remain somewhat less educated, somewhat more traditional, and someone lower on the occupational scale. The difference between workers and peasants was particularly striking.

The liberal coalition also won control of parliament, and Constantinescu was able to appoint his choice for prime minister, mayor Victor Ciorbea of Bucharest.

The first conclusion to be drawn from the election (at least for a sociologist) is the extraordinary persistence, over many generations, of important regional differences. The greater sophistication and higher degree of modernization that existed in Transylvania and the Banat before 1939 survived considerable ethnic migration (Germans leaving, many Romanians entering) and forty years of

Table 5.1 Voting and long-standing urbanism in the Old Kingdom

	% urban in 1974	% voting for Iliescu, 1996[6]
Low Urban (under 30%)		
Botoşani	26	68
Buzau	20	65
Gorj	28	63
Ialomita	26	61
Olt	21	63
Suceava	27	54
Teleorman	25	66
Calaraşi (part of Teleorman in 1974)		64
Tulcea	29	53
Vaslui	24	64
Valcea	23	60
Vrancea	23	58
Average of votes (unweighted)		**61.6**
Medium Urban (30% to 40%)		
Arges	33	58
Bacau	38	54
Dolj	37	54
Iaşi	38	54
Mehedinti	34	54
Neamt	31	56
Average of votes (unweighted)		**55.0**
High Urban (over 40%)		
Braila	47	59
Constanţa	58	42
Damboviţa	48	54
Galaţi	48	49
Prahova	51	46
Bucharest	100	37
Ilfov		43
(Much of rural Ilfov has been turned into the county of Giurgiu, where 56% voted for Iliescu. What remains of Ilfov contains the Bucharest suburbs.)		
Average of votes (unweighted and not counting Giurgiu)		**47.1**

Table 5.2 Voting by population category[7]

	% Constantinescu	% Iliescu
Women	52	48
Men	58	42
Age under 34	66	34
Age over 65	43	57
Completed only Primary School	44	56
Completed High School (Lycée)	60	40
Completed University	66	34
White collar	65	35
Workers	58	42
Peasants	30	70

communism. Attitudes ingrained by generations of change in Hungary, going back perhaps to the Reformation, and certainly to the mid-19th century start of economic and social modernization in Hungary, lasted into the late 20th century.

The second and politically more important conclusion was that these results in late 1996 had to make any observer optimistic for the future of Romanian liberalism. The liberal coalition won the votes of those portions of the population who constituted an ever-growing part of Romania. The liberals were going to privatize the economy once and for all, open Romania to the West, and turn it into a genuinely pluralist democracy. All this would be initiated by the government's first priority, to join the West formally by entering NATO.

Alas, this foreign policy gambit, trumpeted widely by the government as the first step toward full-scale reform renovation of the economy and society, failed. Soon after, liberal optimism turned to gloom. By 1998 the economy was in decline, and by 1999 it seemed close to collapse. In early 1999 there were strikes by miners that prevented restructuring of the coal industry, and the workers in general were threatening the political stability of the country. History had taken its revenge, and Romania was sinking back into what it had always been, at least since it became a player on the European scene in the mid-19th century, a backward, marginalized, tragicomic society unable to perform up to European standards even though its elite tried desperately to pretend that it was a significant part of Europe.

NATO membership would have made it clear to all Romanians that a slide to the far right was no longer an option, and it would have been a precursor to more substantial economic help from the West in the near future. This, no doubt, is why admission to NATO became an obsessive symbol for President Constantinescu.[8]

From the point of view of the United States, which did not anticipate the Kosovo crisis and war of 1999, this Romanian demand to be admitted to NATO verged on the absurd. What security concerns did it address? What could Romania contribute? Was Romania even stable and prosperous enough to sustain any meaningful role in NATO? But for historically aware Romanian intellectuals and politicians, it made perfect sense, because such an admission would have sent a signal to the Romanian electorate that democracy and liberal capitalism were indeed the global wave of the future, and Romania would partake of their benefits. This is why Romania's friends in the United States called for some sort of promise that Romania might, after all, be allowed to enter NATO, sooner rather than later.[9]

There is little question that Romania's leadership was demoralized by the refusal of the United States, backed by the British and Germans, to budge in its policy. The French, backed by Italy, Canada, and Turkey (which alienated the Greeks, of course) had no chance of winning the day on Romania's behalf. Italy and Turkey had security concerns in the Balkans even before the Americans woke up to the fact that the Dayton accord on Bosnia had not resolved all of former Yugoslavia's problems, and France played its usual anti-American game, hoping to get an extra 'Francophone' vote because Romanian intellectuals seem to consider themselves semi-French. But all this was merely symbolic.

Worse was the fact that Romania's liberal leadership had no real back-up plan. Inexperienced in economic matters, unsure of how to stimulate a backward economy, the liberals in power went from one disaster to another. The NATO gambit, with the hope that it would lead to European Union support, was the magic bullet that was supposed to solve the dilemma of reform. Now, with this hope lost, the ineptitude of Constantinescu's reform plans became glaringly obvious. Of course, the failure of a single diplomatic gambit cannot explain very much. What else lies behind the disappointing performance of the late 1990s? Why has the first post-communist decade been so frustrating, and why is it ending so badly after the high hopes raised by the 1996 elections? Answers to these questions can shed much light on what has gone wrong elsewhere, not only in the Balkans, but in much of the former Soviet Union, too.

SOME BLEAK ECONOMIC FACTS

The years immediately after the end of communism were bleak ones in Romania. The economy had been in decline for most of the 1980s, but as in other post-communist countries, the collapse of the system did little, at first, to create either new jobs or to replace the overstaffed, inefficient state firms that had dominated the economy. A moderate recovery seemed to be under way in the mid-1990s, and with the election of the new liberal reformers, it seemed that a real burst of economic growth might be possible. In fact, starting soon after the 1996 elections, Romania began pursuing a liberalization strategy that was highly praised by World Bank and IMF observers.[10] Unfortunately, what has happened is a new period of decline that may be even more serious than the one in the early 1990s.

Even in the best of years, Romania has attracted very little foreign investment. Poland, for example, received about $9 billion in 1998 alone, but in all of the 1990s Romania, with more than half as many people as Poland (23 million to 38 million), has received about $3.4 billion.[11] Furthermore, the rate of foreign investment fell sharply in 1998, and by the fall of that year, it was running at about $5 million a month – an almost insignificant number.[12]

In 1998, industrial production in Romania fell by 17 percent, and Gross Domestic Product fell by about 5 percent.[13] This followed a fall in GDP of 6.6 percent in 1997 (Nine O'clock No. 1780). According to *PlanEcon*, the GDP index since 1980 has been as shown in Table 5.3.[14]: (*PlanEcon* projected stability for 1997, but that turned out to be far too optimistic as a serious decline set in during the middle of that year.)

Table 5.3 Romanian Gross Domestic Product, 1980 = 100

1980 = 100.0
1987 = 120.6
1989 = 113.0
1990 = 106.7
1991 = 92.9
1992 = 84.8
1993 = 86.0
1994 = 89.4
1995 = 95.6
1996 = 99.5

So, if the figures for 1997 and 1998 really indicate a drop of close to 11 percent, the GDP is now heading back where it was in 1994, and in the mid- to late 1970s!

Total GDP, however, tells only a part of the story. *PlanEcon* estimated in July, 1998 that industrial production in Romania at the end of 1997 was only 80 percent of what it had been in 1991, and net real wages only 60 percent of what they were in 1990.[15] Let no one forget that whatever industrial production figures were put forward by the Ceauşescu government in the late 1980s, the real standard of living for Romanians toward the end of that regime was visibly well below what it had been in the 1970s. In fact, any serious comparison of Romania's standard of living in the late 1980s would have indicated that it was significantly below Bulgaria's, and even farther behind the rest of Eastern Europe, except, of course, for Albania. So, a contraction from that period is serious indeed. The only thing that has prevented worse economic hardship is that in recent years there has been somewhat of a return migration to the countryside, and now at least 50 percent of the population is rural.[16] Agricultural production in 1995/96 was about 90 percent of what it had been in 1990; it then rose in 1997, but fell back again in 1998.[17]

Inflation, which seemed to have been brought under control by tight fiscal and monetary measures in 1997, when inflation had fallen to 0.6 percent per month in August (that is, about 7.5 percent per year), was again running at about 3 percent per month (42 percent per year) by early 1999.[18]

Though agricultural production has remained roughly stable in the 1990s, with private production taking up the slack in decline from the failure of state farms, many reports from the countryside in 1998 indicated that there was not enough seed and credit to assure a normal harvest in 1999. The collapse of the cooperatives without the creation of adequate credit facilities for peasants can only further aggravate the problem in coming years. Furthermore, the production of some key industrial crops, and of some meats such as chicken, as well as eggs, had fallen below 1989 levels by 1998! Declines in agriculture since the 1980s have certainly been less than in industry, and food is more plentiful in Romania (partly because of lower exports), but we should remember that during the 1980s Romanian agriculture was thought to be in dire straights.[19]

What actually seems to be happening is reminiscent of the period after World War I when there was a major land reform. The peasants got small parcels of land and were better able to feed themselves than before, when there had been large estates, but total production decreased, and exports fell sharply. This was the heart of the 'peasant problem.' Small, uneconomical plots, an excessively large rural population, and inadequate resources for modernization created a major political dilemma as various governments struggled to improve the situation.[20]

Somewhat the same thing has happened in the 1990s as most of Romania's system of collective farms has been dismantled and land privatized in the 1990s. The land in many areas has been redivided into the long, inefficient, small strips that characterized traditional agriculture in the past. It is startling to fly over Romania and see this historical pattern of field division reappearing in the Old Kingdom, Wallachia and Moldavia. It is like seeing a distant past reappear. This pattern was originally the result of the division of Romania's ancient communal village lands, something accomplished largely in the 18th and 19th centuries (though in some areas going back well before then).[21] It is as if one could witness England's 'open field' structure taking the shape, once more, as it once was before enclosures. But if Romania's agriculture lagged far behind

Central and Western Europe's in the 1930s,[22] to revert to anything like this pattern in the 1990s is catastrophic in a country that is still so rural and depends heavily on its agricultural potential to set its economy right. It is picturesque to see peasants using hand scythes and animal drawn plows, but there are not even enough animals. In Europe in the late 20th century, this sight is an almost unbelievable anachronism. Yet, without credit, and with an increasing rural population that relies on the land for subsistence, there is little likelihood of rapid progress. Furthermore, there is little evidence that the top political officials have much understanding of, or concern for agriculture. The urban intellectuals who form the heart of the liberal parties in Romania are even more removed from the land than were their pre-communist predecessors.

The large state farms, on which the economy had relied for industrial crops and much of its large scale grain growing in communist times are only now being subjected to privatization. Meanwhile, the demoralization and collapse of production on these state farms is dragging down the entire agricultural sector, much as is happening in Russia.

This does not end the bad news. Public revenues are falling as tax evasion increases, parliament passes and rescinds regulations that make it impossible for both domestic and foreign investors to plan ahead, and the banking system may be near collapse. Daniel Daianu, the knowledgeable former minister of finance said in a *European Wall Street Journal* article in late 1998 that the annual current accounts deficit in Romania was running at about 7 percent of the GDP, and that to meet its obligations, Romania's government was having to borrow ever more from increasingly suspicious foreign lenders.[23] Unemployment, officially at about 11 percent, is almost certain to rise, as the present government is only now seriously tackling the problem of what to do with large state firms that were left pretty much unreformed during the Iliescu years.

There are many explanations for the sad situation. One, of course, is that the previous governments run by the reform communists postponed and avoided making the painful choices that were made in the more successful Central European countries, most notably in Poland. Having avoided the pain in the early 1990s, Romania might now be going through precisely the same shock that the 'Visegrad' group (Hungary, the Czech and Slovak Republics, and Poland) went through earlier. Unfortunately, ten years after the revolution, Romanian society may not have the resilience and hope in the future necessary to carry it through such a wrenching adjustment. And then, there is the question of whether or not there is much hope at the other end of this process. (Some, speaking of Russia, have referred to this as the 'tunnel at the end of the light' syndrome.) To begin to know how to approach these questions requires us to take a more long-range view of Romania's trajectory in the 20th century.

Before that, however, it should be noted that in terms of relative progress, neighboring Bulgaria has fared little better. It also postponed reforms in the early 1990s and went through a period of being led by only slightly reformed communists. According to *PlanEcon*, the Bulgarian GDP in 1997 was 69.7 percent of what it had been in 1990, and that situation only slightly improved, to 72.8 percent of 1990 for 1998.[24] This is a relative decline even greater than Romania's. Various estimates of Russia's GDP are that it now stands at no more than 50 percent of what it was in 1990, and Ukraine, Belarus, and Moldova are in even worse shape. So, in a sense, Romania's performance compared to these cases does not look quite as bad. It began poor, has remained poor, and is not getting better, but it has not declined as much as some of its neighbors. Only if Romania is compared to the Central European countries of Poland, Hungary, Slovenia, the Czech Republic, and even Slovakia does its performance seem unusually bad. Yet, as far as the Romanian population is concerned, needless to say, the comparative statistics are meaningless when the brutal fact remains that life is getting harder, not easier, and there is no prospect in sight for immediate relief. Surely this will test the population's will to stick with liberalizing economic reforms and a liberal political regime. As in many other parts of the post-communist world, the trend established in the 1990s in Romania is not propitious for future stability, growth, capitalism, or democracy.

TRYING TO UNDERSTAND THE LONG-TERM CAUSES OF ECONOMIC BACKWARDNESS

Given the bare facts, there are many, even too many possible explanations. The societies that were more advanced before communism ('Central Europe') remained more advanced under communism, and have done better under post-communism. Only Russia made any serious claim to having changed its relative position in terms of economic development under communism, but this was reflected in its military establishment, not in its standard of living which, in real terms, remained below that of Central Europe. It stands to reason, then, that more advanced economies received more foreign investment in the 1990s, and fared better. Romania, one of Europe's most persistently backward societies, has attracted little foreign investment, and has a greater legacy of backwardness to overcome.

This argument is unimpeachable, but it explains little. After all, there are some societies in the world, even in Europe, that have changed their relative economic standing. We do not have to go to the East Asian 'miracles' for examples. The Republic of Ireland caught up with the United Kingdom's Gross Domestic Product per capita (measured by purchasing power parity) in about 1996.[25] So did Italy.[26] There are other cases. Finland, once far behind Sweden, has pretty much caught up. The relative position of Argentina and Chile, of Malaysia and the Philippines, of Australia and Japan, and yet others have changed dramatically since the early and mid-20th century. In this respect, history is not obliged to repeat itself, and development paths fixed in the past are not immutable. But in each of these cases, it is possible to find several generations of preparation that contributed to the modernization of the work force and economy, that changed social attitudes, and set up viable modern institutions. Without such preparation, none of these 'miracles' could have occurred.[27]

A related, but less economically determined argument is that Central Europe, as opposed to the Balkans, had a stronger civil society to begin with, and this has helped it both to resist communism better during the period from 1945 to 1989, and then to progress faster after 1989. This is very close to the old religious argument, as Protestant and Catholic churches had greater powers of resistance to state control under communism than did the Orthodox Christian churches. Indeed, the religious line between Western and Eastern Christianity is so strong that it seems to trump all other cultural and economic divisions. Greece and Greek Cyprus are the only exceptions, and of course, they were never communist. Yet, those two exceptions are quite dramatic, and argue for at least some reconsideration of the historic division of Christianity as an explanatory factor. Perhaps it is the combination of communism and Orthodoxy that has been particularly poisonous. As a backward, largely peasant, primarily Orthodox society before communism, post-communist Romania clearly has a burden to overcome. But again, that does not answer the question of what is going on. Why has this combination of backwardness, Orthodoxy, and communism proved so persistently detrimental?

The Romanians, or at least Romanian intellectuals, and through them, Romanian school books explain their position by referring to past conquests and persecutions. That is the essence of the feeling of aggrieved nationalism that has so often, in Romania and elsewhere, turned into nasty xenophobia.[28] But historical persecution is no explanation at all, as almost every nation except for a fortunate few in the West, and perhaps Japan (at least until 1945), can point to such a past at one time or another. More relevant would be the fact that Romania today cannot count on the kind of aid that Ireland, Portugal, and Spain received from the European Union (in its various incarnations), or that South Korea and Taiwan received from the United States. But to emphasize this too much gets us back to the flaw in the Constantinescu government's attempt to join NATO in order to be in Europe and benefit from aid. It is Romania's very backwardness and unsettled prospects that make full admission into Europe seem unlikely, so exclusion cannot explain a prior problem. In any case, neither

Greek Cyprus nor Finland waited for admission into Europe to make progress, and neither has Poland.

So, what explanations shall we pick? To begin, it is a good idea to be aware of the fact that Romania did not entirely lack a tradition of a civil society or of industrializing capitalism before the communist era. Furthermore, its cultural and political élite, though small, was highly Westernized. But those possible advantages were entirely lost from the 1940s to the late 1980s.

As far as a tradition of civil society in the Western sense is concerned – independent, non-governmental associations and bodies – those that existed in Romania were based on very old, and by the 1930s moribund peasant communities, or on elements in the population who were considered ethnically foreign, mostly German, Hungarian, and Jewish. The Romanian state that developed from the mid-nineteenth century until 1940 was centralized, nationalistic, and increasingly authoritarian. It made a point after World War I of trying to bring under control those independent sources of civil society that it viewed as foreign.[29]

Yet, despite their inauspicious political history, the Romanians certainly elected a very liberal government in 1996, and even under Iliescu, there was a proliferation of NGOs and an astounding revival of an independent press, of political parties, and of intellectual debate.[30] It was precisely this freedom and activism that yielded the political outcome of 1996. So we cannot directly blame its illiberal past for Romania's contemporary dilemma.

In terms of industrialization, it is also hard to lay all blame on the distant past. Romania actually had an impressive growth rate from 1925 to 1937. Even though its standard of living was lower than Bulgaria's and Yugoslavia's (taking an average for the whole of that country) in the inter-war years because its peasant agriculture was more backward, it was more industrialized than either and had one of the highest industrial growth rates in Europe in the 1920s and 1930s. To be sure, a disproportionate number of its industries and much of its trade were owned or managed by ethnic minorities, especially Germans, Jews, Greeks, and Hungarians. As elsewhere in East-Central Europe, there was heavy state involvement in industrialization, and considerable corruption in the assignment of lucrative government contracts. But industrial production doubled from 1925 to 1937. This growth rate was twice the average in all of Eastern Europe during those years, and almost three times Bulgaria's.[31]

Unfortunately for Romania, the period of rapid industrial growth lasted less than one full generation. This was not enough time for many Romanians to learn the skills necessary for operating in a modern economy. Hungary and Poland began their economic modernization at least 30 to 40 years before Romania, and the Czechs earlier than that, so that by the start of the communist period, all had had about three generations of experience. This was enough time so that such skills spread well beyond the ethnic and religious minorities who were the first to adapt to the demands of modern work, commerce, and industry.

As Ivan Szelenyi has shown, in Hungary such skills had spread well into the upper ranks of the peasantry before collectivization, and the period in which commercial abilities were repressed lasted less than a full generation, so that Hungary emerged in the 1980s with a viable class of small entrepreneurs. Szelenyi's data indicate strongly that such skills are partly transmissible to the next generation.[32]

To some extent, the survival of private farming in Poland had a similar effect. Even in Czechoslovakia, which had less independent economic activity than Poland or Hungary, the skills acquired over several generations were not entirely lost in the 40 years of communism. This is what the historical legacy of differential rates of modernization really means: skills are learned, but given only a small period in which to develop them, a society may lose them relatively quickly, too.

The skills we are discussing seem mundane in a developed capitalist economy: basic accounting skills, knowledge of how markets work, a sense that markets are equitable enough so that corruption is not necessary for elementary survival, and a disciplined attitude toward the use of time. An economy also needs a large base of able skilled workers, of engineers, and functioning credit institutions. All of this takes time, an increasingly capable education system, and perhaps most of all, experience to teach individuals how to operate in a non-traditional market environment, both as consumers and as producers.

In Russia, as in Romania, there was barely a single generation in which to develop a large class of commercially oriented farmers, small entrepreneurs, and managers of industrial enterprises. And in Russia, too, a disproportionate share of what was developed was in the hands of ethnic minorities. The process began in Russia in the 1890s, was badly disrupted during the early years of communism, resumed in the mid-1920s, and was cut down after 1928. In Romania it began in a substantial way in the 1920s, was damaged in the 1940s, and eliminated after 1948. In Bulgaria, it barely got under way at all outside of agriculture.[33]

The fact that the skills and habits necessary for operating in a modern economy take at least two or three generations to be solidly acquired explains in part why ethnic minorities (Jews or Germans in East-Central Europe, Greeks and other Christians in much of the Middle East, Chinese in Southeast Asia, and so on) who get a head start because they are somewhat better educated, or more urban, or have traditionally been involved in commerce, can maintain their advantage for considerable periods of time until the societies in which they operate undergo a thorough transformation themselves.[34] Understanding this mechanism of generational change will yield an understanding of why post-communism has had different results in the various parts of post-communist

Europe. It is a matter of competence, not primarily of this or that reform strategy, or of ancient historical legacies as such.

The fact that Romania was so overwhelmingly rural, and that the rural sector was so backward before the communist period meant that its urban base was relatively small, and the short duration of industrialization did not allow enough ethnic Romanians to learn the necessary skills for running a modern capitalist economy. The literary and political skills of the small élite were not adequate training because so little of their training had much to do with economic matters. And the communists, in Romania as elsewhere, produced a very mediocre substitute for a capable, economically modern middle and working class. Whereas there were enough people who remembered what to do in Central Europe, Romania, like Russia, did not have enough of this resource on which to rely.

Historical legacy played a role, of course, because it accounts for the fact that Romania began its industrialization and modernization a good two to three generations after Hungary and Poland.[35] The period of communism made this even worse because it wiped out the substantial progress made before 1939. For Russia, of course, this is even more the case as communism lasted so much longer.

This leads to a conclusion that many academics and intellectuals critical of capitalism, and gloating over the failures of transition, tend to deny.[36] Communism was an alternative path to modernization, and it failed catastrophically. It did so because it did not train a capable population able to deal with modern, industrial, urban life. Communism increasingly evolved toward corruption and inefficiency, not toward rationalization and increasing productivity.[37]

This is the essential fact to understand about Russia. Well before communism there was a notion among Russian intellectuals that it would be possible to find an alternative, non-Western way of modernizing. This sometimes took the form of 'Slavophilism,' though Liah Greenfeld has shown that 'Slavophiles' and 'Westernizers' actually shared many of the same notions with respect to Russia's unique ability to find its own, superior path to progress.[38] Communists in Russia were able to harness this sentiment, and reinforce it. But their failure left Russia without either the skills to run a capable modern economy, or an ideology to guide it.[39]

In fact, the sector of Soviet society best adapted to market conditions during its last two decades operated in the illegal black market. It is no surprise, then, that those with such training emerged quickly as the only viable entrepreneurs in Russia after the fall of communism, and that their methods have proved to be less than honest or rational in Max Weber's sense of rational capitalism.[40]

Romania has experienced a similar failure, though not on so grand or dramatic a scale. Because it is smaller than Russia, because it was ruled by communists for less time, because many of its intellectuals have looked in the past to the West, and because its version of the 'Slavophiles,' namely the xenophobic, nationalist, anti-Westerners have been a quite marginal political force in the 1990s, Romania's political transition has been, so far, more successful than Russia's. Also, its economic decline has not been as severe. But that is not saying much.

WHAT IS TO BE DONE?

It is clear that for those post-communist societies such as Romania that suffer from the basic problem of insufficient competence, the only remedy is time.

During the time it will take, however, every effort must be made to prevent Romania from becoming isolated. All the historical evidence in Eastern Europe indicates that before 1938 the more closely and the longer societies and economies had been associated with the dynamic capitalist West, the better off they were.[41] Rather than being permanently peripheralized, it was close contact that promoted development in 19th century Poland and Hungary. In this respect, simply to help stabilize the Balkans, Europe must keep Romania within its economic, social, and political orbit.

Second, Romanian leaders and intellectuals must themselves understand that there is no unique 'third way' to modernization. It is not that mixed economies never work, or that every successful economy must resemble that of the United States. Nor is it to say that immediate, total trade and financial opening to the larger capitalist world is always good. Rather it is a matter of understanding that the fundamental social and economic skills that make a modern economy work are the same everywhere, and they are best learned when modern education is combined with an open market structure. The latter is as vital for teaching modernity as the former. Most of all, talk about 'third ways' is always accompanied by nationalistic assumptions that make it seem as if it were possible, even desirable, to develop in cultural and economic isolation from the West. That is a prescription for disaster.

So far, when we look at Romania we can be optimistic on this last point. There is little indication that any major political tendency, even the former communists, seriously want to opt out from Europe or a Western, democratic, capitalist way of developing. The case of Russia is far more worrisome in this respect, but that is another matter.

When we look at the European Union and its attitude toward Romania, however, there are some grounds for pessimism. Without some sort of help, if only to facilitate trade with Romania, the Romanian economy will have trouble getting back on its feet. It would be foolish indeed for the Europeans to neglect the peaceful part of the Balkans, Romania and Bulgaria, and to let them deteriorate to a condition similar to Russia's or Serbia's. The key is that a modicum of help and encouragement of openness will, within a generation or two, produce desired results. But a generation is a long time. If the past is any indication, we will have to wait at least that long, perhaps even two generations, for a viable, prosperous, growing economic system to become securely established.

Given all this, there is no reason, yet, to despair and abandon all hope for the Christian Orthodox post-communist societies in Eastern Europe whose transitions to democratic capitalism have been so difficult.

NOTES

1. Vladimir Tişmaneanu (1996).
2. Ştefan Zeletin (1927); Mihail Manoilescu (1997 [1943]); Joseph L. Love (1996).
3. Virgil Madgearu (1940).
4. Stelian Tanase (1996), pp. 35–45.
5. Election data, both official results and exit polling data, are from *Turul 2 Al Alegerilor Prezidentiali: Resultate Finale*, obtained on the 'Virtual Romania' web site, http://www.info.polymtl.ca/tavi/ archive/alegeri.html in 1996, right after the elections.
6. Urban percent from *Anuarul Demografic al Repulicii Socialiste România 1974*, Bucharest: Direcţia Centrala de Statistica, 1974, pp. 5–8. Votes from web site cited above, 'Virtual Romania'.
7. From 'Virtual Romania' web site, cited above.
8. Alfred H. Moses (1998). Moses remains optimistic that if Romania can reform its economy, it will be admitted eventually. The Kosovo war of 1999, in which Romania's government cooperated fully with NATO, despite the unpopularity of that war in Romania, and the pro-Serbian (Eastern Orthodox) sentiment of many of its people, has, no doubt, further increased Romania's chances. But the momentum for economic reform that existed in 1996 has long been lost, so membership now would be less likely to have as positive an effect.
9. Jeffrey Simon and Hans Binnendijk (1997). See also Peter Gross and Vladimir Tişmaneanu (1997), pp. 26–31.
10. *PlanEcon Report* XIII, No. 29–30, p. 1.
11. *Nine O'clock*, No. 1783, October 30, 1998.
12. *Nine O'clock*, No. 1780, October 20, 1998.
13. *România Libera*, (Bucharest) February 9, 1999, article by Adrian Stoica.
14. *PlanEcon* XIII: 29–30, 1997, p. 15.
15. *PlanEcon* XIV: 21–2, 1998, pp. 7–9.
16. Personal communication from former Finance Minister Daniel Daianu, February, 1999.
17. *PlanEcon* XII: 29–30, 1996, p. 5.
18. *Nine O'clock* No. 1784, November 2, 1998 and *Romanian Economic Daily*, February 17, 1999.
19. *Nine O'clock*, No. 1785, November 3, 1998 and No. 1787, November 5. On Romanian agriculture in the 1980s, see Gabor Hunya (1987).
20. Henry L. Roberts (1951); David Mitrany (1930).
21. Henri Stahl (1980 [1969]).
22. Doreen Warriner (1965 [1939]).
23. *Nine O'clock*, No. 1782, October 29, 1998.
24. *PlanEcon*, XIV: 41–2, 1998, pp. 1–16.
25. *Statistical Abstract of the United States 1997*, Washington, DC: Bureau of the Census, 1977, p. 839. The figure here shows Ireland's GDP per capita (PPP Basis) at $17,228, and the UK's

at $17,776, but the same table indicates that in 1996 Ireland's GDP grew by 7 percent and the UK's by 2.4 percent. This would mean that Ireland passed the UK in 1996. Of course, using a straight calculation that did not take into account PPP, the UK would still be ahead. The point is that Ireland was far behind the UK earlier in the century, has essentially caught up, and is now growing much faster. World Bank data shows Ireland still behind the UK, but the argument is not really about fine details here. If Romania were to roughly catch up with Hungary, it would be 50 percent richer than it now is, and if it were at Austria's level, it would be four times richer. The World Bank, *World Bank Atlas 1997*, pp. 36–7.

26. Both the *US Statistical Abstract*, p. 839, and the *World Bank*, pp. 36–7 shows Italy's per capita GDP in 1995 to be ahead of the UK's.
27. On the East Asian economic 'miracles,' which, by and large, persist despite the crisis of the late 1990s, see, among hundreds of works, Danny M. Leipziger, (ed.) (1997). The article by Homi Kharas on the Philippines is useful because of the relative failure of that country to grow. On the other hand, the article in this book on Indonesia ends on a very optimistic note that looks silly in light of the collapse of 1998–1999 in that unfortunate country.
28. Vladimir Tişmaneanu (1998). Tişmaneanu reviews the existence of such resentment throughout the region, but Romanians appear among the worst, exceeded, perhaps, only by the Serbs.
29. On the existence of a 'civil society' in parts of Romania, see Daniel Chirot (1995). On the reaction against 'foreign' cultural institutions, see Irina Livezeanu (1995).
30. Chirot (1995).
31. Chirot (1989), especially pp. 380–84.
32. Szelenyi (1988).
33. The standard economic histories of the Balkans are John R. Lampe and Marvin R. Jackson (1982) and the much narrower, but very carefully done book by Michael Palairet (1997).
34. Daniel Chirot and Anthony Reid (eds) (1997), especially the introductory essays by the two editors.
35. See the essays in Daniel Chirot (ed.) (1989), especially the ones by Peter Gunst, 'Agrarian systems of Central and Eastern Europe', and Jacek Kochanowicz, 'The Polish economy and the evolution of dependency'.
36. For a good example of this attitude see the essays in Michael Burawoy and Katherine Verdery, (eds) (1999).
37. Janos Kornai dissects the many problems of communist economies in Kornai (1992).
38. Liah Greenfeld (1992), pp. 189–274.
39. Tim McDaniel (1996).
40. See the article by Marshall Goldman in this volume (Chapter 9).
41. Chirot, (ed.) (1989).

REFERENCES

Buravoy, Michael and Katherine Verdery (eds) (1999), *Uncertain Transition: Ethnographies of Change in the Postsocialist World*, Lanham, MD: Rowan & Littlefield.

Chirot, Daniel (1989), 'Ideology, reality, and competing models of development in Eastern Europe between the two world wars', *East European Politics and Society*, **3** (3).

Chirot, Daniel (ed.) (1989), *The Causes of Backwardness in Eastern Europe*, Berkeley: University of California Press.

Chirot, Daniel (1995), 'Is civil society enough? Comparing Romania and the American South', in Robert Hefner (ed.) (1998), *Democratic Civility*, New Brunswick: Transaction.

Chirot, Daniel and Anthony Reid (eds) (1997), *Essential Outsiders: Chinese and Jews in the Modern Transformation of Southeast Asia and Central Europe*, Seattle: University of Washington Press.

Greenfield, Liah (1992), *Nationalism: Five Roads to Modernity*, Cambridge, MA: Harvard University Press.

Gross, Peter and Vladimir Tişmaneanu (1997), 'No NATO shelter for Romania', *Transitions*, December.

Hunya, Gabor (1987), *East European Politics and Societies*, **1** (2).

Kornai, Janos (1992), *The Political Economy of Communism*, Princeton: Princeton University Press.

Lampe, John R. and Mavin R. Jackson (1982), *Balkan Economic History, 1550–1950*, Bloomington: Indiana University Press.

Leipziger, Danny M. (ed.) (1997), *Lessons from East Asia*, Ann Arbor: University of Michigan Press.

Livezeanu, Irina (1995), *Cultural Politics in Greater Romania*, Ithaca: Cornell University Press.

Love, Joseph (1996), *Crafting the Third World: Theorizing Underdevelopment in Rumania and Brazil*, Stanford: Stanford University Press.

Madgearu, Virgil (1940), *Evoluţia economiei romaneşti dupa razboiul mondial*, Bucharest: Biblioteca economica).

Manoilescu, Mihail (1997 [1943]), *Roştul si destinul Burgheziei romaneşti*, Bucharest: Athena.

McDaniel, Tim (1996), *The Agony of the Russian Idea*, Princeton: Princeton University Press.

Mitrany, David (1930), *The Land and the Peasants in Rumania*, London: Oxford University Press.

Moses, Alfred H. (1998), 'Romania's NATO Bid', *SAIS Review*, **18** (1).

Nine O'clock (1998), (Bucharest) No. 1780, October 20; No. 1782, October 29; No. 1783, October 30; No. 1784, November 3; No. 1787, November 5.

Palairet, Michael (1997), *The Balkan Economy 1800–1914: Evolution Without Development*, Cambridge: Cambridge University Press.

PlanEcon Report (1996), XII, No. 29–30; (1997) XIII, No. 29–30, p. 1; (1998) XIV, No. 21–2; No. 41–2.

Roberts, Henry L. (1951), *The Political Problems of an Agrarian State*, New Haven: Yale University Press.

Romanian Economic Daily (1999), February 17.

Simon, Jeffrey and Hans Binnendijk (1997), 'Romania and NATO Membership: Reassessment at the 1997 Summit', *Strategic Forum no. 101*, Washington, DC: National Defense University.

Stahl, Henri (1980 [1969]), *Traditional Romanian Village Communities*, Cambridge: Cambridge University Press.

Statistical Abstract of the United States (1997), Washington, DC: Bureau of the Census.

Stoica, Adrian (1999), Article in *România Libera* (Bucharest), February 9.

Szelenyi, Ivan (1988), *Socialist Entrepreneurs*, Madison: University of Wisconsin Press.

Tanase, Stelian (1996), *Revoluţia ca esec: elite & societate*, Bucharest: Polirom.

Tişmaneanu, Vladimir (1996), 'Tenuous Pluralism in the post-Ceauceşcu Era', *Transition*, December, pp. 6–11.

Tişmaneanu, Vladimir (1998), *Fantasies of Salvation: Democracy, Nationalism and Myth in Post-Communist Europe*, Princeton: Princeton University Press.

Turul 2 Al Alegerilor Prezidentiali: Resultate Finale (1996), Obtained on the 'Virtual Romania' web site, http://www.info.polymtl.ca/tavi/archive/alegeri.html.

Warriner, Doreen (1965 [1939]), *Economics of Peasant Farming*, New York: Barnes & Noble.

World Bank (1997), *World Bank Atlas 1997*, Washington, DC: World Bank.
Zeletin, Ştefan (1927), *Neoliberalismul: Studii asupra istoriei şi politicei burgheziei Romane*, Bucharest: Pagini Agrare şi Sociale.

COMMENTS ON DANIEL CHIROT, 'HOW MUCH DOES THE PAST COUNT? INTERPRETING THE ROMANIAN TRANSITION'S POLITICAL SUCCESSES AND ECONOMIC FAILURES'

Jack Edwards

There are some similarities between countries struggling to succeed and companies struggling to succeed. One of the most important similarities is that you can do 80 percent of things right, but achieve only 20 percent of the desired results. Thus it matters very much which 80 percent you get right.

Professor Chirot provided a valuable service to the University of Illinois conference in pushing us to think beyond the two main subjects of economic liberalization and political liberalization, and focus on what else a country needs to get right in order to develop more effectively. In a word, it needs competence.

Professor Chirot's chapter also links to that of Joseph Brada, who states that we must think beyond the twin subjects of economic and political liberalization, and add the social and historical background as well. If Brada and Chirot are right, are their judgments relevant for Latin America as well? Other papers presented at the conference focused on some of the social and historic backdrop of Latin America and the factors which have hindered its development. Economic liberalization has gone hand-in-hand with crony capitalism where 'know who' is more important than 'know how.' Other papers presented a persuasive argument about how this contributed to privatization excesses in Brazil, Venezuela and Mexico. It is also true that in much of Latin America, there are not three generations of experience in dealing with the modern economy and entrepreneurship, and this has clearly been a barrier to development just as it was in Eastern Europe.

Since it appears to be true that a country's development is also dependent on its social and historic background, does this mean that countries are or should be resigned to waiting patiently for a couple of generations in order to overcome these barriers, or is there something that countries can do to overcome the social and historical factors? There are at least five key areas on which governments can focus their efforts to help overcome these historic factors and accelerate their development. They are:

1. Clusters of development. Michael Porter has shown that economies grow more quickly and effectively when there are clusters of development on a regional basis which encourage innovation and entrepreneurship. Sao Paulo, Monterrey, Cali and Medellín are all successful examples of clusters of development for specific industries that have accelerated their country's

development process. While previous governments focused on encouraging and providing incentives for companies to locate in remote, underdeveloped regions, this must now be balanced with a focus on achieving a critical mass of industry in designated regions.

2. Much higher investment in education. Communism did not really emphasize education, but its system clearly benefited from the high levels which already existed. Latin America, with its high illiteracy rates, has had a hard time building a solid enough foundation for its development, especially compared to developing countries in Asia. Increased government focus on elementary education and less focus on high prestige investment in university education is clearly required.
3. Establishing local equity markets. Local entrepreneurs are shackled in growing their businesses because they have to resort to debt or private financing. Local equity markets are very modest in size and are restricted to some of the larger, better known companies. Thus, the larger companies have some ability to grow through equity placements, but the small to medium size companies, which have been an extraordinary source of growth throughout the world, are virtually excluded from these markets.
4. Investing in the informal and entrepreneurial economy. In Latin America and Eastern Europe, small businesses and individual entrepreneurs have sometimes been forced to remain outside the formal economy because of its cumbersome rules and regulations. New government policies that help transition small businesses from the informal economy into the formal economy in ways that accelerate their development, rather than slowing them down, have been successful on a small scale, and need to be applied on a larger scale.
5. Micro-enterprise development. This is clearly an idea whose time has come. Encouraging the development of micro-enterprises, mainly among women, has been shown to be a successful technique to generate income, self-sufficiency, pride, and new jobs in the private and informal sector. However, government finance ministries and government-owned banks are still thwarting the efforts of these micro-enterprise institutes rather than nurturing, encouraging, and financing their development. Based on lending to a sector which has a much higher repayment rate than the huge loans given to government cronies, an effective micro-enterprise policy could pay enormous dividends in terms of job creation and income growth.

COMMENTS ON DANIEL CHIROT, 'HOW MUCH DOES THE PAST COUNT? INTERPRETING THE ROMANIAN TRANSITION'S POLITICAL SUCCESSES AND ECONOMIC FAILURES'

Marcos Holanda

The chapter of Professor Chirot discusses a simple but very relevant question: why has it been so difficult to make economic improvements in Romania? In his view, the difficulties that Romania is now facing to attain a sustainable path of economic growth are strongly related to its past.

Economic development is a process that results from a combination of key elements, such as education, infrastructure, political and macroeconomic stability, an organized system of property rights, and an open economy. Since these elements cannot be developed overnight, the level of their presence in the country's past helps to explain its chance to attain good economic performance in the present. Chirot suggests that such elements were not well developed in Romania in the 1930s, and were greatly weakened by almost 40 years of communism. That would be the major reason for the difficulties that Romania faces at present to achieve high rates of economic growth.

The end of communism and the establishment of a democratic government did not change the reality of a lack of basic economic and institutional elements necessary to promote good economic performance. The newly-elected government soon realized that a liberal political platform is not a sufficient condition for the ready availability of such elements.

As a means of saving time, the government tried a shortcut to the goal of economic development through the acceptance of the country in the NATO alliance. NATO membership would bring economic and political help from the United States and Western Europe, and that certainly would speed up the process of gathering the necessary elements to promote economic growth. Once this risky political action failed, the government had to face the hard reality that the path to economic development would be more difficult and would take longer than was once thought.

The difficulties of the past, and even of the present, do not mean that under-development is insuperable in Romania. As the author correctly points out, the key point here is the 'understanding that the fundamental social and economic skills that make a modern economy are the same everywhere, and they are best learned when modern education is combined with an open market structure.'

The central message of the chapter, to Romania as well to other Eastern European and Latin American countries, is that when it comes to novel approaches to economic development, what is really new is the commitment to an old recipe: modern education, a market-oriented open economy, and political and economic freedom.

6. Hungary's post-communist development in comparative perspective

Béla Greskovits

INTRODUCTION[1]

'Transition to what?' This major puzzle of the transformation studies appears to be solved in Hungary. In 1999 Hungary's social system can be described as democratic capitalism. Viewed in the perspective of Hungary's own past, this outcome is a successful one. The decade between 1989 and 1999 is the longest democratic period of this country's post-World War I history. Furthermore, at the end of the 1990s Hungary's economy is freer than ever before in the 20th century.

In this chapter, first I assess Hungary's present situation in the broader context of overall economic and political developments in post-communist Eastern Europe. I show that in the past decade no country of the region succeeded in getting much farther than Hungary in creating the conditions of economic freedom, while also improving its macroeconomic performance. Another indicator of Hungary's success is its integration into the political and economic structures and institutions of the West. Where does the secret of Hungarian success lie? I shall argue that both the past and the present matter: the success is both due to the favorable legacies of the Hungarian version of socialism, and the patterns of resolving the conflicts between the capitalist and democratic components of transformation. Hence, in the third part I shall demonstrate how both the communist legacy and the post-communist democratic politics affected the process and the outcome of capitalist transformation. Given that the interaction between politics and the economy was shaped by the risks and opportunities of the international environment, external factors will also get ample weight in my explanation.

However, the comparison of Hungary's recent performance with that of the Mediterranean countries and a number of Latin American states reveals the modest degree of this post-communist success story. Given that in 1997 in terms of GNP per capita at purchasing power parity, Hungary was significantly lagging behind both Mediterranean Europe and a number of Latin American countries. The Hungarian case also indicates the limited perspectives of capitalism after communism in general. How can we make sense of the observation that so far Hungary's struggles for catching up with Europe by adopting the institutions of European market economy resulted in worse aggregate development performance than that of many Latin American countries? This is my question in the last part, which is devoted to the assessment of the political and economic costs and worrisome side-effects of Hungary's road to freedom.

HUNGARY IN POST-COMMUNIST EASTERN EUROPE

The regional perspective suggests that in terms of parting with state socialism and building capitalist democracy, Hungary and a few other countries, such as Poland, the Czech Republic, and Slovenia, represent the maximum of success any former socialist state could achieve between 1989 and 1999. Let us compare the Hungarian data with the performance indicators of other East European states which gave high priority to achieving democratic capitalism and incorporation into Europe, ultimately aspiring to full EU membership.

Table A6.1 in the Appendix shows the well-known fact that following the collapse of communism, Hungary underwent a transformational recession (Kornai 1994), which, however, was milder than the recession in many other East European countries, both in depth and length. Inflation was high in Hungary throughout the transformation period, but its rate was among the lowest in the sample, and had been decreasing over the past decade. While the recession resulted in impoverishment and increasing social inequality, the alarming degree of social dislocation characteristic of countries of the Balkans, the Baltic states, and even more of many other ex-Soviet states, was absent in Hungary. (However, the available evidence indicates that after 1995–6 the implementation of a draconic stabilization and adjustment package resulted in a large deterioration of the standards of living in Hungary.)

Table A6.2 in the Appendix reveals that while losing less than many other ex-communist states in terms of deteriorating GDP, inflation, and social inequality, Hungary succeeded in liberalizing its foreign trade and foreign direct investment regime, eliminating domestic price controls and the barriers to private-sector entry, and diminishing state intervention in the economy. It is common in the comparative literature on post-communist economic transformations to explain the relatively favorable economic and social performance indicators by the implementation of a radical and rapid liberalization strategy (Aslund 1997; Fish 1998; Hellman 1998). Thus, 'radical and rapid liberalizers' are expected to perform better than 'slow or laggard reformers,' and Hungary is often placed in the first group of countries. However, the data in Table A6.2 highlight the need for more complex explanations. Measured by the distance covered from their fully state-controlled systems in 1989 to their thoroughly liberalized economies in 1994, Estonia, Latvia, and Lithuania – but even Romania or Bulgaria – in fact underwent more rapid and radical policy shifts than Hungary, Slovenia, or Poland. Yet, their efforts did not result in comparably low GDP-losses, slow inflation, and modest increases of poverty and inequality. Hence reform radicalism alone does not seem to account for good economic performance under post-communism. But what does, then, have a better explanatory power?

First, what separates Hungary from the less successful radical reformers is that this country did not have to start economic liberalization from ground zero. On the contrary, the Hungarian success might have been facilitated by a number of institutional and behavioral legacies of its long 'market-socialist' period. Thus I share the view of those analysts who stress the importance of the initial conditions for our understanding the variation of economic performance under post-communism, and believe that, to put it simply, 'them that has, gets' (Bunce 1998, p. 12). One of these scholars, Fabrizio Corricelli found that

> the prereform liberalization index is a good proxy of the extent of development of markets and of private sector activities. The index mainly reflects the occurrence of partial reforms within the old regime. Interestingly, these partial reforms, meant to improve the efficiency of the planned economy, failed to achieve their primary objectives but created the seeds for a better performance during the period of market reforms (Corricelli 1998, p. 35).

Second, most ex-communist states, including several countries in my sample, had been affected by the massive political and administrative collapse associated with the dissolution of the Communist Bloc, the USSR, or the communist versions of federal states of Czechoslovakia, and Yugoslavia. This collapse often slowed down the pace of transformation, derailed the initial successes of stabilizing and freeing the economy, or dramatically magnified its costs. New national states, new administrative entities, providers of national identity had to be created, and this process often conflicted with the consolidation of market society (Bunce 1999). Many states in East- and South-East Europe imploded before, or parallel with, the start of the transformation. As also visible in Table A6.2, these states lost much of their centralizing capacity on the revenue-side with the effect of their dramatic weakening as providers of public goods including sustainable and well-performing market regimes. Whatever remained of state capacity was mobilized for the most urgent needs of state-(re)building in administrative terms, but even more often, state formation was subordinated to the task of providing the major collective good favored by the domestic élite: national identity.

Contrary to this trend Hungary, and a few other states in North-Western Eastern Europe could vigorously advance on the trajectory of simultaneous political and economic transformation, and could implement, under democratic rule, what Murrell names 'the most dramatic episode of economic liberalization in economic history' (Murrell 1996, p. 31). Occasionally, state capacity suffered heavy losses there as well; still, these states remained capable of democratic and economic reforms. I believe the relatively minor salience of the challenge to adjust to the new conditions of national sovereignty has itself strongly contributed to the Hungarian success. While the collapse of Soviet rule meant national liberation in Hungary as well (Bunce 1998, p. 12), neither the formation of national identity nor building of a new, independent state from scratch were important items on the Hungarian transformation agenda.[2] One implication is that the Hungarian transformation process can be properly analyzed in terms of a single logic, the interaction between democratization and marketization during transformation.

Yet the Hungarian case is unique even in comparison with other success stories of the post-communist transformation. This country – to a much larger extent than other ex-communist states – became a major target for foreign direct investment (Table A6.2). This was owing to a number of factors: Hungary's strategy regarding its foreign debt, macroeconomic management, privatization, and the foreign investors' and creditors' own expectations. However, the resulting large capital inflow had a major impact on the features of Hungarian capitalism. While everywhere in the East the new ownership structure displays various combinations of foreign owners, 'national capitalists,' and the scattered property rights of workers, the proportions dramatically differ. In much of the East the cohort of foreign investors is entirely missing, while national capitalists of mostly *nomenklatura* origin acquired overwhelming share and influence. At the other extreme, in the former GDR virtually the whole business élite is 'foreign,' that is, West-German or of other Western origin. On this scale Hungary, with a third of its largely private economy in foreign hands in 1997 is closest to the former GDR, and at the same time farthest from the other extreme exhibited by Eastern 'national capitalism.' This location significantly contributes to the specificity of the Hungarian case, and hints both at the risks the country avoided and the ones it took.

Finally, Table A6.3 in the Appendix shows that throughout the period of struggling with the economic change, and despite the social hardship associated with the crisis and the reforms implemented, the Hungarian transformation proved to be unexpectedly and remarkably peaceful and non-violent. All in all, what makes the Hungarian case specific and interesting is this country's sustained commitment to comprehensive transformation strategies; its legacies facilitating democratic capitalism after communism; its sustained state capacity to reform; the dominant overtly foreign element in its new business élites, and the remarkable political patience of its citizens, throughout the decade. It is the details of this broad explanatory framework to which I turn next.

1989–99: TEN YEARS OF SOCIAL PATIENCE

Hungary, unlike other countries, did not have to form a new nation and its efforts at state (re)formation have not been challenged by ethnic and regional identities, or contestation over the national borders, so it could focus its transformation on building democratic capitalism. Therefore, to understand how and at what cost Hungary has become a market economy, it is best to ask how it succeeded in balancing the political and economic dimensions of social change.

Let us recall first that initially most observers did not give much credit to the viability of democratic capitalism after state socialism. Indeed, scenarios of destabilization or breakdown under post-socialism have been more profoundly elaborated than those of the collapse of socialism ever were. Often, these gloomy prophecies contradicted each other. First, a number of liberal economists and policymakers worried that delays or deadlocks of radical economic reforms could lead to political and economic destabilization and even to populist authoritarianism. Second, on the Left, social scientists and politicians argued the opposite: that it is excessive economic liberalism, where the danger to freedom and democracy ultimately lies. Third, many historians and political scientists believed the political, cultural, and social legacy of state socialism had been almost entirely negative, and could become a massive obstacle to the emergence of the new social system. Finally, there were fears that democracy came 'too early,' and that political competition could undermine state capacity to radical reform.

Contrary to these latter views, my argument is that both a number of important socialist legacies, and democracy itself, did contribute to stability rather than to destabilization in the first period of the Hungarian transformation. They did so in three ways: (1) by creating winners who supported (or at least did not oppose) the transformation; (2) by creating patient losers who granted reformist politicians with relatively long 'grace periods,' and (3) by leaving behind domestic and external constraints to deviating from the mainstream transformation strategy.

Empowered Winners

First, Hungarian socialism improved the chances of powerful economic élite-groups, whose behavior was important if democratic capitalism was to survive, to become winners of the privatization process. Thus for them, capitalism paid, and democracy was acceptable: they were not interested in derailing the transformation process. I refer to the empirically well-documented argument that the last Hungarian socialist governments created and left behind the legal and institutional infrastructure – laws regulating the commercialization and privatization of public firms – helping the most competitive elements of the managerial stratum to become powerful in the emerging capitalist élite (Urbán 1991). There were other elements of their legacy which both enhanced their competitive advantages against domestic rivals – small private entrepreneurs, and 'expectant' client-capitalists – and enabled the domestic winners to ally more easily with external challengers: foreign direct investors. One of their important skills inherited from Hungarian reform socialism was their experience as 'public entrepreneurs' with mixed formal–informal, state-market strategies, organizations and institutions which 'got the job done' of keeping economic activity afloat (Róna-Tas 1997; Stark and Bruszt 1998, p. 128). Their other advantage was their familiarity with foreign markets, investment, licensing contracts, partnerships, and joint ventures which became a common practice by the 1980s, and which explains the remarkable openness of the Hungarian managerial élite to foreign capital, and specifically to alliances and cooperation with foreign investors. As a consequence the emerging business élite exhibited a more moderate and less insatiable domestic managerial element, whose acquisition strategies considered privatization less as a zero-sum game, than actors of other Eastern capitalisms. Second, as mentioned above, in Hungary, unlike in some countries, the state did not collapse in 1989–90. (Murrell 1996). Furthermore, the most powerful cohorts of the Hungarian administrative élite – the policymaking and financial bureaucracy – was in relatively good shape and in a favorable position to enforce the administrative changes required to the conduct of the market-oriented economic strategy.

Patient Losers

Other elements of the socialist legacy contributed to the overwhelmingly patient attitude of losers in the transformation process. I believe it was mainly due to them, that the political dynamics of the Hungarian transformation exhibited a different pattern from the disruptive social response to the first wave of radical crisis-management and adjustment in the late 1970s and early 1980s in many Third World countries.[3] Fears of similar developments have frequently been expressed in the Eastern context by politicians, political analysts and social scientists alike. However, these fears missed two important points. One is that the 'IMF-riots' of Latin America of the 1980s typically challenged authoritarian regimes, and signalled the turn to democracy, rather than to dictatorship. Moreover, the violent economic revolts lost momentum by the late 1980s: in this sense many new Latin American democracies appeared to be more crisis-proof than the old military regimes. Another neglected aspect was that the post-socialist countries differed from the more rebellious societies of the Third World in a number of structural, cultural and institutional aspects. These differences in the 'East' have become a basis for political patience even in critical situations when potentially explosive political protest was the more probable response in the 'South.' To put it differently, in part, the socialist legacy has had a demobilizing, and, consequently, politically stabilizing effect. The explanation that socialism left behind societies characterized by a relative lack of the structural, cultural and institutional factors associated with violent collective action seems to be especially powerful in the Hungarian case. It is the following legacies and effects that deserve particular attention.

When the changes began, large popular sectors in Hungary had yet at their disposal relatively substantial reserves to survive hard times. To be sure, their resources were modest in absolute terms: but at least they had not been devoured by hyperinflation or confiscation of the population's forced savings.[4] In this sense the fact that the state did not 'wither away', and did not lose control over the macroeconomic fundamentals was another positive element of the socialist legacy. As a consequence, the absence of extreme income inequality and of poverty of a Third World type – that is, concentrated in overpopulated and politically explosive informal urban settlements – may have contributed to weakening the threat of violent political mass actions. Even if poverty and inequality dramatically increased during the last decade, it continues to be far below Third World standards both in terms of its extent, and its concentration (Table A6.3). To put it simply, Budapest has not become Lima, Quito or Djakarta. These effects could be reinforced by cultural factors such as the substantially higher education standards, or by a characteristic element of the Hungarian political memory: the experience that – as it happened in and after 1956 – revolutionary violence breeds horrifying counter-revolutionary retaliation.

Such structural legacies as the country's demographic characteristics certainly mattered as well. The Hungarian population is more aged and less urbanized than most of the rebellious Third World nations. Elderly people in general, and pensioners in particular, could not strike or riot, even if they felt aggrieved, and typically neither could members of the rural society who lived dispersed in the countryside. When urban socialist industries in Hungary collapsed, redundant labor migrated back to villages and other small-scale settlements, contributing to the emergence of 'pockets of rural poverty'. These were economically depressed and marginalized regions lacking any public infrastructure and jobs as well as the opportunities and resources for collective protest. Consequently, major social groups, like the poor, the pensioners, and much of the rural population, have had to tolerate economic hardships. If they have associated their grievances with the strategy of economic transformation, their most available avenue of protest has been to vote against the reformist governments.[5]

Labor protest, the contentious political action of the lower, and lower-middle classes of the Kádár-regime, did not significantly shape Hungarian transformation politics either (see Table A6.4 in the Appendix). At the beginning this might have happened, because the potential organizers, the ex-communist National Federation of Hungarian Trade Unions (MSZOSZ) and its allies, were suffering both from a dramatic loss of union rank-and-file members, and credibility problems. Their lost credibility was due to their socialist legacy: their intimate ties with the Communist party. It is also true that the few new unions that were credible, among them the League of Democratic Trade Unions – similar to Poland's Solidarnosc – initially favored reform. Later, however, the transformational recession – the decline in living standards and the loss of job security coupled with rapidly growing unemployment – has curbed labor's contentious mood. One more institutional factor, also originating partly in the Hungarian socialist past, namely the tradition of collusion between labor unions and management, may have contributed to the cooperative rather than confrontational stance adopted by most unions.[6]

Finally, in different forms and to different degrees, all social groups, including the workers, the poor, the elderly, and the rural population, have had an important alternative to protest: 'going informal.' Led by cultural and behavioral norms left behind by socialism, for example, that laws do not matter and theft from the state is morally permissible, a third of the Hungarian population (and not only the poor) stayed in or retreated into the informal economy: another socialist legacy, also revitalized by the crisis and massive social dislocation. Non-criminal exit forms may also have had a positive stabilizing effect, at least in the short run (Sík 1994).[7]

All in all, instead of protesting violently and directly, Hungarians remained patient and either 'went informal' or exploited their employers' capacity to enforce protective state intervention until this was possible. Whatever social tensions remained, their direct influence was neutralized either by government tactics aiming at dividing losers by partial compensation, or by the democratic political institutions. Over the decade Hungarian democratic governments abundantly used pre-emptive partial compensation: from political payoffs to unions to politically targeted pension-, wage- or social benefit-increases. However, I believe it was likewise important that democracy institutionalized the protest vote as the standard weapon to express economic grievances; it became much more popular (and was less costly) than riots, strikes, or violent demonstrations. In politics, Hungarians typically preferred this form of resistance, channeling their demands through democratic institutions rather than using more disruptive tactics. Thus the democratic system contributed to the success of economic transformation by providing a safety-valve for socio-economic tensions.

The characteristic political dynamics presented above – the alternation between extended periods of political patience with protest and retaliation only during elections – is one of the keys to the politics of the Hungarian economic transformation. On the one hand, society's overwhelmingly patient attitude has provided democratic reformist governments with longer grace periods and longer time horizons in which to implement difficult reforms.[8] On the other hand, the politicians' fear of a protest vote is a partial explanation for why reforms were sometimes delayed, 'watered down,' or lost their radicalism in other ways. Finally, the fact that social discontent was expressed mostly in legal forms contributed not only to the success of economic transformation, but also to the stabilization of the main institutions and actors of democracy, for example the political parties.

Was the protest expressed by the voter effective? Were electorates able to radically change the transformation strategy? Did the economic hardships of the Hungarian population substantially decline during the past decade? My answer is rather negative. What mostly happened was that Hungarians voted out economic policies injurious to their immediate interests, only to witness their recurrence under different party banners: in Hungary first in that of the Christian-Democrats, then that of the (ex-communist) Socialists, and that of the Liberals, and most recently in those of a center-right and Liberal coalition.[9]

Inherited Constraints and New Commitments

Finally, I believe the fact that the mainstream of the transformation strategy could be maintained is partly explained by the – external and domestic – constraints left behind by state socialism. Specifically, in the early period of Hungarian transformation the economy affected politics mainly by the constraints of threatening macroeconomic and external imbalance. Although Hungary started its transformation with a relatively less devastated economic landscape than most other post-socialist states, its macroeconomic situation in 1991, 1992 and 1993 was far from permitting any populist or social democratic 'deviation' from the mainstream of stabilization and structural adjustment policies. From the beginning, the effect of domestic macroeconomic constraints had been reinforced by external constraints, namely the international 'rules of the game' to which Hungarian politicians became increasingly committed during the 1990s.

Let me illustrate this contention in detail by giving examples of Hungary's foreign policy orientation, and examples of the country's strategies of debt management, privatization and banking sector reforms. These policies show how the constraints and commitments left behind by state socialism impacted the transformation path, and how such legacies were reinforced by the new political commitments in the 1990s.

In continuity with the late Kádár regime, but also taking advantage of the new situation, the first democratic government lead by József Antall in 1990–94 made crucial political commitments, reinforcing Hungary's aspiration to reintegrate into the world economy and outlining increasingly concrete agendas for Hungary's return to the West and, specifically, to Europe. Regarding foreign affairs and economic diplomacy, by signing the Association Agreement with the EU in December 1991, by creating the CEFTA with the Visegrád-countries in early 1993, by maintaining and intensifying Hungary's membership in the World Bank, IMF, WTO and GATT, by expressing Hungary's wish to become full members of the NATO and the EU, the Antall government completed the country's departure from socialism, increased the cost of deviating from the chosen path, and paved the way for the integration efforts of the second government under Gyula Horn (1994–8). Thus Hungary joined the OECD in Spring 1995, NATO in Spring 1999, and came closer to full EU-membership.

Most importantly, by the mid-1990s Hungary's leading political parties, for their part, fully internalized the constraints and opportunities inherent in Hungary's actual economic situation, and the country's old and new international economic and political commitments both in their election and coalition programs. Specifically, the parties were much more keen on collecting protest votes than seriously suggesting or implementing policies satisfying the short-term demands of aggrieved constituencies. Rather than making bombastic economic promises, or challenging the path of international integration, the parties across the political spectrum proved to be capable of governing and building legislative majorities, or even issue-specific alliances bridging the divide between government and opposition around similar policy objectives.[10]

The economic transformation strategy was also embedded in the emerging new structure of bureaucratic power – and this is where the continuity between Hungary's past and present is most accentuated. Due to the long traditions of Hungary's relative external openness – stemming, irony of ironies, not least from the heavy external debt, and Hungary's resulting early IMF, and World Bank membership – Hungarian policy-making and financial bureaucracy from the early 1980s became integrated into international professional, policy-making and financial networks. This created skills – dealing with IMF and World Bank staff and policy programs, negotiating and bargaining with foreign creditors[11] or investors – which were not less, but even more needed when the changes came. Rather than losing out with economic transformation, this reformed communist bureaucracy consolidated its influence in politics and policymaking. By the mid-1990s its power was also institutionalized in the dominance of the Ministry of Finance and the Hungarian National Bank over rival bureaucratic strongholds, the independent status of the Hungarian National Bank, and the power of the Finance Minister over the 'spending ministries.' Also supported by the consensus of most economists on 'what was to be done' the reform bureaucracy had become a strong advocate of capitalism, including decisive steps in economic hard times.

A similar continuity, and a reinforcement of the inherited constraints with new commitments, can be observed in Hungary's strategy regarding privatization, and the reform of the banking sector. I argue that both strategies had been thoroughly influenced by Hungary's approach to its external debts. In stark contrast with Poland, Hungary opted against asking for rescheduling and debt-forgiveness.[12] This choice might explain much of the later divergence between the Hungarian and Polish performance in privatization and foreign direct investment, and, as a consequence, of the ownership dynamics and pattern of their emerging capitalisms. Because of its debt, Hungary from the start was highly dependent on hard currency cash receipts from privatization, which implied strategies of massive selling-off of state property to foreigners. Specifically neither could Hungary 'afford' systematic delays in privatization, nor could it opt for massive free property distribution, nor for labor's extensive inclusion in the privatization process. Poland and Czechoslovakia applied the latter two more extensively. On other hand, it is partly the Hungarian way of debt-management that impressed foreign investors, allowing Hungary to count on much larger capital inflows initially than Poland could.[13]

However, selling for hard-currency cash was not easy: on the one hand there was an intensive process of 'spontaneous privatization' underway, and on the other, the Hungarian state-owned enterprises (SOEs) suffered from excessive bad debts, and the banking sector experienced crippling problem-loans in the early 1990s.[14] All this posed the Antall government the difficult tasks of both regaining control over spontaneous processes, and improving the financial standing of both the SOEs, and the banking sector.

First, at the beginning of its term the Antall government (re)centralized privatization by placing the State Privatization Agency (SPA) under government control.[15] Second, from late 1991 till 1994 the government took several controversial steps resulting in 'creative destruction,' and later structural policies to cope with the challenge. In December 1991 the government implemented the law on financial institutions, which 'brought Hungarian practice up to those of the European Union. This was the first serious legislation on banking in the region, and ... uncovered much of the financial strain inevitable under restructuring and recession' (Csaba 1995, p. 224). This was soon followed by the implementation of the law on accounting stripping away much of the fictive revenues which had helped the firms to cover their losses before. As a combined effect both the banks and the SOEs became more interested in enforcing payments from their debtors (Jelentések az alagútból 1994, pp. 74–5). The institutional vehicle of enforcement was provided by the implementation of a severe bankruptcy legislation which produced 16 000 cases of bankruptcies between April 1992 to December 1993, a number unprecedented in the whole region. Some analysts argue that the combined implementation of the three laws created an unnecessarily hard shock, and 'wanton' but not 'creative destruction' (Stark and Bruszt 1998, p. 131), especially because the timing was unfortunate – the firms' budget constraints were hardened just at the moment when their Eastern markets collapsed – and because the bankruptcies had a domino-effect: healthy firms were made insolvent by the decline of their debtors (Jelentések 1994, p. 35).[16] From 1992 the processes of structural change were both shaped and mitigated by two more structural policy measures: during 1992–4 several packages were launched to consolidate the banking sector, and to reorganize a number of SOEs, including 14 large firms and 55 other companies by 1994. (Later these numbers substantially increased.) In 1993–4 the government bailed out the largest state banks while requiring them to clean their balances and implement crucial, efficiency-enhancing changes in their organization, financial structures, and business strategies. Large debtor SOEs in turn had to contract reorganization plans with their creditor banks and other creditors, the Social Security Funds, and the Tax Office. In exchange they were granted debt forgiveness and new capital inflows that in part meant recycled revenues from privatization.[17]

To sum up the combined positive effect of the measures above: the cleaning up of their balances and their improved capitalization subsequently made Hungarian SOEs and banks more attractive for foreign strategic investors. There was another development originating in the structural policies of the Antall government, which – while it was worrisome from the viewpoint of indigenous firms – had a positive effect on greenfield foreign investment. Both the recession accompanying the wave of bankruptcies in 1992–3, and the hardening of the Hungarian banks' budget constraints, implied that Hungarian companies had to withdraw from their traditional markets both in Hungary and abroad.[18] The gaps were quickly filled by the acquisitions and new, greenfield investment of multinational corporations, and fully foreign owned subsidiaries of large and small banks. All in all the policies implemented under the first democratic Hungarian government paved the way for the acceleration of privatization of the financial sector between 1994 and 1998. One result is that, in 1998, the Hungarian banking system was roughly 75 percent private, and, reflecting both the effect of privatization and the expansion of foreign banking, almost two-thirds foreign owned.[19]

WHAT KIND OF DEMOCRATIC CAPITALISM HAS EMERGED?

Summarizing all the above, by 1999 Hungary's socioeconomic system is that of democratic capitalism. Hungary is a success both in terms of its own past, and in comparison with other countries in post-socialist Eastern Europe. This success is the combined result of many factors. One factor is nothing but 'virtue of lack':[20] unlike the situation in many other countries of the post-socialist region, neither the peaceful or forceable formation of national identity nor of a new, independent state were important items on the Hungarian transformation agenda. Another important factor was that even if the Hungarian economy did not always perform much better than other economies, it has more or less constantly been perceived by the actors in international capital and financial markets as a potential success story. To the extent that this was important, then, the Hungarian success, in part, can be attributed to 'the power of path-finding expectations' abroad.[21] There was still a third set of advantageous preconditions: Hungary inherited relatively favorable legacies from state socialism. One of them was that the Hungarian state did not collapse as the transformation speeded up. Other legacies also contributed to stability rather than to destabilization in the first period of the Hungarian transformation, and improved the viability of the crucial policy choices and the efficiency of continually balancing the democratic and capitalist aspects of transformation.

Given that the Hungarian success story is a combined result of the most favorable constellation of various domestic and external factors, of enabling communist legacies and crucial post-communist strategic choices, the last thing to be asked is: how far could Hungary advance in terms of its new social system's quantitative, and qualitative performance?

Hungary did not get very far. The comparison of its recent performance with that of the Mediterranean countries and a number of Latin American states reveals the very modest degree of this post-communist success story. In terms of GNP per capita at purchasing power parity Hungary's catching up with Europe's Mediterranean periphery seems to be out of the question in the next few decades. Furthermore, according to the same indicators, Hungary is also lagging behind a number of Latin American countries (See Table A6.5 in the Appendix).[22] Moreover, the available data indicate that it is the past decade of post-communist transformation in which Hungary fell behind Latin America's best performers: in 1987 the aggregate performance of both Chile and Mexico was still worse than Hungary's, while Argentina's lead over Hungary was much less accentuated. Also, Mediterranean Europe's performance advantage appeared to be much smaller in 1987 than in 1997.

How do we make sense of the fact that Hungary, one of the few winners in post-communist transformation Hungary, ended up in Europe's second-rate periphery, and in terms of its aggregate output indicators currently performs worse than the leading countries of Latin America? First, one cannot confidently assume that the performance gap is nothing but a transitory phenomenon. Rather there are reasons to be worried that catching up – even with the Latin American leaders – will take time. Second, it is not convincing to argue that Hungary's extensive informal and illegal sectors – which are not reflected in the aggregate statistics – reduce the actual degree of backwardness, because the informal economies of the Latin American states are of comparable size.

Yet, the crucial question to be put is: to what extent do Hungary's current economic, social and political structures exhibit the backwardness indicated by the poor aggregate performance data? Clearly, this question implies a vast research agenda, and for the time being I have only tentative answers. However, a closer look at the Janus-faced character of Hungary's democratic capitalism and at the emergence of contradictory and dualistic features of its polity, economy and society suggests that we have no way to deny the discomforting image of Hungary's peripherization under postcommunism.

Against the gloomy expectations, Hungarian democracy survived the transformational recession and also contributed to the success of economic transformation. But, to begin with, the crisis left behind much political damage. Democracy in Hungary could take root only at the cost of some of its qualitative aspects, such as its representativeness, inclusionary features, and its capacity to uniformly provide and protect civil liberties. Many important ingredients of fully developed Western-type democracies continue to be in short supply in the new Hungarian political system.

Throughout the past decade it was obvious that – because of the dire economic situation bequeathed by socialism and aggravated by the transformational recession – the emerging system would be incapable of meeting even some of the justified demands for acceptable living standards and security of large social groups. Thus the major dilemma the political system had to face was the political representation of the millions pushed to the margin by the crisis and the transformation strategy. If their demands had received strong political representation, they would have paved the way to economic chaos, and a short-lived populist democracy. Conversely, if the essential democratic institutions and capitalism had simultaneously taken root under economic stress, the political system had to exclude justified but infeasible economic demands from the discourse as political non-issues. In this sense with a bit of exaggeration: the emerging Hungarian democracy had simultaneously to perform the democratic agenda of political integration, and the authoritarian agenda of political and economic exclusion. It succeeded in both, consolidating a democracy with strong exclusionary features.[23] This is the price Hungarian democrats paid for building capitalism in democratic settings after socialism. As to the institutional and organizational consequences of the above political logic, I mention only two: (1) there is a pervasive lack of both civil organizations representing various losers's groups, and channels – other than voting in elections – for civil control over state policy in general. (2) While the elite-echelons of ex-communist labor unions were to some extent included in power, using their allliance with élites to defeat rival civil organizations and the new non-communist trade unions, labor at the shop-floor is mostly ignored, and unrepresented. The victory of the ex-communist unions and the transformational recession in combination resulted in the decline or dissolution of all new trade unions: the Solidarity Workers' Alliance, the League of Democratic Trade Unions, and the Workers' Councils. Based on the evidence of these developments in Hungary, and according to the concept elaborated by Acuna and Smith (1994) in the Latin American context, I classified Hungarian democracy as a 'dual democratic regime' where the system's stability is based on the alliance of political and state élites with a strategic minority of the potential opposition to economic policies. The purpose of the alliance is to exclude 'the majority of the remaining social actors by disarticulating and neutralizing their capacity for collective action' (Acuna and Smith 1994, p. 47; Greskovits 1998, ch. 9). As a consequence, large sectors of the Hungarian society continue to be both marginalized in the economy, and excluded from political representation. Moreover, those who are on the margin economically and are largely unrepresented in politics, typically lose as well in terms of provision and protection of their human and civil rights. Is this new market society durable? Is the 'low-level equilibrium' between the incomplete democracy and the type of the emerging market economy stable? How long will the tension between the integrative and the exclusive, anti-democratic features of the political system prevail? Can economic transformation further advance in the atmosphere of social patience in the next decade?

Hungarian democratic capitalism seems to be consolidated in the sense that while there is an ongoing debate on its details, no robust political challenge to either its democratic or capitalist component is in sight. Moreover, as I stressed above, the past decade brought about crucial international political commitments which magnified the costs of abandoning the chosen path. Thus there are good chances that the new system will continue in the medium term as it is now: without much probability of an authoritarian turnabout, but also without automatic guarantees of development toward a democracy of better quality. On the one hand, reform élites need not be enticed by authoritarian temptations to defend their interests because the transformation strategies they favor will not be effectively challenged by the society. But on the other hand – and for similar reasons – I think there will not be strong societal pressure for more inclusion, nor more liberalism either.

I base my above hypotheses on the emerging evidence of the economic and social structural impact of the transformation strategies implemented throughout the decade. In brief my argument is that the structural changes induced by the chosen transformation path further impaired the capacities for collective action of its losers, particularly large segments of labor, and other lower-income groups. I think in the Hungarian context it is the following changes that deserve particular attention: one of the most visible structural adaptation processes is the dramatically increasing share of private non-industrial employment, and a rapid decrease of the average plant size.[24] One dimension of this process, the emergence of many hundreds of thousands of small or medium sized firms and their growing role in output and employment (Laki 1998), is visible not only in Hungary, but elsewhere in Eastern Europe as well. But it is a Hungarian specificity that at the opposite end there has been a rapid rise in the scope of operations of the local subsidiaries of large multinational corporations which now clearly dominate a number of important sectors. (See Törékeny stabilizáció 1997, and Hegymenet 1998, for the details of the Hungarian multinational export sector). Both types of economic organization prefer forms of employment with limitations on institutionalized representation of interest or collective protest.[25] About one-third of Hungarian employees are covered by collective agreements – mainly the employees of the shrinking public or semi-public industry and services. Roughly a second third of the workers, including those employed by the multinational corporations, have individual contracts, while many of the rest, including migrants, do not have any: they are hired and fired under precarious conditions by the (often informal) small-scale economy. The presence and activity of trade unions in the firms and at the shop-floor level confirms this: specifically, about two-thirds of the Hungarian labor force is not (or at least not directly) represented by unions: they are mostly absent in the sectors dominated either by the small-to-medium firms, or by the multinational corporations. Where the unions are, however, present at the shop-floor, they are mostly silent. This is in striking contrast with the vocal and noisy élite unionism in the political parties, parliamentary factions, national tripartite corporatist forums, and a number of important redistributive centers of the government administration, such as the self-governing bodies of pension and health-care funds. Apparently, dual democracy and dramatic economic structural change, in combination, resulted in a dual system of labor representation and industrial relations. As for the work conditions of those employed on the 'margins' by the small- and medium-scale economy, there is a strong sense of the absence of both collective representation and state control. In general, the defenselessness of labor maintains low levels of job stability, dependence upon income from piecework, poor working and health-conditions, little access to training, impediments to collective negotiation, and not infrequently subjection to outright oppression in the workplace. As the case of Chile, the most advanced neo-liberal reform-country in Latin America, shows, such anomic and unhappy situations may long prevail, provided that the strategic export sectors of the economy[26] consider the low cost and 'flexibility' of labor employed under precarious conditions by their suppliers as a major factor of their international competitiveness (Díaz 1993). The lesson from Chile's pattern of integrating its dual economy is this: a more cohesive and efficient capitalist economy does not automatically lead to better work- and life-conditions. It may lead to the opposite, if the improved cohesion and international competitiveness of the national economy occurs in part at the cost of oppressing large segments of labor.

In the above sense, the degree of internal cohesion and integration of the Hungarian economy has not yet achieved the Chilean standards. For instance there is little contact and even less cooperation between the MNC-dominated leading export sectors and the Hungarian firms oriented to a larger extent towards the domestic market, including the small and medium sized companies. Instead, the most powerful and influential, largely foreign, cohorts of Hungarian capitalism reside in an economic and political 'off-shore' status. They operate off-shore, mostly in the more developed West-Hungarian Transdanubia or in Budapest, where they enjoy tax-relief, low-price real estate for locating their plants, and other incentives provided by the central and local governments. Rather than acquiring inputs from domestic firms, they typically buy foreign: their suppliers are either firms abroad, or foreign firms setting up their Hungarian production facilities next to their buyers. These firms have their own associations but are not members of Hungarian business organizations, nor do they participate in the national tripartite corporatist bodies and negotiations. Supposedly they are able to influence the government with their economic policy preferences, but they apparently do not use the more or less formalized and visible channels of interest intermediation for these purposes.

These large firms are almost exclusively export-oriented, hence it is not the conditions of the Hungarian, but of their export markets upon which they ultimately depend, and which govern their decisions on investment, production and sales. Consequently, they are also largely autonomous from government policies shaping the domestic economic conditions – be their effect recessionary or expansionary. Their autonomy resulted in benevolent effects in 1995–6, when, notwithstanding the recessionary impulses of the harsh stabilization and adjustment plan, the foreign multinationals completed massive investment projects (Töréspontok 1996). But what about the opposite situation: how to protect the Hungarian economy in the case of a larger recession abroad? The latter situation could cause really big troubles, given that the Hungarian export-sector became more concentrated, and thus more vulnerable, than it was: its most strategic part, manufacturing, essentially means ten firms and ten products. To deal with the effects of a recession abroad seems to be substantially more out of the reach of Hungarian economic policy than ever before.

For the foreseeable future, Hungary's major risks seem to lie in its economic vulnerability and social and political dualism. The major lesson for Hungarian politicians and policymakers, then, is: there is much yet to be 'democratized' in Hungarian democracy, and more to be done for a more cohesive, integrated and diversified economy. Finally, we must note that an efficient, integrated, and dynamic economy does not automatically result in more equitable and liberal democracy. The corrective and inclusive function of the political system cannot be substituted for pure economic strategies. Rather, there is a need for more politically inclusionary institutions, and for mechanisms of sharing the gains when they materialize. Clearly, Hungary's search for 'pathways from the periphery'[27] is not over, but received a new impetus from the collapse of communism.

APPENDIX

Table A6.1 Economic and social indicators of 10 post-communist countries

	1 Depth of the transformational recession: 1997 GDP as % of 1989 GDP	2 Length of the transformational recession: number of years of GDP-decline	3 Inflation in 1990–95, geometric average, % a year	4 Population below USD 1 a day, %	5 Gini coefficient 1993–95 (income per capita)
Poland	111.8	2	34.9	6.8	28
Slovenia	99.3	3	62.1	–	25
Czech Rep.	95.8	3	18.3	3.1	27
Slovak Rep.	95.6	4	16	12.8	19
Hungary	90.4	4	22.3	<2	23
Romania	82.4	4	158.4	17.7	29
Estonia	77.9	5	151.4	6.0	35
Bulgaria	62.8	6	81.2	2.6	34
Lithuania	42.6	5	241.4	<2	37
Latvia	56.8	4	149.1	–	31

Sources: Columns 1, 2, and 5: G. Kolodko, 'Nouveaux Riches vs. Nouveaux Pauvres: Equity Issues in Policy-Making in Transition Economies', *Emergo*, **5**. (2), Spring 1998, pp. 30–31. Column 4: V. Popov, 'Internationalization of the Russian Economy: What Went Wrong?', *Emergo*, **5**. (2), Spring 1998, p. 81. Column 4: World Bank, *World Development Report 1998–9*, New York, Oxford University Press.

Table A6.2 Indicators of economic freedom, state capacity, and foreign direct investment in transition economies

	1 Index of economic freedom. Ranking in 1999 in a sample of 160 countries	2 Legacy of economic liberalization: degree of economic freedom in 1989	3 Speed of economic liberalization: change of the degree of economic freedom between 1989–94	4 Government revenues, % of GDP, change between 1989–94	5 FDI inflow in 1989–96, % of 1995 GDP
Poland	65	23	64	5	4.2
Slovenia	81	43	50	5	3.9
Czech Rep.	12	0	90	–11	14.8
Slovak Rep.	75	0	87	–12	4.4
Hungary	62	37	50	–7	30.3
Romania	95	0	73	–18	4.0
Estonia	18	7	83	–8	17.6
Bulgaria	106	13	60	–22	3.6
Lithuania	72	3	80	–25	4.3
Latvia	61	3	77	–16	9.7

Sources: Column 1: T.B. Johnson, K.R. Holmes and M. Kirkpatrick (1999), *Index of Economic Freedom*. The Heritage Foundation, and *The Wall Street Journal*, 1999. Columnns 2, 3, and 4: calculation based on Murrell (1996), Column 5: Popov. op. cit.

Table A6.3 Indicators of social inequality in Eastern Europe and Latin America

	Ratio of percentage share of household income, held by the richest 20%, and poorest 20% of households		Population below $2 a day
	early-mid-1980s	early-mid-1990s	early-mid-1990s
Hungary (1983, 1993)	3.0	3.9	10.7
Poland (1987, 1992)	3.6	3.9	15.1
Romania (1992)	n.a.	3.8	70.9
Russian Fed. (1993)	n.a.	5.2	10.9
Brazil (1983, 1995)	26.1	25.7	43.5
Colombia (1988, 1995)	13.2	19.8	21.7
Costa Rica (1986, 1996)	16.5	12.9	43.8
Peru (1985–86, 1994)	11.8	10.3	n.a

Sources: *World Development Report 1991*, *1997*, New York; Oxford University Press.

Table A6.4 Labor protest in transition economies

	1 Number of strikes and lockouts: 1990–95	2 Workers involved in strikes and lockouts (1000s)	3 Workdays lost as a result of strikes and lockouts (1000s)
Poland	7914	1702	4235
Slovenia	–	–	–
Czech Rep.	10	97	26
Slovak Rep.	28	22	199
Hungary	23	232	306
Romania	99	134	680

Source: *World Labour Report 1997–98*. ILO, Geneva.

Table A6.5 Relative income position of Hungary measured in GNP per capita at PPP in 1987 and 1997 (%)

1987		1987, 1997	1997	
				Spain 225
				Portugal 198
				Greece 187
Spain 175			Chile 173	
Greece 150			Argentina 142	
Portugal 144			Venezuela 122	
	Venezuela 114		Mexico 116	
	Argentina 109		Panama 101	
		Hungary 100	Uruguay 100	
	Mexico 96			Turkey 92
	Panama 90			
	Chile 85			
	Uruguay 84			
Turkey 71				

Source: Calculation based on *World Development Report 1997*, *1998–9*, New York: Oxford University Press.

NOTES

1. I am indebted to Grzegorz Ekiert, Jacek Kochanowicz, John Lampe, Joseph Love, Gerardo Munck, and Lawrence Whitehead for their helpful comments on the draft version of this chapter.
2. Until 1998 populist politicians who tried to run on the nationalist platform against capitalism and democracy were even less successful in the Hungarian political competition than their colleagues in Poland, the Czech Republic, Slovakia, Romania, or Belarus.
3. Often, the initial response to crisis and adjustment in Latin America and elsewhere in the Third World was severe, massive and violent protest: food riots, general and political strikes, clashes with the armed forces, and escalation of guerrilla-warfare resulting in declarations of state of emergency and impositions of martial law, or, alternatively, in withdrawing economic reform measures, replacing key ministers, ousting governments, or returning to civilian rule (Walton and Seddon 1994).
4. Obviously, Poland, where the changes were preceded by galloping inflation, was less fortunate in this respect – a fact which partly explains why Polish society was somewhat less 'patient' than the Hungarian.
5. There was, however, some rural protest in Hungary, organized by the Smallholders Party, and later by an emerging association of better-off farmers. Also, with respect to the political behavior of Polish peasants I am aware of the fact that they – or at least their representatives in politics – were in general less patient than the rural population in Hungary. Clearly, what matters is not just the geographic dispersion of the population, but its interaction with organizational and cultural factors of mobilization.
6. Here again Hungary differs from Poland, where labor was more contentious. Nevertheless, strike activity in Poland did not paralyze the economy, and its intensity fell throughout the last decade (Ekiert and Kubik 1996).
7. Another similarity between Poland and Hungary: data show a large extent of informalization of the economy.
8. Mainly for political institutional reasons – the initial absence of a minimal threshold of political support required to enter parliament – the Polish political process was more 'hectic', and policymakers were granted much shorter 'grace periods' than in Hungary (Balcerowicz 1995). However, after the threshold was introduced, Polish politics in this respect became similar to the Hungarian.
9. This seems to have happened in similar ways in Poland where not only center-right and liberal, but also ex-Communist coalitions parties implemented largely market-oriented economic policies.
10. Save for the communist Workers' Party, and the racist Party of Hungarian Justice and Life which, however, until 1998 could not mobilize significant political support. However, even the Smallholder Party, which is generally termed 'populist' in the Hungarian political discourse, ultimately embraced many suggestions of the Washington consensus in its 1995 party program. Economic populism, then, was 'the dog which did not bark' in Hungary. A similar phenomenon in the Polish context was pointed out by Leszek Balcerowicz (1995, p. 300).
11. These skills might even have entalied capacities of outmaneuvering the external actors by domestic bureaucrats (Csaba, p. 1995), or designing policy programs with a large domestic intellectual value-added. Greskovits (1998) concludes that Hungarian, Polish and Czechoslovak policymakers enjoyed higher degrees of relative autonomy of policy formulation than their colleagues in less integrated Romania, Bulgaria, or for that matter, the Baltic States.
12. Indeed, Hungary could not follow the Polish road because its major creditors were mainly commercial banks rather than foreign governments, and because Hungary was less politically important for the West than Poland was. However, Hungary did not even push strongly for debt relief.
13. A similar view is expressed in Brada (1996, p. 78).
14. The bad debts forced by non-payments of the debtors to their suppliers, and the social security system raised the stock of problem loans in the banking sector and had multiple negative

effects: they delayed structural change, slowed down the effect of macroeconomic stabilization measures, and became an obstacle to both financial stability and privatization in the firms' sector, and the banking system.

15. While these measures received passionate criticism for their statist and centralizing features, and for allegedly slowing down privatization, looking back from the perspective of the late 1990s, I believe this move was reasonable: it was arguably wise to reinforce state control over spontaneity and state capacity against the tendency of loss of control experienced in many other cases in the East.
16. While these claims are justified, and the structural policies of the Antall government indeed had an element of 'overkill', I wonder whether better solutions were really feasible. Specifi cally, I believe that the Czech attempt to solve the problem favored and conceptualized by Stark and Bruszt (1998), restructuring by 'deliberative associations', was neither superior to the Hungarian solution, nor feasible under the Hungarian conditions of heavy indebtedness and macroeconomic instability.
17. The programs of bank consolidation and firm reorganization received severe and justified criticism for their high costs, the protectionist style of state intervention, and the rent-seeking and moral hazard involved.
18. By 1991 the Antall government also completed trade liberalization by mastering its most difficult phase, and exposed the most sensitive parts of the Hungarian economy to import competition. However, the bankruptcies had especially severe effects in the Hungarian export industries. Of course, the loss of external markets was not a simple outcome of the policies implemented: clearly the most important factor was the collapse of the Soviet economy in 1992–3. What brought especially hard times for Hungarian firms was the simultaneity of the processes.
19. As I argued above, the expensive reorganization of the banks and their debtors under the Antall government was an important condition for this success: earlier attempts at privatization mostly failed because of the banks' precarious financial standing. However, this large share of foreign ownership in banking is rather unprecedented in the whole of Europe: there are only three other countries – Belgium, Luxemburg, and the UK – where foreign ownership was substantial around 1990 (Törékeny stabilizáció 1997, p. 103). I believe this unusual feature of Hungarian capitalism and the risks and opportunities inherent in having a foreign-owned banking sector – also accompanied by a 100 percent foreign ownership in the insurance sector – deserve more scholarly attention. Nevertheless, the first analyses report on intensive investment activity and improvements in financial services.
20. The expression, in a different context, is used by Grant (1998).
21. And, of course, to many other, partly domestic, political and economic factors, which I highlighted above. I borrow the above expression from Federowicz (1997).
22. The gap is even larger if the comparison is based on GNP or GDP per capita at actual exchange rates rather than GNP per capita at purchasing power parity.
23. Hungarian democracy is, to some extent, 'undemocratic' not only in terms of the tension between its exclusionary and inclusionary dimensions. To use Guillermo O'Donnell's and Phillippe Schmitter's famous concept (1986), Hungary also represents a case of democracy building by 'undemocratic means': specifically by exclusive élite pacts.
24. See for the negative effect of similar processes on labor in Western Europe, Pontusson, 1995.
25. For the description of the Hungarian labor relations see Ladó (1996), and Ellingstad (1997).
26. In Chile, the bulk of exports is provided by 8–10 large, export-oriented and internationally integrated conglomerates.
27. The idiom is used in a different context by Haggard (1990).

REFERENCES

Acuna, H.C. and C.W. Smith (1994), 'The political economy of structural adjustment: the logic of support and opposition to neoliberal reform' in William C. Smith, Carlos

H. Acuna and Eduardo Gamarra (eds), *Latin American Political Economy in the Age of Neoliberal Reform. Theoretical and Comparative Perspectives for the 1990s*, New Brunswick (USA) and London (UK): Transaction Publishers.

Aslund, A. (1997), 'Possible future directions for economies in transition', in Joan M. Nelson, Charles Tilly and Lee Walkers (eds), *Transforming Post-communist Political Economies*, Washington, DC: National Academy Press.

Balcerowicz, Leszek (1995), *Socialism, Capitalism, Transformation*, Budapest, London, New York: Central European University Press.

Brada, J. (1996), 'Privatization is transition – or is it?', *Journal of Economic Perspectives*, **10** (2), Spring, 67–86.

Bunce, V. (1998), 'The political economy of postsocialism', Cornell University, mimeo.

Bunce, V. (1999), *Subversive Institutions. The Design and the Destruction of Socialism and the State*, Cambridge: Cambridge University Press.

Corricelli, F. (1998), *Macroeconomic Policies and the Development of Markets in Transition Economies*, Budapest: Central European University Press.

Csaba, L. (1995), 'Hungary and the IMF: The Experience of a Cordial Discord', *Journal of Comparative Economics*, **20**, 211–34.

Díaz, A. (1993), 'Restructuring and the new working classes in Chile: trends in waged employment, informality and poverty, 1973–90', Discussion Paper 47, UN Research Institute for Social Development, Geneva: Switzerland.

Ekiert, G. and J. Kubik (1996), 'Strategies of collective protest in democratizing societies: Hungary, Poland and Slovakia since 1989', Paper presented at the 10th International Conference of Europeanists, Chicago, March 14–16, (mimeo).

Ellingstad, M. (1997), 'The Maquiladora Syndrome: Central European Prospects', *Europe-Asia Studies*, **49** (1), 7–21.

Federowicz, M. (1997), 'The power of path-finding expectations', presented at the IV ESF-workshop: 'Institution Building in the Transformation of Central and Eastern European Societies', Budapest: 1997, December 5–7, (mimeo).

Fish, M.S. (1998), 'The determinants of economic reform in the post-communist world', *East European Politics and Societies*, **12**, Winter, 31–78.

Grant, B. (1998), 'The virtue of lack. Russian elites in transformation', Lecture presented in The Institute for European Studies, Cornell University, October.

Greskovits, B. (1998), *The Political Economy of Protest and Patience*, Budapest: Central European University Press.

Haggard, S. (1990), *Pathways from the Periphery. The Politics of Growth in the Newly Industrializing Countries*, Ithaca and London: Cornell University Press.

Hellmann, J. (1998), 'Winners take all: the politics of partial reform in post-communist transitions', *World Politics*, **50**, January, 235–65.

Kornai, János (1994), 'Transformational recession: the main causes,' *Journal of Comparative Economics*, **19** (1).

Ladó, M. (1996) 'Continuity and changes in tripartism in Hungary', in Attila Ágh and Gabriella Ilonszki (eds), *Parliaments and Organized Interests: The Second Steps*, Budapest: Hungarian Center for Democracy Studies, 158–72.

Laki, M. (1998), *Kisvállalkozás a szocializmus után* (Small enterpreneurs after socialism), Közgazdasági Szemle Alapítvány, Budapest.

Murrell, P. (1996), 'How far has the transition progressed?', *Journal of Economic Perspectives*, **10**, (2) Spring, 25–44.

O' Donnell, G. and P. Schmitter (1986), *Transitions from Authoritarian Rule: Tentative Conclusions about Uncertain Democracies*, Baltimore, London: Johns Hopkins University Press.

Pontusson, J. (1995), 'Explaining the decline of European social democracy: the role of structural economic change', *World Politics* (47), 495–533.

Róna-Tas, Á. (1997), 'Social engineering and historical legacies: privatization and the business elite in Hungary and the Czech Republic', in Beverly Crawford and Arend Lijphart (eds), *Liberalization and Leninist Legacies: Comparative Perspectives on Democratic Transitions*, Research Series No. 96. University of California at Berkeley, pp. 126–41.

Sík, E. (1994), 'From the multicolored to the black and white economy: the Hungarian second economy and the transformation', *International Journal of Urban and Regional Research*, **18**, 46–70.

Stark, D. and L. Bruszt (1998), *Postsocialist Pathways: Transforming Politics and Property in East Central Europe*, Cambridge: Cambridge University Press.

Urbán, L. (1991), 'Why was the Hungarian transition exceptionally peaceful?', in György Szoboszlai (ed.), *Democracy and Political Transformation*, Budapest: Hungarian Political Science Association, pp. 303–9.

Walton, J. and D. Seddon (1994), *Free Markets & Food Riots. The Politics of Global Adjustment*, Oxford, UK and Cambridge, USA: Blackwell.

Fordulat és folytonosság (1995) Pénzügykutató Részvénytársaság, Budapest.
Hegymenet (1998) Pénzügykutató Részvénytársaság, Budapest.
Jelentések az alagútból (1994) Pénzügykutató Részvénytársaság, Budapest.
Törékeny stabilizáció (1997) Pénzügykutató Részvénytársaság, Budapest.
Töréspontok (1996) Pénzügykutató Részvénytársaság, Budapest.

7. Trajectories of East European transformation: global influence and local legacies

Jacek Kochanowicz

INTRODUCTION

Communism collapsed in an era of globalization. This last word may be vague and overused, but it reminds us that it seems extremely difficult today to set as an agenda the creation of an economic system that would differ in principle from a capitalist market economy. It is also implausible to declare the intention of creating a political system other than democracy. Thus, leaders of societies leaving communism behind found themselves under pressure to construct democratic capitalism. In a most direct way, this pressure came from international financial institutions and from governments of the most developed countries. In a more subtle way, it was exerted by the dominant ideology of the end of the 20th century, liberalism, as well as by the attraction of the life style of western consumer societies. In some post-communist societies, this pressure also came from below, from the middle classes, which had emerged at the later stages of communism. The price of not taking this route looked high – marginalization within the international community and exclusion from the possibility of modernization. Thus, many of the leaders declared at the beginning that they intended to take the liberal-democratic, capitalist route.

After ten years, it is worthwhile to take stock, to see who achieved what, which routes were actually taken, and where they led. This is what this chapter intends to do, looking from a bird's eye perspective on the European part of the post-communist world. The purpose is, first, to single out these countries which look as if they are on a trajectory of change convergent with the Western world. Second, it is to speculate on the possible reasons for particular countries' success in achieving these converging trajectories, while others are placing themselves on clearly divergent trajectories, and a third group is drifting aimlessly. (I am saying, 'to speculate,' because it is clearly impossible in a short chapter to go much beyond asking hypothetical questions.)

Before starting, it is important to note that the end of communism, being political as much as social and economic change, brought about a substantial redrawing of the Eurasian map, as well as wars and violence. Three federal states – the Soviet Union, the Federal Republic of Yugoslavia, and Czechoslovakia – broke down, adding almost 20 new states to the political map of the world. In former Soviet Asia and in the Balkan Peninsula, ethnic tensions – suppressed under communism – led to bloody conflicts with no end in sight. Protracted wars and violence seem to preclude, for the time being, constructing viable market economies. In what I am saying below, I therefore omit countries at war.

I begin with a brief statistical comparison of post-communist countries, then I discuss the character and phase of transitions for the different regions, and I end with an interpretation of divergent trajectories they took.

TAKING STOCK

The most obvious way of classifying post-communist societies is regional, as it reflects common characteristics of a geographical, political, and cultural character. The broadest regional classification is: Eastern Europe, Russia, and the Asian states which were former republics of the Soviet Union. Today, however, Eastern Europe is too broad a category. As a concept, it was widely used during the Cold War, referring to satellite countries of the Soviet Union or to countries that split away from the USSR – Albania and the Federal Republic of Yugoslavia. This category stressed similarities brought about by communism and the Soviet system. At the same time, it neglected important geographical, cultural, and historical differences. It is worthwhile to mention that, broadly understood, Eastern Europe is divided by the Carpathian mountains; it encompasses regions of different natural endowments, and has populations of four religions (Roman Catholic, Protestant, Orthodox, and Islamic), belonging to many ethnic groups; and its inhabitants speak more than a dozen languages. In the modern period, it belonged to four different empires (Turkey, Russia, Austria, and Germany), and during World War II its peoples found themselves on different sides of the political–military cleavage. With the process of corrosion of the Soviet Empire, visible by the 1970s, the differences among these countries became more pronounced – differences relating to cultural and political inheritance, as well as to the feelings of common identity. Thus, for example, Hungarian and Czech intellectuals introduced the category of Central Europe, stressing important cultural similarities of countries, which for a long time had formed a part of the Habsburg empire, and implying important differences with 'more Eastern' Europe, particularly Russia.

Taking into consideration these cultural and geopolitical differences, the region is now often divided into Central (or East-Central) Europe, Eastern Europe in a narrower sense (see below), the Balkans, and the Baltic States. Inclusion or exclusion of particular countries into this or that sub-region may not be obvious. The Czech Republic, the Slovak Republic, and Hungary belong to Central Europe, while Poland's claim to such an inclusion may seem dubious, taking into consideration the fact that only part of its present territory belonged to the Austrian empire and shared its particular cultural influence. Still, I include Poland, as it has always looked to the West culturally, particularly because of the Roman Catholic religion. It seems sensible to add Slovenia to this group as well. On the day that the Czech Republic, Hungary, and Poland joined NATO, a Ljubljana journalist, writing for a Polish paper, observed with regret, that – culturally – his country belongs to Central Europe too (Gogala 1999). Geographically, his country, Slovenia, is on the Balkan Peninsula, but historically it was much closer to the West than the rest of the former Federal Republic of Yugoslavia, as it was part of the Habsburg Empire. For a time being it also was a part of the Napoleonic Empire. During the last decades of the former Yugoslavia, Slovenia maintained close economic and cultural contacts with Austria.

Eastern Europe in a narrow sense consists of Belarus, Ukraine, and the European part of Russia. Russia, however, should be treated as its own category, not only because geographically it lies both in Europe and in Asia, but also because of its political weight. The Baltic States – particularly Estonia and Latvia – are culturally closer to Scandinavian than to Slavic countries. They have a tradition of political independence between the two world wars (as they were forcibly integrated into the Soviet Union only in 1939). They were also the first among the Soviet Republics to have their claims to independence recognized by the West. Finally, Croatia, Bosnia-Herzegovina, the present Yugoslavia (Serbia and Montenegro), Macedonia, Albania, Bulgaria, and Romania belong to the Balkans. Technically, only part of Romania lies on the Balkan Peninsula. Still, Romania is commonly included in the Balkans, as, together with the rest of the group, it shares the legacy of the Ottoman empire, and obtained its independence through the Balkan wars. It is worth reminding ourselves, however, that a substantial part of what constitutes Romania today – Transylvania in particular – was outside the Ottoman Empire, and under Western rule for most of its modern history.

While the interest of this chapter is primarily in Eastern Europe in its broad sense, we shall include, for comparative reasons, some data relating to Asian states which were formerly republics of the Soviet Union: Armenia, Georgia, Azerbaijan, Kazkhstan, Kyrgyzstan, Turkmenistan, Tajikistan, and Uzbekistan. The last five are often referred to as Central Asian republics.

If one looks at the indices of economic performance during the last ten years, Central European countries stand out. However, it is important to remember that quantitative data – if available at all – are often not reliable.[1] It is also important to note that several countries have recently been or are still embroiled in civil strife, a situation which so strongly affects their economies that it is impossible to make any judgments about their systemic transitions. This is the case with a number of countries that were formerly parts of the Yugoslav Federation, particularly Bosnia-Herzegovina and Serbia. This is also the case of Armenia, Azerbaijan, Georgia, and Tajikistan.

Table 7.1 Post-communist countries ranked by GDP per capita (PPP) in 1997

Country	US$
Slovenia	12 520
Czech Republic	11 380
Slovak Republic	7 850
Hungary	7 000
Poland	6 380
Estonia	5 010
Belarus	4 840
Lithuania	4 510
Romania	4 290
Russia	4 190
Kazkhstan	3 920
Bulgaria	3 860
Latvia	3 650
Uzbekistan	2 450
Armenia	2 280
Ukraine	2 170
Kyrgyzstan	2 040
Georgia	1 980
Azerbaijan	1 520
Turkmenistan	1 410
Tajikistan	930

Source: World Bank 1998, Table 1.

Table 7.1 ranks post-communist countries according to GDP per capita (measured according to purchasing power parity – PPP). Central Europe has the highest per capita incomes among the post-communist countries; these incomes are also higher than the average GDP per capita income for all the middle income countries of the world, which for 1997 was 4450 US dollars (World Bank 1998). While noting this advantageous position of Central Europe, one has to remark that these countries were 'misdeveloped' in the same sense as all communist countries, being over-industrialized, relying on outdated technologies, having insufficient service and consumer sectors, and so on. Moreover, while they underwent a considerable process of economic and social modernization during communism, they nonetheless lagged enormously behind Southern Europe (which, before World War II, had a similar level of development) (Berend 1996). While no doubt communism brought some modernization to the region, this modernization was much less effective than the one produced by capitalism in Southern Europe during the same period.

Table 7.2 Lowest level of GDP in comparison with 1989

Country	Index	Year
Turkmenistan	97.1	1991
Poland	82.2	1991
Hungary	81.9	1993
Uzbekistan	80.5	1995
Slovenia	79.9	1992
Czech Republic	78.5	1993
Slovak Republic	75.0	1993
Romania	75.0	1992
Bulgaria	73.3	1993
Croatia	65.4	1993
Estonia	63.2	1994
Belarus	61.5	1995
Albania	60.4	1992
Russia	56.6	1996
Kyrgyzstan	53.2	1995
Macedonia	52.9	1995
Latvia	51.0	1993
Kazkhstan	49.0	1995
Armenia	45.7	1993
Ukraine	41.6	1996
Lithuania	37.2	1993
Azerbaijan	36.9	1995
Tajikistan	33.2	1996
Georgia	17.2	1994

Source: *UN Economic Commission for Europe* (1997), p. 225.

All post-communist countries, after the collapse of the old regime, went through a phase of extreme recession, which – in comparative terms – was much deeper than the Great Depression (Milanovic 1998). There were various causes of this recession, and the relative importance of such causes is widely and fiercely debated. Three main reasons are mentioned: the first is shedding redundant output (military production, as well as unwanted goods). The second is a breakdown of cooperation links, characteristic for the old command economy, as well as for the Comecon. The third reason is the decrease of internal demand, related to macroeconomic adjustment programs. It is very difficult to measure the exact role these factors played in each individual case. Without going into this debate, it is enough to mention that the loss of output, related to the first cause, is less of a worry than the second, and particularly the last one. Once again, as Table 7.2 shows, the Central European countries suffered the least severe shock (apart from two Asian republics). By contrast, Belarus, Russia, and Ukraine suffered very heavy losses. Central European countries were also relatively quick to resume growth, with Poland emerging as a leader (growth began in 1992), and the first country to achieve pre-transition levels. The Central European nations also had relatively high growth rates (Table 7.3). If one takes the period 1990–97, Poland remains the only one among the group to have a positive average rate of growth; the rest of the Central European countries had to contend themselves with the fact that their negative rates of growth were relatively low. This may be contrasted with very high negative rates of growth for Russia, Belarus, and Ukraine. How stable and sustainable these positive rates of growth are, is hard to say. Taking the Polish case as an example, there are reasons to worry: growth was to a large extent driven by consumer rather than producer demand; furthermore, a negative balance of trade is accumulating, savings remain low, and there are signs in 1999 that the growth will slow down significantly. Still, all the worries of Central European countries are nothing when compared with those of Russia or Ukraine. The former group of countries was also successful in managing inflation. As Table 7.4 shows, their yearly average inflation was lower than in the rest of the post-communist countries, and this includes Poland, which began in 1989 with hyperinflation.

In comparative terms, therefore, the Central European transformation looks successful. There have been, obviously, high social costs related to economic change. Indeed, many Western observers worried at the beginning of the transformation that these costs would be so high that post-communist societies would not be able to bear them, and that social tensions would provoke riots, the breakdown of democratic regimes, a return to authoritarianism, and a derailing of economic reforms. Those fears were, to a large extent, based on a comparison with the reform process in Latin America in the 1980s (Greskovits 1998). It was argued that Eastern Europe, having much less of a social memory of

Table 7.3 Average yearly rate of growth in 1990–97

Country	Rate of growth
Poland	3.9
Albania	1.8
Slovak Republic	0.4
Romania	0.0
Hungary	–0.4
Mongolia	–0.6
Czech Republic	–1.0
Bulgaria	–3.5
Uzbekistan	–3.5
Estonia	–4.3
Lithuania	–4.5
Belarus	–6.5
Russia	–9.0
Turkmenistan	–9.6
Kazkhstan	–10.5
Latvia	–10.7
Kyrgyzstan	–12.3
Ukraine	–13.6
Azerbaijan	–15.1
Tajikistan	–16.4
Armenia	–21.2
Georgia	–26.2

Source: World Bank (1998).

capitalism than Latin America, would prove unable to introduce it, which would mean that hardships of macroeconomic adjustment would serve no purpose. Those dark scenarios have not materialized, at least in Central Europe, but indeed the social costs are enormous.

The most important are unemployment, social inequality, reduced incomes, and poverty. Under state socialism, the official doctrine of full employment accompanied the functioning of the 'economics of shortage' and 'soft budget constraint' (Kornai 1980), which meant that almost everybody below a certain age would have a job. While such policy hid under-employment, it also guaranteed a minimal income and basic social security. The 1989 recession, coupled with a rationalization of enterprises, produced overt unemployment all over the region. As unemployment did not exist under state socialism, its emergence was a dramatic change for which these societies were psychologi-

Table 7.4 Average yearly inflation, 1990–97

Country	Implict deflator
Slovak Republic	12.7
Czech Republic	17.7
Hungary	22.5
Poland	29.5
Slovenia	32.1
Albania	58.1
Bulgaria	79.8
Mongolia	89.3
Estonia	92.1
Latvia	112.0
Romania	124.5
Lithuania	139.9
Macedonia	149.4
Croatia	218.1
Kyrgyzstan	256.2
Moldova	307.7
Russia	394.0
Tajikistan	394.3
Azerbaijan	447.8
Uzbekistan	546.5
Belarus	564.8
Kazkhstan	604.9
Ukraine	800.5
Armenia	860.5
Turkmenistan	1074.2
Georgia	2279.5

Source: World Bank (1998).

cally and institutionally unprepared. Characteristically, it is still higher today in the Central European countries, which are more advanced in transformation than in Russia, Ukraine, or the Asian countries. In the latter areas, higher employment is caused by a slower pace of economic transformation, as well as by the policy of keeping redundant workers in factories for social reasons – often, however, without paying them wages for months at a time.

Inequalities rose everywhere, as data collected by Branko Milanovic show (Table 7.5) (Milanovic 1998). Figures given here relate to incomes, not wealth. Transformation in post-communism countries also caused massive shifts of

Table 7.5 *Rise of inequalities in post-communist countries*

	Gini coefficient	
Region and country	1987–88	1993–95
Central Europe		
Czech Republic	19	27
Hungary	21	23
Poland	26	28
Slovak Republic	20	19
Slovenia	22	25
Baltic countries		
Estonia	23	35
Latvia	23	31
Lithuania	23	37
Eastern Europe		
Belarus	23	28
Moldova	24	36
Russia	24	48
Ukraine	23	47
Balkan countries		
Bulgaria	23	34
Romania	23	29
Asian countries		
Kazkhstan	26	33
Kyrgyzstan	26	55
Turkmenistan	26	36
Uzbekistan	28	33

Source: Milanovic (1998), p. 41.

assets (due to privatization), and considerable inequalities undoubtedly emerged as well. On the other hand, it is worthwhile to remember that such inequalities also exist in highly developed countries. As far as income disparity is concerned, Central European nations remain within the range of the OECD countries, for which the average Gini coefficient is around 30 (Milanovic 1998). In Russia or Ukraine it is close to 50, not far below Brazil or South Africa, infamous for their social inequalities. Comparison with the OECD countries on the basis of income concentration alone is, however, misleading. The situation of the lowest quintile in well-off France is somewhat different from that of the lowest quintile in Poland, which has one fourth of France's GDP per capita. And, indeed, poverty rose considerably everywhere, as Table 7.6 shows. Poverty is defined in this table as a situation in which per capita household income per day is less than 4 US dollars, measured according to purchasing power parity, and the poverty gap is the percentage of people living below this level (Milanovic 1998). Poverty in post-communist countries emerged as a result of declining nominal and real incomes; for many families it was a direct result of unemployment. Real incomes declined because of recession and dramatic price rises, resulting from macroeconomic stabilization. Still, apart from Poland, it is not very significant in the Central European countries, while it is quite dramatic in Russia and Ukraine.

Table 7.6 Increase of poverty gap in post-communist countries

	Poverty gap	
Region and country	1987–88	1993–95
Central Europe		
Czech Republic	0	<1
Hungary	1	4
Poland	6	20
Slovak Republic	0	<1
Slovenia	0	<1
Baltic countries		
Estonia	1	37
Latvia	1	22
Lithuania	1	37
Eastern Europe		
Belarus	1	22
Moldova	2	66
Russia	2	50
Ukraine	2	63
Balkan countries		
Bulgaria	2	15
Romania	6	59

Source: Milanovic (1998), p. 68.

Looking at the statistical data it is fair to say that by and large Central Europe is relatively most successful in transition, and it is followed by the Baltic countries, particularly Estonia. One form of recognizing that fact is putting the Central European countries, as well as Estonia, on a short list of applicants to the European Union. In a certain way, another proof is the recent admission of Czech Republic, Hungary, and Poland to NATO. The somewhat striking omission of Slovakia from both these groups is due to the political turbulence occurring in this country under the Meciar presidency; there is a hope now that Meciar is gone, that the chances of Slovakia will improve.

AIMS AND PHASES OF TRANSFORMATION

It is now proper to pose the question, what strategies of transformation, or rather what patterns of change lay behind these results? What was attempted depended, among other things, on project outcome, or on ideas of the politicians trying to implement changes. Without a deeper study of the most recent intellectual history of post-communist countries, it is difficult to be very precise about these ideas. Very roughly, it can be said that two competing views on the transition have been articulated. One may be called neo-liberal, and the second, 'the Third Way.' The first one was close to what, after a decade of experience with reforms in Latin America, came to be known as 'the Washington consensus,' although the term itself has rarely been used in post-communist countries. (Williamson 1990, 1993). It stressed the need to achieve a macroeconomic stability, to open and deregulate the economy, to privatize as quickly as possible, and to confine the role of the government in the economy to protecting property rights, to maintaining a regulatory framework, and to pursue correct macroeconomic policies. An active role of the state, apart from this, should be restricted to investing in human capital, and to establishing social safety nets. There is no need to restate here that this view became extremely well articulated in mainstream academic economics during the last thirty years, as well as in policy by international agencies and Western governments. The early version of the Washington consensus was later modified, stressing the importance of effective – which does not necessarily mean large – governments. The state, according to post-Washington consensus view, should be not so much interventionist as regulative. (Stiglitz 1998; Sen 1997; World Bank, 1997).

There has been a widespread perception in the West that this view was imposed from outside upon those countries by international financial institutions (the International Monetary Fund and the World Bank in particular), and by foreign experts. At least as far as Central European countries are concerned, this perception is not fully correct, as support for economic liberalism was also quite widespread internally, even well before the political turnabout of 1989. (Szacki 1995). In a large measure, it was a product of disillusionment with earlier attempts of market socialism reforms.

The second view – that of a Third Way – has never been well articulated and codified, and it is therefore much more difficult to reconstruct.[2] In most of the cases, it was formulated rather in polemics with the prevalent ideology. In some sense, the idea of a Third Way consisted, at least initially, on combining good aspects of capitalism and socialism. Opponents of the neo-liberal approach thus have identified themselves either as social democrats, or – in countries with strong Catholic tradition, such as Poland – as adherents to the social teachings of the Church. Social cohesion, the importance of community, an incomes policy, a redistributive role for the state, a mixed economy, and the participation of workers in economic decisions have been stressed as important goals of transformation. The Third Way, however, has never achieved a coherent intellectual framework, while at the same time it has often been entangled in populist rhetoric.

Not all the opponents of the Washington consensus approach, it may be added, would agree on classifying them as adherents to the Third Way model. Some among them would rather say that while there is no sensible alternative for capitalism in general, that system could notwithstanding take different shapes, accordingly to historic and cultural traditions. Societies which shed communism should, therefore, search for their own versions of capitalism. Others, who would also agree with capitalism as an ultimately correct model, would have doubts about a quick route to the final destination, arguing rather for a gradual or evolutionary approach, and they attribute Poland's initial deep recession to the excesses of 'shock therapy' (Poznanski 1996; Kolodko 1999). Arguments have also been put forward for an active role of state in restructuring state firms even before privatization, with an aim of pushing transforming economies into more competitive position *vis-à-vis* the rest of the world (Amsden et al. 1994). Still, it is probably correct to say that, on a rhetorical level, the neo-liberal or Washington consensus view emerged as the winner of the debate. In a practical sense, a much more evolutionary approach was taken, perhaps apart from the case of Polish shock therapy. The latter, nonetheless, applied to only one aspect of transition, namely the macroeconomic stabilization. It was probably inevitable, taking into consideration a near hyper-inflationary situation of this country. The evolutionary approach, however, was much more a product of a political situation than of a conscious choice.

Looking into the transformation process from a somewhat longer perspective, it is convenient to make a distinction between a phase of initiation of reforms and a phase of their consolidation. This is a distinction that has been introduced into studies of transformation of the political sphere in countries moving from authoritarianism to democracy, and it is often applied to the study of economic transformation as well. In an often-quoted expression of Adam Przeworski, democracy is consolidated when it is 'the only game in town.' It is difficult to translate this approach literally to the economic sphere and, by analogy, to speak about the market as the only game in town. Even in the most developed economic systems, the market is not the sole mechanism of economic coordination, as many important economic decisions remain within the political sphere. The market, therefore, has to be treated rather as *the most important* game in town for a transformation to be completed or reforms consolidated. The state, at the same time, while important, must be 'market-friendly,' securing and facilitating its operations. Finally, the market must be legitimized, in a sense of the public at large accepting the outcomes produced by the market, even if they tend to be unpleasant for given individuals or groups. The focus of policies in the initiation phase is, on the one hand, on restoring macroeconomic balance, and, on the other, on letting economic agents – entrepreneurs first of all – act freely. In the second phase, that of consolidation, the focus has to be much more on institution-building, as well as on securing social consent for reforms and legitimizing capitalism.

If 1989–90 is to be treated as a starting point of transformation, it is important to note that the initial situation was not a full-blown command economy of a Stalinist type, but rather various forms of late-phase communism. Some countries had an important record of reforms, attempting some kind of market socialism. Even in those that did not try reforms, the command economy underwent various kinds of evolution, often making it internally incoherent and dysfunctional in comparison with an original, highly hierarchical order. 'No market, no plan' was a shorthand expression, characterizing this situation. State-socialism economies suffered acute internal imbalances, of which hidden or open inflation was a visible sign, and also long-term stagnation. They were unable to produce much technological change, to improve standards of living and consumption, or to adjust to the requirements of the international economy. The task facing the reforming governments was as much to restore stability as to put economies on the reform track, having as an ultimate aim building full-blown capitalist system.

Taking into consideration the state of affairs at the beginning of the transformation (understood here as a moment of political change), it is sensible to treat the initiation phase as focusing primarily upon macroeconomic stabilization, external liberalization, deregulation, and setting off the privatization process. Macroeconomic stabilization included a reduction of subsidies and of the budget deficit, and easing price controls, sometimes introducing wage controls in the state sector to depress demand. An aim of liberalization is to allow foreign competition to discipline domestic producers. It was commonly agreed that these measures should be accompanied by the introduction of social safety nets, targeted as precisely as possible at the unemployed and the very poor. It was important, because state socialism – while it produced its own kind of welfare state – was institutionally unprepared for coping with unemployment and poverty.

Continuation of the process of privatization of state-owned enterprises is a very important task of the consolidation phase. At phase two, there must be much more institution-building than was the case in phase one. Schematically, four aspects of institution building may be singled out. First is the introduction (or re-invocation) of laws and legal institutions supportive of markets. This means constitutional guarantees for private property, civil codes, commercial codes, laws regulating banking and the securities exchange, and so on. Needless to say, for all these laws to be effective, a given country needs courts and other law enforcing institutions, as well as trained lawyers. Of particular importance among institutions, guaranteeing the proper operation of banking, is a central bank.

A second, relatively easier task is reconstruction of the economic functions of the central government. Under state socialism, the operation of a command economy was realized through a hierarchical system of central planning authorities, responding to party bosses, and a system of branch ministries (energy, agriculture, industry, and so on), acting as super-enterprises. This pattern had to be abolished, while capacities of functional agencies (finance, for example), had to be redesigned and upgraded.

The third task is to establish a modern tax system. Under state socialism, the most important tax was the so-called 'turnover tax,' collected through state-owned enterprises. It was a mark-up on costs, and served as a means of the realization of government's redistributive policies. Since it was the government that set all prices and wages, and in such a way also determined the costs, the turnover tax was relatively easy to operate. It is, obviously, totally unsuitable to the exigencies of market economy, which requires taxes on net values – personal income taxation and value added on consumer goods. The introduction of such new taxes calls for the establishment of a whole new bureaucratic machinery.

The fourth aspect, or task, is a need to reconstruct the 'socialist welfare state.' This requires a longer comment: under state socialism, part of what is called in Western Europe a welfare state was provided through the workplace. Full employment not only guaranteed a minimal income to almost all the members of the society, but also acted as a channel of distribution of many goods and services (housing, coupons for cars, or holidays). Another element of social policy was embedded in establishing prices and wages, which enabled the government to influence income levels and consumption patterns of the population (cheap milk, expensive cars, for example). Health care and education, free of charge, were provided through all-encompassing bureaucratic organizations. Finally, all the working population was covered by universal pension schemes, organized as a 'pay as you go' system. Certain parts of this system disintegrated during the early phases of transformation: full employment and guaranteed incomes, as well as a system of subsidies for consumer goods. What remain to be reconstructed are the pension, health care, and education systems. As they currently function in most of the post-communist countries, they are both inefficient and ineffective.

The distinction between the two phases is very schematic, and obviously the cutting points between them are not clear-cut. Still, it makes sense to ask the question, which post-communist countries have completed the first phase, entered the second one, and are in the process of strengthening the market economy?

CENTRAL EUROPE AND THE REST

It is safe to say that the Central European countries, particularly the Czech Republic, Hungary, Poland and Slovenia, and – among the Baltic countries – Estonia, have completed the initiation process and are now in the consolidation phase. They managed to achieve macroeconomic stability and, moreover, to establish institutions controlling the money supply. Their economies are open, and they have developed a fairly efficient private sector of trade and services. The privatization of the state sector is advancing, and many '*de novo*' firms are emerging. In some of these countries, the private sector produces more than half of GDP today. (Nellis 1999, p. 5). There is an ongoing process of legal changes, which are motivated as much by the needs of building capitalism as by the wish to make legal standards compatible with that of the European Union. These countries are politically stable, and tensions attributed to the social costs of reforms are being managed in a democratic way. That, obviously, does not mean that all is well in the Central European economies, and that their future prosperity is secured. Internal political and economic debate in these countries points to weaknesses, and even to possibilities of derailing reforms. These societies remain poor, far below the standards of even the weakest members of the European Union, which they aspire to enter. On the other hand, when compared with the rest of the post-communist world, they look much better.

However, the process of institutional change, which constitutes the bulk of the consolidation phase, is a long and protracted one, even in these most successful countries. One way of explaining the slow pace of change is related to the political economy aspects of transition: vested interests may defend the status quo, groups endangered by the forces of the market may defend their position by political means, politicians may slow down the pace of change in order to avoid political problems – or simply, to get more votes because of 'populist' promises. Another way of explaining the problem is to make use of an institutional and evolutionary approach to economics and social science in general. If we agree that – as Hayek or North hold– institutions are the rules of the game and that they embody tacit and local knowledge, then a long process of learning is required to move from one set of social arrangements to another.

In a short chapter it is impossible to touch upon all aspects of legal and institutional transformation. A brief comment on certain important aspects must suffice. The three, singled out here, are privatization of state owned enterprises, reform of the 'welfare state,' and the problem of social support for the changes.

Privatization, not surprisingly, proved to be more difficult than enthusiasts expected at the beginning, and even when it advanced, it did not necessarily increase efficiency (Blaszczyk and Woodward 1996; Nellis 1999). There have been technical, economic, and political obstacles in the way. Technical obstacles included those related to the process of assessment of the firm's book and market value. This is relatively simple in the market environment, but much more difficult when a market is only emerging. It also requires skills which have been in dramatically short supply in the early phases of transformation. Lawyers, accountants, and managerial consultants became, as a result of this shortage, among the important early 'winners' of the transition process. Among the economic obstacles, the most dramatic have been a short supply of capital in the countries that have been poor, where level of saving have been low, and where few private assets have been accumulated. For this reason, ingenious schemes were devised for managerial buy-outs, for selling shares to employees, and for mass (coupon) privatization, while at the same time prospective foreign owners were courted.

Some of these measures also served political purposes. At the beginning, there was great opposition to privatization. Many workers feared that they would lose their jobs as a result of rationalization of employment, or that they could not cope with the higher expectations of the managers for high-quality work. There were also widespread feelings that people well connected to the old system (*nomenklatura*) would have much better chances of profiting from the process of divesting state assets. Selling shares to employees, as well as mass privatization schemes, were supposed to work as a compensation, and to make the process more attractive to ordinary people. From a strictly economic point of view, such schemes were criticized, because privatization serves its purpose, generally speaking, when it leads to the creation of well-defined owners, having a stake in the success of the firm. Still, with all these obstacles, the process of privatization continues in Central Europe, although results might be more modest than statistics show. Firms are usually considered in 'private' hands if the state share is below 50 percent, so the proportion of firms privatized exceeds the share of capital in private hands. There is the gray zone between the state and the private. Many firms still in state hands, but now working under market conditions, do not perform significantly worse than those that were privatized. As a rule, firms privatized by an important foreign investor perform the best.

Reconstruction of what remained from the 'socialist welfare state' is even more difficult than the privatization (Kochanowicz 1997). The socialist welfare state consisted of a combination of incomes guaranteed by full employment and the universal provision of social services by the state. Incomes were guaranteed by easy access (indeed, almost a duty) to work and by the system of administered prices, combined with rationing. This part of the socialist welfare state disappeared quickly during the process of deregulation, privatization, and macroeconomic adjustment. Job security disappeared, and subsidies to basic consumer goods were abolished. What remained were state-provided pensions, free health care, and free education. Pension systems were organized on a 'pay-as-you-go' (redistributive) principle, and state budgets came under pressure when employment (that is, the contribution base) shrank, while at the same time pensioners became more politically vocal. Health and education are provided in a standardized form by comprehensive, bureaucratic structures, hardly responsive to specific needs and oblivious to cost-benefit analysis. However, though these systems were considered as costly and ineffective, reform was postponed, and they still lag behind the change of institutions regulating the 'productive' sectors of the economy. There are a number of reasons for the slow start of the reform of the public services sector. One is that there are no clear blueprints. The West did supply clear models for how to organize a bank, or a business enterprise, or how to set up a stock exchange. In contrast to these, public sector services, or the welfare state in general, are everywhere in crisis. The general idea is to change pension systems from a pay-as-you-go basis to a funded system; to introduce management practices into the health sector, parallel with reforms of the way they are financed; and to give schools more flexibility, changing their finances by introducing educational vouchers and even tuition fees for university students. From these general ideas to operating principles, however, is a long road. Another reason for delay is a perception, shared by many post-communist governments, that reforming these institutions, while making them more efficient and effective, may also make them more costly to consumers. This occurrence provoked political reactions which, at the very least, may cost votes. Finally, there is resistance to these reforms from the providers, particularly teachers and medical personnel, fearful of possible adverse effects to themselves (Nelson 1998).

The importance of broad societal support for reform does not require justification. In the early nineties, a number of observers expressed quite pessimistic opinions as to the chances of the successful introduction of Washington-consensus reforms. They argued (a) that post-communist societies, having no experience with capitalism (no institutions, no entrepreneurial tradition, and so on), would be unable to adjust in a positive way, and (b) that, being accustomed to a paternalistic, egalitarian social order, they would not accept growing social insecurity, as well as social inequalities. Pessimists forecasted a de-railing of reforms, and/or the emergence of authoritarian politics. In fact, these fears have not materialized. Opposition to reforms emerged in Central Europe, but it did not stop the economic changes, nor did it endanger the democratic order (except in Slovakia). No doubt, the re-emergence of former communists, re-defining themselves as social democrats and winning electoral support, is proof of a certain dissatisfaction with the reform outcomes in countries such as Poland or Hungary. Extremists have not gained much support, however, and the social democrats (actually, coming from the ranks of the most reform-minded former communists) have kept the same type of macroeconomic policies, even if they slowed down the pace of reforms. More generally, the politics in Central Europe became 'normalized' in the sense that the number of important collective political actors decreased, as coalitions replaced a very fragmented political spectrum in the first years of transition.

Explaining the relatively peaceful process of transformation in Central Europe, Bela Greskovits (1998) stresses that this process 'created winners,' while at the same time neutralizing losers, particularly through an apt process of compensation (such as workers' inclusion in the privatization process). Creating winners means the emergence of a middle class which would support a further market transformation. Yet the issue of who might be included in the middle classes, how large they are, and what might be their likely political behavior, is quite complicated in Central Europe. In comparative terms, however – if other post-communist countries are taken into consideration – it may indeed be claimed that an embryonic middle class has emerged in this region. But there are losers as well. Their mobilization potential is often limited, as is the case with the rural population in Poland, which generally did not gain much. One may add that a slow process of dismantling the socialist welfare state, as well as hidden subsidies to inefficient state enterprises, which allowed them to keep workers on the payroll, might also have reduced social tensions – albeit at a certain cost in economic efficiency. On the ideological level, there is no clear, attractive alternative to the ideas of transformation, approximating the Washington consensus model.

To sum up what has been said about Central Europe, it is appropriate to say that the Washington consensus was followed more in rhetoric than in practice. Deviations, however, were related not so much to the ultimate model, as to the way it was followed. These deviations were not a product of a different world-view, but the result of a political situation and of a certain pragmatism. Gradualism was one such deviation. Another has been the application of elements of industrial policy, while preaching (as one of the Polish cabinet ministers said at the beginning of the nineties), that 'the best industrial policy is no industrial policy.' Such policy partly had a negative character – protecting 'sunset' industries for social and political reasons. But there has also been a sort of 'picking the winners,' when promising state firms were singled out for privatization. Yet another example is the very slow process of scaling down the socialist welfare state, done mostly for political reasons. Central European countries apparently managed to strike a proper balance in slowing down the change for political reasons, while at the same time still moving in the right direction.

In sum, the Central European countries, and perhaps the Baltic countries, seem to be on a convergence path with Western Europe. The picture looks different in the rest of the post-communist world. Bulgaria and Romania are much less advanced; reforms are carried out in an inconsistent stop–go way, seldom producing positive outcomes, while at the same time social costs are rising. This produces political tensions, particularly in Romania, and the recent miners' unrest is an example.

Even worse is the situation in Russia, and in post-Soviet East European states. In Russia, we deal not so much with failed or de-railed reforms, but rather with an emergence of altogether different, highly dysfunctional system (if a word 'system,' assuming some form of order and homogeneity, is appropriate). Russia seems to be on a route that diverges from the Western model. Despite several attempts at reforms (especially at the early stages of transformation), most of the macroeconomic indices reveal a disaster – growth is negative and inflation high. This is accompanied by an enormous rise in inequality and poverty, which makes Russia almost a Third World country, and by deteriorating social indicators, such as diminishing life expectancy. The picture that emerges from the statistics, is daily supplemented by press accounts of extremely grim social conditions in the Russian provinces. A market economy of a sort is developing, to be sure, both on the elementary level of bazaars and shops and in the form of large corporations. But the economic system is becoming a mixture of rampant, unregulated capitalism, in a large measure targeted on the exploitation of natural resources, and of remnants of unreformed state socialism. Privatization seems to have advanced substantially (in terms of the number of firms in non-state hands). This fact masks, however, a situation in which state assets have found their way into shady holding companies, established by people well connected to the old regime. Massive amounts of capital have been transferred abroad. The system is not only riddled with corruption, but is also perverted by organized crime ('mafiyas'), which apparently control significant segments of the economy. Violence, including killings as a way of 'disciplining' those targeted by organized crime, have become a norm. The state is in disarray, unable to collect taxes and to meet its basic obligations. The whole idea of transformation to capitalism is de-legitimized, while populist and extremist political movements are gaining popularity. The political system seems as dysfunctional as the economic one. After the financial crisis of late 1998, Russia was insolvent, and its fate depends as much on the doubtful ability of its élite to straighten out the reform process, as on the West's willingness to put up the necessary sums of money.

Russia is a case in itself, and a concern for the world because of its size, its former superpower status, and – last but not least – its nuclear arsenal. The pathologies mentioned might take an extreme form there, but they are present in other post-Soviet states of Eastern Europe, namely Belarus, Moldova, and Ukraine (Kuzio 1998). In Ukraine, foreign investment is around 1.4 billion US dollars, while it is estimated that up to 20 billion US dollars have left the country illegally since the country split away from the USSR. 'The most pernicious element of the crime phenomenon in Ukraine is the criminal–political nexus, the alliance among former Party elite members of the law enforcement and security apparatus, and gangs of organized criminality.' (Shelley 1999, p. 6). While Ukraine, despite its stagnation and corruption, at least preserves basic elements of the democratic system, Belarus under President Lukashenko has turned into a semi-authoritarian state, trying – within the economic sphere – to return to some form of command economy.

HISTORY MATTERS

We started with an observation that it is possible to classify postcommunist countries into three groups: those that are on trajectory of change which make them institutionally converge slowly on the Western model, those that are on a clearly divergent track, and those that appear to be drifting aimlessly. Central Europe and the Baltic countries appear to be on a route convergent with the West – although it is another question how long they will lag behind the West. Russia and Belarus, and perhaps Ukraine as well, are on a trajectory that is divergent from that of the West. It may also be the case with the Central Asian States. Finally, the Balkans (Romania and Bulgaria), and Moldova seem to be drifting aimlessly. When the question is asked as to why those patterns of change are so different, the easiest answer is that there was not enough good economic policy in the less lucky places. Indeed, economic advisers have tended to argue that if only proper deregulation would be introduced and correct macroeconomic policies set up, almost any country would have a good chance for growth and future prosperity. The relative success of Central Europe has often been cited as a proof of this argument. While agreeing that the Washington consensus (or post-Washington consensus) prescriptions are basically sound, one may ask, however, why was it that a number of leaders took them only with reluctance; and why in some cases (notably Russia) even when its leaders tried, did the prescriptions not produce the expected outcome?

Possible answers are that the less lucky countries did not have good economic leaders, or that challenges set off by reforms did not produce enough correct entrepreneurial response, or that – lacking the underlying institutional infrastructure – even correct policies could not produce positive outcomes. All of these answers are probably true. For success in economic transformation, it is important to have a high-quality political élite as well as an efficient state. It is also important that, in society at large, there are positive attitudes toward the market and capitalism, a readiness to take certain risks, as well as beliefs that individual enterprise and hard work can lead to personal success. Finally, the underlying rules of the game, sets of formal and informal rewards and punishments for individual behavior must be such – as Douglass C. North says – that they make for a convergence of the individual and the social rate of return.

All these conditions are very difficult 'to introduce,' as they are products of history. It is proper to recall the debate on the original emergence of capitalism in the West. Today, there is a consensus that emergence of capitalism was, in a sense, accidental – an outcome of the unlikely coincidence of ecological, cultural, and political circumstances, that occurred in late medieval Western Europe (Jones 1981; Braudel 1981–4). To put together a complete list of necessary conditions is, of course, impossible, but among other things such factors include the individualization of property, its protection by the state, the rule of law, an ethics of thriftiness, a high prestige of commercial activity. Nobody planned these institutions; capitalism was rather an unintended consequence of social actions, taken for different purposes. When Montsquieu argued for *doux commerce* – as Albert Hirschman reminds us – he had not done so in order to increase the wealth of nations, but to tame the passions of rulers. But, in effect, he contributed to an ideology, which made capitalism more likely. We are, of course, in a better position today, because – knowing more or less how capitalism works and what conditions are necessary – we may at least try to design institutions to transform countries in a proper way. And it is possible, to a degree, with legal-formal institutions. It is less so with those institutions which are informal, or embedded in local culture. It is possible to argue for the introduction of an independent central bank. It his hardly possible to persuade people to convert, say, to Protestantism.

In the West, where capitalism was invented, attitudes and institutions helpful for its operation developed spontaneously. If one speculates about the more profound reasons for the differences in degree of success that particular post-communist countries have had with the transformation to a market economy, it looks as if the proximity of the West – mental or historical perhaps more than spatial – helps. Even a cursory look at the history of Central Europe shows that it was much more exposed to the West than the rest of the post-communist world. Looking from the West, the countries of Central Europe are peripheral, but no doubt they are a periphery of the West (Chirot 1989). Contrary to Western Europe, most of Central Europe was outside the *limes Romanum* of Antiquity, but Christianity came there from Rome, and in the 13th century German colonizers brought in Western legal institutions. Universities were established in Prague and Cracow in the Middle Ages, and educated upper strata of society were formed within the Western intellectual tradition. Italy was a cultural model in the 16th century, to be replaced later by France. No doubt there were interruptions in the history of Western influence. Hungary fell under Ottoman rule in the 17th century, and Poland set itself on a somewhat divergent political track at the same time, inventing a dysfunctional republic of the nobility instead of the absolutism common in those times. Central Europe industrialized in the second half of the 19th century, the Czech lands achieving standards comparable to those of the West. Parts of Central Europe's territories were then under Western political rule – Hungary, Bohemia, Slovenia, and the south of what is now Poland under Austria, the west of today's Poland under Prussia. In the relatively lax conditions of the Habsburg monarchy, it was possible for political and ideological pluralism to develop; a certain pluralism was also possible under German rule, which taught respect for the *Rechtstaat* and raised literacy considerably. It is worth noting that in the Balkans those regions that were under Western rule for a considerable span of time – as was the case with Transylvania – show patterns of social and political behavior closer to the liberal and democratic ideas (cf. Daniel Chirot's chapter in the present volume, Chapter 5, pp. 103–22).

Under communism, Central Europeans kept many of their western traditions, and maintained closer contacts with the West than the rest of the post-communist world. (In the case of Poland, Stalinist isolation had lasted only for about six or seven years, between 1949 and 1956.) This is, however, more true in Poland, Hungary, or Slovenia, than in Czechoslovakia, which after the Prague Spring of 1968 suffered a long span of neo-Stalinism. For all its isolationism, the experience of 1968 seemed to bury whatever sympathies existed in Czechoslovakia for Marxism–Leninism, contributing at the same time to the emergence of the civil liberties movement of Charter 77. To give yet another small but important example: during all the years under communism, law students in Polish universities were obliged to take courses in Roman law and Latin. Poland and Hungary were also open to the Western ideas in several senses. Intellectuals were allowed to travel, and foreign books were translated. Marxism as an ideology was practically finished after 1968, and was gradually to be replaced by Western liberalism, with the help of numerous unofficial publications (Skilling 1989). Both Poland and Hungary have large expatriate communities, staying in close contact with the home countries. Both countries tried to introduce extensive market reforms – Hungary during the 1970s, Poland in the 1980s. Both maintained close economic contacts with the West, and both enjoyed a high degree of interest and sympathy of the West – because of the Hungarian revolution of 1956, because of the Polish Solidarity movement of 1980–81, and because of the two countries' relative Westernization. Both nations have had, since the sixties, a sizable private small-scale sector, and both have developed a large parallel economy. In the Polish case, in the eighties, it consisted to a large degree on work abroad and so-called 'commercial tourism' – Poles using opportunities of recreational travel abroad for semi-legal business purposes. Furthermore, Poland, apart for the advantages already mentioned, had a record of developing civil society. Its Catholic Church was independent even during Stalinism, and in the seventies, and particularly the eighties, a so-called democratic opposition developed, stressing human rights and civil liberties. In sum, it is possible to say that the Central European countries were relatively well prepared for the encounter with capitalism, both intellectually and culturally. Not surprisingly, their transformation has gone relatively smoothly.

This pattern contrasts with those areas of Eastern Europe, Russia included, and the Balkans, where there was less contact with the West, both before and after communism was introduced. Christianity came from Byzantium, not from Rome, and the idea of the separation of secular and sacred powers – and thus a possibility of creating a larger sphere for the individual – was absent. In addition, the Balkans were much longer under Ottoman rule than was the case in Hungary – almost until the end of the 19th century. While there were thin strata of Westernized intellectuals in these countries, they were much more separated from the rest of their societies than was the case in Central Europe. Before communism, there was relatively little experience of Western liberalism, of the rule of law, and of democracy. Industrialization and modernization, to the extent that they occurred, were even more confined spatially and socially than was the case in Central Europe. In pre-communist and communist Russia, modernization was most often not so much a result of spontaneous social forces, as of acts of government – with Peter the Great, Count Witte, Peter Stolypin, and Josef Stalin symbolizing this pattern. Although Russia had its phase of capitalist development between 1890 and 1914, these experiences were erased from social memory by the long history of Communism, spanning more than two generations (Malia 1994). In its early, Stalinist phase, Communism was particularly harsh and cruel, while in the long, late, Brezhnevite phase, it was corrupt and demoralizing. If one is persuaded by Tim McDaniel and many other writers that Russians tend to see their civilization as fundamentally different from the West, than there is no doubt that it is difficult to legitimize capitalism (McDaniel 1996).

The above argument on the role of the long-term influence of the West on the success of post-communist transformation – by necessity, sketchy and superficial – undoubtedly leaves a rather pessimistic impression about the chances for future successes for the less lucky countries. One should not be overly deterministic, however. Certain types of development may be more or less likely, but, as Alexander Gerschenkron (1962) had convincingly argued in another context, certain missing preconditions may be substituted by different social arrangements. Unexpected positive change happens in economic history as well, as we know from recent experience from East Asia and Ireland. While there is a lack of market infrastructure in many countries, it is not impossible to create this infrastructure, if incrementally. While certain cultural traditions may be adverse to Western capitalism, there is also the enormous attraction of consumer society, and liberal ideology finds a sympathy among many people as well. For the time being, various parts of the post-communist world seem to be taking divergent routes – but 'the time being' is not eternity.

NOTES

1. Regarding the tables in this text, one should note that data referring to Asian republics and Belarus are less reliable than those related to European countries.
2. The Third Way has interwar precedents. In Romania, for instance, corporatist theorists spoke of balancing monopoly capital against monopoly trade unions. One of the most prominent defenders of the Tierce Solution was the French economist François Perroux (1938). Hungarian populists in the 1930s were inspired by similar ideas, criticizing large-scale estates but making clear that they supported neither collectivization nor large-scale farming. Hungarian novelist Laszlo Nemeth resisted industrialization for industrialization's sake and defended an idea of 'Garden Hungary' (Szelenyi 1988).

REFERENCES

Amsden, Alice, Jacek Kochanowicz and Lance Taylor (1994), *The Market Meets Its Match: Restructuring the Economies of Eastern Europe*, Cambridge, MA: Harvard University Press.

Berend, Ivan T. (1996), *Central and Eastern Europe 1944–1994: Detour from the Periphery to the Periphery*, Cambridge, Cambridge University Press.

Blaszczyk, Barbara and Richard Woodward (eds) (1996), *Privatization in Post-Communist Countries*, Vols **1** and **2**, Warsaw: CASE.

Braudel, Fernand (1981–84), *Civilization and Capitalism*, New York: Harper & Row.

Chirot, Daniel (ed.) (1989), *The Origins of Backwardness in Eastern Europe: Economics and Politics from the Middle Ages until the Early Twentieth Century*, Berkeley: University of California Press.

Gerschenkron, Alexander (1962), *Economic Backwardness in Historical Perspective*, Cambridge, MA. and London, England: Cambridge University Press.

Gogala, Viljem (1999), 'Slowenia wraca do Europy Srodkowej' [Slovenia returns to Central Europe], *Rzeczpospolita*, March, 13–14.

Greskovits, Bela (1998), *The Political Economy of Protest and Patience: East European and Latin American Transformation Compared*, Budapest: Central European University Press.

Hirschman, Albert O. (1977), *The Passions and the Interests: Political Arguments for Capitalism before Its Triumph*, Princeton: Princeton University Press.

Jones, E.L. (1981), *The European Miracle: Environments, Economies and Geopolitics in the History of Europe and Asia*, Cambridge: Cambridge University Press.

Kochanowicz, Jacek (1997), 'Incomplete demise: reflections on the welfare state in Poland after communism', *Social Research*, **64** (4) (Winter).

Kolodko, Grzegorz (1999), *Od szoku do terapii: Ekonomia i polityka transformacji* [From shock to therapy: Economics and politics of transformation], Warsaw: Poltext.
Kornai, Janos (1980), *Economics of Shortage*, Amsterdam: North Holland.
Kuzio, Taras (ed.) (1998), *Contemporary Ukraine: Dynamics of Post-Soviet Transformation*, Armonk and London: M.E. Sharpe.
Malia, Martin (1994), *The Soviet Tragedy: A History of Socialism in Russia, 1917–1991*, New York: Free Press.
McDaniel, Tim (1996), *The Agony of the Russian Idea*, Princeton, NJ: Princeton University Press.
Milanovic, Branko (1998), *Income, Inequality, and Poverty during the Transition from Planned to Market Economy*, Washington, DC: The World Bank.
Nellis, John (1999), 'Time to rethink privatization in transition economies?', *Transition*, February.
Nelson, Joan (1998), *The Politics of Pension and Health Care Delivery Reforms in Hungary and Poland*, Budapest: Collegium Budapest, Discussion Paper Series, Discussion Paper No. 52.
North, Douglass C. (1990), *Institutions, Institutional Change and Economic Performance*, Cambridge and New York: Cambridge University Press.
Perroux, François (1938), *Capitalisme et communaute de travail*, Paris: Librairie du Recueil Sirey.
Poznanski, Kazimierz Z. (1996), *Poland' s Protracted Transition: Institutional Change and Economic Growth in 1970–1994*, Cambridge: Cambridge University Press.
Przeworski, Adam (1991), *Democracy and the Market: Political and Economic Reforms in Eastern Europe and Latin America*, Cambridge: Cambridge University Press.
Sen, Amartya (1997), 'Development thinking at the beginning of the XXI century', in L. Emmerij (ed.), *Economic and Social Development in the XXI Century*, Washington: IDB.
Shelley, Louise I. (1999), 'Organized crime and corruption are alive and well in Ukraine', *Transition*, February.
Szelenyi, Ivan (1988), *Socialist Entrepreneurs: Embourgeoisement in Rural Hungary*, Madison, WI: University of Wisconsin Press.
Skilling, H. Gordon (1989), *The Samizdat and an Independent Society in Central and Eastern Europe*, Columbus: Ohio State University Press.
Stiglitz, Joseph (1998), 'More instruments and broader goals: moving toward the post-Washington consensus', The 1998 WIDER Annual Lecture (Helsinki, Finland), Mimeo.
Szacki, Jerzy (1995), *Liberalism after Communism*, Budapest–London–New York: Central European University Press.
UN Economic Commission for Europe (1997), *Economic Survey of Europe in 1996–1997*, New York–Geneva: United Nations Economic Commission for Europe.
Williamson, John (1990), 'What Washington means by policy reform', in John Williamson (ed.), *Latin American Adjustment: How Much Has Happened?*, Washington, DC: Institute for International Economics.
Williamson, John (1993), 'Democracy and the "Washington Consensus"', *World Development*, **21** (8).
World Bank (1997), *World Development Report 1997: The State in the Changing World*, Oxford: Oxford University Press.
World Bank (1998), *World Development Report 1998/99: Knowledge for Development*, Oxford: Oxford University Press.

COMMENTS ON JACEK KOCHANOWICZ, 'TRAJECTORIES OF EAST EUROPEAN TRANSFORMATION: GLOBAL INFLUENCE AND LOCAL LEGACIES'

Larry Neal

First, let me present another overview of the transition process, comparing the levels of real Gross Domestic Product which the Central and East European transition economies have achieved since the collapse of their central planned economies after 1989. This is a series of Figures derived from the 1996 Transition Report of the European Bank for Reconstruction and Development that starts each country at a level of 100 in 1989 and updated from the versions that appear in my textbook on the economics of the European Union (Neal and Barbezat 1998).

These figures simply reinforce the argument made by Professor Kochanowicz, namely that Poland, alone among the transition economies, has managed to regain the level of output it had before the transition and to be on the kind of growth path expected of West European economies when they start from such a low level of per capita income. It is striking that all the economies experienced much the same decline in levels of output during the first five years

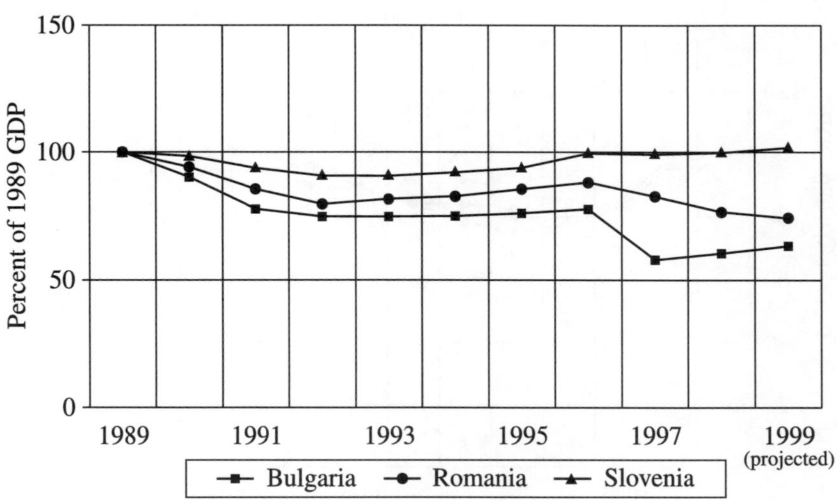

Source: EBRD (1996) and Neal and Barbezat (1998).

Figure 7.1 GDP in transition (1)

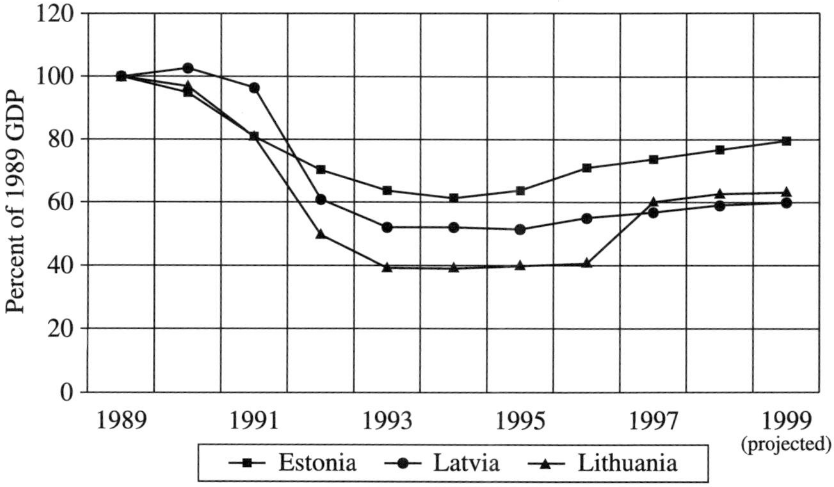

Source: See Figure 7.1.

Figure 7.2 GDP in transition (2)

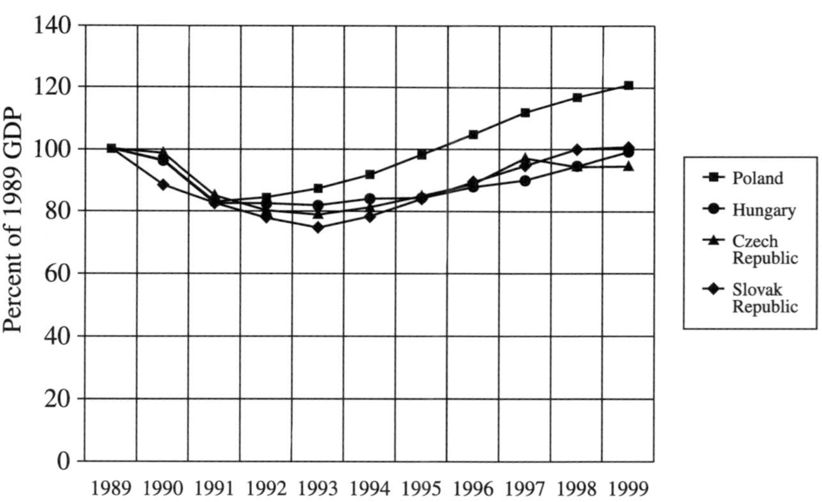

Source: See Figure 7.1.

Figure 7.3 GDP in transition (3)

following the collapse of the planning mechanism; the differences have emerged clearly only in the past five years. Even so, the decade that it has taken Poland to regain its pre-collapse level of output is not so impressive when we reflect that after the collapse of command economies in Europe following the end of World War I and World War II, it typically took only five years to regain their pre-war levels of output and to resume the pre-war growth path.

I want to pick up on one aspect of the argument made by Kochanowicz that, somehow, it was 'closer previous ties with the West' that helps account for the different transition experiences now. Why should this be the case for Poland and not for, say, Hungary or Romania? And, just how close were these ties for Poland? I recall one of our early Polish visitors contrasting the Polish bureaucratic élite with that of South Korea. He argued that the Poles received their training in Moscow while the Koreans had gone to the US. He also thought that the reform process would stagnate if the former Communists regained control of the government in the election of 1993. As it turned out, they did win control, but the Polish reforms and recovery continued on course, even as the transition began to falter in other Central and East European countries.

What then is so different about Poland? What makes their post-transition ties to the West so much more effective than those of, say, Hungary and Romania, two countries that promoted increased trading ties with the West before the collapse of the Soviet Union? For that matter, why is acceptance of western-style institutions taking so long and meeting so much resistance in East Germany? In short, what internal shock absorption mechanisms or institutions make some countries able to rebound from the shock of transition while other countries continue to stagger?

I would like to offer a conjecture that the nature of the dominant religion within a country or region is the critical factor. The very word, religion, after all, comes from the Latin verb 'religare,' to tie together things, places, people. If the dominant religion ties the majority of the people in a country to Western co-religionists, then it surely helps them cope with the shock of being suddenly opened up to western economies and being cut off from their previous source of external support. To see if there was anything to this wild idea, I tried to compare the religious make-up of the transition economies in Europe. To do this, I turned to the most secular, and therefore most objective, source I could think of, the CIA World Factbook, available on the Web. The results are in Table 7.7.

The connection between homogeneity of religion and relative success in transition is, I suggest, pretty striking. The exception may be Lithuania, with a population that is primarily Roman Catholic, but which seems to have faltered again after a strong rebound in 1997. Estonia's relative success, despite its religious heterogeneity, may be due in part to its contiguity with an existing EU country, Finland.

Why should a dominant Roman Catholic population be helpful in Eastern Europe when the popular impression is that the dominance of Roman Catholicism was actually harmful in Latin America? Perhaps in Central and Eastern Europe, the Roman Catholic religion offered a coherent monitoring and information structure that served as an alternative to the dominant Communist party. Such a continuing structure could lead to acceptance and trust by the population that the radical changes underway would bring positive outcomes for all or, if they didn't, that corrective measures would soon be taken.

Table 7.7 Religions in the transition economies

Poland

Roman Catholic 95% (about 75% practicing), Eastern Orthodox, Protestant, and other 5%

Hungary

Roman Catholic 67.5%, Calvinist 20%, Lutheran 5%, atheist and other 7.5%

Czech Republic

Atheist 39.8%, Roman Catholic 39.2%, Protestant 4.6%, Orthodox 3%, other 13.4%

Slovakia

Roman Catholic 60.3%, atheist 9.7%, Protestant 8.4%, Orthodox 4.1%, other 17.5%

Estonia

Evangelical Lutheran, Russian Orthodox, Estonian Orthodox, others include Baptist, Methodist, 7th Day Adventist, Roman Catholic, Pentecostal, Word of Life, 7th Day Baptist, Jewish

Latvia

Lutheran, Roman Catholic, Russian Orthodox

Lithuania

Primarily Roman Catholic, others include Lutheran, Russian Orthodox, Protestant, evangelical Christian Baptist, Islam, Jewish

Slovenia

Roman Catholic 70.8% (including 2% Uniate), Lutheran 1%, Muslim 1%, atheist 4.3%, other 22.9%

Romania

Romanian Orthodox 70%, Roman Catholic 6% (of which 3% are Uniate), Protestant 6%, unaffiliated 18%

Bulgaria

Bulgarian Orthodox 85%, Muslim 13%, Jewish 0.8%, Roman Catholic 0.5%, Uniate Catholic 0.2%, Protestant, Gregorian-Armenian, and other 0.5%

Source: CIA World Factbook. www.cia.gov/cia/publications/factbook.

Trust would be reinforced by the hierarchical structure of the church that extends into the West, which dominates the overall structure of that religion.

By contrast, the Protestant religions lack a hierarchical structure and the Orthodox lack external ties. Hence we have the Romanian Orthodox church in Romania and the Bulgarian Orthodox church in Bulgaria. The various Muslim groupings have the external ties, although not to the West, but they lack the hierarchical structure that would provide an effective alternative to the rule of Communist parties.

The argument above is quite independent of the particular theology of a given religion, as important as that may be for motivating the responses of individuals to external shocks. To me the important quality is the ligature that ties people of different locales, families, and languages into a relationship based on impersonal trust in one another. It is this ability to place trust in distant people who have no personal contact that enables, for example, open capital markets to develop for providing finance. It is not surprising then that the society which has the strongest basis for mutual trust in one another following the collapse of state socialism, should also have the strongest and most active stock exchange. The Warsaw Stock Exchange was the first to open in the transition economies, taking back its building that had been commandeered by the Communist Party for its headquarters after World War II. Moreover, the Warsaw Stock Exchange has been the first among the emerging markets of central and east Europe to recover from the common shock of the Russian default in August 1998. It is this financial marketplace where Polish and foreign stockbroker firms can put into effective operation the trust in one another's integrity that is needed to mobilize the financial resources of the West for the benefit of the Polish economy.

References

European Bank for Reconstruction and Development (EBRD) (1996), *Transition Report*, London: EBRD.

Neal, Larry and Daniel Barbezat (1998), *The Economics of the European Union and the Economics of Europe*, New York: Oxford University Press.

COMMENTS ON JACEK KOCHANOWICZ, 'TRAJECTORIES OF EAST EUROPEAN TRANSFORMATION: GLOBAL INFLUENCE AND LOCAL LEGACIES'

Alessandro Merli

The chapter by Jacek Kochanowicz provides an excellent overview of the transition of Central and Eastern Europe, especially from a historical and institutional perspective.

A comparative assessment of the economic consequences of the transition in the region is made difficult partly by the initial unreliability of statistics and partly by the different stages of the reforms in different countries. According to the most recent estimates by the EBRD (1999), only two or three countries have recovered the GDP levels of 1989. But, while 1989 is an important reference point as the watershed of political change, the choice of this starting date tells us nothing with respect to the progress of economic reforms. Some countries (Hungary, Poland) had already embarked on the path of reforms before 1989, others started later and then backtracked, and still others cannot claim to have started them in earnest even now.

As much as history matters, as Kochanowicz tells us, and geography matters too, they are very useful in explaining where these countries come from, but not necessarily where they are going in their process of transformation. It is therefore important that we focus as well on other determinants of the transformation, such as policy on the one hand and global influences on the other.

In the European context, a good example on both counts is Portugal in the 1980s and 1990s, a country with certain historical similarities with those of Central and Eastern Europe (small, closed economy, emerging from a long dictatorship) and possibly at a geographical disadvantage compared to them (Lisbon is further away in many respects from the core of Europe than Bratislava or Warsaw). However, sound policies implemented steadily for a decade and accession to the European Union have provided Portugal with a much speedier transformation than even the most successful Central and Eastern European economies.

The aspiration to be admitted into the EU and the international capital markets are indeed the two most powerful global influences on the transformation of Central and Eastern Europe. The enlargement of the EU to the East is the most obvious factor in the quickening of the transition both for its effect on policy (witness again the case of Portugal, but also of Greece and other late entrants) and its direct impact on trade and financial markets. On average, 52 percent of exports and 40 percent of imports of Central and Eastern European countries are with the Euro area.

As for the financial markets, the risk premium effect of EU enlargement is well demonstrated in Baldwin, François and Portes (1997). However, it is entirely possible that, if the less optimistic forecasts are proved correct, enlargement is delayed and some form of 'enlargement fatigue' sets in, affecting both policy and financial markets, generating a counterproductive effect on Central and Eastern European pretenders.

The influence of international capital markets cannot be overlooked and indeed other chapters in this volume (especially the one by Victor Bulmer-Thomas, Chapter 2) make a reference to it. This is not, however, because they are the most evident manifestation of globalization, and globalization – in Kochanowicz's line of reasoning – seems to lead to democratic capitalism almost by default. After all, globalization is a now-fashionable word, but hardly a new phenomenon. Private capital flows were at least as large, in relative terms, at the turn of the twentieth century as they are today. Their relevance as an ingredient of the economic success or failure of different countries and regions is, however, increasing, much more than that of the international financial institutions mentioned by Kochanowicz. The financial firepower of the IFIs is actually on the wane (in 1997 official flows were but a fraction of private flows) and even their influence on policy and the behavior of private agents is now hotly debated.

The countries of Central and Eastern Europe seem so far to have had only modest success in attracting capital flows. Foreign direct investment of $16 billion attracted by Central and Eastern European and Baltic states in 1998 was a record figure, but compares very poorly with Latin America. The privatization of Telebrás alone, in July 1998, produced revenues of about $20 billion, largely from foreign investors. Figures for other categories of capital flows tell a similar story about the difference between Latin America and Central and Eastern Europe, as shown in the BIS annual report (1999).

From a short-term perspective, being marginal players in the international capital markets may have helped Central and Eastern European countries to weather the financial turbulence of 1998–99 better than more involved participants, such as Latin American countries. However, looking forward, it is impossible to see the institution-building that Kochanowicz rightly puts at the core of the transformation process not being deeply altered by the concurrent pressures of the EU and the global financial markets.

References

Baldwin, R., J.F. François and R. Portes (1997), 'The costs and benefits of Eastern enlargement: the impact on the EU and central Europe', *Economic Policy*, 24.

Bank for International Settlements (1999), *69th Annual Report*, Basle.

European Bank for Reconstruction and Development (1999), *Transition Report Update*, London.
International Monetary Fund (1998), 'Impact of MEU on selected non-European Union countries', Washington (mimeo).
Zecchini, S. (ed.) (1997), *Lessons from the Economic Transition. Central and Eastern Europe in the 1990s*, Dordrecht: Kluwer Academic Publishers/OECD.

8. Neo-liberalism revisited in the light of the Brazilian crisis

Lawrence S. Graham

During the last two decades profound changes have been sweeping through Latin American economics, politics, and government. In economics we have moved from an era in which state control of the economy was common throughout the region to one where market economies now dominate. In politics, we have moved from a world in which authoritarian regimes were in the majority to one where democratic regimes are in the ascendancy. In government, we have moved from a context in which the state controlled the development policy agenda to one where initiatives outside government have more and more weight in determining economic outcomes. In this new setting, reform initiatives are under way throughout much of the world. Reductions in the labor force are occurring in industrial as well as industrializing societies; attention is being given to the establishment of smaller and more professional public services, and new thinking in public management is in vogue, emphasizing cooperation with organizations outside government, especially when it comes to tackling social issues for which public resources are all too limited.

THE REFORM WAVES

In responding to these challenges, three different waves of reforms can be identified in Latin America. First, with the exception of Cuba, authoritarian regimes have undergone liberalization or collapsed, and democratic transitions have gained the upper hand. Where the military was dominant and economic performance did not measure up to expectations, pressure grew to return power to civilian leaders. During the 1970s, especially in South America, military governments built technocratic alliances in which macroeconomic projections supported by economists in key ministries and private-sector business leaders looked to the state to create the conditions for sustained economic growth, and to maintain order. In this setting the state largely dictated the conditions under which foreign investment operated, stimulated internal economic growth through establishing close ties between business and government, and accelerated import-substitution industrialization in efforts to make internal markets function more effectively. Yet in very few cases did these policies produce the economic breakthrough these technocratic alliances promised through the concentration of economic decision-making in the center, political control of dissidents, and public investment projects in which the state encouraged cooperative undertakings with domestic and foreign firms. In each of these settings inflationary pressures accumulated, either gradually (as in the case of Mexico) or rapidly (as in the case of Argentina and Brazil), until major adjustments had to be made in the distribution of political power.

There is, of course, one notable exception to these generalizations: Chile. There military rule coincided with an economic reform agenda based on a return to markets and extensive privatization, so that by 1980 an economic recovery had taken place. But in 1981–82 the military and economists within the government faced a new crisis. Their success in economic reform had left the country so vulnerable to international economic forces that when there was a precipitous drop in the price of copper, a severe economic recession set in that threatened to bankrupt domestic firms and banks. In this setting the government's response was to bring the state back in, by designing and implementing a new set of policies increasing the government's capacity to regulate oscillations in the market and to protect domestic firms and banks from international pressures which threatened their survival as productive enterprises, while reducing the size of government. In this regard, Chile anticipated what has become a new development elsewhere in the latter part of the 1990s: the coupling of state reform with economic reform in order to produce the structural changes necessary to sustain markets. Within Chile, these reforms are summed up in the shift in economic policymaking from the 'Chicago Boys' to the 'Santiago Boys.'[1]

At the same time, during the 1980s, the South American military began to look for ways to exit from their leading role in determining the course of public policy. Faced with internal dissension as a consequence of major differences over economic and social policies and protest movements by opponents of military rule that could not be suppressed indefinitely, the military opted to return to the barracks. How this was accomplished varied widely from country to country.

In Argentina, where it had become apparent that the country could be governed neither by suppressing the Peronistas nor by controlling their return to active participation in public life, the military first attempted to remove civilian dissidents by force and then by elimination. Finally, when it became evident that they could not suppress civilian political forces indefinitely, they embarked on a war with Great Britain to regain control of the Falkland Islands and to rally civilian support behind a largely bankrupt regime, only to discover that they were no match for British armed forces. As a consequence, civilians returned to power by virtue of the collapse of a military defeated in armed conflict.[2]

In Brazil another pattern emerged. There the military maintained its cohesion as an institution, but continued and increasing civilian opposition to authoritarian rule convinced the military and its civilian allies eventually that there was no alternative but to open up the political system to participation by the opposition and to schedule open elections to determine the country's leadership. Failing to control the transition, even though they were successful in postponing direct elections of the President until 1989, they secured sufficient prerogatives in the subsequent democratic regime to block punishment of military and civilian leaders involved in the previous regime. From this base they moved on to influence politicians and to elect individuals who would protect their interests.[3]

Coincidental with these political openings and the euphoria surrounding the return to democratic rule, the new round of leaders coming to power during the 1980s and 1990s all had to engage economic issues without delay. Chile's return to democratic rule constituted the last case in South America of prolonged authoritarian rule, when in January 1989 General Augusto Pinochet signaled to the armed forces that they should return to the barracks. But he did so in the context of consolidated market reforms that could be matched nowhere else in Latin America. Similar to the Brazilian case, but much more openly and directly, military and civilian hardliners secured a pacted democracy in which the right was guaranteed continued representation in congress and the military was placed beyond effective civilian control. In any event, except for Chile, the newly constituted democratic regimes that emerged in the 1990s as legitimate governments throughout South America all faced severe economic problems requiring drastic measures. In most cases government had a difficult time securing economic stabilization programs.[4] A second wave of reforms ensued that entailed major adjustments in economic policy.[5] However, the manner in which these new regimes engaged the new economic orthodoxy focused on the supremacy of markets and privatization initiatives varied widely. In most quarters economic policies which were identified with neo-liberalism took precedence. However, since these economic reforms required Draconian measures and entailed severe social dislocations, only Chile, under authoritarian rule, and Mexico, with its long-standing authoritarian practices, were initially able to implement these new policies successfully, until a new style of 'reform-mongering' politics began to emerge within the context of democratic governance.[6]

Mexico was different from the three South American cases discussed above in that it had been ruled by a dominant single party, controlled by civilians, for decades. There the regime likewise experimented with political reforms designed to open up politics in such a way as to secure sustained rule by the Institutional Revolutionary Party (PRI). But, as in other instances of authoritarianism, the most dangerous moment in maintaining the PRI's hegemony came with the attempt to change the power base of the regime by engaging economic transparency: the Party discovered too late that transparency in economics had inevitable consequences for transparency in politics. Although the PRI continues to control the presidency, there can be no doubt that a democratic transition is also underway there, because the opposition parties took control of congress in July 1997.

During the 1990s, the pace of economic reform accelerated and, with the exception of Cuba, this took place while engaging democratic practices. All these governments – new democracies as well as the older established democracies of Costa Rica, Colombia, and Venezuela – found the neo-liberal emphasis on free markets and a reduced role for the state in determining economic outcomes, unavoidable. Once again, however, the new orthodoxy in economic thought did not necessarily produce immediate and direct results in reviving long-term economic growth. Generally what became known as the Washington Consensus, reflecting US hegemony throughout the Western Hemisphere, focused on halting acute inflation, stimulating privatization initiatives, and attracting new foreign investment as governmental regulations were cast aside.[7] Yet economic stabilization packages, respecting supply and demand mechanisms, were not sufficient to engender sustained economic growth nor to deal with severe economic dislocations. This necessitated additional adjustments in economic policymaking.

By the mid-1990s a third wave of changes in the political economies of the Latin American states was underway.[8] The focus of this round of changes in the economy and the state has been on wider and more fundamental institutional reforms, involving the construction of new economic institutions and/or major restructuring of existing ones to strengthen the market mechanism. Since these reforms have involved vested interests, the reform of political institutions likewise has become necessary. While downsizing the state remains a priority, this third wave of changes has had to acknowledge the limits of economic stabilization programs and has had to adopt the view that in order to attain new economic growth, the state must become an actor in the economy, albeit with a much more limited role than in the past. This has involved regulating extremes in market fluctuations, setting monetary policy, and determining social policies designed to offset inequities in society. This active role assigned to the state, first, in dealing directly with poverty alleviation and, second, in bringing the state back in as a crucial actor in stimulating new economic growth, is nowhere better recognized than in the 1991 and 1997 World Development Reports.[9]

THE BRAZILIAN CASE

The Latin American country which perhaps best illustrates the convergence in the new political economy, with its emphasis on markets, democracy, and institutional reform is Brazil, under the presidency of Fernando Henrique Cardoso. In this regard, it is important to see Brazil in a new light. While Brazilian specialists have long called attention to the size and diversity of Brazil, which make it the largest country in the region – in geography, in population, and size of its economy – what is different about the present era is that Brazil's continental dimensions have come to match its economic weight and influence within South America, despite periodic crises. Matching its growing economic importance is its regional political influence, a development not generally perceived or understood within the United States, either in established governmental or private sector circles. Like the US a century earlier, Brazil in the 1990s has been making its first real entrance into world politics as a regional power, though not through its military projection, but rather by virtue of the sheer weight of its economy within South America. Consequently, be it with an expanding economy or one that is in recession and in crisis, Brazilian developments now have reverberations outside national borders, not just in adjacent South American areas but in North America and Europe as well.

As in the circum-Caribbean, where US action or inaction has an immediate effect in that region, so too today in South America no country can afford to calculate its options internationally without taking a growing Brazilian presence into consideration. This shift has been enhanced by the development of Mercosul (in Spanish America: 'Mercosur'), the regional trading association composed of Brazil, Argentina, Uruguay, and Paraguay as full members, and Chile and Bolivia as associate members. Increasingly, despite the attractiveness of Argentine markets, foreign investors are finding in Brazil an advantageous setting for situating themselves in South American markets, because by locating in Brazil they access both the Brazilian domestic market (the largest in Latin America) and the other Mercosul countries, in those areas where trade agreements now provide for a single common market – one that is being built according to the model of the European Union, with all its delays, constraints, yet continuing progress.

During these years, the government (that is, the two administrations of Fernando Henrique Cardoso, 1995–98 and 1999–2002) has followed the new orthodoxy in structural reform. First, it achieved economic stabilization through the *Plano Real*. Then it undertook an aggressive program in privatization that required political reform as well, that is, amending the constitution in those areas where public enterprise has been linked most closely with economic nationalism. Subsequently, once Cardoso had achieved reelection, his government increased its fiscal control over the states by restricting their indebtedness. In the process of implementing these changes and confronting the problems of controlled exchange rates, Brazil became the Latin American country most in the international news during the first quarter of 1999. Its devaluation of the *real* on January 13, the economic turbulence that ensued as a consequence of the decision to float the country's currency on the 15th, and its acceptance of a *de facto* loss in the value of the *real*, mounting initially to approximately 40 percent, had reverberations throughout the world. Yet, while the government acted quickly and decisively and by late March had a new international agreement in place, a correction in the value of the *real* proved to be only temporary, and by the second half of the year it was fluctuating between 1.8 and 1.9 *reais* to the dollar. Cardoso's political image quickly passed from a positive assessment in the polls to an increasingly negative one. He ran into more and more opposition in congress, and an image of national stalemate and stasis replaced the earlier one of reform and change.

Background

Cardoso's mixed record, however, mirrors the ambiguities that have long been present in Brazilian politics and economics. Redemocratization in Brazil in the mid-1980s did not get off to a good start, either in terms of consolidating democratic practices or in encouraging free markets. Rather, the Brazilian transition during these years appeared to be captured by those forces most resistant to change.[10] Groups favoring the comfortable corporatist practices of the past – in which government and domestic firms maintained a symbiotic relationship – were not disappointed. Extensive and rampant clientelism reappeared, through which newly elected officials at the federal, state, and local level provided public employment for their electoral cadres. During these years the opposition movement, which had been so successful in mobilizing mass protests against authoritarian rule, became demoralized. First, their leader, Tancredo Neves, who was designated via indirect elections to take power in March 1984, died on the eve of assuming office. Replacing him was his vice president, José Sarney, a man identified with the more liberal wing of the authoritarian coalition. He had been put on the ticket to balance the reformist and opposition politics with which Tancredo Neves was identified, as the leader within the state of Minas Gerais of the main opposition party, the PMDB. Second, the newly elected congress (which also served as the constituent assembly) became hopelessly bogged down on the issue of constitutional reform. The initial draft of the constitution gave real voice to democratic forces within Brazil, only to become watered down with amendment after amendment. What emerged in 1988 was a complex document that protected vested interests, while reaffirming the government's commitment to human rights and democratic liberties. Third, the first direct presidential election in Brazil in more than 25 years, that of 1989, brought to power a politician from the small northeastern state of Alagôas, Fernando Collor de Mello, who, despite his appeal as a young, attractive candidate, once in office carried corrupt practices and patronage politics to a level hitherto unknown in Brazil. In December 1992, rather than face impeachment proceedings stemming from extensive corruption, Collor resigned. Fourth, the man who became president as a consequence of his position as vice president, Itamar Franco, was yet another national leader tied to the status quo. With inflation running well above 1000 percent annually, Brazil drifted aimlessly.

Cardoso's Reforms

At the moment when Brazil bordered on economic collapse, Itamar Franco appointed Fernando Henrique Cardoso as finance minister and charged him with the need for immediate action. In contrast to previous finance ministers, who had devised schemes that promised extensive economic reforms only to see their plans frustrated by anti-reform forces, Cardoso produced an economic stabilization plan that worked: the *Plano Real*. The ending of acute inflation opened the way to major economic reforms – reforms that placed Brazil on the road to a free market economy. The economic turnaround produced by Cardoso led in turn to his candidacy for president and his election at the end of 1994.

On taking office in January, 1995, Cardoso embarked on a strategy of constitutional reform, one designed to remove those articles in the 1988 Constitution which limited the impact of the privatization policies to which he was committed. As he approached the end of his first term of office in 1998, Cardoso had achieved economic success by embracing markets and aggressively pursuing privatization, to the point that Brazil was now engaged in the largest privatization process in the region. With economic stabilization measures in place and the economy open to foreign investment without constraint, foreign capital poured into Brazil to take advantage of the sale of numerous public enterprises and the opening of the Brazilian economy.

To achieve the constitutional reforms necessary to sustain his commitment to privatization, Cardoso built and maintained a broad-based coalition that brought together reformers and moderates on the center-right. Key to this coalition was an alliance among his own party, the PSDB (the Brazilian Social Democratic Party), the PMDB (the Party of the Brazilian Democratic Movement), and the PFL (the Liberal Front Party), to which can be added a number of other smaller parties and representatives in Congress, sufficient to muster the three-fifths vote required, in each house, in two successive votes in each chamber. The core of this coalition held throughout Cardoso's first term of office. The accomplishments were notable, not just in introducing privatization into public enterprises hitherto identified with Brazilian economic nationalism (electricity, telecommunications, and oil and gas), but also in gaining support for amending the constitution, so that he could stand for a second term. In the latter case, however, the trade-off in votes led to the writing of an amendment in which all incumbent executive officers could stand for re-election, not just the president but governors and, in the next round of mid-term elections, mayors. Central to the success of this strategy was Cardoso's ability to sustain the support of the PFL and its leader, Antônio Carlos Magalhães. What was notable about this success was Cardoso's ability to build and sustain a broad-based coalition that could deliver the necessary votes on crucial issues.

As national elections approached in late 1998, the country had to face a major challenge in the global economy, beginning in August. With a badly overvalued currency and with increasing doubts that the government could maintain its fixed three-tiered exchange rate by gradual adjustments, capital flight ensued. Given the government's commitment to maintaining the free flow of capital, the result was a dramatic fall in the country's foreign reserves during the last four months of 1998, as well as sharp increases in domestic interest rates, in the region of 45 percent. While there were splits within the cabinet, Cardoso's decision was to maintain the value of the *real* until he was re-elected and had his new ministerial team in place. Thus on 13 January, 1999, the government announced a devaluation of the *real* and on the 15th made the decision to allow the currency to float on international markets.

Consequently, as Cardoso moved into his second term, Brazil faced major difficulties. He had already been criticized for implementing market reform and privatization at the expense of social reform. And, as the new budget took shape, it was clear that there would be even larger cuts in health, education, and social welfare. By July, major splits within the government and problems with the administration's coalition in Congress produced an alliance that was notably farther to the right, and more dependent than ever on the support of Antônio Carlos Magalhães and his PFL. The immediate cause of this shift was political realities. While the coalition supporting Cardoso in Congress consisted largely of the same parties, in the new Congress, the conservative PFL had the most representatives, followed by a PMDB whose centrist position produced more ambiguity than ever. In third place was Cardoso's PSDB, with Michel Temer as president of the Chamber of Deputies. The coherency of the PFL and Magalhães' leadership as president of the Senate meant that he had become an even more important political factor in Cardoso's second administration. The net result was Cardoso's increasing dependence on Magalhães for legislation and a virtual closing off of social legislation. Negotiating further reforms ceased to be an option.

REFORM-MONGERING IN BRAZIL: SUCCESS AND FAILURE

While Cardoso's sustained commitment to economic and political reforms within the framework of democratic politics was notable during his first administration, his difficulties with sustaining reform initiatives in his second administration calls attention to the limits of 'reform-mongering' in democratic Brazil. Increasingly lacking power in Congress to support further economic reform, Cardoso has had to opt for a strategy in which further economic reform has been occurring only by allowing market forces to determine economic outcomes. Herein lies the anomaly of an economy that generally continues to do well, despite increased unemployment and economic dislocations, linked to protests and demonstrations against the economic changes underway.

In such a context, it is important to understand that, while the Brazilian transition to democratic rule is over, one should not conclude that Brazil is a consolidated democracy. The more appropriate terminology for the present moment is a 'democratic situation,' analogous to the moment for which Juan Linz developed the term 'authoritarian situation' almost two decades ago.[11]

Nevertheless, notable progress has been made over the last ten years in increasing the commitment to democratic rule. Thus, before one raises the specter of a populist breakthrough reversing current government action, as has been the case with Hugo Chávez's government in Venezuela, or the scenario of Cardoso having to govern by opting for a 'state of exception' (which under Brazilian practice permits a president to govern by decree law), one should keep in mind the major landmarks established to date:

1. before Cardoso took office, the indictment of a president (Collor de Mello) for corrupt electoral practices and illicit fundraising by the Brazilian Chamber of Deputies, as well as his resignation, rather than facing trial in the Senate
2. the design and implementation of a major change in economic policy during the Franco government under Cardoso's leadership as finance minister, its continuation under Cardoso as president, and its expansion and enhancement during his first term of office
3. the achievement of major structural reforms. These included amending the Brazilian constitution to expand the scope of privatization initiatives, and getting congress to increase the federal government's control over fiscal and monetary policy, including curbing the right of states to incur debt in early January 1999.

During his first term, Cardoso accomplished his reform agenda by building a multi-party coalition, based on the realities of the distribution of power within the states and regions and centered around reformers and moderates in the congress. To achieve this, Cardoso and his advisors had to abandon ideological commitment to the social democratic principles to which they were committed while in opposition, and instead to construct a center-right coalition. The key factor in this strategy was attracting and keeping the support of Antônio Carlos Magalhães. While this necessitated reshaping reform priorities to match the more conservative preferences of the PFL during the first administration, it became more apparent in Cardoso's second administration that this support had been purchased at huge cost, once the PFL emerged with the largest bloc of representatives in congress in the December 1998 elections. In 1999 the PFL's power obviated any chance of a meaningful government social agenda, once devaluation and fiscal austerity had been accepted as priorities.

The dilemmas Cardoso faced in his first administration have been compounded in his second. His response to those dilemmas – the use of the power of the president to bypass congress, except when he needed the support of a broad-based coalition to amend the constitution – suggests that bypassing the legislature will become increasingly necessary in his current term. The power to issue provisional measures (*medidas provisórias*) without consulting Congress, however, remains controversial. Those critical of these actions see them as inherently authoritarian and a legacy of the era of military rule. Others argue that this is a necessary power to make presidentialism work in Brazil, given the fluidity of political parties and the continual shifting of alliances in a complex multiparty system. To require the president to go to Congress on every aspect of his policies would paralyze government. Those defending this practice also maintain that this is a limited power since it can be overridden by a simple majority.

During his first administration, Fernando Henrique Cardoso balanced his use of provisional measures with congressional initiatives to sustain the votes he needed on crucial legislation. When the government encountered decisive opposition, it had to come back with a revamped package to obtain the necessary votes; this was the case with social security reform. In his second administration, however, the President has had to face reversible policy changes. Yet, the current political game continues to be a search for the proper mix between reform initiatives and acceptance of the political realities linked to the PFL's ascendancy. Despite discontent with the government's continued commitment to economic restructuring through privatizations and the use of market forces, a more fundamental reversal comparable to the election of Hugo Chávez in Venezuela at the end of 1998 remains unlikely. To date, the left in Brazil has been unable to win control of the presidency. In the last three elections, the leading contender on the left has been the leader of the Labor Party (the PT),

Luís Inácio ('Lula') da Silva. While he argued in each contest for a more aggressive social policy to deal with the enormous inequities of Brazilian society, he has failed to win. Meanwhile, Brazilian federalism since 1988 has effectively decentralized power and passed much of the capacity to act to state and local governments, unlike the relatively centralized governments of Spanish America. Where reformist agendas can be mounted at the subnational level, it has been possible to make major changes. This can be seen in the enormous difference between the PT's effective governance in the state of Rio Grande do Sul and its capital, Porto Alegre, and the Party's limited capacity to build an effective alternative national coalition in a national arena in which ever-larger urban areas are underrepresented. At the federal level continued 'muddling through' with economic restructuring is likely, despite political protest. Meanwhile, pressure for social change will be partly siphoned off into other arenas at the state and local levels.

CARDOSO COMPARED AND CONTRASTED WITH OTHER LATIN AMERICAN PRESIDENTS

Analysis of these uncertainties in Brazil can be enhanced by surveying the impact of neo-liberalism elsewhere in Latin America on domestic politics. Four country cases involving presidential rule, market and structural reforms and democratization warrant comment in particular: Chile, Argentina, Mexico, and Venezuela. The premise underlying the use of these cases is that, while there is a common set of economic policies identified with market-oriented strategies, the policy reforms encountered within Latin America vary widely as a consequence of national politics within the context of what can be called a 'consolidated state system.'[12] The pace of economic reform, democratic initiatives, and shifts in the relations among parties, presidents, and legislatures have responded to very different national realities.

In Chile, since redemocratization, the administrations of Patricio Aylwin and Eduardo Frei Ruíz-Tagle (the son of former President Frei, 1964–70) have consolidated the market reforms initiated during the Pinochet era, by completing privatizations initiated more than a decade earlier. The last remaining area of direct state involvement in the economy was the social security system. By the end of the Aylwin administration the privatization of the social security system had been completed; Chilean nationals were offered a wide range of market-based retirement accounts, and the government now regulates these investments to protect these accounts from speculation. In terms of monetary policy, as the Asian crisis progressed, the government tightened up exchange controls over buying and selling dollars in Chile, as a way of regulating currency speculation.

At the international level, realizing that it was highly unlikely that the NAFTA agreement would be expanded and that Chile would be given further access to North American markets, these administrations negotiated closer cooperation with Mercosul, while retaining Chile's associate member status. They did so on the grounds that Chile's commitment to a market-based economy and free trade is much further advanced than that of the member countries.

On the political front, democratic rule has continued to be reinforced. Congress has devoted attention to human rights abuses and disappearances that occurred under Pinochet, with the government adopting the stance that individual cases must be adjudicated within the country's court system. In social policy, while the public monies available for poverty relief have been limited, attention has been focused on decentralizing social service delivery and increasing social programs in poor neighborhoods. Much slower has been the pace in establishing civilian control of the military. But, as the Frei administration drew to an end in 1999, one could note the establishment of the accountability of military officers to the civil courts in the cases of human rights abuses committed before the return of democratic rule. The leading instances in this case were the arrest and the trial of General Manuel Contreras Sepúlveda in May 1995 and the arrest of Brigadier General Pedro Espinoza Bravo the next month, followed by his trial and conviction. While the issue of their imprisonment after conviction dragged on many more months, the government's insistence on their serving prison sentences eventually prevailed over military resistance. Likewise, despite tensions in early 1998, Augusto Pinochet did step down on 10 March as commander in chief of the country's armed forces and, over the opposition of the left, assumed his place in the Chilean Senate as a senator for life. In short, despite opposition from the right and the left in Chilean politics toward the moderate policies of the Frei administration, the political pact held, confirming the commitments to democratic rule under civilian leadership. While there remains a chasm between the right and the left in Chilean politics over the Pinochet era, the resolution of issues according to democratic norms has progressed to the point that, within the Democratic Alliance, not only was Socialist Ricardo Lagos chosen as the presidential candidate, but also, after winning, he took office without military opposition.

In Argentina, President Carlos Menem advanced market-based strategies and privatizations during his two terms to such an extent that commitment to a market-based economy there now seems to be consolidated. As a consequence, although Brazil's devaluation of 13 January 1999 adversely affected the Argentine market, Argentina's economic position appeared to be much more secure than Brazil's. Despite the fact that Argentina's economic reforms remained linked to the personal style of Menem, under President Fernando de la Rua it is unlikely that Menem's reforms will be significantly reversed.

Nevertheless, while both markets and democratic practices look good in Argentina at the moment, these developments are much less secure there than in Chile, as a consequence of past legacies: the reliance on personalities rather than parties in politics, the weakness of political party organization, and the continued dominance in Argentine politics of the Peronistas and Radicales as movements rather than disciplined party organizations.[13] But meanwhile Argentina's restructuring of its armed forces continues to move ahead, as a new professionalism through international cooperation and good relations with the US military has gone a long way toward changing the internal attitudes of the officer corps. This stands in contrast to a Chilean military that remains captured by its authoritarian legacy, the prestige accorded to Pinochet, and its focus on internal military affairs. As a consequence, while Chile is further along than Argentina in consolidating democratic rule by civilians, neither country can be classified as a consolidated democracy. Both, as is also the case with Brazil, have what might be called 'democratic situations' in which current international and domestic conjunctural circumstances sustain democratic rule. All three countries remain vulnerable to prolonged economic and political crisis. Again, Juan Linz's observation regarding the failure to institutionalize authoritarian rule in Brazil during the 1970s, for which he coined the term 'authoritarian situation,' can be adapted for the 1990s: although enormous progress has been made toward the redemocratization of the Southern Cone countries, their regimes seem no more consolidated than were the preceding authoritarian regimes of the 1970s.[14]

The same may also be said of Mexico. There economic liberalization and the shift to market-based strategies to secure economic stabilization and structural adjustment reforms began earlier under civilian-led authoritarian rule. All this took place in what was virtually a single-party system: in Mexico the mass political base of the governing Institutional Revolutionary Party (PRI) gave the regime far more legitimacy than was ever the case with the right-wing authoritarian governments of the Southern Cone during the 1980s. Also, despite the opening up of Mexican politics in the early 1990s, a good case can be made for saying that Mexico's democratic transition did not really begin until July 1997, when, in off-year congressional elections, the opposition parties in coalition secured control of the Mexican congress for the first time. In short, the convergence of economic and political reform policy has followed a very different sequence in Mexico. There economic reforms preceded political reforms, and a much longer period of political liberalization was required before Ernesto Zedillo, the current president, made public his commitment to democratization, both as head of state and head of the still-dominant PRI. There also, but for very different reasons, the movement toward a full market economy appears to be as decisive as has been the case with the Southern Cone countries, where Chile remains the farthest advanced. Likewise, a strong preference for democratic rule has remained salient under Zedillo, in his role as President since 1995 and as the Mexican leader who has made the clearest commitment to democracy. But movement toward a consolidated democratic regime remains as uncertain there as in the foregoing cases. It is far from clear that the major opposition parties, the conservative PAN and the more left-oriented PRD, will succeed in developing an alternative political and economic agenda that will earn either of them the presidency in the next election.

For this reason, the case that offers the most in the way of contrast with the reformist policies now dominant in Brazil is Venezuela, where a major rupture has occurred in national politics. The political and social strains engendered by its neo-liberal economic reforms have upset the consensus and the procedures built up over the years for resolving conflict within Venezuelan society. Whereas Brazil fits very much within the framework of the democratic situations and market strategies dominant in the Southern Cone, Venezuela does not. Brazil's delays in implementing economic and political reforms are largely a consequence of its more complex and larger federalist institutional context, whereas Venezuelan politics during the 1990s highlight the social explosion and the significant realignment in national politics that is likely to occur elsewhere, if government fails to deal decisively with the growing gap between rich and poor. Should elected governments fail to respond to the mobilization of the excluded poor, who make up a major segment – if not the majority – of the population in each country, social conflict is a real possibility. The 1998 election of Hugo Chávez, the former military officer who led a failed military coup in 1992 to overthrow the President, Carlos Andrés Pérez, has shaken the Venezuelan political system to its foundations.

What remains to be seen is whether or not Venezuelan democracy can survive the accession to office of a leader and his followers identified with a radical alternation in politics and a break with the economic and political strategies of the past. Here the reference to Przeworski's analysis in an earlier endnote warrants reconsideration. Although civilian control of the military does not appear to be at issue in the realignment underway in Venezuelan politics, what is not clear is how Chávez will fulfill his electoral promises, and whether Venezuelan economic élites will accept his new social and economic priorities. Will they accept a redistribution of income and wealth, will they frustrate or deflect the President, or will they favor a repressive coup, as did the economic élites of Chile when faced with the Marxist government of Salvador Allende in the early 1970s?

The Draconian economic measures implemented in the early 1990s to deal with Venezuela's economic crisis and to engender market-friendly economic strategies, created a series of social explosions which ultimately led to widescale attacks on the prevailing political order. After more than three decades of constitutional government, younger officers – sensitive to the economic hardships imposed on the poor by liberalization measures – attempted two coups in 1992.

Subsequently, as the economic crisis worsened and bank failures loomed, the government accepted conditions set by the IMF and World Bank for economic liberalization. To make matters worse, corruption charges against President Pérez, whose term would end in 1994, reached such intensity that he was impeached. The political fallout of these scandals was a thorough discrediting not just of Pérez but of his party Acción Democrática (AD). Furthermore, the other major party, COPEI, was also implicated. As a consequence, when Rafael Caldera, the longtime leader of COPEI, won the 1993 elections, he did so not primarily as the standard-bearer of his party, but as the candidate of a coalition rejecting the traditional two-party dominance of national politics. But Caldera was no more able than Pérez to revive the economy and respond to demands for greater equity.

As the line-up of presidential candidates firmed up during 1998, it became clear that the public had rejected the two traditional parties, for neither of the leading candidates identified themselves with them. The presidential election at year's end resulted in a resounding majority for Hugo Chávez, the ex-military officer who most identified with the demands for social justice. Though his followers drafted a new constitution in 1999 and got it approved by a majority of voters it is still unclear to what extent Chávez will pursue a new social agenda for those long marginalized in Venezuela's oil-based economy.

CONCLUSIONS

In Chile, Argentina, Mexico, and Venezuela, as in Brazil, the division between those who have participated in the economic progress and those who have remained at the margins is long-standing. All five experienced earlier cycles of sustained economic growth that placed them in the upper tier of the developing world without redressing major income disparities between the social groups and regions of each country. At best, the economic liberalization reforms of the 1980s did little to improve this basic configuration.

After Chile, Mexico was the first to embrace the neo-liberal ideology. The response to the 1982 peso crisis, when the decision was made to move from a fixed exchange rate to a free market rate, was acceptance of neo-liberalism: economic stabilization, followed by structural adjustment policies designed to remove constraints on markets and promote privatization. The president most identified with the opening up of the Mexican economy was Carlos Salinas de Gortari (1988–94). During these years Mexico was identified as a success story, albeit these economic changes coincided with enormous political changes as

Mexico also began to open up politically. While limited at the outset, as the government relaxed controls over the media and gave the opposition greater freedom to participate in elections, a political transition began which the PRI could no longer control. The new transparency in politics brought to light an enormous degree of corruption, the consequence of which was that Salinas ended his presidency in the midst of a major scandal, calling into question the quality of his leadership and the expectation that the PRI would ever relinquish its hold on power. Yet by the time Ernesto Zedillo took office, following a round of political turbulence and assassinations of prominent Mexican officials not seen since the revolutionary era, it was clear that a political transition was underway that was in many ways more profound than Mexico's economic transition. While there are still questions about how legitimate the presidential election of 1994 was, by the time mid-term congressional and local elections occurred in July 1997, it seemed clear that attempts at controlling elections were at an end. As a consequence, the opposition was able to secure control of the Chamber of Deputies. More than any other political change, the 1997 elections signaled that a full-fledged democratic transition was underway.

Let us return from this digression to the Brazilian case: whereas Brazil had been the laggard in responding to the new orthodox economic thinking in the 1980s and early 1990s, once Fernando Henrique Cardoso was elected in 1994, he moved Brazil toward neo-liberalism. With stabilization in place under the Real Plan, which he had developed as finance minister, Cardoso inaugurated one of the most ambitious privatization programs in Latin America, culminating in the 3.4-billion-dollar sale of the state-owned regional development authority, the Companhia do Vale do Rio Doce (CVRD) in the first half of 1998. Even Petrobrás, the state-owned oil company which had long been untouchable, found it necessary to open the oil sector to foreign competition and to privatize many of its downstream services.

Cardoso's success in inaugurating economic and political restructuring during his first administration, however, stands in contrast with his failure to sustain this restructuring since. But this is in part a reflection of the democratic framework within which he has had to function. Although democratic rules had been secured before he took office, more than the Mexican presidents Cardoso has had to contend with a rapidly changing political environment. Initially he was able to come up with a politically feasible strategy achieving economic and political reforms, precisely because the issue of how the political system was to be opened up had already been resolved. But once conservative forces gained the upper hand in the Chamber of Deputies and especially in the Senate, he also had to confront political realities constraining his capacity to initiate further reforms.

What the Brazilian case shows, together with the others, is that much depends on the ability of Latin American presidents to balance internal and external political and economic forces. Mexico initially had an easier time making unpopular economic reforms under its authoritarian system. But further progress in Mexico's economic reforms is now tied to a very complex but much more democratic political process.

Although Cardoso is weaker as a second-term president and speculation abounds concerning his successor, market reforms are likely to continue because of the absence of viable alternatives. Here the Venezuelan case is more instructive. It shows that in a democratically structured society, a president can come to power publicly committed to a radical redistributionist program. But Chávez is almost certain to find his options sharply limited by financial constraints, internal and external.

My own conclusion is that the Brazilian experience, in which Cardoso first gave priority to working out new governance practices that could be broadly embraced, and then engaging economic reform, has proved effective compared to other paths, despite the short-term costs of delayed reforms. Yet the Brazilian case has provided no easy escape from the dilemmas of reform-mongering in a federal republican system – one saddled with a divided government and weak support in congress.

The Latin American states are alike in their dependency on international investments and capital transfers if their domestic economies are to remain afloat in the first decade of the next century. The development of Brazil, and, by extension, that of the other Latin American republics, is probably most likely to be secured by acknowledging the reality of their dependency on policies linked to associated development. The irony is that the very patterns of 'associated-dependent development,' of which Cardoso was so critical in the past and which he rejected in favor of 'constructing paths toward socialism,' have been exemplified more clearly than ever before in the policies of his first administration – namely, in building new relationships among government, private firms, and not-for-profit organizations, while strengthening external ties with multilateral and international actors.[15]

In short, 'reform-mongering' in Brazil did make it possible for a while to design and implement new economic, political, and social programs, only to become mired again in the realities of practical politics when conservatives regained control of congress. Yet, Brazil in the 1990s is very different from the Brazil of the 1970s in one fundamental respect: groups and individuals struggling to make democracy work have now been able to constitute and reconstitute viable alternative coalitions committed to reform and change. There the struggle to promote democratic practices, in substance as well as in procedures, continues to offer viable alternatives at the federal, state, and local levels.

NOTES

1. Alfred Stepan (1985).
2. Carlos H. Waisman (1989).
3. Thomas Bruneau (1992).
4. The book which best sums up this first round of economic reforms and the divergent politics which ensued is Joan M. Nelson (ed.) (1990).
5. Derick W. Brinkerhoff (1997).
6. This term 'reform-mongering' is borrowed from Albert Hirschman, who called attention to the prospects for democratic reform in Latin America in the early years of the Alliance for Progress. See Hirschman (1963) and especially Daniel Triesman (1999).
7. John Williamson (ed.) (1994).
8. Brinkerhoff characterizes this third wave of reform as one that has profited from the policy dialogue and reform experience of the past decade; the emphasis is now on policy as a process. Reformers in this context, he writes, recognize 'the complex interactions among policy statutes, target populations, implementers, and sociopolitical environments' and make social and institutional factors more central to the analysis of policy issues (Brinkerhoff 1997, p. 6).
9. World Development Report (1991), especially Chapter 7, 'Rethinking the State,' pp. 128–47, and World Development Report (1997).
10. Frances Hagopian (1992).
11. Linz argued that an authoritarian regime was not consolidated, because it lacked an ideology which could replace the legitimacy accorded to democratic rule. Analogously, Adam Przeworksi argues that, although there is a general preference for resolving the issue of who should rule at the ballot box, electoral outcomes have not generated a setting in which economic conflicts have been resolvable within a democratic framework; further, there is no certainty that the military has been placed effectively under civilian control. See Przeworski (1991) (see especially p. 106), and Juan J. Linz (1973).
12. Lawrence S. Graham (1998). The case used to illustrate this point is Mexico.
13. For a more extended discussion of these legacies which argue against democratic consolidation in Argentina, see Marcelo Cavarozzi (1992).
14. Linz (1973).
15. For the quoted phrases, see Fernando Henrique Cardoso (1973) and Cardoso and Enzo Faletto, (1979), p. xxiv.

REFERENCES

Brinkerhoff, Derick W. (1997), 'Integrating institutional and implementation issues into policy decisions: an introduction and overview', *Policy Studies and Developing Nations*, **5**, New York: JAI Press, pp. 1–18.

Bruneau, Thomas (1992), 'Brazil's political transition', in John Higley and Richard Gunther (eds), *Elites and Democratic Consolidation in Latin America and Southern Europe*, New York: Cambridge University Press, pp. 257–81.

Cardoso, Fernando Henrique (1973), 'Associated-Dependent Development', in Alfred Stepan (ed.), *Authoritarian Brazil*, New Haven, CT: Yale University Press.

Cardoso, Fernando Henrique and Enzo Faletto (1979), *Dependency and Development in Latin America*, Berkeley: University of California Press.

Cavarozzi, Marcello (1992), 'Patterns of elite negotiation and confrontation in Argentina and Chile', in John Higley and Richard Gunther (eds), *Elites and Democratic Consolidation in Latin America and Southern Europe*, New York: Cambridge University Press, pp. 208–36.

Graham, Lawrence S. (1998), 'The state in retreat in the administrative field', in Menno Vellinga (ed.), *The Changing Role of the State in Latin America*, Boulder, CO: Westview Press, pp. 149–62.

Graham, Lawrence S. (1999), 'New dynamics in economic restructuring: cross-national patterns in regional accommodation and the Brazilian response', 3rd International Conference on Technology Policy and Innovation, Austin, Texas, LBJ School of Public Affairs, 30 August–2 September.

Hagopian, Frances (1992), 'The compromised consolidation: the political class in the Brazilian transition', in Scott Mainwaring, Guillermo O'Donnell and J. Samuel Valenzuela (eds), Issues in Democratic Consolidation: *The New South American Democracies in Comparative Perspective*, Notre Dame, IN: University of Notre Dame Press, pp. 243–93.

Hirschman, Albert O. (1963), *Journeys Toward Progress: Studies of Economic Policy-Making in Latin America*, New York: Twentieth-century Fund.

Linz, Juan J. (1973), 'The future of an authoritarian situation or the institutionalization of an authoritarian regime: the case of Brazil', in Alfred Stepan (ed.), *Authoritarian Brazil*, New Haven, CT: Yale University Press, pp. 233–54.

Nelson, Joan M. (ed.) (1990), *Economic Crisis and Policy Choice: The Politics of Adjustment in the Third World*, Princeton, NJ: Princeton University Press.

Przeworski, Adam (1991), 'The games of transition,' in Scott Mainwaring, Guillermo O'Donnell and J. Samuel Valenzuela (eds), *Issues in Democratic Consolidation: The New South American Democracies in Comparative Perspective*, Notre Dame, IN: University of Notre Dame Press, pp. 105–52.

Santiago Nino, Carlos (1996), 'Hyperpresidentialism and constitutional reform in Argentina', in Arend Lijphart and Carlos H. Waisman (eds), *Institutional Design in New Democracies: Eastern Europe and Latin America*, Boulder, CO: Westview Press, pp. 1612–74.

Stepan, Alfred (1985), 'State power and the strength of civil society in the southern cone of Latin America', in Peter B. Evans, Dietrich Rueschemeyer and Theda Skocpol (eds), *Bringing the State Back In*, New York: Cambridge University Press, pp. 317–43.

Triesman, Daniel (1999), 'Hirschman on Reform', in *APSA-CP: Newsletter of the Organized Section in Comparative Politics of the American Political Science Association*, 10: I (Winter 1999), pp. 10–13.

Waisman, Carlos H. (1989), 'Argentina: autarkic industrialization and illegitimacy', in Larry Diamond, Juan J. Linz and Seymour Martin Lipset (eds), *Democracy in Developing Countries: Latin America*, Boulder: Lynne Rienner Publishers, pp. 59–109.

Williamson, John (ed.) (1994), *The Political Economy of Policy Reform*, Washington, DC: Institute for International Economics.

World Development Report 1991: The Challenge of Development, New York: Oxford University Press.

World Development Report 1997: The State in a Changing World, New York: Oxford University Press.

COMMENTS ON LAWRENCE S. GRAHAM, 'NEO-LIBERALISM REVISITED IN THE LIGHT OF THE BRAZILIAN CRISIS'

Eduardo Fernández Delgado

The success of the Plano Real in putting an end to the inflationary process in Brazil provides Professor Graham with the opportunity to examine the leadership and political skills of Fernando Henrique Cardoso, the current President of Brazil and author of the strategy. After achieving economic stabilization President Cardoso was able to introduce market-oriented reforms while preserving democratic rule.

The results of these measures can be fully appreciated in the rise of the rate of growth of the economy, as well in the weathering of the Asian Crisis. Also on Cardoso's behalf one should add the confidence of foreign capital and multilateral agencies in his handling of Brazil's economic policy.

Unfortunately much more cannot be said on the impact of those same reforms on the living conditions and well-being of a large proportion of the population. The increasing percentage of Brazilians living below the poverty level and the growing inequality constitute a danger to social stability.

Although the chapter focuses on the Brazilian case, Graham also considers the experiences in Argentina, Chile, Mexico and Venezuela in providing a broader picture of Latin America's return to democracy. As in Brazil, the authoritarian regimes of Argentina and Chile were able to step down smoothly, while in Mexico the PRI initiated an internal democratization process. In those countries rampant economic disarray, growing social unrest, and mounting political pressures explain the change in regime and mark the beginning of the transition process to democracy.

Despite differences in timing, Argentina, Chile, Mexico and Venezuela reacted to the problems left behind by the authoritarian regimes by embracing the neo-liberal paradigm. Since then, those countries have been struggling to enhance the supremacy of the market while eliminating the distorting intervention of the State. Special emphasis was given to adjust fiscal deficits and misguided monetary policies. According to the neo-liberal recipe, it was not possible for the market to work well unless the ongoing macro imbalances were eliminated.

Despite the good results achieved initially (the elimination of inflation and the decline of balance of payments problems), deeper economic problems and social unrest have revealed the inability of the market alone to promote sustainable economic growth and equitable societies. As Joseph Stiglitz (1998) bluntly put it, the Washington Consensus failed because of its confusion of means with ends. Since then it has been recognized that there is a need to make market policies compatible with social justice.

Paradoxically, it was the supporters of the neo-liberal paradigm who discovered that it was necessary to bring the State back in, albeit a more efficient State, with well-defined tasks and largely led by technocrats. Mexico and Chile were first off the blocks with a commitment to a set of structural reforms that emphasized economic gains at high social costs. Both being under authoritarian regimes, political reforms leading toward the consolidation of democracy suffered. In Mexico there is still some uncertainty as to the degree to which the PRI bosses really want to depart from old political practices in the face of growing competition from the PAN and the PRD. Chilean democracy faces a test of its institutionalization if the next president emphasizes greater social justice and income equality.

In sharp contrast to Mexico, Venezuela shows the type of explosive social situations that are occurring wherever the conditions of the least favored have been worsened by market-oriented reforms. Likewise, large social groups are emerging in Colombia, Ecuador, and even Brazil, sharing a complete disregard for the political system and a growing skepticism about the market's ability to redress their grievances.

In light of these experiences, Graham arrives at the critical question being asked in academic, political and business circles: would Latin American countries under democratic rule ever be able to implement a set of reforms that permits them to achieve economic growth *and* better living conditions of the poor, who constitute a majority of the region's population?

The vast majority of the people in the southern cone countries are deeply committed to democratic solutions. They have not forgotten the suffering associated with the denial of civil rights and economic failure brought in by previous authoritarian regimes. However, in the northern cone of South America (Colombia, Venezuela, Ecuador and Peru), and to some extent in Brazil, there is a growing belief, especially among upper income-receivers, that democracy is a costly luxury, and that it might be appropriate to follow the Chilean path to economic reform.

It is under these circumstances that Cardoso's consensus building – reform-mongering – is presented by Graham as counterweight to authoritarian practices.

Certainly, the Brazilian experience and especially the immense efforts in building political coalitions by President Cardoso to advance economic and political reforms could be a lesson for countries in similar predicaments. However, a brief look at the determinants of this political practice and its achievements will help to assess its relevance for the transition and consolidation of democracy in Latin America.

Cardoso's 'reform-mongering' cannot be fully understood without taking into account Brazil's political system, and in particular the institutional weakness of the parties not on the 'left.' Mainwaring (1999) provides a picture of the high volatility of these parties, their weak roots in society and limited legitimacy, their feeble organization and individualistic nature and their lack of discipline and loyalty, which finally results in the fragility of party support for the legislative agenda of the president. The result is the continuing proclivity of the Brazilian political regime, quite common in Latin America, to build short-lived coalitions, mostly by granting State favors.

Moreover, the proliferation of political parties, promoted by recent institutional changes, increases the difficulties of establishing a coherent government program, consolidating the traditional policy bias in favor of high and middle-income groups. This explains the growing mistrust of political parties that appear everywhere in Latin America. Rampant corruption of party leaders, a final consequence of the weak institutionalization of parties, noted by Mainwaring (1999), finally triggers social upheaval and political disruption like those recently observed in Venezuela and Ecuador.

Under these circumstances, Cardoso's success in stabilizing the economy and introducing the structural reforms is quite remarkable. It says a lot about Cardoso's abilities to maneuver politically. Nonetheless, these same factors contribute to explain the tremendous difficulties faced by the regime in its attempts to move beyond the 'quick fix' stage. Certainly, the facts tend to confirm the concern expressed by Nelson and others (1989) at the beginning of this decade about the ability of the post-authoritarian regimes to solve the social and economic structural problems associated with the transition process.

While Brazil's transition process is usually associated with economic success, it has also meant widening disparities in living standards and increases in absolute poverty. According to the UNDP report (1999), 28 percent of Brazil's population is living below the poverty level. Brazil's efforts to reduce the shortfall in the human development index value have been less than those realized in Argentina, Uruguay and Peru. Moreover, the ranking in terms of human development (79) is well below Brazil's possibilities as the ninth economic power in the world. Not surprisingly, Brazil shows the worst income distribution in the world as measured by the ratio between the GDP per capita of the richest 20 percent to that of the poorest 20 percent.

Moreover, despite several efforts made by Cardoso to introduce a comprehensive fiscal reform, it is not yet clear who is going to bear the brunt of the fiscal adjustment. The resilience of fiscal deficits and consequently pressure for foreign resources aggravates the dependency of the economy on foreign capital, finally threatening the efficacy of the Plano Real, as the recent devaluation showed. High interest rates and equally volatile exchange rates may slow down the rate of the economic growth, provoking increasing unemployment and social tensions.

These results should not shock anyone. As has been noticed repeatedly since Marx, political, economic and social institutions cannot avoid reflecting the power structure of the society from which they originate. The lack of effective political representation indubitably contributes to the assertion of such a tendency. Until now, it could be said that the democratization process has favored the policy-making of the traditional ruling élite.

Notwithstanding the positive picture presented by Graham, there does not seem to be a future for the type of personal reform-mongering shown by Cardoso and Menem as an alternative to traditional Latin American authoritarian regimes. Personality cults add to an already fluid political environment swinging outcomes either way, as the Menem case shows in Argentina.

Yet, despite the limitations of reform-mongering, this short review of the democratization process in Latin America does not necessarily lead one to despair. A careful reading of Graham's chapter allows for some hopeful insights into the re-entry of the masses into the political arena.

Contrary to what some fear about the collapse of democracy, there is much to be learned from what recently happened in Venezuela. After an unsuccessful coup attempt, Chávez reached the Presidency at the head of a social movement in a clean democratic contest. This is the result of Chávez's commitment to address the demands of the political majority for social justice. Similar lessons can be derived from the commitment to social progress of Argentina's Alianza coalition and the consequent election of Fernando de la Rua to the country's presidency, and from the choice of socialist Ricardo Lagos as candidate for the center coalition in Chile. There seems to be a trend in Latin America for political parties and coalitions to gain political muscle by upholding social causes which may bring some balance to the current uneven struggle. This is a radical change which was probably not expected by either the backers of neo-liberalism or by its foes.

This is a highly risky turn to the left, which has grim antecedents in many countries of the region. These include outcomes that vary from populist movements, passing from the strengthening of patronage and clientelistic bondage to the return of military cadres. However, it also presents the opportunity to match the privileged treatment of the few against the plight of the majority of the population in Latin America.

Politics in democratic societies means the search for consensus among conflicting interests and opinions. What we are about to see in several Latin American countries is the rapid consolidation of a political market where people want to be better represented. With more equitable representation, politics is likely to produce fairer responses to collective problems. As incipient as it may be, it looks like a better alternative than the reigning neo-liberal model.

However, for the successes of the democratization process two complementary factors are needed: a favorable international environment and the institutionalization of the rules of the game. On the one hand, the open support for democratic rule given by the United States and the multilateral agencies should be preserved. On the other hand, the élites must practice self-restraint and not turn to the military to avoid undesired policies. In such circumstances there could be a region-wide wave of reform-mongering where social justice and equality gain the upper hand.

References

Mainwaring, S.P. (1999), *Rethinking Party Systems in the Third Wave of Democratization. The Case of Brazil*, Stanford: Stanford University Press.

Nelson, J.M. (ed.) (1989), *Fragile Coalitions. The Politics of Economic Adjustment*, Washington, DC: ODC.

Stiglitz, J. (1998), 'Towards a new paradigm for development strategies, policies and processes', (1998 Prebisch Lecture at UNCTAD, 19 October), Geneva, Switzerland.

United Nations Development Program (1999), 'Human Development Report 1999', Oxford: Oxford University Press.

COMMENTS ON LAWRENCE S. GRAHAM, 'NEO-LIBERALISM REVISITED IN THE LIGHT OF THE BRAZILIAN CRISIS'

Mary Arends-Kuenning

In his chapter, Larry Graham examines the experiences of Argentina, Brazil, Chile, Mexico, and Venezuela with political reform and economic reform in the 1990s. He focuses on the case of the Cardoso administration in Brazil. First of all, he argues that Brazil has made great progress in the last ten years in developing democracy, so that now the country is in a 'democratic situation' – democratic rule has not been consolidated, but the prospects for a future democratic state are bright.

Second, he argues that Cardoso's strategies have been the most successful in implementing a neo-liberal agenda, compared to the other Latin American countries. Prospects for success with economic liberalization and with expanding democracy are most favorable when the political changes precede economic changes. Chile and Mexico present cases where economic liberalization occurred before necessary political changes. In Brazil, first democracy developed through events such as Fernando Collor's removal from office, Itamar Franco's presidency, and Cardoso's election. It was only after Cardoso secured political support and built coalitions that he attempted to liberalize Brazil's economy through policies such as privatization of large state-run enterprises. However, in Cardoso's second term, economic and political reform has been slowed by the increased strength of the conservative parties in Congress.

The chapter raises many questions. After reading about Cardoso's skillful political maneuvering, one question that arises is, what precisely do we mean by democracy? Is it the rule of law? Brazil's record in this respect is mixed. An important moment for Brazil's political development was the indictment and resignation of Collor, which upheld rule by law. Cardoso accomplished a sweeping constitutional reform that sought to make states accountable for their spending. However, Cardoso also changed the constitution so that he could run for another term of office, perhaps taking a cue from Alberto Fujimori in Peru and Carlos Menem in Argentina. Keeping power was more important than setting a legal precedent.

In a Latin American context, is an essential part of democracy having civilians control the military? In Brazil, the military ruled from 1964 until 1985. The chapter affirms that military interests had enough power within the democratic regime to block any accusations of wrong-doing in the military regimes. The military also managed to influence politicians who would represent their interests. So, effectively, the military seems still to be above civilian control. Is democracy the ability to make economic changes like pegging the currency to the US dollar without being turned out of office? This would seem to be a very narrow definition of democracy. Or by democracy do we mean that grassroots organizations share power with the traditional élites? That all groups are represented in the political process? It appears that the left has not been a part of Cardoso's coalitions. What is happening with groups like the Movement of the Landless (MST)? Is Cardoso engaging or ignoring them? Although Graham does mention that Cardoso's social programs and ability to work with the left have been constrained by the recent electoral victories of conservative parties, did Cardoso ever make a strong effort to engage the left and bring about social reform?

Should a definition of democracy include addressing the formidable social debt of Brazil? Brazil has one of the most unequal distributions of wealth in the world, with the wealthiest 10 percent of the population owning 48 percent of the income. The bottom 10 percent has only 1 percent of the income, according to the US State Department. Educational levels also lag behind other nations with similar levels of GDP per capita – the average 18 year old male has 5.6 years of schooling, and the average 18 year old female has 6.5 years. These figures vary greatly by region, with the northeastern states faring especially badly. What progress has Cardoso made in addressing this 'social debt'?

The increase in the power of the conservative parties indicates Cardoso's political problems. The Brazilian voters did not elect representatives who were committed to addressing the problems of income inequality and insufficient education. Cardoso failed to convince voters of the importance of these issues, or he refused to spend political capital to get social policies passed. He did expend political capital to change the law and run for a third term. Certainly, controlling inflation helped the entire economy, although some evidence suggests that the poor are not as negatively affected by inflation as the middle class.

Finally, the question of Cardoso's democratic legacy will obviously depend on what happens after Cardoso leaves office. Are economic and political reforms dependent on his particular skills as a negotiator? Does Cardoso represent a move away from the personalism that has affected Latin American politics so profoundly in the past? Is Cardoso associated with a strong political party, and will the coalitions he has forged endure after he is gone?

9. The Russian oligarchs: not your typical robber barons

Marshall I. Goldman

I

It is widely accepted that the transition, as it is called in Eastern Europe, or liberalization, as it would be in Latin America, will bring with it a reduced government involvement in economic matters and a more effective operation of the economy. By reducing the scope of political patronage, non-government and independent policymakers are more likely to base their decisions on economic rather than political or personal criteria.[1] That brings with it greater efficiency, higher productivity and rates of economic growth, and more widespread prosperity. This does not guarantee a higher standard of living for everyone in a society, but that certainly is a possibility, and in many countries it has indeed happened. Just such expectations explain why, after the collapse of communism, Boris Yeltsin's commitment to economic reform and a market were so widely applauded both within and outside Russia.

The key elements of this reform effort, just as in other countries undergoing similar moves to the market, are price liberalization and the privatization of state assets. Since price reform and privatization are central to all such efforts, it might appear, superficially at least, that the process in Russia should not have been very different from what went on elsewhere in Eastern Europe and Latin America. However, this was definitely not the case. Seventy years of communism and the fact that the market in Russia had only just begun to take shape prior to World War I meant that the transition process would evolve in a markedly different way from that taking place in countries with a market infrastructure already in place, partly in place, or in place at one time but now dormant. In Poland, for example, the transition, while problematic during the early months after it began in January 1990, quickly took off and by the late 1990s Poland was the fastest growing country in Europe. Proponents of similarly rapid reform in Russia insisted that like Poland, by 1992 the Russian economy – although in a deep sleep for many decades – was ripe for transition. All that it would take was for a princess to come, kiss the sleeping prince and he would awake from his trance ready to go. The problem, however, was that after seventy years of not only a ban but also the suppression of all forms of market activity under communism, the prince was not dormant, he was dead – and no amount of kissing would revive him. As a result, the transition in Russia was not only a failure, but it resulted in changes that in many ways resulted in no improvement, and in some respects such changes have made future retro-fitting reform all the more difficult. Privatization in particular was a disaster.

Privatization in Russia is a major exception to the conventional wisdom that privatized enterprises are necessarily more efficient and productive than state owned enterprises. That does not necessarily mean that countries that were once communist cannot privatize successfully. In Poland, privatization was a notable success. But in Russia, privatization became an instrument by which a select few 'oligarchs,' as Russians call them, managed to seize ownership of what had been valuable state properties at a fraction of their real value. In some cases, these oligarchs were former government officials and in other cases, private businessmen, many of whom had been arrested for economic crimes in the Soviet era. The difference in how privatization was implemented in Poland and Russia highlights what can happen when privatization is handled in the wrong way. Privatization in the period of transition, when and how to do it, and when and how not to do it will be the focus of this chapter.

Privatization that is widely accepted by the public is almost a contradiction of terms. As we shall see, Poland comes close to being an exception. Resentment is likely to be particularly bitter when it is a communist country that is doing the privatizing. Inevitably, privatization will result in the creation of a small group of suddenly very rich people – the new managers, and in the case of Russia, a narrow circle of new and super-rich oligarchs. That is not to suggest that in the communist era there was perfect or even approximate equality. The party and government hierarchy or *nomenklatura*, as it was officially termed, had very sharply defined access to services and privileges such as special stores, homes, cars, travel, and even medical care. As inegalitarian as that may have been, that was a flow of privileges, not a stock; the communist élite had little in the way of net worth or wealth. The difference after privatization is that in Russia today there is not only a sharp differentiation of flow or access to services and consumption, but also of stock or net worth. Thus five Russian oligarchs made the *Forbes Magazine*'s list of the world's 200 richest billionaires on 6 July, 1998. This is all wealth acquired since 1987, at which time none of them had a net worth more than $20 000. Moreover, most of the assets they now possess once belonged to the nation as a whole and with rare exceptions were appropriated or snatched by the current owners for nothing or, at best, a fraction of the true value.

Unlike the robber barons in the US, however, few of the Russian oligarchs seemed to feel it was wise to keep all of their newly acquired stocks and assets inside Russia. Thus there was a massive outpouring of capital; according to some estimates, it exceeded $1.5 billion a month. Nonetheless, the fact that they could strip those assets and convert them into flight capital is a form of asset control. This was something that rarely happened in the Soviet era when factory directors (and for that matter even the highest ranking party and government officials) may have had control over the flow of income but were unable to dispose of the assets for their or their heirs' personal consumption.

It would be misleading to argue that such daylight theft was unique to the countries that made up the former Soviet Union – far from it. Privatization in Latin America has frequently resulted in similar abuses. On 17 March, 1999 an article in the *Wall Street Journal* recounted how anger at earlier privatization efforts in Mexico hampers current privatization, 'Many lower class Mexicans see the privatization binge of the early 1990s as having enriched a few and impoverished the rest. That is particularly so in the case of the country's banks, sold off in the early 1990s to a handful of well connected businessmen.'[2] Substitute Russians for Mexicans and the article could come close to describing what happened in Russia, including the subsequent paragraphs which went on to describe the chaos that followed Mexico's (Russia's?) currency devaluation. In Mexico, as well as Russia, the devaluation led to the collapse of many of the banks, but rather than let them die, the Russian government stepped in once again to rescue many of the banks' owners. They did this despite the fact that many of the bankers looted their banks. But in contrast to the protected bankers, most ordinary depositors ended up with little or nothing.

That is not to say that if they had only tried harder, Russian privatization could have been designed so that everyone was allocated an equal share of the new wealth. That probably would have necessitated renationalization. But there is little doubt that despite initial assertions about how successful the Russian process was,[3] there is now widespread acknowledgement that it was a disaster, and indeed, an alternative approach such as the one in Poland might have resulted in far less abuse and inequity. We will first examine the Russian experience and look at why it went so wrong, and contrast that with the Polish effort, an approach which should serve as a model for all future privatization procedures.

II

As they look back at the mess they have made, those in charge of the Russian privatization effort justify their approach by insisting that if they had not acted as they did, Russia may well have reverted to communism. The architect of Russia's privatization efforts, Anatoly Chubais, explained that when he began the process in 1992, there was widespread resistance to his efforts.[4] The factory directors who had considerable influence in the Supreme Soviet were dead set against privatization, because they correctly perceived that it would result in a loss of their power and privilege. In addition, there seemed to be no widespread consensus among the public as to what direction to take. After 70 years of communism, there were a substantial number of Russians (as much as 25–30 percent consistently voted for a return of the communist party) who seemed to prefer the old central planning system. This more or less equaled those who strongly supported the switch to the market. Under the circumstances, Chubais felt that his first priority was to build up a larger constituency with a vested interest in privatizing state enterprises. If not, the managers of state enterprises and communist members of the Supreme Soviet would dig in their heels; thus, there would be no privatization and the entire system would remain dominated by the state.

Chubais' first goal, therefore, was to create as large a block of supporters for privatization, and as quickly as possible. One way was to allow factory directors and their workers to gain easy access to a controlling share of their enterprise's stock; in effect to make them stake-holders. In addition, Chubais also announced that each Russian, regardless of age, would be issued a voucher at a nominal charge but with a face value of 10 000 rubles. That voucher would entitle the holder to exchange it for a share of stock in a state enterprise or some other tangible piece of property. Alternatively, the voucher holder could sell or swap it with other individuals or investment funds if he or she desired, or, if nothing else, trade it for a bottle of vodka. The goal, however, was to build a constituency with a vested interest in transforming state enterprises into private enterprises, and keeping them that way.

Chubais was aided and guided in his program design by several foreign advisors, particularly a team from the Harvard Institute of International Development led by André Shleifer, a specialist in Western corporate finance.[5] The guiding philosophy of these advisors that private ownership is always preferable to state ownership was based on the works of Frederick von Hayek and others associated with the University of Chicago School.

The Russian reformers, led by Yegor Gaidar, who was to become the acting Prime Minister, assumed that Russians would respond to the decision to privatize, just as their counterparts would in other parts of the world. The problem was that the Shleifer/Chubais approach made no allowance for the chaos that characterized the Russian economy in the wake of the collapse of the Soviet Union, the resignation of Mikhail Gorbachev, and the decision to abolish central planning.

It is difficult for those who have always lived in a market economy environment to appreciate the magnitude of the problem. In 1991 and 1992 something approaching market anarchy prevailed in Russia. Central planning and the dominant actors such as Gosplan (the central planning agency), Gossnab (the central supply agency), the Ministry of Prices, and the industrial ministers who heretofore had made all decisions about what to produce, what to use in the production process, who should produce it, and for whom, were being phased out. But after 70 years of determined suppression of virtually all private business and individual initiative, there was no market infrastructure to take their place. That meant that there was no meaningful or operational price system, wholesalers, marketers, labor markets, commercial codes, or civil court procedures. This was understandable, given that for 70 years the Soviet authorities sought to ban private activity, going so far as to declare that private economic activity would be classified as an economic crime punishable by death. Of course, no such decree could be completely enforced, but periodically there would be economic show trials, and those found guilty were often executed. It was understandable therefore that Gorbachev's decree in 1987 authorizing the formation of cooperatives and private businesses took a little getting used to. Thus there was no immediate rush by the bulk of the population to open up their own businesses. Indeed, given that Gorbachev seemed to have no trouble reversing himself – in 1986 for example he went to the other extreme and launched a far-reaching crackdown on all private activity – there was widespread concern that the 1987 opening to private activity would not last for long. Consequently only a relative few were willing to risk taking advantage of the new opening.

It was not easy going. With no Gosplan or Ministry of Prices, there were no ready sources of supply and no way to judge what the price would be when supplies were found. To fill the vacuum, desperate traders created commodity markets all over the country, and at one point there were several thousand in existence. And unlike their modern day counterparts in the West, these were really commodity, not futures, markets. Sellers offered small lots of things such as lumber, nails, paper, towels, tires, or even basic food and clothing supplies. After all there were no hardware stores or wholesale suppliers, much less discount stores or supermarkets. The state market coordinators and supply traffic regulators had been stripped of power, but initially at least, there was nothing to take their place.

This was a daunting and a potentially explosive time, but for a small number of those who were prepared to risk failure or a return to political repression, it was a golden opportunity. It was like a six-way major traffic intersection when suddenly the traffic lights go out. For most drivers it is a time of caution but for the bold it is a dream come true. No restraints – just plow through and scatter everyone else in your wake. For the new Russian private entrepreneurs, there were no government regulations of businesses and markets (all existing regulations were designed for state enterprises), and there were no entrenched business competitors. This meant that there were virtually no boundaries restricting those who survived. Except for the chaos of the market and the absence of institutionalized sources of supply, there were no limits to what these buccaneers could achieve, if they could only find ways to provision themselves. This in part explains how some of the oligarchs who started out with so little could accumulate so much in such a short period of time. Of course they also had to devise ways to acquire their initial capital stake and subsequent infusion of capital. Moreover, the absence of state authorities also meant that they would have to fend for themselves against criminal and Mafia groups as well as against rival marauders embarked on the same path of acquisition.

III

It is a bit of a simplification but there were essentially three categories of Russian oligarchs. First, there were the factory directors/owners. Taking advantage of the fact that their employees were seldom well organized, most factory directors were able to manipulate proxy contests so that they could dominate the make-up of the board of directors. This was possible because the managers and the employees were in a position to acquire a majority of the shares. In some cases, the factory directors simply bought up the proxies from their employees on the street although on occasion, some directors would coerce their employees to sell their shares with threats to fire those who didn't.

Vladimir V. Kadannikov and Nikolai A. Pugin are two factory directors who in effect became the principal stockholders in their companies. After graduating from the Gorky Polytechnical Institute, Mr Kadannikov went to work for the Gorky Automobile Plant. In 1967, he moved to Volga Automobile Plant in Tiglutti, which produced the Zhiguli and Lader. After privatization, he became the President and Chair of the Board of what was to become the Avtovaz Joint Stock Corporation. In much the same way, Mr Pugin, also a graduate of the Gorky Polytechnical Institute, served as the Director of the Gorky Automobile Factory (GAZ) from 1981 to 1983. From 1986 to 1988, he headed the Ministry of the Automobile and Agricultural Machinery in Moscow, but returned to what was called Nizhni Novgorod when he again took over GAZ – only this time as President of the GAZ Joint Stock Company. Although he was in Moscow during the privatization process, and thus did not partake in the initial allocation of enterprise stock, he nonetheless made up for his absence once he returned as Plant Director; by 1995 he was the enterprise's largest stockholder.[6]

The factory directors were lords of their domains with the ability to strip assets from their own factories or otherwise build up their personal net worth. But on the whole, their wealth was localized. They limited themselves to their specific factories and did not qualify to enter the ranks of the super-rich. Some joined together to create regional banks which were then used as personal loan funds to provide the money used to buy up the workers' shares. Since they lacked banking skills or failed to bring in those with banking skills, many of these banks failed quickly or were absorbed by larger Moscow banks in the aftermath of the various financial panics, such as Black Tuesday, 11 October, 1994, or Black Monday, 17 August, 1998.

The second category of oligarchs consists primarily of former members of the communist era *nomenklatura*. Usually these were former senior officials in some government ministry or regional industrial administration. Sensing the opportunity, these officials arranged to set up a private entity and then they promptly got themselves appointed as the president. On the surface, this was not very different from the factory directors who gained control of enough vouchers to make themselves the effective owners. The difference, however, was that in this case the properties usually involved control of raw materials, and in the extreme case, these new private executives ended up as some of the country's richest oligarchs.

The prime example of a bureaucrat made billionaire is Rem Vyakhirev. A long-time official in the Ministry of the Gas Industry, he rose ultimately to the post of Deputy Minister. His boss, the Minister of the Gas Industry, Viktor Chernomyrdin, decided early on in 1989 to convert the Ministry into a private entity, which he named Gazprom (Gas Industry). Shares of stock were printed, but were not initially made available to the public as part of the voucher program. Eventually, 33 percent of the shares were exchanged for vouchers and purchased by 747 000 people including Chernomyrdin and Vyakhirev.[7] Gazprom purchased 10 percent of the company's shares for itself, and the executives and staff were allowed to buy up to 15 percent for their own account. The state retained 40 percent of the shares, although that 40 percent ownership has not bought the state much in the way of material help. For example, the state received only $3.5 million as a dividend on its investment in 1995 and 1996.[8] Until 1997, foreigners were limited to holding no more that 9 percent of the shares issued in exchange and sold to the staff.[9]

Yeltsin appointed Chernomyrdin Deputy Prime Minister in mid-1992 and then Prime Minster in December 1992. When he left Gazprom to become Deputy Prime Minister he turned control of Gazprom to Vyakhirev. Under a secret agreement signed in 1993 agreed to by the Prime Minister at the time and his former colleague Chernomyrdin, Vyakhirev was given the power to vote not only his shares but also the government's shares. It was clearly a sweetheart deal which in essence allowed Vyakhirev to run Gazprom as if he were the majority stockholder. The 1993 agreement was also written in such a way that Vyakhirev could not only vote all the government's shares, but sometime in the late 1990s, Vyakhirev and the Gazprom board would have been able to buy out 30 percent of the state's shares at the pre-inflation initial face value of the securities.[10] Yeltsin was alerted in time by Boris Nemtsov that this transaction was about to take place and this 'theft,' as Yeltsin put it, was thwarted.[11] This did not affect Vyakhirev's already substantial holdings, however, nor prevent his inclusion among the Forbes list of the world's richest.

As for Chernomyrdin, despite widespread skepticism, he has insisted that while Prime Minister he owned no shares of Gazprom. However, after being forced out as Prime Minister in August 1998, he was selected as the government's representative on the Gazprom Board of Directors. In mid-1999 he was voted Chairman of the Board of Directors, replacing Vyakhirev, who nonetheless retained a seat on the Board. While Chernomyrdin's function was to vote the government's shares, presumably he has now purchased or been given shares for himself. The net worth of Gazprom is estimated to be anywhere from $250 to $950 billion.[12]

Vagit Alekperov's story is much the same. A native of Baku, a city which was a pre-Revolutionary center of Russia's petroleum production, Alekperov graduated from the Azerbaijan Institute of Oil and Chemistry and went to work directly in the oil fields. He moved into an administrative post in 1984 and in 1990 became Deputy Minister of Fuel and Energy and ultimately Acting Minister. From there he was in a key position to oversee the privatization of the petroleum industry. In the process he carved out for himself three of the choicest production fields: Langepaz, Urengoi, and Kogalym. Along with some other oil fields which were added subsequently, as well as some distribution and servicing facilities, these fields became the core of his new firm LUKoil, now Russian's largest oil company with Alekperov assigning himself the largest number of shares. With these resources, Alekperov and LUKoil easily moved on into banking and control of television stations and newspapers.

Not all of the second category of oligarchs owe their new wealth to their official status in the communist era or evolved out of the raw material and energy sectors. For example, Vladimir Potanin's empire, by contrast, began in Soiuzpromexport, one of the foreign trade organizations of the Ministry of Foreign Trade. This FTO specialized in the export of non-ferrous metals. In 1991, after it became legal to establish cooperative and private businesses, he established INTERROS which exactly duplicated what Soiuzpromexport did. In effect, Potanin privatized Soiuzpromexport. With the capital he accumulated at INTERROS, he went on to create MFK (the International Finance Company). Calling once again on his connections from the communist era, Potanin was helped in this effort by gaining access to the funds of Vneshekonombank, the foreign trade bank, which he then combined with capital funds from MKF in 1993 to open up what he called Oneximbank.

After he was elected President in 1996, Boris Yeltsin appointed Potanin as First Deputy Prime Minister. Potanin had joined with six other bankers in organizing, promoting and financing Yeltsin's victory, and this appointment was Potanin's reward. Ostensibly, Potanin took a leave of absence from his bank, but in fact he used this post to enhance the 'Loans for Shares' program he had initially proposed in 1995. Loans for Shares became the major vehicle for privatizing some of Russia's largest enterprises, and Potanin secured for himself some of the choicest plums. In theory, Loans for Shares was intended to help the government over a funding shortfall. Because the government was not collecting enough tax revenue to cover its expenditures, Potanin suggested that it make up the deficit by borrowing money from banks like his. As collateral for the loans, the government would provide shares of stock in some of the companies which it still controlled. When the state collected the necessary taxes, it would then pay off its loans and retrieve the collateral. Realistically, however, the bankers at least understood that the taxes would probably never be collected (since they, like almost everyone else, were also not paying them), and the loans would never be repaid. But to protect the government, the banks agreed that if the loans were not repaid, the government would still benefit because the banks would auction off the stocks and that would yield a price considerably larger than the initial size of the loans. However, only the naïve were shocked to discover that in almost every case, the auctions turned out to be a charade, and that the banks holding the collateral and conducting the auctions would emerge as the winner at a price that barely exceeded the price of the initial loan.[13] When others tried to bid, they found that the airport at the site of the auction was closed for the day or that the bidders were disqualified for some other reason. This was larceny on a grand scale. In Potanin's case, because of such opportunities, he ended up controlling 30 major properties including Norelsk Nickel, Sidanko Petroleum, Perm Motors, Northwest Shipping, and Magnitogorsk.

IV

That privatization should give birth to new owners who previously had been the factory directors or senior government ministers seemed only natural. Seizing what was already there also explains why it was that these oligarchs acquired so much wealth so quickly. Unlike the robber barons in the United States who built their empires by building steel mills, railroads and refineries, the Russian oligarchs simply purloined what previously belonged to the state and in the process became instant millionaires, if not billionaires. For that reason, it is the third category of oligarch that is most interesting. Generally, they were not part of the main *apparatchik* cadre of the Soviet era. If anything, they were more outside than inside the law prevailing in the communist era. Some of them indeed had been charged with economic crimes, and some even served time in jail. That they grew so wealthy so rapidly, despite what had been their previously low social standing, again is something unique.

To understand how so many of the new rich could emerge so quickly out of such humble and even despised origins (in many ways they were like the untouchables of India), it is necessary to recall the economic and ethnic policies of the Soviet government in the 1970s and 80s. Except for the sale of food grown in the peasant small garden plots, all private business activity was prohibited. Those violating the laws were charged with economic crimes, the punishment for which, as noted earlier, could even be death. Despite the harshness of the penalty, many nonetheless ran such risks. Most of those who did so were members of different ethnic groups such as Jews or Muslims who, with rare exception, were otherwise excluded from mainstream positions of authority within the party, the military, the KGB, the Foreign Service, or even as factory directors. Rather than accept low level work, some of the more ambitious among them set up their own businesses, even if it meant flaunting the law at great risk. Hardly anyone expected that this attitude towards what the Russian's called *fartsovshchiki* (currency speculators, black market operators, and so on) would ever change. But with Gorbachev's decision to reverse course in 1987 and to allow private and cooperative trade and business activity, what had previously been treated as antisocial behavior became praiseworthy overnight. For those who were not in jail, it meant that they could come out from the underground and launder what had been ill-gotten assets. Rather than find themselves disadvantaged in the post-1987 society, the ethnic opportunists in effect had become advantaged.

By contrast, few Russian nationals in the Soviet era had risked trading or speculative behavior. They had more to gain by entering the mainstream. Thus they lacked the experience of the minority ethnic groups. As Russia moved to the market, the Russians who wanted to take advantage of the new circumstances, as we saw, simply seized the assets they had been working within the government. But few ethnics could do that: They lacked access. Instead, they had to build on their trading skills and accumulate a capital stake that way. With that capital, as meager as it might have seemed to a Western businessman, it was often enough to start up one of the new private banks, which suddenly sprouted across the country. Most of these banks acted as little more than personal ATM machines. But this allowed their owners to enter the race to buy up state property.

The perfect prototype for this model was Alexander Smolensky. Although he graduated from a provincial geological technical institute, Smolensky spent as much or more time at work moonlighting as he did in ordinary state employment. For example, in addition to illegally working on the side in a bakery, he also took advantage of his access to government printing presses and ink to publish bibles, a practice explicitly prohibited by the atheist state. When caught, Smolensky was arrested in 1981 and charged with economic crimes. Although he was sentenced to two years at hard labor, Smolensky served only one day.

Unintimidated by his brush with the KGB, Smolensky shifted his efforts to the unofficial construction industry, an activity that nicely lent itself to off-the-books activity. After the Gorbachev decree of 1987, Smolensky moved quickly into construction and construction supply. The next step was to find a place to put his now legitimate wealth. Since he didn't trust state banks, in February 1989 he opened his own, which he called the Stolichny Bank. He focused his attention on expanding his banking network and successfully bid to gain control of the state owned Agroprombank, a largely rural network of banks with 1250 branches. He then changed the name of the bank to SBS/Agro (Stolichny Bank Savings/Agro). Some charged that his bid was given special consideration by Anatoly Chubais, then First Deputy Prime Minister. Those accusations were made all the more plausible when Smolensky provided that same Chubais with an interest-free loan of $3 million.

The devaluation of the ruble, the crash of the Russian stock market, and the moratorium on the repayment of Russian treasury bills on 17 August, 1998, were devastating blows for most Russian bankers, including SBS/Agro. Technically, Smolensky's bank became insolvent, but calling on his ties with Viktor Geraschenko, the head of the Russian Central Bank, Smolensky, now an insider, successfully pressured the Central Bank to provide him with a series of large loans. Such a move was meant to reassure the bank's depositors that he had sufficient funds to remain solvent, and thus to prevent a further run on the remaining deposits. That turned out to be too little, too late, so more loans were requested and obtained. To protect himself, Smolensky, like most of the other oligarch bankers, set up a new banking shell and shifted most of his viable assets out of SBS/Agro into the new banking entities, Soyuz and the First Mutual Society.

Vladimir Gusinskii emerged from the underground economy in much the same way. He too trained in a technical field, the Institute of Petrochemicals and Natural Gas, but then went into theatrical productions. Reportedly, he also drove a cab on the side and engaged in peddling. He has denied reports that at one time he had been charged with embezzlement. In 1988, Gusinskii decided to set up a cooperative consulting firm. He focused on working with prospective foreign investors. The Washington law firm of Arnold and Porter was seeking just such advice, and in 1989 its subsidiary APCO agreed to form a joint venture with Gusinskii. This joint venture provided Gusinskii with a generous source of dollar earnings that he quickly converted to rubles at a very favorable rate. These funds were further supplemented with funds which the cooperative derived from the sale of office supplies. Gusinskii, like Smolensky, also moved into construction and renovation. This brought him into contact with Yuri Luzhkov, then the Deputy Mayor of Moscow. Luzhkov agreed to let Gusinskii manage key properties owned by the city. This coincided with the influx of foreign businessmen eager to rent prime office and housing space. Luzhkov also agreed to deposit Moscow city revenues into Most Bank, Gusinskii's new banking affiliate established in 1992. Given the way banks operated at the time, this meant that Most Bank could hold on to the deposits (work the float) on an interest-free basis for weeks and sometimes months at a time. Since interest rates on federal securities yielded from 150 to 200 percent, this was a guaranteed source of income.

Gradually, however, Gusinskii tired of banking but, unlike the oligarchs who bought up already existing industrial properties, Gusinskii established a media empire. He opened up several television stations, which he then turned into NTV. This soon became Russia's second most important television network. Before long, he had become Russia's leading media baron, owning not only television and radio networks, but also newspapers and magazines. These were all properties established anew.

All the oligarchs who worked their way up via the corporate route are controversial, but perhaps the most shady of the lot is Boris Berezovsky. In a sense this is surprising because, unlike the others, Berezovsky had not been involved in currency speculation or the 'second economy' (underground or illegal) during the communist era. On the contrary, he had earned a Ph.D. and became an expert on systems control and operations research. He even did some research work at the Harvard Business School in the 1970s.

Berezovsky too began his move by creating a cooperative, namely Logovaz, a consulting firm, in 1989. For some time he had been providing advice on operations to Avtovaz, the Soviet Union's largest automobile manufacturer. It was a natural step therefore when Gosplan was abolished for Berezovsky to work out a marketing arrangement to help Avtovaz sell its automobiles. With no Gosplan or economic ministries, most factories, as we have seen, were at a loss as to how to sell their product. Now the factories were on their own with no experience to draw upon. Berezovsky stepped into the vacuum with Logovaz, and offered to market a substantial share of Avtovaz's output. Under this arrangement, Avtovaz consigned its cars at a substantial discount to Logovaz which sold them at a substantial mark-up. It is reasonable to assume that the senior management of Avtovaz did not suffer from this arrangement. Using Avtovaz's output as a base, however, Berezovsky quickly branched out to establish franchises for the sale of foreign built cars as well.

Once others came to appreciate how much money Berezovsky was making from such arrangements, there were several attempts to muscle Berezovsky out of his near-monopoly. Attempts were made on his life, and in return by coincidence several rivals were killed. That in part is what led *Forbes Magazine* on 30 December, 1996, to assert that Berezovsky was the head of the Russian Mafia. (Berezovsky has denied these accusations and is attempting to sue

Forbes for libel.) In any event, Berezovsky used his profits to finance partial ownership in several banks as well as Aeroflot, the oil company Sibneft, and most important, the largest television network in Russia, ORT.

Through skillful manipulation, Berezovsky used his wealth and his partial control of key assets to ingratiate himself with President Yeltsin, as well as with Yeltsin's family and staff. The president of Aeroflot, for example, was Yeltsin's son-in-law. More important, Berezovsky took the lead in organizing six other banking oligarchs including Potanin, and they worked together during the 1996 presidential campaign to support Yeltsin. This was done at a time when Yeltsin could barely attract 10 percent of the voting public, and it looked as if the communist candidate might defeat him. Yeltsin eventually won the election with a solid victory and rewarded not only Potanin, but also Berezovsky, with political appointments. For a time, he even named Berezovsky Deputy Secretary of the Security Council.

With his access to Yeltsin, Berezovsky came to view himself as a king-maker, and on occasion he was a major force in the ousting of senior government officials, including Sergei Kiriyenko, the Prime Minister, in August 1998. Alert to the danger, Kiriyenko's successor Evgeny Primakov moved to neutralize Berezovsky. As part of an anti-corruption campaign, Primakov arranged for the firing of several Berezovsky loyalists from Aeroflot, Sibneft, and ORT, and sent in tax inspectors and auditors to intimidate those who remained. Yet indicative of his power, Berezovsky managed to free himself from possible arrest and to arrange for the ousting of Primakov as Prime Minister.

Primakov's attack on Berezovsky was possible in part because like all the other oligarchs, Berezovsky was badly weakened by the economic meltdown of August 1998. As for the other oligarchs who had lower political profiles, they lost considerable sums of money, but most of them, especially the bankers, managed to shift their still viable assets to new shells. Smolensky, as we saw, created two new entities, Soyuz and the First Mutual Society. In this way he protected himself, while most of the depositors in SBS/Agro, as well as many of the other banks, found it impossible to withdraw their funds. As Gregory Yavlinsky, the head of Yabloko, one of Russia's political parties, put it, 'In the United States the banks take the money from the public and lend it to businesses. By contrast, in Russia the banks take the money and send it to Switzerland.'[14]

V

The privatization mess in Russia stands in sharp contrast to the considerably more positive accomplishments in Poland. In part the Polish success was due to luck. Originally the newly installed Solidarity government intended to privatize their major industries immediately after the beginning of their shock therapy in January 1990, just as the Russians did two years later. Fortunately for Poland, because of political disagreements within the government, their efforts stalled, and they were not able to move forward in any substantial way until about 1995. In the interim the government focused instead on facilitating the start-up of new businesses, so that in five years, 2 million or so had opened. As a consequence, the Poles were able to create a market infrastructure with checks and balances both from business competitors and the government. It probably helped that the Poles had only endured communism for about 45 years, not 70 as in Russia. Moreover, Polish farms had resisted collectivization, and there had always been a small private service and manufacturing sector. Thus by the time the authorities finally moved ahead on their privatization effort, Poland had a market and political infrastructure in place, not a vacuum, as was the case in Russia.

The Poles were also fortunate in that the architect of their privatization effort, Janusz Lewandowski, anticipated what might happen in the absence of a carefully designed program; therefore, he set out to achieve certain critical objectives:

1. He wanted to prevent the factory directors from gaining direct or indirect ownership of their enterprises. If the factory directors took over, they would have almost certainly stymied any effort to restructure the enterprise – both in terms of changes in personnel, including the firing of the factory directors themselves, or closing down or selling off parts of the enterprise.
2. He wanted to bring in foreign specialists and advisors, to provide guidance to managers unequipped for dealing in a market economy.
3. He also sought to insure that every Pole – average citizens as well as workers in the factories being privatized – could derive tangible benefits from the privatization process. That meant not only having access to an initial stake in the privatized enterprises, but also sharing in any increase in value that might come from the future operation of such enterprises.

This was a very different agenda from the Russian one which, as mentioned, seemed more political than economic. Among other differences, there would have been almost no chance that the Russian government, even in its pro-Western days, would have allowed foreign advisors to supervise the utilization of Russian assets. Moreover, no one in Russia seemed to care about preventing the managers from becoming the owners at the expense of the general public.

Like similar schemes in Russia and the Czech Republic, the Polish model involved the issuing of vouchers to everyone, and the creation of mutual or investment funds. What was different, however, was that each of the 15 National Investment Funds (NIFs) set up by the state was assigned a 33 percent interest in 34 of the 512 companies selected for privatization. This way one NIF had a dominant interest in each of the privatized companies. The other 14 NIFs were given a 1.9 percent share interest in each of the remaining 478 enterprises undergoing privatization. This was different from the practice in other countries whereby all the shares were divided equally, so that each mutual or investment fund received the same percentage share in each one of the privatized companies. When that happens, it usually means that no one ends up in a controlling position, and no one can take responsibility. Therefore, the factory director in effect becomes the factory owner. In the Polish model, with one NIF controlling 33 percent of the shares, each factory director found himself accountable to a specific fund, and had to include representatives of the foreign investment firms in the factory's management.

The Polish managers and the Polish workforce were allocated 15 percent of each enterprise's shares for their outright ownership. Under normal circumstances that would provide them with some incentives, but would not be enough for them to assert ownership. Therefore they remained subordinate to the NIF assigned to them. Thus the profits earned by the enterprise accrud to the shareholders, which included not only the director and his staff but also those who had exchanged their vouchers for shares in the NIF. Another difference between the Polish plan and the others is that the government retained a 25 percent interest in each of the 512 enterprises so that the state, and by extension the public, would share in whatever profits there might be. Even more appropriate, two-thirds of the state's 25 percent share would be assigned to state and social pension funds. This was very different from Russia, where the public received no benefit from the ongoing operations of the former state enterprises, once they were privatized. (Recall the complaints that Gazprom paid little or nothing in the way of dividends on the stock the state still owns in such companies.)

VI

One of the most sacred tenets in economics is that private ownership is almost always preferable to state ownership. What the Russian experiment shows, however, is that there may be a major exception to such a rule when privatization takes place in an economy where there is no existing market and regulatory infrastructure. Without checks, balances and a viable environment of competition in operation, there is a real danger that state property will be seized or stolen by those in a position of influence from the old regime. Even when newcomers do manage to break through, the absence of restraints means that they too will find there is almost nothing to impede their empire-building. With their own banks, they can fund additional acquisitions, almost all of which are already existing assets.

Privatization in Russia need not have brought with it a clique of oligarchs. As the Polish case shows, it is possible to privatize in a communist country without such a perversion of policy, but only if the proper prerequisites are in place. Those who insist on the shock therapy approach to reform, by which everything must be done at once and simultaneously, use the analogy that those wishing to jump over an abyss had best do it in one leap. What they forget is that such a rule applies to those standing on the brink of the abyss, not those standing in a pit below the peak. For those without the proper market infrastructure, that is, those in the pit, it is first necessary to create the infrastructure. They must take a preliminary leap up to reach the edge of the abyss; in other words, at least two jumps are required. Future policymakers would do well to remember this important exception to the conventional wisdom.

NOTES

1. For a fervent exposition of that point of view see Maxim Boycko *et al.* (1995).
2. *Wall Street Journal*, 17 March, 1999, p. A22.
3. Boycko *et al.* (1995).
4. Marshall I. Goldman (1996).
5. Boycko *et al.* (1995).
6. *Nizhni Novgorod*, 8 June, 1995.
7. *Ogonek*, December 1995, no. 79, pp. 22–3.
8. *Financial Times*, 1 April, 1996, p. 17; 14 May, 1997, p. 14.
9. *Financial Times*, 30 June, 1997, p. 1.
10. *The Jamestown Foundation*, 23 December, 1997, p. 2; *The Economist*, 5 July, 1997, p. 65.
11. *Financial Times*, 17 May, 1997, p. 7.
12. *Moscow News*, 13 February, 1999.
13. *Russia Review*, 26 February, 1996, p. 26.
14. Yavlinsky to author in personal interview.

REFERENCES

Boycko, Maxim, Andrei Shleifer and Robert Vishny (1995), *Privatizing Russia*, Cambridge, MA: MIT Press.

The Economist, 5 July, 1997.

Financial Times, 1 April, 1996; 14 May, 1997; 17 May, 1997; 30 June, 1997.

Goldman, Marshall I. (1996), *Lost Opportunity: Why Economic Reform in Russia Has Been so Difficult*, New York: Norton, pp. 133–35.

The Jamestown Foundation, 23 December, 1997.

Moscow News, 13 February, 1999.

Nizhni Novgorod, 8 June, 1995.

Ogonek, December 1995, no. 79.

Russia Review, 26 February, 1996.

Wall Street Journal, 17 March, 1999, p. A22.

COMMENTS ON MARSHALL I. GOLDMAN, 'THE RUSSIAN OLIGARCHS: NOT YOUR TYPICAL ROBBER BARONS'

Edmund Amann

I read this chapter with great interest for two main reasons. In the first place, the chapter offers a series of intriguing points of comparison with the Latin American case while, secondly, it paints a number of fascinating portraits of individual oligarchs and their paths to wealth and influence. What appears to stand out in this chapter is the peculiar nature of the Russian privatization process. In particular – and I think this is a key distinguishing feature from the Latin American experience – privatization was seen as a way of locking in political change. This helps to explain why the privatization process in Russia was carried out with such haste and with so little regard to such conventional privatization objectives such as greater efficiency or market competitiveness. But did the sweeping privatization program achieve its core political objectives?

While a transfer to the private sector was speedily realized, what is rather more doubtful is whether the concentration of economic power that ultimately resulted acted as a propelling force of democratization and pluralism. Instead, what seems more likely is that the effective parceling out of assets to a few individuals has created the conditions for the emergence of an oligarchic, factionalist political culture reminiscent of that endured by Paraguay. Turning to the economic implications of the privatization process, I am struck by two of Professor Goldman's observations; the non-existence of market institutions and the lack of any vigorous regulatory framework. I am certainly sympathetic to the point that a major problem of the Russian privatization process – in contrast to those of Poland and the Czech Republic – was that its shock therapy style of execution took no account of the facts 1) that markets were missing, and 2) that the legal and property rights framework needed for the efficient functioning of markets was also largely absent. Thus, enterprises were launched into the private sector without suitably developed market institutions or effectively functioning price signals. Unsurprisingly, therefore, chronic productive inefficiencies persisted, assets were sold on at grossly undervalued levels, and deals that were struck between individual oligarchs over sales of output took the place of open, price-driven market transactions.

Although differences abound, I am struck by certain similarities between the Latin American and Russian privatization experiences. In the case of Latin America, the Brazilian experience comes particularly to mind. Specifically, I think we should recognize that the absence of a formal, rigorous regulatory framework for large privatized enterprises, especially in the energy sector, is not a purely Russian phenomenon. In Brazil, the privatization process, driven in large part by fiscal imperatives, has been executed in a manner that poses major questions for long term economic efficiency. In particular, the regulatory frameworks for telecommunications and electricity, although in place at the time of privatization, are regarded by many as too weak and lacking in the technical and institutional capacity to secure badly needed efficiency gains. The privatization process in Brazil, in partial consequence, has seen the transfer of major assets to the private sector without any yet recognizable improvements in quality of service or keenness of price. At the same time, and once again driven by the fiscal imperative, too little account has been taken of the degree of industrial concentration in sectors where privatizations have taken place. In the case of steel and minerals, it is possible to see the emergence of 'oligarchs' presiding over large chunks of an industry. In this connection the case of Benjamin Steinbruch, the head of CVRD and CSN, comes particularly to mind. A similar pattern of concentrated holding is evident if we examine the Mexican case, where the telecommunications sector is an outstanding example of the phenomenon.

The major difference between the Latin American 'oligarchs' – as we might very loosely term them – and their Russian counterparts lies in the mode of their emergence and wealth accumulation. By and large the key domestic individual players in Latin American privatizations have sprung from long established family conglomerates, the 'Grupos.' As Goldman's chapter makes clear, the Russian oligarchs have a very different provenance.

One particularly interesting question surrounding the privatization of large individual enterprises is that of technology. Understandably, the chapter – given its primary focus on the nature of the oligarchs themselves – omits discussion of this theme. However, it would be interesting to establish the extent to which the Russian privatization process – and the peculiar pattern of ownership which has subsequently resulted – has affected the level of domestic technological self-reliance. Most of the evidence of which I am aware indicates that technological strategies among enterprises tend to become more conservative after privatization, for reasons that mainly stem from the necessity to reduce risk and raise the short-term rate of return.

Returning to the more direct concerns of the chapter, it is hard not to be affected by a certain despair when one reflects upon the nature of the privatization process in Russia, and the nature of those who have risen to the top as a result of its operation. I think one of the key questions facing the Russian economy now is whether, with the passage of time and the maturing of market institutions, the damage wrought by the privatization program can be rectified. If patterns of oligarchical concentration remain ingrained, it seems that the process of competitive renewal within Russian industry will continue to be retarded, preventing the economy from fully realizing its growth potential.

However, this scenario may be unduly pessimistic. If, over the next few years domestic capital markets deepen and broaden, inward investment increases, and legal and regulatory institutions strengthen, then it seems likely that the robber baron phase of capitalism will pass as concentration diminishes and structural efficiency improves.

COMMENTS ON MARSHALL I. GOLDMAN, 'THE RUSSIAN OLIGARCHS: NOT YOUR TYPICAL ROBBER BARONS'

Diane P. Koenker

The title of Marshall Goldman's chapter, his talk, and the conference itself raise a central issue of the study of Russia and the post-Soviet Union, an issue that is especially acute for economic analysis of the Russian economy. This issue can be expressed, in a word, as the question of universality versus uniqueness when it comes to this or any economic structure. A key premise of terms like 'liberalization,' 'transition' and 'democratization,' is the *assumption* of global processes and universal human behaviors. There is no *Homo Sovieticus*, only *Homo Economicus*. A market is a market is a market. The 'transition' market involves a set of processes that are replicable and transferable. Opposed to this argument of universality is an argument that Russia and its predecessor are unique, *sui generis*. Russia cannot be compared with anywhere else, and it cannot be the object of theoretical analysis based on economies and societies with different cultures, traditions, and histories. The premise of this conference is that cases can be compared, but the premise of the cases is that they have unique attributes. Goldman's chapter offers a number of reasons why Russia is peculiar, without saying that it is incomparable. The title itself implies there is a 'typical' robber baron, or ideal-type robber baron from which the Russian type diverges. The chapter assumes as well that there are well-established models of privatization, and that Russia's experience can be fitted into one of the models.

Because I am a specialist on the Soviet Union, the list of Russian peculiarities comes most naturally to me. A key point raised by Goldman is the lack of infrastructure for private enterprise: no commercial code, no civil court procedure, no labor market, no marketers, no wholesalers, no price system, no law on private property, no regulatory infrastructure, no checking accounts. We might consider as well the relationship of civil society to the market. Historians are now debating whether and when Russia developed a civil society – a public network of associational life outside the control of the state. Maybe the late 18th century Free Economic Society could have been a progenitor of such a civil society, or the late 19th century *zemstvos*, or the associations that emerged at the end of the 19th century and early 20th when the expansion of commercialism led to the growth of professional and trade associations. Civil society in the Soviet period lacked even these institutions: autonomous public organizations were very few, especially in any commercial sphere. Thus Russia lacked a robust civil society that could have furnished networks, consumers and self-regulators. Those who wish to consider Russia's special or divergent path of economic development need to ask how this absence of a civil society tradition affects contemporary capitalist endeavors. And we are entitled to ask whether the oligarchs continue to preclude the development of a rich civil commercial society by monopolizing enterprise and wealth.

Another area to ponder Russian uniqueness lies in Russia's traditional values and attitudes that shape responses to reform, whether market, political, or otherwise. Here is more grist for the 'uniqueness' mill.

1. Observers of post-Soviet society note a strongly developed sense of egalitarianism, which was promoted under communism everywhere, but which has been apparently easier to shed in Poland than in Russia. We could worry about the 'negative egalitarianism' imputed to Russian peasant culture, in which the preference is for both to be poor, rather than for one to be better off than another. Such egalitarianism is an important disincentive to participate in market reforms.
2. The social history of unemployment in the Soviet Union is yet to be written, but another attitude is a strongly entrenched fear of unemployment. Unemployment was widespread in the first ten years of the Soviet experiment, and the sense of insecurity and inequality that it created fostered social support for the five-year plans.[1] In the post-Stalin period, unemployment was depicted as an example of the evil of capitalism. Gorbachev's early reforms promised bankruptcy and unemployment – and the reforms stalled because of the insecurities they raised. Underemployment and going without wages for months at a time seem today preferable to unemployment.
3. Agricultural welfarism is a third set of values that affects Russian prospects for reform. Chinese economic reforms were spurred by agricultural reform that was embraced by the primary producers, and the case is similar for Poland. By contrast, Russian producers – the collective farmers – have been dependent on the state for subsidies and support since 1930; they have no interest in independence or in entrepreneurship. The agricultural belt has supported the Communist Party of the Russian Federation in recent elections, and it has been easier for entrepreneurial rural residents to take their initiative elsewhere. The remainder resent change and growth, and agriculture remains stagnant.
4. This fear of change is related more generally to a history of resistance to reform in Russian and Soviet history, a theme that can be traced back to the time of Peter the Great. In Soviet times, a good example is provided by the reconstruction plans following World War II, in which the Seven-Year Plan of 1945 called for massive investment in new industries – consumer goods and petrochemicals, and in new regions – the Urals and Siberia. But local economic and party managers sabotaged the plan, and as a result the old

smokestack industries were rebuilt in the already worn-out territories of the western, European regions of the USSR.[2] In 1965, reforms were proposed by the economist Evsei Liberman, focusing on 'profitability,' and that changed the incentive structure; but these foundered by 1968 because managers preferred old certainties to new efficiencies. Gorbachev's early reforms – both to accentuate cost-accounting and to raise production discipline by switching from vodka to mineral water – reflect the same old story. One can see the resistance to reform even today, in the lack of an economic plan produced by the succession of Yeltsin's prime ministers, and the resistance of the Duma to any prior proposals.

5. Finally, perhaps another prevalent Russian value is the tradition of embezzlement: here is another socio-cultural history waiting to be written. What the state owns, nobody owns, or everybody owns – and so it has been easy for Soviet citizens to abscond with state property and state rubles. There were a tremendous number of cases of embezzlement reported in the Soviet press in the 1920s – we need to look further to determine whether this was an invented crime, like Trotskyism, or a real social phenomenon. Steven Solnick's new book, *Stealing the State*, brings the story up to the late Soviet period,[3] by analyzing what he terms a 'massive bank run' on state assets by rational bureaucratic actors. The flow of money from Russia to the Bank of New York – evidently cash converted by state officials from government bonds about to suffer devaluation in August 1998 – continues this tradition into the present.

Do such peculiarities mean that Russia is impervious to reform and genetically incapable of a market transformation? Goldman's close study of the oligarchs offers a useful point of entry into the questions of universality versus particularism. We might look elsewhere in history for how economic oligarchies did or did not transform economic structures on the road to capitalism. Is the close relationship of oligarchs to the State, as is the case in Russia, a common pattern? Was this in fact a feature of Stalin's Russia, with the leaders of key industrial ministries and conglomerates playing the roles of Boris Berezovsky and Vladimir Potanin? Are there historical precedents for the process by which warlords become respected citizens? We could ask further questions as well about the embeddedness of these oligarchs in Russian culture and tradition: were there educational cohorts that produced this generation of robber barons, and if so, what kind of cultural milieu is producing the next generation? Perhaps with further comparative and historical analysis of the phenomenon of robber barons, we might be in a better position to understand the prospects for Russia's economy to privatize, to collapse, or to return to a renationalization and to start all over again.

Notes

1. L.S. Rogachevskaia (1973).
2. On this, see Timothy Dunmore (1980).
3. Steven L. Solnick (1998).

References

Rogachevskaia, L.S. (1973), *Likvidatsiia bezrabotitsy v SSSR 1917–1930 gg*, Moscow: NAUKA.

Dunmore, Timothy (1980), *The Stalinist Command and Economy: The Soviet State Apparatus and Economic Policy, 1945–53*, London: Macmillan.

Solnick, Steven L. (1998), *Stealing the State: Control and Collapse in Soviet Institutions*, Cambridge, MA.: Harvard University Press.

10. Privatizing the commons: liberalization, land and livelihoods in Latin America

Anthony Hall[1]

INTRODUCTION

Privatization has become a key ingredient in the market-based, neo-liberal recipe for development of the 1990s and beyond. Starting slowly in the South as an integral part of structural adjustment packages negotiated during the1980s debt crisis, the process of privatization has accelerated rapidly over the past decade. Privatization now forms part of a wider strategy for achieving a global free market and is considered a powerful antidote to problems associated with earlier policies of state-directed development and populism (Cook and Kirkpatrick 1995; Gray 1998).

Privatization is usually considered to be synonymous with the direct transfer of government owned assets to the business sector. This normally involves the sale of companies in areas such as public utilities, mining, communications and others. However, asset transfer from the public to the private domain also embraces terrestrial, aquatic and subterranean natural resources. Such 'privatization of nature' (Goldman 1998) has accompanied the spread of agro-livestock activities, commercial fishing and oil exploration in the developing world. It may involve, for example, the direct sale to private individuals or companies of state-owned agricultural land held by communities, as in the cases of Mexico, Peru and Ecuador, which are discussed briefly below. This process will here be labeled *direct privatization*.

This chapter, however, focuses primarily on another important dimension of resource control by the private sector, termed *indirect privatization*. This refers to the gradual penetration of private enterprise, especially into new frontier regions, and the subsequent incremental appropriation of land and natural resources hitherto controlled by local traditional groups for livelihood purposes. This process may be associated with a general policy move towards privatization, as in the case of oil exploration in western Amazonia during the 1980s and 1990s and the granting of concessions to private oil companies.

Alternatively, it may not be linked to any formal privatization initiative as such but is, rather, strongly encouraged and subsidized by the State in its search for solutions to the challenge of developing rural areas and promoting economic integration. In the case of Brazilian Amazonia, for example, indirect privatization was initiated during a period not of liberalization, but of increasingly powerful State control over regional development under military dictatorship (1964–85). Such policies were sustained by subsequent civilian governments during the 1980s, but have been called into question in the 1990s by those local populations whose livelihoods have been adversely impacted.

THE PRIVATIZATION OF COMMON PROPERTY RESOURCES IN LATIN AMERICA

Large areas of rural Latin America comprise common property regimes, in which the notion of individual property ownership has been largely irrelevant to the forms of resource-use developed there by indigenous and other traditional populations. This category includes not just Amerindian populations, but also other traditional groups which have over the past two centuries or more settled in the region. In accordance with the above distinction, privatization of common property resources (CPRs) may themselves be sub-divided into *direct* and *indirect*. The first of these two sub-categories describes State action backed up by changes in the law, and even the Constitution, to transfer or sell communally administered areas into private hands on the grounds of economic efficiency. Perhaps the best known example of direct privatization of rural common property is that of Mexico's *ejidos*, gradually privatized since 1992. However, Peru and Ecuador have undergone similar policy changes in the rural sector.[2]

Yet as significant as these government measures are, this chapter is concerned in particular with the gradual appropriation or indirect privatization and enclosure of rural common property. Common property can be defined in three major ways:

1. the *global commons*, all-embracing assets such as the atmosphere or international seas, which cannot be legally appropriated or privatized
2. *Open access* resources such as unclaimed lands which are freely available to all, but which might eventually be placed under some form of public or private ownership, and
3. *Closed access* resources which are, *de facto* (if not necessarily *de jure*), governed by structured, common property regimes which have been developed informally over generations by indigenous and other traditional

populations. Community-managed forests and inland fisheries in Amazonia, discussed below, fall squarely into this third category.

Vast swaths of Latin America, especially in the Andean highlands and in the Amazon Basin, constitute common property regimes in which the notion of individual, private property ownership has so far been relatively unknown. Systems of collective resource governance have been developed over generations by the users themselves as a means of managing fragile ecosystems, in what would in today's parlance be called a 'sustainable' manner. That is, by allowing local populations to gain their livelihoods without destroying the natural resource base upon which those livelihoods depend. Closed access CPRs contain common-pool natural assets which underpin the livelihoods of large sectors of Latin America's rural population.

State-sponsored development has often been preceded by the enclosure of common lands, creating a property market and providing cheap labor to fuel the process of urban-based industrialization.[3] In Latin America generally and Amazonia in particular, collectively managed terrestrial and aquatic resources have come under increasing pressure. In a more fundamental sense, of course, the history of Latin America is a history of enclosure by colonizing powers, during which indigenous populations have been displaced from their traditional lands, with terrible consequences.

This process of dispossession has continued ever since but has become particularly marked during the past two decades. It is a product of various related factors, from the political turbulence and civil war experienced in some countries such as Guatemala, Peru and Colombia, to the economic modernization policies adopted by most Latin American governments. These have failed to seriously address rural poverty, landlessness and insecurity but have, instead, sought to encourage settlement of frontier zones as a quick-fix solution to development problems, where old problems of inequity have been faithfully reproduced. In Brazilian Amazonia, for example, the latifundium-biased nature of land distribution now faithfully mirrors the national situation.[4]

The present analysis will focus on the indirect privatization of land and natural resources in Amazonia by commercial groups that have threatened the livelihoods of local populations. In particular, the specific cases of rubber tappers and artisanal inland fishing populations in Brazilian Amazonia will be considered, as well as that of indigenous tribes affected by oil and gas exploration in the jungles of Ecuador and Peru. Most importantly, given the failure of both the private sector and State adequately to protect the environment and in the face of these privatization pressures, it will be shown how these groups have, in conjunction with other key institutions, been involved in designing new and locale-specific strategies of resource protection and development. These have comprised not just short-term vigilance and resistance to counter the initial incursions by outside commercial interests, but also long-term environmental management proposals which build upon and formalize collective governance procedures.

PRIVATIZING THE COMMONS IN AMAZONIA

Amazonia has for millennia been home to indigenous and other related traditional populations, which have used the region's natural resource base to sustain their livelihoods in a non-destructive manner. The concept of private property was largely unknown and much of the terrestrial and aquatic resource base was used collectively for the benefit of both individuals and their respective communities. For Amerindians, rubber tappers and riverine fishing populations, informal systems of collective resource governance were, and in many cases still are, not just common but the norm. Despite the eradication of indigenous populations, increasing rates of rural out-migration and the loss of once communally administered areas, common property regimes are still a vital source of livelihood to significant populations. Research in the Brazilian Amazon has shown clearly how peasant livelihoods are often based on a mixture of common (extractive) and private property resources, and that people become highly vulnerable once they lose control over access to these resources (Hall 1997; Eve and Eve 1998).

The processes of colonial occupation and state-directed frontier development in Amazonia have steadily undermined the viability of common property regimes. Unlike the case of the US where the Homestead Act of 1862 provided for the equitable allocation of small plots to frontier settlers, in Brazil the Portuguese Crown distributed land in huge concessions (*sesmarias*) to its political representatives and allies. This highly unequal structure was further legitimized by the Land Law (Lei de Terras) of 1850, which prohibited squatting on unclaimed territory. A series of other Constitutional changes in 1891, 1937 and 1969 gave federal and state governments legal control over frontier lands and the right to give land to private claimants. In 1971, Decree-Law 1164 placed under federal jurisdiction all lands within 100 km of existing and future federal highways in Amazonia (Alston et al. 1995). These legal changes paved the way for a mixed Amazonian settlement strategy which catered, in varying degrees over time, to the interests of both small and large land claimants.

DEVELOPING BRAZILIAN AMAZONIA

Since the 1960s, national governments have systematically encouraged settlement of the Amazon Basin in order to serve a number of economic, social and strategic development objectives. This process has been particularly marked in Brazil, which occupies some four-fifths of the region. Economically, Amazonia came to be seen as a resource frontier to be exploited in order to stimulate regional development while generating export earnings to service the growing foreign debt. Strategically located in 'development poles,' from which the benefits of growth would irradiate outwards, cattle ranching and, later, mining were seen as the leading sectors (Becker and Egler 1992).

Politically, federal intervention was viewed as a means of controlling the power of state governors and regional élites. In social terms, Amazonia was conceived as a 'safety-valve,' giving 'land without men to men without land.' It offered a politically attractive alternative to agrarian reform by providing cheap land to the landless or land-poor, victims of drought as well as land concentration and conflict in the North-East and Centre-South of Brazil. In addition, human settlement was considered fundamental from a geo-political standpoint, in terms of consolidating national control over the Amazon, although nowadays State and military perspectives on this question have become more sophisticated and multi-dimensional (Dreifuss forthcoming).

Although financial incentives for cattle ranching commenced when SUDAM, the regional development agency, was set up in 1966, a major boost to human occupation came with the construction of two major roads. These are the Belém-Brasília, built in the early 1960s, and the Transamazon highway, initiated in 1970 under the Plan for National Integration. The *Transamazônica* has been a relative failure in terms of relocating poor farmers from the North-East and South in planned settlements. Disillusionment soon set in with the inability of INCRA, the resettlement agency, to provide adequate production and social infrastructure. There was a high rate of turnover and just 4 percent of its original goal of 100,000 settled families by 1974 was met (Smith 1982; Moran 1983). Soon after, the World Bank-funded POLONOROESTE settlement program for the state of Rondônia attracted a further wave of poor farmers to INCRA settlement projects along the infamous BR364 highway, with disastrous economic, social and environmental consequences (Martine 1990; Millikan 1994). Furthermore, for every officially sponsored colonist in the Brazilian Amazon, at least ten independent settlers were attracted to the region in their wake.

Notwithstanding the emphasis during the early 1970s on directed colonization for small farmers, the top Amazon development priority of successive military governments remained the large-scale livestock sector. After 1974, under pressure from the agrarian lobby in Congress, official policy switched openly towards favoring corporate undertakings in the region. Land along the Transamazon highway previously reserved for small cultivators, condemned as destroyers of the forest, was now quite openly sold off at bargain prices to large landowners and private investors who would 'modernize' the region. In the apparent belief that cattle ranching could spearhead the process of regional development, over $5 billion in official subsidies was allocated to this sector from 1971–87 (Schneider 1992). However, the largely speculative nature of these investments was revealed by an official evaluation which found that only 92 of 631 such 'enterprises' had been properly implemented and that many were simply fronts for obtaining fiscal incentives (Gasques and Yokomizo 1986). Although now drastically reduced, such incentives have not been altogether eliminated (Fearnside forthcoming). This latifundium-biased policy seriously aggravated problems of land conflict, violence and land concentration in Brazilian Amazonia, especially in southern Pará and Mato Grosso (Hall 1989).

A major indicator of the rapidly increased pace of settlement is the overall level of deforestation, which rose from 2.4 percent in 1970 to 10.5 percent by 1993 and over 13 percent (532 000 km^2) today. Annual rates have varied considerably, from an average of 21 000 km^2 during the peak years of government-subsidized settlement from 1978 to 1988, falling to 11 000 km^2 in 1991 at a time of recession. This rose to 29 000 km^2 in the peak year of 1995, falling again to 18 000 km^2 in 1996 and 13 000 km^2 in 1997. However, this figure rose to 17 000 km^2 by the end of 1998, an increase of 27 percent over the previous year (Hall 1999; INPE 1998; ESP 1999). Although 87 percent of its Amazon rainforest is still relatively intact, Brazil now has the highest *rate* of tropical forest loss in the world. This is exacerbated by increasing vulnerability to forest fires, experienced in 1997 Roraima state and more widely on the southern fringes of Amazonia along the so-called 'fire arc' during 1998. This has been due to a combination of the extended dry seasons caused by El Niño, as well as to the use of fire linked to slash-and-burn agricultural practices and associated logging activities.

A further indicator of the increased pressure on land generally in Brazilian Amazonia has seen a rapid rise in deaths associated with land conflicts. This has taken various forms. In the early years of colonization, it was common for peasant squatter families to be summarily evicted from their plots by powerful landowners (Branford and Glock 1985). Later, small producers developed often quite sophisticated defensive tactics to resist these pressures (Hébette and Colares 1990). Such was the case of the rubber tappers' movement with its stand-offs (*empates*) against ranchers and loggers during the 1980s, and fishing communities' resistance to commercial boats in the middle and upper Amazon, studied below.

Most recently, the Movement of the Landless (MST) has taken an even more pro-active stance by occupying unproductive lands that it wants included in the agrarian reform program for redistribution. According to an INCRA report, in Amazonia the MST has 10 000 members occupying an area equivalent in size to Alagoas state (*Veja*, 4 February 1998). The 1000 land conflict-associated murders in southern Amazonia during 1982–92 have in recent years been complemented by several massacres of peasants at the hands of hired gunmen and military police.

In the Brazilian Amazon, therefore, official development policy since the 1960s has actively encouraged occupation by both small and larger land claimants. Government subsidies have stimulated earlier and more rapid migration by lowering costs or increasing anticipated revenues, permitting significant rent-seeking (Alston, Libecap and Schneider 1998). This has resulted not just in uneconomic enterprises such as cattle ranches being artificially sustained, but in a series of social and environmental pressures on the land and its natural resources, as reflected in persistently high levels of deforestation and rural tension. Such indirect privatization of the land, with either explicit or tacit official support, has adversely impacted individual landholders, given their insecurity of tenure and vulnerability. In addition, however, private appropriation has placed growing pressures on communally administered lands and waterways.

OIL IN THE JUNGLE

Oil and gas exploration in western Amazonia reveals a similar government strategy of facilitating access by private enterprise, for national development purposes, to lands administered communally by traditional groups. The demands of structural adjustment have required the increased export of primary commodities such as oil to generate capital for international debt servicing. The national economic importance of the industry is illustrated by the fact that oil accounts for 40–50 percent of Ecuador's national budget and export revenues, depending on the international price (Kimerling 1996).

Ecuador and Peru are both striving hard to expand oil and gas production, the bulk of which presently comes from their respective Amazon regions in areas of virgin rainforest. A thousand mile-long petroleum front stretching from southern Colombia to southern Peru is now characterized by almost contiguous blocks of industrial penetration into the rainforest. This process is inducing major social and ecological impacts, and poses a severe threat to the livelihoods of native peoples who depend on the forest for their sustenance. Some 50 indigenous nationalities live within oil and gas concessions in the region. Not only does oil and gas development generate severe direct environmental hazards, as detailed below; in addition, the road networks built to support petroleum development have greatly facilitated small farmer settlement and associated ecological degradation (Hicks et al., 1990).

In Ecuador, Texaco discovered commercially valuable oil deposits in 1967, extracting almost 1.5 billion barrels before leaving the country in 1992 when its license expired. A substantial fall in oil income after the 1986 price collapse as well as dissatisfaction with the performance of State oil companies and the need for new technology led to the sale of exploration rights in frontier zones to foreign enterprises (Philip 1994).[5] Ecuador left OPEC in 1992, allowing it to increase its crude oil production levels.[6] The State oil company (Petroecuador) produces the bulk of Ecuador's oil, while four official subsidiaries manage all upstream and downstream activities. However, a number of foreign oil companies have purchased exploration rights, including Arco, Elf Aquitaine, Maxus, Occidental, Oryx and YPF. Virtually all the country's oil production comes from the Oriente (Amazon) region, which has some 60 operating fields, although 40 percent is concentrated in three – Shushufindi-Aguarico, Sacha and Auca. The government plans to develop other reserves in north-eastern Ecuador (USEIA 1997).

Oil exploration has had major negative ecological and social consequences in the Amazon, where large indigenous populations have been driven from their homelands or otherwise adversely affected by the resulting pollution. This has been particularly true in Ecuador, where Texaco spearheaded oil development during two decades, at a time when State environmental controls did not exist and standards were set by private companies themselves. Texaco drilled 339 wells over an area of 443 000 hectares, dumping tons of toxic waste and more than 19 billion gallons of water waste into the local environment. Some 235 wells are still active, pouring out an estimated five million gallons of toxic wastes every day. Containing heavy metals, hydrocarbons and toxic salts, these wastes are discharged untreated into unlined pits in the earth. Toxic substances from pits infiltrate the groundwater, while rainwater enters the open pits causing them to overflow into the environment (Kimerling 1991, 1996, forthcoming; Kane 1996).

There have been other immediate environmental impacts. Oily waste substances are also applied to oilfield roads for the purposes of dust control and maintenance. Gas extracted with the oil is burned off with no controls, thus polluting the atmosphere with greenhouse gases and acid rain ingredients such as nitrogen oxides and sulphur dioxide. Oil spills from pipelines, wells and tanks sent a total of almost 17 million gallons of crude oil into the environment during the Texaco period, (compared, for example, with 11 million gallons spilled during the Exxon Valdez incident). So lax were environmental controls and so poor was company training that oil workers for Texaco and Petroecuador applied crude oil to their heads to prevent balding. 'They sat in the sun, or covered their hair with plastic caps overnight. To remove the crude, they washed their hair with diesel' (Kimerling forthcoming).

The impacts of these developments on the local environment and population have been dramatic. Rivers and streams that supply water to communities in the Oriente region of Ecuador have been severely contaminated, virtually wiping out formerly abundant aquatic life in many areas. Pollution has also destroyed crops, animals and forest flora, while indigenous people and new farmer settlers attribute specific health problems to the widespread pollution by oil, including headaches, rashes, nausea, fevers and miscarriages. Seismic mapping involves cutting straight, 2.5 metre-wide paths through the forest on which explosives are placed to test for oil deposits. The explosions disturb and frighten off local wildlife (Project Underground, 1998a). Oil exploration has involved the felling of thousands of hectares of rainforest, while access roads built by oil companies have facilitated colonization by peasant farmers practicing inappropriate slash-and-burn techniques, thus aggravating the problem. Valuable natural resources used by indigenous people for food, medicinal and religious purposes have been destroyed, while the broader negative implications for biodiversity loss can only be guessed at.

Although the Ecuadorian government has titled many Amerindian lands, it claims full ownership of all subsurface hydrocarbons and minerals. Indigenous land titles usually state that owners may not impede oil or mining activities on their lands. Consequently, pressures on land have continued and whole indigenous groups have become extinct or significantly reduced in numbers as the result of oil exploration. The Tetetes, for example, were forced to flee their homeland when Texaco developed its first field in Ecuador. Indigenous Cofan, Quichua and Secoya also lost their lands to oil infrastructure development and the flood of settlers that followed. The Cofan have been reduced from 15 000 to just 300 as the result of oil exploration (Jochnick 1995).

The nomadic Huaorani were 'pacified' and relocated to distant Christian settlements with the aid of the Summer Institute of Linguistics and the government (Kane 1996; Kimerling forthcoming). The Huaorani, their number reduced from an original 25 000 to 3000, have also reportedly suffered in the 900 000-hectare Asuni National Park, a UNESCO Biosphere Reserve. Several companies are presently drilling here, including Elf of France as well as YPF, the Argentine State oil company. Construction of pipelines, heliports and oil platforms are expected to disrupt life in the park, while road building will encourage colonization (*Drillbits and Tailings*, 7 June, 1998).

Peru's oil industry goes back to the 1930s but production surged from 1990 when President Alberto Fujimori was elected and started a widespread privatization program, which raised over US$5 billion between 1992 and 1995. This was to include the country's State oil enterprise, Petroperu (which started operating in 1993), by the end of 1998. Peru's total oil production of 123 000 barrels per day (bbl/d) is but one-third that of Ecuador's, but the government is anxious to make new discoveries and international tenders are being prepared for the Ucayali Basin and elsewhere. As of March 1998, 34 promising areas in the Peruvian Amazon covering 21 million hectares were contracted out to oil companies, including Royal Dutch/Shell, Exxon, Mobil, Chevron, Occidental, Hyundai, Philips, ARCO, Elf Aquitaine and others (Kimerling forthcoming).

Development of the Camisea gas field, the largest in Latin America, is expected to turn Peru into a net exporter of hydrocarbons (USEIA 1998).

As in the case of Ecuador, most of Peru's oil and gas reserves are located in the Amazon region in areas of virtually inaccessible rainforest inhabited by indigenous peoples. However, the serious ecological problems witnessed in Ecuador as a direct consequence of oil exploration have not so far been experienced in Peru. This is due not just to the more recent nature of Peru's oil industry expansion into the Amazon; more importantly, Peru has profited from the harsh lessons of the Texaco experience in neighboring Ecuador, which have made government, oil companies and indigenous peoples more aware of the potential pitfalls and high environmental costs of uncontrolled development.

Nonetheless, research evidence confirms that indigenous groups in Peru have suffered, one of the most notorious cases being that of the Nahua, who were decimated by a serious epidemic during the 1980s as a direct result of penetration by oil companies onto their lands. The lands of the Mashco-Piro and Kugapakori peoples are also reported as having come under pressure from oil exploration (Project Underground 1998a). Problems between mining companies and traditional populations in Peru will undoubtedly increase, since the amount of land solicited for exploration has increased rapidly from three million hectares in 1992 to over 20 million hectares today, affecting some 2000 rural communities (*Drillbits and Tailings*, 21 October, 1998).

RECLAIMING THE COMMONS

For many years, a common reaction of traditional populations to the kinds of pressures described above was passivity and conformity. Disorganized, politically inarticulate and historically repressed, indigenous and other groups frequently lacked either the willpower or the capacity to offer any form of resistance. This situation was reinforced throughout years of military dictatorship in the 1970s and 1980s in the Amazon Basin countries. In the 1990s, this has changed dramatically and new social movements have arisen to resist encroachment by outsiders on traditional territory and the valuable resources contained therein. Three cases will be considered; the Brazilian rubber tappers, fishing communities along the river Amazon and indigenous populations in the oil exploration zones of Ecuador and Peru.

The Rubber Tappers

One of the most significant movements in modern times to defend access to common property resources has been that of the rubber tappers (*seringueiros*) of Brazilian Amazonia. A thriving rubber industry had developed in the region during the latter half of the 19th century based on the extraction of latex (*Hevea brasiliensis*) to serve the booming European and North American markets, attracting thousands of poor farmers to Amazonia fleeing the North-Eastern drought and poverty. The economic collapse of Brazilian wild rubber came after 1912 when the British conspired to transplant seeds (via Kew Gardens in London) to Malayan plantations, drastically reducing production costs, in what was probably the world's first major act of 'biopiracy.' As traditional Brazilian rubber estates were gradually abandoned by their owners, so tappers became autonomous producers, earning their livelihoods through a combination of extractivism and modest subsistence farming in what was still a relatively undisturbed environment.

This situation was to alter dramatically in western Amazonia with the previously mentioned construction of highway BR364 in the early 1970s, which connected the rubber-producing, north-western states of Rondônia and Acre to the South. This was paid for in part by the World Bank-funded POLONOROESTE, a regional development program. Encouraged by the generous official subsidies already described, cattle ranchers, logging companies and land speculators moved in to take over land, legally or otherwise. The intact rubber stands of the *seringueiros*, with their vast reserves of land and timber, soon became an attractive target for outside corporate as well as individual land-grabbers as the 'cattle front' moved northwest.

The first land conflicts in southern Acre drove out many Brazilian families into neighboring Bolivia. However, aided by strong leaders such as Wilson Pinheiro and Francisco 'Chico' Mendes (both assassinated, in 1980 and 1988 respectively), rubber tappers took a firm stance against this major threat to their livelihoods. *Seringueiros* organized themselves into rural trades unions and developed systematic grassroots resistance in the form of largely peaceful stand-offs (*empates*). Men, women and children confronted field hands hired by cattle ranchers and logging companies to clear the land, usually persuading them to depart. From 1976 to 1988, some 45 such *empates* are credited with having saved 1.2 million hectares of rubber stands from deforestation (Gross 1989; Arnt 1994). Furthermore, the National Council of Rubber Tappers was set up in 1985 to further the rubber tappers' cause.

Matters came to a head in December 1988 with the murder of Chico Mendes by a local rancher in Xapuri, southern Acre. Coming in the midst of intense international debate and media focus on high levels of deforestation in the Amazon, the first civilian administration in Brazil for over two decades was pressed into urgent action. Using existing land reform legislation, the government expropriated ten rubber estates during 1989 to set up 'Extractive Settlement Projects,' covering a total of 900 000 hectares and home to 3000 families. The following year, with the assistance of the Rubber Tappers' Council, new legislation was drafted within Brazil's first National Environment

Program to establish 'Extractive Reserves,' rapidly formalized by Presidential Decree. At present, four federal reserves (*reservas extractivistas*, abbreviated to 'resex') in Amazonia embrace two million hectares with a population of some 23 000.[7] A number of state-administered extractive reserves have also been set up covering a further 1.7 million hectares, and more are planned (Hall 1996, 1997). In effect, extractive reserves are a form of 'collective privatization,' in which the land is leased by the government on a long-term basis to local rubber tappers' organizations to administer on behalf of the local population.

The rubber tappers' struggle is especially significant since, for the first time in Brazil, a major policy innovation was introduced as a result of grassroots defensive action combined with international campaigning and lobbying to devise a land-use model specifically to meet the needs of traditional groups. It marked the beginning of a new environmental policy phase for Brazil in which the livelihood requirements of local populations would be incorporated into a conservation strategy. The four largest federal reserves mentioned above currently receive support from the US$300 million 'G7 Pilot Programme to Conserve the Brazilian Rainforest.' Over US$9 million has so far been earmarked for assistance for baseline socioeconomic and biodiversity studies, boundary demarcation, strengthening of infrastructure for education, health, production and transport, as well as improving local organizational and management capacity.

The setting up of extractive reserves is still in a relatively early phase, and major problems threaten to undermine their sustainability (Hall 1996, 1997). Some of these relate to the ability of geographically dispersed, socially diverse, inexperienced and poorly educated populations to effectively manage these vast areas. Most immediately pressing is the question of economic self-sufficiency. Declining international rubber prices together with the gradual withdrawal of government subsidies have caused tappers' incomes to fall substantially, inducing out-migration to urban centers and the search for alternative sources of employment.

Efforts are currently underway to diversify production into other areas such as higher quality rubber, 'organic leather' (*couro vegetal*),[8] agroforestry, Brazil nuts and even selective logging. Investment in health and education services is also needed to help minimize out-migration. It is also essential that the federal government provide a more favorable policy context in terms of tax breaks and incentives for sustainable development. These are major challenges which have to be faced if the extractive reserve concept is to be adopted more broadly as a policy tool for protecting the livelihoods of rubber tappers and other traditional extractivist groups against the pressures of both direct and indirect privatization.

Inland Fishing Communities

Although land conflicts of various kinds have attracted most attention, communally-managed aquatic resources in Amazonia have also come under intense pressure from commercial interests. The Amazon floodplain or *várzea* is home to a significant population of riverine communities who earn a living from subsistence farming, forest extractivism and, increasingly, artisanal fishing using simple technology. For generations, these descendants of indigenous and white farmer settlers (known as *caboclos*) have operated an informal resource management system of the aquatic commons which has successfully avoided depletion of fish stocks. From the late 1960s, however, as the drive to develop Amazonia got underway, community fishing grounds were invaded by commercial boats from large towns such as Belém, Santarém and Manaus. Catering for demand from rapidly growing urban centers and for export overseas, especially to the US, these craft employed more modern technologies (such as gill nets and refrigerated processing plants) which increased yields but at the same time threatened the livelihoods of local fishers.

Even before rubber tappers had used the *empate* to ward off land-grabbers, fishing communities actively confronted commercial vessels during the 1960s and 1970s in what became known as the 'fish wars', which were sometimes fatal (McGrath 1993).[9] The growing seriousness of these conflicts led fishers, with the aid of local NGOs and the radical sector of the Catholic church, to formalize traditional community management procedures by declaring 'lake reserves' in order to monitor activities more systematically. However, under the Brazilian Constitution, all inland waterways, although often recognized as 'lake reserves' by municipal law, are the property of the State and are *de jure* open access. The challenge to development practitioners is therefore how to make such *de facto* community initiatives viable, with a view to changing the law and developing government-backed policies for sustainable inland fisheries management to reconcile subsistence and commercial extraction without depleting stocks.

Building upon these earlier conflicts and experiences, attempts are now underway to develop formal, community-based management systems for inland fisheries in the Amazon Basin. The oldest and best known of these is the Mamirauá project, located in western Amazonas, near the town of Tefé (Hall 1997). It covers 1.12 million hectares of seasonally flooded forest situated in a triangle formed by the confluence of the Rivers Solimões and Japurá, an area of extremely high biodiversity, with several species endemic to the area, and said to house the richest aquatic system on Earth. Originally designated an Ecological Station, it is now Brazil's first 'Sustainable Development Reserve,' declared under Amazonas state law. Project activities are concentrated in a focal area of

200 000 hectares, which has 600 lakes and is used by a population of over 5000 fishers, about one-third of whom live within the reserve boundaries.

Although the Catholic church had helped fishing communities to establish an informal monitoring system during the 'fish wars' of the 1970s, owing to a lack of funding and personnel it was of limited effectiveness. The Mamirauá Project was therefore set up in the early 1990s, on the initiative of a Brazilian primatologist who had been working in the area for several years, as a multi-disciplinary, collaborative exercise involving natural and social scientists (Ayres 1993). A scientific research program was commenced to study both terrestrial and aquatic resources, especially in relation to the conservation of fish and aquatic mammals. In parallel, socioeconomic research was carried out to examine livelihood strategies. More immediately, vigilance and monitoring was strengthened through the construction of 11 floating guard posts strategically placed at the entrance to lake complexes, linked by solar-powered radios to project headquarters and to the local environmental control agency office (IBAMA). After several confrontations with commercial boats, this strategy has proved to be highly effective in protecting fish stocks.

Over a five-year period, with funding of some US$3 million from a range of official international aid organizations and NGOs, an environmental management plan was developed in consultation with local communities (Mamirauá 1996).[10] This embraces a zoning system which designates areas for subsistence, commercial and conservation purposes, guidelines for resource-use based on scientific and local knowledge, continued vigilance as well as research and extension plans for the project's second phase. This last category includes proposals, as in the case of rubber tappers' extractive reserves, for economic diversification into other areas such as agriculture, bee-keeping, agro-forestry and handicrafts. Community representatives are formally integrated into the Mamirauá management committee.

Mamirauá and similar projects on the Amazon floodplain face a number of problems (Hall 1997). Immediate protection and vigilance activities are in many ways the easiest activities to implement, while other development and management initiatives may prove more difficult to follow through. Developing and marketing a broader range of products to increase incomes will present a formidable challenge, in the face of urban attractions. Executing an effective participatory consultation and decision-making strategy which reflects resource-user needs may also prove elusive. More broadly, developing a co-management institutional structure which incorporates community lake reserves into the formal structure for managing Amazonian fisheries will present a major challenge (McGrath forthcoming). Communities consist of little more than small groups of huts on the river's edge, hours or even days away by canoe from their nearest neighbors. Care must also be taken to avoid imposing a top-heavy management structure controlled by administrators and scientists, at the expense of the grassroots. Finally, dependence on overseas aid will continue unless alternative financial support can be arranged, such as a Trust Fund for Mamirauá.

Amerindians and Oil

As in the above Brazilian cases, local populations elsewhere which have been adversely affected by private, commercial resource extraction in Amazonia have also mounted increasingly vociferous campaigns against the threats thus posed to their livelihoods. Indigenous groups in the Amazon region of Ecuador and Peru, in collaboration with representative bodies and local non-governmental organizations have engaged in various forms of direct local protest. These include international legal action, negotiation with oil companies and international lobbying, and campaigning in order to ameliorate some of the harsher economic, social and environmental impacts described above. Consonant with the serious nature of their predicament, Ecuadorian indigenous organizations have spearheaded this process.

When Texaco pulled out of Ecuador in 1992, it left a massive trail of ecological damage that involved the contamination of substantial areas of rainforest in the Oriente. In 1993, a class action lawsuit (Aguinda vs Texaco) was filed in federal court in New York against the company on behalf of 30 000 local settlers and Amerindians of the Oriente, claiming US$1.5 billion in damages. Texaco was accused of 'negligence, public and private nuisance, strict liability and trespass,' and clean-up operations and compensation were demanded by the plaintiffs (Kimerling 1996, p. 65). Texaco denied any wrongdoing, and the lawsuit was dismissed in November 1996. However, this decision was itself challenged in October 1998 in the US Court of Appeals and a new ruling is expected in the near future on whether Texaco is liable under US law for its actions in Ecuador. If this judgment is favorable to the indigenous communities, it will set a major legal precedent. Texaco will be obliged to undertake a proper clean-up and pay much fuller compensation than it has so far offered. While a Court decision is awaited, an alliance of environmental, settler and indigenous organizations is calling for a consumer boycott of Texaco until it implements a thorough clean-up.

The Texaco case has led to a voluntary response from several major oil companies such as Mobil and Chevron in Peru, and Occidental, ARCO and Maxus in Ecuador, to undertake 'best practice' environmental measures and community relations programs when developing new fields. However, neither the Ecuadorian nor the Peruvian government has effective means of independently monitoring the efficacy of these procedures. Indigenous groups such as the Huaorani and Quichua have learned to negotiate directly with oil companies and sign agreements for compensation. These aspects have come under heavy criticism as constituting no more than a relatively cheap means of 'buying off' local communities and denying them lasting benefits. Furthermore, as Kane (1996) has documented so vividly in the case of Maxus' dealings with the Huaorani, such negotiations can be employed by oil companies to divide indigenous communities and curtail protest.

Direct action at local level has frequently been used as a means of resisting penetration by oil companies. The Cofán people were dispossessed of their lands by the first Texaco commercial oil strike in Ecuador and, although their number has been severely reduced to 700, they are now active in protecting what remains of their holdings. Part of this includes the Cuyabeno Wildlife Reserve, from which they were originally excluded. Having put pressure on the government, the Cofán have been deputized as reserve guards, and have established a zoning plan for land-use (Kane 1996). The Doreno and Quichua peoples of Ecuador have also impeded oil company operations at the exploratory and production phases. In Peru, 250 people from the Vicco community demonstrated in front of the Ministry of Mines and Energy in Lima in 1998 in protest against the pressure on them by the government to lease 3000 hectares of village land over 50 years for a paltry sum (Kimerling 1996; *Drillbits and Tailings*, 21 October, 1998).

More generally, lobbying at national and international levels against the actions of oil companies in the western Amazon continues apace. For example, a campaign is being waged for a moratorium against further drilling within Ecuador's Yasuni National Park and on Huaorani lands. The country's two major indigenous confederations, CONAIE and CONFENAIE, have demanded a 15-year moratorium against further oil development, but with little effect so far. Regional socio-environmental monitoring programs are being developed by CONFENAIE in collaboration with the NGO Acción Ecológica, based in Quito. Local groups such as OPIP in Pastaza have also been effective in lobbying for indigenous interests. In fact, OPIP led the historic march to Quito in 1992 of Amerindian and peasant farmer groups, which resulted in the legalization of over 1.1 million hectares of indigenous territories.

In Colombia, action by the 5000-strong, semi-nomadic U'wa of the Sierra Nevada has challenged the exploration rights granted by the government in 1995 to Occidental Petroleum on the tribe's Samore ancestral homeland. These were, it is alleged, obtained without proper local consultation. The Superior Tribunal of Bogotá ruled in favor of the U'wa in 1995, a decision which was immediately challenged by the company and revoked by the Colombian Supreme Court. In 1997, however, the Constitutional Court ruled that proper consultation, as required by law, had not in fact been carried out.

A complaint was then made to the Inter-American Commission on Human Rights, a branch of the Organization of American States, claiming that U'wa rights were being violated. In mid-1998, Occidental withdrew from the Samore project and is currently seeking to renegotiate terms with the Colombian government and the U'wa for exploration rights to a smaller area (Project Underground 1998b; Uribe Marin 1999). Since the early 1990s, the indigenous people's protests have been complemented by action on the part of a national lobby of environmentalists, journalists and lawyers as well as a vociferous coalition of NGOs in the US (the 'U'wa Defense Project'). Significantly, the translation of U'wa is, 'intelligent people who know how to speak'!

It was mentioned above that, following the turbulent Ecuadorian experience, oil companies in Peru have adopted a more cautious approach in dealing with indigenous communities and potential environmental hazards. Nowhere is this better exemplified than in the case of the US$3 billion Camisea project, located in the Lower Urubamba Valley, which was to have been developed by Royal Dutch Shell and Mobil. Camisea contains the largest known gas deposits in Latin America, enough to meet Peru's needs for over a century, or over 11 trillion cubic metres (Shell 1997). An area of major biodiversity, Camisea is home to several indigenous populations, primarily Machiguenga.

An environmental impact assessment study (EIA) was started in 1996 for the appraisal stage of the project and preliminary drilling commenced in the following year, with a view to deciding by mid-1998 whether to proceed with full field development. This would include isolated, clustered wells producing natural gas and liquids (with little or no local road construction to minimize disturbance), a local separation plant and two 520-kilometre pipelines across the Andes to the Pacific coast. The Camisea project was warmly welcomed by environmentalists because, for the first time, such an enterprise made systematic provision for consultation of local stakeholders as well as implementation of a 'health, safety and environment management system' which would minimize impacts and provide community health-care. However, environmental groups continued to criticize the company for failing to consult properly with local native groups and build in appropriate safeguards (EWGA 1998; CEIA 1998). Shell and Mobil withdrew from Camisea in July 1998 on the grounds that they wanted greater control over gas distribution than the Peruvian government was willing to concede. It is a matter of conjecture as to how environmental complications might have affected this decision to withdraw (Wright 1998).

PROTECTING THE COMMONS FROM BELOW

The above case studies illustrate how common-pool Amazonian natural resources, once explored collectively to meet long-term livelihood needs, have been appropriated by private interests for short-term commercial profit. Whatever the merits of such resource exploration in terms of regional or national development, the social and environmental impacts of indirect privatization in these instances have been highly negative.

Yet this conclusion is paradoxical since, according to conventional thinking, privatization should be one major *solution* to the problem of common-pool resource degradation, not the source of the problem. A number of theories, the best known of which is the 'tragedy of the commons' hypothesis (Hardin 1968), maintain that environmental destruction is inevitable where resources are openly accessible and jointly used. Individuals are thought to be incapable of pursuing long-term, collective welfare goals but will use the system to maximize individual benefit, leading inevitably to its collapse. As self-regulation is presumed to be 'irrational' (since it goes against individual, short-term interests) and therefore unworkable, it becomes necessary to introduce external regulation. This may be achieved either through the imposition of State controls or by providing incentives to individuals through the privatization of once collectively-held assets. It is therefore assumed that private owners will be automatically induced to preserve what once they might have destroyed.

Clearly, the conservation of Amazonia's natural resources was not uppermost in the minds of planners and politicians during the 1970s and 1980s, when aggressive policies of frontier settlement were being pursued in the name of regional and national development. In practice, a 'frontier economics' paradigm (Colby 1990) was followed, in which Amazonia was viewed as an infinite source of physical resources and as a sink for ecological degradation. After 1974 in particular, the private sector was officially portrayed as the key to modernization and economic progress in Brazilian Amazonia. Private enterprises were praised as inherently sound, while small farmers were openly criticized by the Planning Minister of the time for their 'predatory occupation,' and a policy of 'blaming the victims' prevailed (Wood and Schmink 1978). Such propaganda belies research evidence, which shows that some two-thirds of environmental destruction in terms of deforestation and associated impacts is caused by larger, commercial development rather than by subsistence farmers (Fearnside forthcoming).

It is not difficult to see why the appropriation by private interests of natural resources once administered collectively has led not to conservation but to degradation. The whole ethos of Amazonian frontier development has been based on generating quick commercial profit to serve both private and State interests, with scant regard for resource preservation. As mentioned above, vast financial subsidies have been offered to private ranchers, loggers, agribusiness concerns and mining companies to exploit the region as an infinite supplier of physical resources – terrestrial, aquatic and subterranean, in the case of oil. The changing macroeconomic situation has also offered powerful incentives to speculate in land and seek economic rents rather than productive development. Though making little sense in terms of balanced economic development, viewed through a 'rational choice' lens (Bates 1988), the strategy is logical in terms of the powerful political and personal interests being served.

If the private sector was expected to play a leading role in promoting economic development in Amazonia, the main responsibility for environmental management fell to the State. Since the early 1970s, the designation of protected areas such as national parks, national forests and ecological reserves has formed the backbone of environmental policy in Brazilian Amazonia. Almost 10 percent of the region (45 million hectares) is set aside in such 'conservation units' (Hall forthcoming(a)). This protectionist approach is backed up by surveillance, monitoring and control of deforestation by federal and state environmental agencies. Yet financial and human resource constraints often make it extremely difficult to enforce such centralized, protectionist policies.

Neither privatization nor government intervention has, on its own, offered an effective antidote to the poison of environmental destruction in Amazonia. On the contrary, both have, arguably, often exacerbated the problem, as this chapter has attempted to demonstrate. Confronted by a predatory private sector attempting to take control of common property resources on the one hand and, on the other, an ineffectual State machine, those communities whose livelihoods are threatened have had no choice but to take direct action.

Nowadays, the most significant policy innovations for resource conservation in Amazonia originate at the grassroots level. Mobilization by traditional populations in defense of their collective resource base has become increasingly common across the Amazon Basin, as commercial pressures have mounted. The key to resource protection lies in the hands of resource-user populations themselves. In operational terms, therefore, it is important to identify some of the specific roles that local communities are now playing in this process.

The 'tragedy of the commons' myth has now been widely debunked. It has been demonstrated how societies have developed their own informal, closed access resource management systems to provide for both individual and group needs (Bromley and Cernea 1989; Ostrom 1990). Under pressure from State-backed, private interests, traditional communities have been obliged to take the initiative and to develop their own strategies for countering these threats. These normally take the form of multi-institutional arrangements for CPR environmental management, tailored to meet the requirements of specific situations. They usually embrace a range of organizations working together, including community associations, government agencies, non-governmental organizations and international donors.

However, it is invariably local resource-user groups themselves which provide the initial stimulus for developing these new and dynamic strategies, born of the need to protect their own livelihoods. It is now realized that such groups possess social capital in terms of social structures, assets and relationships which form the foundation upon which adapted environmental management strategies may be constructed (Hall 1998). Drawing upon the examples discussed above from Brazil, Ecuador and Peru, key community roles may be briefly identified (Hall 1997, forthcoming(a):

1. Self-defence and vigilance. Since the Conquest, Amazonian populations have had a history of defending their territories against external threats. In more recent times, as noted above, the rubber tappers and fishing communities of Brazil have successfully challenged incoming commercial ranchers, loggers and fishing boats in face-to-face confrontations. Thus, the territorial integrity of large areas of common-pool resources has been secured. In Ecuador and Peru, indigenous groups have challenged oil companies, both on the ground as well as through national and international campaigning, embarrassing the enterprises concerned into adopting more environmentally sensitive practices. In Ecuador, the massive and still unresolved lawsuit against Texaco bears witness to the resilience of this movement, in collaboration with Ecuadorian and US environmental allies.

   Furthermore, reactive self-defense is increasingly being replaced by communities' systematic involvement in vigilance and monitoring as part of structured management plans, on the grounds that resource users are the best custodians of the rainforest. As part of management procedures in Brazil's four major federal extractive reserves, which cover over two million hectares, environmental monitors are recruited from the ranks of rubber tappers. On the Mamirauá fishing reserve, radio-equipped floating guard posts are manned by community members, to exclude commercial fishing vessels and report infractions to the authorities.
2. Articulating local needs in management. The failure to consult and involve beneficiaries has been a major reason for the failure of development projects generally. Threats to livelihoods have catalyzed Amazonia's traditional populations into a more proactive stance, forcing local demands onto the agenda for negotiation with development authorities and private interests. On the extractive reserves, community associations have been set up to facilitate the involvement of local populations (some 30 000 people) in designing and executing management plans. A similar principle underlies community organization at Mamirauá, where 1700 lake-users are being incorporated into the long-term management process. In Peru, Shell sought to develop a path-breaking consultative project at Camisea which, as mentioned, has now been abandoned by the company. Despite such setbacks, however, these cases demonstrate the potential role of local resource-user communities to become actively involved in environmental management.
3. Using traditional ecological knowledge. Part of the social capital brought by traditional CPR users into modern management set-ups comprises the knowledge of local ecology handed down over generations (Hall 1998).

This is crucial to any understanding of how ecosystems function and to determining their carrying and production capacity. Richards (1997) notes, for example, how in Amazonia there have been few attempts to draw from traditional knowledge on indigenous principles of land management. At Mamirauá, however, natural scientists have consulted with fisher folk over the complex dynamics of fish and aquatic mammal populations, feeding this local knowledge into the lake reserve zoning plan which designates areas for subsistence, commercial and re-stocking uses. Other traditional populations such as the rubber tappers on Brazil's extractive reserves and the Jaú national park (2.3 million hectares), as well as the Cofán and Huaorani in Ecuador, have also integrated local knowledge into management and zoning activities.

CONCLUSION

Privatization pressure upon Amazonia's common-pool resource base during the past two decades has provoked grassroots responses from a diversity of traditional populations whose lands and livelihoods have been undermined in the development process. Grassroots action thus constitutes a complement to state-controlled protectionism as an answer to the growing problem of resource degradation. Reconciling the economic use of natural resources to benefit traditional populations while conserving the natural resource base for present and future generations, a process which has been called 'productive conservation' (Hall 1997) thus offers some hope for the future. However, although laudable in principle, the potential problems of implementation should not be underestimated.

Initiatives such as the extractive and fishing reserves face numerous obstacles in operationalizing the notion of 'productive conservation.' Although social capital exists, it is not always easy to mobilize in traditional populations, which are often poor, geographically isolated, politically excluded and socially fragmented. It is difficult to sustain collective action for longer-term management purposes once the immediate external threat disappears. Organizational and managerial skills are extremely thin on the ground. Dependence on local NGOs and other intermediaries for these purposes carries the real danger that community needs can be easily undermined by outside agendas. Another major challenge which underpins all others is that of achieving economic sustainability and enhancing local incomes, thus providing users with incentives to reduce pressures on local resources. Diversifying production away from traditional crops such as rubber, finding markets for alternative non-timber forest products and strengthening commercial links with the private sector are all issues which practitioners are only just coming to grips with.[11]

Resistance to the privatization of Amazonia's natural resources has resulted not simply in *ad hoc* productive conservation projects. These initiatives have also helped to generate policy changes in their respective economic sectors. The rubber tappers' movement was instrumental in forcing the creation of a major policy change in Brazil, creating the 'extractive reserve' as a new category of conservation unit specifically for extractivist populations. Similarly, the Mamirauá project has been designated a 'sustainable development reserve' under Amazonas state law, the first of its kind in Brazil for fishing communities. As a result of such experiences, draft legislation is currently being considered in the Brazilian Congress to introduce a National System of Conservation Units, which would create new categories of protected area to allow for the planned integration of local communities into their management.[12] In the oil exploration areas of Ecuador and Peru, private companies are now having to take a far more cautious and conciliatory approach due to the organization and influence of the indigenous movement, although serious pollution problems remain. This mirrors developments in other exploration areas of the world such as the Canadian Arctic where, for example, during the 1980s, oil companies sought to establish community consultation procedures with the Inuit.[13]

For decades, privatization in Amazonia has been synonymous with social conflict and ecological degradation as individual corporate private interests have sought to extract profit from the resource base at minimum financial cost. Paradoxically, however, privatization must also form part of the solution to the environmental problems it has helped to create. Extractive reserves and fishing reserves are, after all, a form of collective private property over which local communities have control, although they do not enjoy outright ownership. If 'productive conservation' projects adopting new production forms such as agroforestry are ever to become economically viable, they must involve the business sector to market their products. On the Andean side, private companies such as Shell, despite the recent Camisea setback, will sooner or later probably be obliged to accept participatory forms of environmental management, as oil reserves elsewhere become scarce.

In a more general sense also, the private sector may well hold a major key to environmental sustainability in Amazonia. Current multi-billion dollar development plans to invest in transport, energy and communications infrastructure under the *Brasil em Ação* ('Brazil on the Move') program are currently being implemented (Brazil 1995; Hall 1999).[14] Concentrated along development 'axes' (*eixos de integração*), these investments are designed to integrate Amazonia into *Mercosul* and beyond, providing outlets for key exports such as soybeans from the cerrado region and iron-ore from Carajás. Certain public and private investments have been slowed down because of the economic crisis, as well as government embargoes imposed to punish alleged financial impropriety on the part of some institutions involved.[15] However, development of these major projects is underway and will accelerate in the near future.

Yet despite the legal obligation on companies to undertake environmental impact assessments, there is little or no incorporation of them into the planning process (FOE 1998; Egler 1998). Several major projects have already been implemented with such requirements playing a minimal role. The BR174 highway in Amazonas state was built with no environmental impact assessment, for example. Such lacunae need to be urgently addressed, as private capital is attracted to Amazonia in the wake of public incentives. Otherwise, the integration of Amazonia into the continental and global economy will surely lead to massive deforestation, environmental pressure and livelihood loss on a scale scarcely witnessed so far.

NOTES

1. Reader in Social Planning in Developing Countries, Department of Social Policy, London School of Economics, Houghton Street, London WC2A 2AE. Email: a.l.hall@lse.ac.uk
2. For further details on Mexico's *ejidos* and their privatization, see Sanderson (1986), Grindle (1990), Stephen (1998), Russell (1995), Barry (1995) and Ross (1997). For Peru, see Manrique (1996), and for Ecuador, Pacari (1996).
3. The best known example is of course that of 18th century Britain. Several thousand acts of enclosure resulted, by 1876, in 0.6 percent of the population owning over half of agricultural land in England and Wales (*The Ecologist* 1992).
4. According to the latest figures, the Gini coefficient of land concentration for Brazilian Amazonia (Northern Region) in 1992 stood at 0.83, compared with 0.85 for Brazil as a whole (Brazil 1997).
5. The price of oil on the international market plummeted from US$30 per barrel in 1986 to around US$10 in early 1999.
6. From 321 000 barrels per day (bbl/d) in 1992, to 390 000 in 1997.
7. These are: Chico Mendes and Alto Juruá in Acre, Rio Ouro Preto in Rondônia and Rio Cajarí in Amapá. Another five federal extractive reserves were set up in Maranhão, Tocantins and Santa Catarina, covering a total of 127 000 hectares and with a population of some 5600.
8. 'Couro vegetal' comprises framed sheets of cotton which are coated in latex, smoked intensively in small ovens, soaked in water and then vulcanized by the contracting company. A range of commercial products made from this material now exists, including shoes, bags and other items of clothing.
9. The most notorious of these have been at Lake Januacá in 1970, when six people were killed, and at Monte Alegre, near Santarém, in 1966, when 100 men attacked invading commercial fishing boats. By 1989, 44 Amazon lakes in Brazil had experienced such major confrontations (McGrath 1993).
10. Donors include the British Overseas Development Administration (ODA), now renamed the Department for International Development (DFID), World Wildlife Fund (WWF), Wildlife Conservation International, and the Brazilian government's scientific research council (CNPq).
11. For further information on sustainability issues, see Hall (1997, Chapter 6), Richards (1997), Smith *et al.* (1998).
12. Additional details on this project can be found in Hall (1997, Chapter 6) and Ramos and Capobianco (eds) (1996).
13. For further information, see Clark *et al.* (1997), especially Chapter 7 by Chris O'Neill on 'Community relations.'

14. Projects include, for example: (1) paving of major highways such as the BR364 to Rondônia and Acre, with extensions to link up with trans-Andean highways, thereby providing export access to the Pacific, the BR174 from Manaus to Venezuela and the BR156 from Amapá to Surinam; (2) development of the Urucú gasfield in Amazonas; (3) development of waterways on the rivers Madeira, Tapajós and Araguaia-Tocantins; and (4) extending the North–South railway, already connected to the Carajás–Itaqui railway, southwards from Imperatriz.
15. Two cases of projects that have been suspended pending investigation are the paving of the BR364 in Acre between Rio Branco and Cruzeiro do Sul, and the Araguaia–Tocantins waterway.

REFERENCES

Alston, Lee J., Gary D. Libecap and Robert Schneider (1995), 'The demand and supply of property rights on the frontier: the cases of North America and Brazil', in Terry Anderson and Peter Hill (eds), *The Privatization Process: A Worldwide Perspective*, Boston and London: Rowman and Littlefield, pp. 203–36.

Anderson, Terry and Peter Hill (eds) (1998), *The Privatization Process: A Worldwide Perspective*, Boston and London: Rowman and Littlefield.

Arnt, Ricardo (ed.) (1994), *O Destino da Floresta: Reservas Extrativistas e Desenvolvimento Sustentável na Amazônia*, Rio de Janeiro: Relume/Dumaré.

Ayres, Márcio (1993), *As Matas de Várzea do Mamirauá*, Brasília: CNPq.

Barry, Tom (1995), *Zapata's Revenge: Free Trade and the Farm Crisis in Mexico*, Boston, MA: South End Press.

Bates, Robert (ed.) (1988), *Towards a Political Economy of Development: A Rational Choice Perspective*, Berkeley, Los Angeles and London: University of California Press.

Becker, Bertha and Paulo Egler (1992), *Brazil: A New Regional Power in the World Economy*, Cambridge: Cambridge University Press.

Branford, Sue and Oriel Glock (1985), *The Last Frontier: Fighting Over Land in the Amazon*, London: Zed Books.

Brazil (1995), *Brasil Em Ação: Investimentos para o Desenvolvimento*, Brasília: Presidency of the Republic.

Brazil (1997), *Atlas Fundiário Brasileiro*, Brasília: INCRA.

Bromley, Daniel and Michael Cernea (1989), *The Management of Common Property Natural Resources: Some Conceptual and Operational Fallacies*, Washington, DC: World Bank Discussion Paper 57, World Bank.

CEIA, Commission for Environmental Impact Assessment (1998), *Advisory Review of the Environmental Impact Statements of the Hydrocarbon Appraisal and Development in Camisea, Peru*, Netherlands.

Clark, Karin, Cory Hetherington, Chris O'Neil and Jana Zavitz (1997), *Breaking Ice With Finesse: Oil and Gas Exploration in the Canadian Arctic*, Calgary: The Arctic Institute of North America of the University of Calgary.

Colby, Michael (1990), *Environmental Management and Development: The Evolution of Paradigms*, Washington, DC: World Bank Discussion Paper 80, World Bank.

Collinson, Helen (ed.) (1996), *Green Guerrillas: Environmental Conflicts and Initiatives in Latin America*, London: Latin America Bureau.

Cook, Paul and Colin Kirkpatrick (eds) (1995), *Privatisation Policy and Performance*, London: Prentice Hall.

Diegues, Antônio Carlos (ed.) (1994), *Deforestation and Livelihoods in the Brazilian Amazon*, São Paulo: UNRISD/NAPAUB.

Dreifuss, René (forthcoming), 'Strategic perceptions and frontier policy in Brazil', in Anthony Hall (ed.), *Amazonia at the Crossroads: The Challenge of Sustainable Development*, London: Institute of Latin American Studies, University of London.

Drillbits and Tailings, various issues.

The Ecologist (1992), 'Enclosure in Britain', **22** (4), July/August, 132–33.

Egler, Paulo (1998), *Improving the Environmental Impact Assessment Process in Brazil*, PhD thesis, School of Environmental Sciences, Norwich, UK: University of East Anglia.

ESP, Estado de São Paulo (1999), 'Desmatamento volta a crescer na Amazônia', 11 February.

Eve, Evaldice and Christoper Eve (1998), 'Resource base of peasants in the Brazilian Amazon: planning solutions for current problems of sustainability', *Bulletin of Latin American Research*, **17** (3), September, 387–407.

EWGA, European Working Group on Amazonia (1998), 'Report of the Camisea Decision Workshop', Institute of Latin American Studies, London, 26 June, *mimeo*.

Fearnside, Philip (forthcoming), 'Deforestation impacts, environmental services and the international community', in Anthony Hall (ed.), *Amazonia at the Crossroads: The Challenge of Sustainable Development*, London: Institute of Latin American Studies, University of London.

FOE, Friends of the Earth (1998), *Políticas Públicas para a Amazônia: Rumos, Tendências e Propostas 97/98*, São Paulo: Amigos da Terra Internacional Programa Amazônia, Grupo de Trabalho Amazônico (GTA).

Gasques, José Garcia and Clando Yokomizo (1986), 'Resultados de 20 anos de incentivos fiscais na agropecuária da Amazônia', *XIV Encontro Nacional de Economia*, ANPEC 2: 47–84.

Goldman, Michael (ed.) (1998), *Privatising Nature: Political Struggles for the Global Commons*, London: Pluto Press.

Goodman, David and Anthony Hall (eds) (1990), *The Future of Amazonia: Destruction or Sustainable Development?*, London: Macmillan.

Gray, John (1998), *False Dawn: The Delusions of Global Capitalism*, London: Granta Publications.

Grindle, Merilee (1990), *Agrarian Reform in Mexico: A Cautionary Tale*, in Roy Prosterman, Mary Temple and Timothy Hanstad (eds), *Agrarian Reform and Grassroots Development: Ten Case Studies*, Boulder and London: Lynne Rienner Publishers, pp. 179–204.

Gross, Anthony (1989), *Fight for the Forest: Chico Mendes in His Own Words*, London: Latin America Bureau.

Hall, Anthony (1989), *Developing Amazonia: Deforestation and Social Conflict in Brazil's Carajás Programme*, Manchester: Manchester University Press.

Hall, Anthony (1996), 'Did Chico Mendes die in vain? Brazilian rubber tappers in the 1990s', in Helen Collinson (ed.), *Green Guerrillas: Environmental Conflicts and Initiatives in Latin America*, London: Latin America Bureau, pp. 93–102.

Hall, Anthony (1997), *Sustaining Amazonia: Grassroots Action for Productive Conservation*, Manchester: Manchester University Press.

Hall, Anthony (1998), 'Enhancing social capital: productive conservation and traditional knowledge in the Brazilian Rainforest', *mimeo*. Paper presented at the conference on 'Human Impacts on the Environments of Brazilian Amazonia. Does Traditional

Knowledge Have a Role in the Future of the Region?', Linacre College, Oxford, 5–6 June.

Hall, Anthony (1999), 'Deforestation in Brazilian Amazonia: trends, causes and policy implications', *mimeo.*

Hall, Anthony (forthcoming(a)), 'Environment and development in Brazilian Amazonia: from protectionism to productive conservation', in Anthony Hall (ed.), *Amazonia at the Crossroads: The Challenge of Sustainable Development*, London: Institute of Latin American Studies, University of London.

Hall, Anthony (ed.) (forthcoming(b)), *Amazonia at the Crossroads: The Challenge of Sustainable Development*, London: Institute of Latin American Studies, University of London.

Hardin, Garret (1968), 'The tragedy of the commons', *Science*, **162** (13), December, 1243–48.

Hébette, Jean and Antonio Colares (1990), 'Small farmer protest in the Greater Carajás Programme', in David Goodman and Anthony Hall (eds), *The Future of Amazonia: Destruction or Sustainable Development?*, London: Macmillan, pp. 288–305.

Hicks, James F., Herman E. Day, Shelton H. Davis and Maria de Lourdes de Freitas (1990), *Ecuador's Amazon Region*, World Bank Discussion Paper 75, Washington, DC: World Bank.

INPE (1998), *Desflorestamento 1995–1997*, São Paulo: Instituto Nacional de Pesquisas Espaciais.

Jochnick, Chris (1995), 'Amazon oil offensive', *Multinational Monitor*, **26**, (1–2), January–February.

Kane, Joe (1996), *Savages*, New York: Vintage.

Kimerling, Judith (1991), *Amazon Crude*, New York: Natural Resources Defense Council.

Kimerling, Judith (1996), 'Oil, lawlessness and indigenous struggles in Ecuador's Oriente', in Helen Collinson (ed.), *Green Guerrillas: Environmental Conflicts and Initiatives in Latin America*, London: Latin America Bureau, pp. 61–73.

Kimerling, Judith (forthcoming), 'Oil development in Ecuador and Peru: law, politics and the environment', in Anthony Hall (ed.), *Amazonia at the Crossroads: The Challenge of Sustainable Development*, London: Institute of Latin American Studies, University of London.

Mamirauá (1996), *Mamirauá – Plano de Manejo*, Brasília: CNPq.

Manrique, Nelson (1996), 'The two faces of Fujimori's rural policy', *NACLA Report on the Americas*, **30** (1), July/August 39–43.

Martine, George (1990), 'Rondônia and the fate of small farmers', in David Goodman and Anthony Hall (eds), *The Future of Amazonia: Destruction or Sustainable Development?*, London: Macmillan, pp. 23–48.

McGrath, David (1993), 'Varzeiros, geleiros e o manejo de recursos naturais na várzea do Baixo Amazonas', *Cadernos do NAEA*, 11, November, 91–125.

McGrath, David (forthcoming), 'Avoiding a tragedy of the commons: recent developments in the management of Amazonian fisheries', in Anthony Hall (ed.), *Amazonia at the Crossroads: The Challenge of Sustainable Development*, London: Institute of Latin American Studies, University of London.

Millikan, Brent (1994), 'The agricultural frontier and deforestation in Rondônia', in Antônio Carlos Diegues (ed.), *Deforestation and Livelihoods in the Brazilian Amazon*, São Paulo: UNRISD/NAPAUB, pp. 70–107.

Moran, Emilio (1983), *The Dilemma of Amazonian Development*, Boulder, Co: Westview Press.

Ostrom, Elinor (1990), *Governing the Commons: The Evolution of Institutions for Collective Action*, Cambridge: Cambridge University Press.

Pacari, Nina (1996), 'Ecuador: taking on the neoliberal agenda', *NACLA Report on the Americas*, **29** (5), March/April, 23–32.

Philip, George (1994), *The Political Economy of International Oil*, Edinburgh: Edinburgh University Press.

Project Underground (1998a), *Drilling to the Ends of the Earth*, 13 September.

Project Underground (1998b), 'U'wa in Crisis', August.

Prosterman, Roy, Mary Temple and Timothy Hanstad (eds) (1990), *Agrarian Reform and Grassroots Development: Ten Case Studies*, Boulder & London: Lynne Rienner Publishers.

Ramos, Adriana and João Paulo Capobianco (eds) (1996), *Unidadades de Conservação no Brasil*, São Paulo: Instituto Socioambiental.

Richards, Michael (1997), *Missing a Moving Target? Colonist Technology Development on the Amazon Frontier*, London: Overseas Development Institute.

Ross, John (1997), 'Zapata's children: defending the land and human rights in the countryside', *NACLA Report on the Americas*, **30** (4), January/February 3–33.

Russell, Philip L. (1995), *The Chiapas Rebellion*, Austin: Mexico Resource Center.

Sanderson, Stephen (1986), *The Transformation of Mexican Agriculture*, Princeton: Princeton University Press.

Schneider, Robert (1992), *Brazil: An Analysis of Environmental Problems in the Amazon*, Washington, DC: World Bank.

Shell (1997), *People and the Environment: the Camisea Project, Peru*, Health, Safety and Environment Performance Report, Shell Prospecting and Development.

Smith, Nigel (1982), *Rainforest Corridors: The Transamazon Colonization Scheme*, Berkeley: University of California Press.

Smith, Nigel, Jean Dubois, Dean Current, Ernst Lutz and Charles Clement (1998), *Agroforestry Experiences in the Brazilian Amazon: Constraints and Opportunities*, Pilot Programme to Conserve the Brazilian Rainforest, Brasília: World Bank/Ministry of the Environment.

Stephen, Lynn (1998), 'Between NATFA and Zapata: responses to restructuring the commons in Chiapas and Oaxaca, Mexico', in Michael Goldman (ed.), *Privatising Nature: Political Struggles for the Global Commons*, London: Pluto Press, pp. 76–101.

Uribe Marin, M. del Pilar (1999), 'Where development will lead to mass suicide', *The Ecologist*, **29** (1), January/February, 42–6.

USEIA, United States Energy Information Administration (1997), 'Ecuador country analysis brief', December.

USEIA, United States Energy Information Administration (1998), 'Peru country analysis brief', January.

WF, Worldwide Forest/Biodiversity Campaign News (1998a), 'Occidental Petroleum will give up oil search on U'wa land'.

WF Worldwide Forest/Biodiversity Campaign News (1998b), 'Peru Indians Protest Shell Pullout'.

Wood, Charles and Marianne Schmink (1978), 'Blaming the victim: small farmer production in an Amazon colonization project', *Studies in Third World Societies*, **7**, February, 77–93.

Wright, Shannon (1998), ' Shell pulls out of Peru gas project', Rainforest Action Network, *Press Release*, 24 November.

COMMENTS ON ANTHONY HALL, 'PRIVATIZING THE COMMONS: LIBERALIZATION, LAND AND LIVELIHOODS IN LATIN AMERICA'

Hadi Esfahani

The central point of Anthony Hall's chapter is that, in the zeal for privatization as a solution to the problems of public and communal ownership, policymakers and policy analysts have tended to overlook the ills of private ownership in the presence of significant environmental externalities. The result has been environmental and social disaster in some parts of Latin America and, I would add, elsewhere around the world.

The main intellectual ammunition for the superiority of private ownership over collective ownership comes from the property rights school of thought, whose central proposition is based on the Coase Theorem. The proposition states that resources would be most efficiently allocated and incentives for productivity would be maximized if property rights of the individual over those resources are well defined and enforced. I don't think there are many economists who would quarrel with that proposition as long as its conditions are met. After all, with the commonly accepted specification of objective functions and property rights, the proposition is a matter of logic. What is important is the way the proposition has been interpreted for policy purposes. The property rights school has tended to interpret the key condition of the proposition, that property rights must be well defined and enforced, as a policy implication and a basis for the plan of action. The proposition has been taken to imply that to achieve efficiency and productivity, we must assign property rights over resources to individuals. This makes sense when we can define, properly assign and effectively enforce private property rights. The trouble is that assigning and enforcing private property rights is not always practical. And that is what Anthony Hall tries to show through a variety of examples concerning production activities that have significant environmental hazards.

Whether it's oil exploration or cattle ranching or agriculture, economic activities in the Amazon have significant environmental impact. The property rights over pieces of land can be easily privatized, but property rights over the environment are not easy to define and enforce on a private basis. You cannot sustain a rainforest in five acres of land if the rainforest all around it has been cleared. In this sense, part of the necessary conditions for the property rights proposition does not hold. So, the conclusion that private ownership would be better than public ownership is not necessarily warranted. Of course, one can argue that even if the necessary conditions are not fully met, private ownership may still be superior to public or communal ownership. But, as Anthony Hall argues, in situations such as Amazonia, the environmental externalities are too large to make that conclusion palatable.

The cases that Anthony Hall analyzes further suggest that in such situations there are potentially more efficient alternatives to private ownership. Common pool resources may be managed more efficiently through community organizations. This should not come as a surprise when one takes note of the fact that historically the resources of Amazonia have been collectively managed. It is natural to think that the indigenous people who have lived in those areas for millennia must have found reasonable institutional mechanisms to manage their resources. But the success of the property rights view in other areas, where the definition of property rights is relatively unambiguous and enforcement is relatively easy, has blinded many to the potential hazards of privatization in the presence of significant externalities. The success has made them forget that there may be a valid rationale for communal ownership mechanisms.

This is particularly surprising since as economists we always assume that people act rationally and take advantage of opportunities for mutual gain. When we see a particular organization survive through time, our normal null hypothesis is that there must have been good reasons why rational individuals have maintained that organization and followed its rules. But those of us who have been carried away by the success of the property rights idea forget about its limitations and quickly jump to the conclusion that communal ownership is an inefficient form of organization. The result has been that the property rights proposition has become the rationale for the plan of action by governments or individuals who see gains in the dismantling of the community ownership of common pool areas.

Of course, the old institutional arrangements have not been flawless, and with changing socioeconomic conditions they may not be working efficiently. But, as we are finding out, and Anthony Hall carefully demonstrates, the reform of those arrangements does not necessarily mean switching to a private property regime. There are many other alternatives that we can pursue, and these may best be found through experimentation by the local population.

The problem with respect to the application of the property rights proposition is not unique in the economics profession and warns us about some of our other judgments. Another prominent example that reflects the failure to apply the rationality axiom to the phenomena that we want to understand is the analysis of sharecropping. About a century ago, Alfred Marshall condemned sharecropping as a stupid arrangement that only the French would adopt! Marshall's analysis of incentive problems under sharecropping remained standard practice until about thirty years ago, when the economists expanded their perspectives beyond the European landscape and found out that many other people around the world share that kind of 'stupidity.' Some practitioners had gone even further and had guided governments to ban sharecropping in countries such as India.

Eventually, a few economists started wondering why so many people in so many different places do the same stupid thing. Then suddenly came the revelation that there may be very good reasons why people systematically favor sharecropping over fixed rent or fixed wage contracts. Nowadays, of course, the advantages of sharecropping are well understood and no one goes around banning it as an irrational practice.

The same thing appears to be happening with respect to community management of environmental resources, of course, after letting improper and imperfect property rights do a great deal of damage to the environment and to the indigenous populations.

11. Privatization and the public interest: partial theories, lopsided outcomes

Laurence Whitehead

I. INTRODUCTION

Throughout the 20th century, if not before, Latin American governments have been searching for the right overall development strategy (one might even say philosophy of development) that would achieve accelerated economic growth, structural modernization, social integration, and a respected status among the advanced countries in the international community. This search has given rise to a number of at least partially successful experiences of modernization 'from above, and without,' but it has also encountered a succession of disappointments, with the result that successive initially popular development strategies have subsequently entered into discredit and then been vigorously repudiated. The international liberalism of the 1870–1914 period was increasingly rejected in the inter-war years, and displaced by inward-looking strategies that became prevalent by mid-century. In the 1960s and 1970s there was division over whether these no longer flourishing strategies should be 'deepened' (in an increasingly state-dominated and potentially socialist direction, although anti-Communist regimes such as the Brazilian military might also favor 'deepening' on nationalist grounds), or reversed. Following the 1982 debt crisis and the global discredit of central planning, the 1990s has witnessed the emergence of a strong and broad-based consensus around a liberal and outward-oriented development strategy, sometimes referred to (in short-hand) as 'neo-liberalism' or the 'Washington Consensus.'

Within this new framework privatization (the divestiture of state assets) occupies a central role. It can perform a variety of strategic functions: creating new management incentives; enhancing competition: relieving fiscal burdens; eliminating subsidies and price distortions; attracting flight capital back, or drawing in new multinational investors; strengthening local capital markets; providing reliable assets for privatized pension schemes; funding huge otherwise unaffordable capital investment programs; and more generally signaling irreversible commitment to the prevailing philosophy of development. Privatization is best understood as an integral component of a broader liberalization process, rather than viewed too narrowly and in isolation. It is also important to keep in mind the longer-term historical context. If Latin America has now finally ended its search, and settled on the right development strategy for the indefinite future, then privatization is a foundational element in the new order. But if the features that gave rise to disillusion with earlier development models have still not been fully overcome, then the Latin American tradition of first promoting and then rescinding alternative patterns of property rights could eventually reassert itself.

Overall there is not much prospect of an early and major reversal in the privatization trend. It might be slowed or redirected, but except in extreme situations it is unlikely to be frontally challenged, at least for some time yet. After all, the most clear-cut and recurrent factor triggering privatization decisions across the sub-continent has been the overstretched state of public finances, and that impetus shows no signs of coming to an end in any part of the region. In the absence of adequate tax revenues government after government has been forced to recognize its incapacity to supply all the resources needed to finance public enterprise investment or to supply the goods and services demanded by citizens and consumers. Privatization has thus swept the sub-continent, not just as a source of short-term revenue enhancement, but as the only way to tap private capital markets and so pay for economic modernization. Whether it will ultimately clear the backlog of unmet demands cannot yet be established in most cases. However, it has now been underway long enough for some provisional judgments to be made. This chapter attempts such a preliminary review.

The next section defines the phenomenon under study (the boundaries of which are less clearcut than one might suppose) and draws attention to the various issues of public interest that are not resolved merely by expressing a preference for privatization. The third section considers some questions of timing and sequencing that are related to the alternative styles of privatization that have been attempted. The fourth offers a 'snapshot' of the current scene, indicating where the momentum is still building up, and where the main points of difficulty and resistance are emerging. The fifth section reviews a series of alternative theories of privatization, comparing each with the Latin American experience so far.[1] The conclusion returns an as yet open verdict on the relationship between privatization and the public interest, and on the prospects for a permanent pro-market policy consensus. The various theories of privatization seem to provide only partial and incomplete accounts of the story so far. They do not suffice to establish that the current consensus is necessarily an irreversible break with the past, in particular since the prospective outcomes are often lopsided and in disequilibrium. On the other hand, the forces promoting privatization are largely unabated, the alternatives are sketchy and unconvincing, and so the present tide of pro-market reform almost certainly has further to run.

II. 'PRIVATIZATION' AND 'THE PUBLIC INTEREST'

Compare the following two definitions, taken from recent publications on privatization in Latin America by respected US-based academics:

> I define *privatization* to include all types and increments of transfer of ownership, partial or complete, from the government to the private sector. Privatization also occurs when previously excluded persons or groups, such as foreigners or limited liability corporate entities, are recategorised as 'eligible' private owners (Leslie Armijo).[2]

> We are using *privatization* to include divestiture, the liquidation of uneconomic public enterprises, the conversion of government-owned ventures into mixed enterprises or joint ventures with private investors on the basis of market performance, the contracting out of management or subsidiary operations, and the requirement that parastatal managers meet ordinary standards of profitability in discharging their functions (William Glade).[3]

Now consider a third formulation, offered by a leading analyst of privatization in Britain:

> The privatization programme . . . was a much broader policy than asset sales, involving a host of measures including the withdrawal of industrial aid, deregulation, and franchising. The policy followed a number of phases, as did the emphasis on its intellectual justification. At first, the State withdrew aid and subsidies, radically pruning industrial policy as traditionally conceived. ... The next step was to increase competition in the State sector . . . The next phase concentrated more directly on ownership and the transfer of public assets to the private sector . . . In addition, there were a number of other variants of the new competition policy. These included the contracting-out of services traditionally performed by State organizations (such as dustbin collection and health service laundry) as well as more ambitious franchising arrangements. Thus, what started out as a relatively well-defined policy came to be directed towards the achievement of other objectives which sometimes conflicted with competition.

This author then extends the analysis to include legislation against trade union 'monopoly' and in favor of the private provision of health care, and education, and the disposal of the social housing stock (Dieter Helm).[4]

Each of these three definitions has its advantages, but they differ substantially in their respective boundaries and focus. It is therefore important to be alert to these variations when applying the term. The first definition is the narrowest, concerned only with ownership transfer (and explicitly disavowing 'privatization of management' in the absence of ownership change). Although it acknowledges complexity, and posits a continuum rather than a dichotomy, it takes as given a set of legal categories ('state' ownership and 'private' ownership) which other analysts have viewed as contested and problematic. For example, if the Honduran military pension fund owns strategic productive assets, is that adequately characterized as state ownership? If shares in Bolivian state enterprises are transferred to collective pension funds administered by private foreign financial managers, is that a shift into 'private' ownership in the same sense as quoting YPF shares on the New York Stock Exchange? (If so, what are the rights of the ultimate owners? In 1998 Bolivian pensioners proved bereft of legal protection when their government unilaterally changed the pension contract.) Armijo's definition has the advantage that it is empirically observable, but there is room for doubt over the true meaning of what is thereby observed.

Glade's definition apparently includes everything covered by Armijo, but it adds two further elements that considerably redefine the issues. If an enterprise can be privatized through *liquidation*, then we need to pay much more attention to bankruptcy procedures and to the residual claims of the various creditors and stakeholders. If privatization can include some continuation of state ownership, moderated by the requirement that enterprise managers are subject to market disciplines, then at least some of the public enterprises operating in Latin America before 1982 would have to be classified as privatized (for example PDVSA after the Venezuelan oil nationalization of 1976, or the Puerto Rican Telephone Company between 1973 and 1998, when it was finally 'privatized' in Armijo's sense).

Acknowledging the 'strikingly entrepreneurial behavior' of the Venezuelan state petroleum company, Glade describes this as 'a form of simulated privatization when managers of state-owned enterprises must conform to the behavioral constraints applied by the market to private firms.'[5] Glade's definition invites further consideration of various aspects of the 'public interest' (for example concerning bankruptcy, and the social behavior of market-oriented managements) to which we will return in Section VI below. He also stresses the points that privatization must be seen as part of a broader package of market-oriented policies, and that its effects must be evaluated in terms of the general signals it transmits, as well as the specific economic results it delivers. But his analysis is structured around the dichotomy conveyed in his title, and he therefore tends to assume that the broad thrust of current policy is both positive and irreversible.

The third definition (or more strictly evaluation) followed Glade on some key points, but includes various qualifications that he downplays. Thus, privatization is viewed as a broad policy orientation, with an initial pro-market theoretical foundation, but the theory is held to fall short of accounting for successive policy applications and variations. Privatization is not necessarily pro-competitive; it may be distorted to serve political necessity (Armijo also makes this point, although in a reductionist manner); it can centrally involve the redistribution of social power against welfare dependants, and organized labor, and so on. Again these are points we shall return to below, since they redirect our attention to various aspects of the 'public interest'.

Having reviewed these three alternative definitions, it is necessary to indicate the approach used in this chapter. Here 'privatization' is an umbrella term, encompassing a number of sub-categories and national variations. As it has grown in popularity over the past 20 years, the term has also been extended in scope, so that it can now be used to include social security and welfare provision and even a range of government services in addition to directly productive activities. Even prisons and police forces may be contracted out to private suppliers, though not (at least yet) the legislative or judicial functions of the state. At the same time as this inflation of the term, broader changes in economic ideology and organization have been taking place, so that the policy significance of any particular measure of privatization needs to be assessed in a specific policy context. In one setting the main objective might be to reduce fiscal subsidies or to strengthen management incentives, whereas elsewhere the rationale could become to eliminate vestiges of state socialism, or to attract modern technology and direct foreign investment. Privatization might be a central pillar of economic strategy in one context, or simply one alternative option within a market-oriented reform program in another. What gives this disparate range of possibilities some underlying unity is not so much any precise, let alone technical, meaning as a prevailing pro-market internationally-oriented mood in favor of liberalization – a *zeitgeist* as much as a calculated choice. What matters from a public interest perspective is precisely how this general orientation is worked out in particular contexts. Here we need to make some further distinctions.

For example, privatization has different implications when applied to a natural monopoly as opposed to a competitive industry. Its significance varies when the product is in relatively fixed supply (such as water) or when the product is in headlong expansion (say, telecoms). We can illustrate the point using the following two examples:

1. The Chilean Water Code of 1981 is widely regarded as a pioneering initiative in privatizing water rights. It set up a legal framework for the free trading of water rights, transferring oversight from administrative agencies to the judicial system, and leaving the rest to private initiative. It has been generally interpreted as a faithful application of the theories of the 'Chicago' school to one particular conflictual area of public policy, and regarded as a vindication of those theories. However, this understanding has not been based on much careful examination of the experience on the ground. A

recent study of the rural water system in Chile by Carl J. Bauer seeks to rectify that deficiency. Bauer found that in practice the Code was something of a compromise aimed at accommodating traditional conservative and military interests, rather than a wholehearted application of neo-liberal theory. Although trading in water rights was introduced, little actually occurred. The really difficult issues involved socio-political conflict (for example, between power companies which sought to store water in the summer in order to meet peak electricity demand in the winter, and irrigators who aimed to store water in the winter to meet agricultural demand in the summer). Neither the markets nor the Chilean judiciary were particularly well placed to resolve these disputes (as the 1998/9 drought and power cuts in much of rural Chile made clear). More generally, Bauer concluded that

> To define property rights to natural resources simply as commodities tramples on difficult issues. Such property rights cannot be private, exclusive, and transferable, because different resource uses are physically inter-connected and people's activities directly and indirectly affect one another. New definitions of property rights affect not only their owners but also other resource owners and users. Thus property rights to nature affect collective interests, and consist partly of overlapping rights to use shared resources, rather than private freedom to alienate and exchange.

Resolving water conflicts 'requires qualitative measures and comparisons of value, and a qualitative logic to weight and choose among a web of rights, rules, purposes and interests. This again is an inherently judicial and political task for which private bargaining and exchange cannot substitute.'[6] Bauer concludes that as competition for scarce water increases in Chile, the sclerotic and tradition-bound judicial system will need to be reformed. Public interest considerations will demand greater weight, and the market-determined allocation of private rights over water will have to be reformulated. Bauer's study refers only to the rural sector. It should also be noted that in Santiago the municipally owned water utility has succeeded in balancing market constraints with social objectives to a greater extent than elsewhere in Latin America.[7]

2. Telecom companies occupy pride of place in Latin America's new corporate rankings. According to the London *Financial Times*, 29 out of the region's top 100 companies, ranked by market capitalization as of 30 September 1998 were in this sector.[8] Topping the list was Telmex; fifth and sixth were the two São Paulo components of Telesp; seventh and tenth were the rival Argentine telecom private monopoly; Chile's CTC was fourteenth; and so on. But the fact that private investors can buy and sell such shares on the stock exchange by no means tells the whole story about the scope and limits of private ownership in this most strategic and dynamic of industries. Even

the old state-owned monopolies frequently released a proportion of their equity to the investor public. More important have been legislative changes to introduce competition and perhaps subject managements to the possibility of challenge and even takeover. In Mexico the transformation was partly driven by the need to satisfy business demands on the US–Mexico border, and to cater for the explosive growth of international traffic. In the Dominican Republic the demands of the tourist industry were paramount, and so forth. In any case, according to Noam's recent study,

> once governments make the decision to liberalize markets and to permit multiple providers, they can organize domestic telecom markets to allow various amounts and types of competition. The licensing of operators can be used to limit the number of competitors and services and to impose obligations on providers. Licenses for spectrum access can be allocated according to specific use or assigned according to specific users. Once multiple providers are permitted in domestic markets, governments can restrict the extent of collaboration among competitors within limits on vertical and horizontal integration and separation of territories of operation. Foreign PTOs . . . can be regulated as common carriers and required to meet minimum quality of service and investment criteria specified by the regulatory entity. Particularly important in developing countries with low teledensities is the mandate to strive for universal connectivity.[9]

In summary, the world of privatized telecoms is about as far removed from *laissez-faire* as one could imagine. If we accept the stereotype that state interventionism encourages rent-seeking and collusion, then of itself privatization of this sector can offer no guarantees that the public interest will be more honorably served. If possible at all, this can only be achieved through vigorous supervision provided by a well-structured and well-resourced system of regulation.

The issue of regulation arises in many guises, depending on the specific characteristics of each industry. Here we shall pursue the telecoms example, because of its quantitative importance and its exemplary complexity and relevance to the public interest. But this is illustrative of a broader pattern. When Telmex was sold by the Mexican government (between 1990 and 1994) the privatized enterprise was granted a domestic concession until 2026, and a monopoly on long-distance services until 1997. The largest shareholder, Grupo Carso, has been accused of acting as a front for the most powerful politicians responsible for the privatization (Mexico's long-standing governing party, the PRI, is almost universally perceived as having manipulated privatization in order to secure party and patronage benefits). In Venezuela, in 1991, 'the government and the state telecom company, CANTV, renegotiated the company's contract prior to the privatization to ensure CANTV's monopoly for the first 9 years after its sale and its continued contribution to the National Treasury; this policy was supported by the major political parties in Venezuela.'[10] (Venezuela's traditional parties have since been comprehensively repudiated by an electorate which judged them to have become irredeemably corrupted). In Argentina, Alejandra Herrera writes that, 'the government increased tariffs prior to the sale of ENTel to increase the basic rates from which future increases would be calculated. Also, in Argentina, entrenched suppliers were able to secure continuance of existing contracts in order not to lose market share.' She concludes that

> the post-privatization period in Argentina is inherently unstable because of the institutional weaknesses of the national telecom regulatory agency; the two regional monopolies are virtually unregulated. The agency has been excluded from all major disputes among companies and between the companies and the government since privatization. The companies have used the regulatory vacuum to their advantage to consolidate their position in the major service areas.[11]

My own interviews with telecom regulators in La Paz, Bolivia in April 1997 foreshadowed the likelihood that regulatory deficiencies would emerge there too. Overall, Noam's assessment is that 'as a result of privatization, private monopolies, sometimes foreign-owned, have, in many countries, replaced the old state monopolies.' (Noam, 1998). Arguably this policy was necessary to provide sufficient incentive in the form of monopoly rents to promote high levels of investment and greatly expanded network coverage. Also, the policy contributed to the high price realized by the state for the privatization. But a problem amply documented in the Noam volume is that adequate, consistent regulatory controls of private monopolies have yet to be instituted. Furthermore, as part of the initial sale terms, buyers of telephone companies demanded policy changes that undercut many of the alleged benefits for the public of sector reorganization. Noam's final observation is that

> governments have pledged to regulate private companies in a way that will expand and modernize the public network and eventually extend service to all who want it, but to date, the authors have found little evidence that government officials have made the necessary political and financial commitments to create and to sustain credible regulatory agencies. In some cases, regulatory agencies were supposed to have been established prior to the sale of the state companies but either became entangled in domestic political disputes or, according to the cynical view, were purposefully not created and/or not funded in order to give the new owners a free hand.[12]

As in the case of water, Chilean telecoms privatization has been regarded as exemplary. It began earlier than elsewhere in Latin America, and went further. It was based on laws barring monopoly and periods of exclusivity, authorizing international involvement, and promoting competition among equipment suppliers. Noam describes Chile as the closest in Latin America to developing an institutionally advanced federation of subnetworks, or what he calls a 'pluralistic stage network.' But although privatization has resulted in a tremendous increase in the quality, variety, and quantity of services, it has also exposed the problem of the institutional weakness of the regulatory regime.

> Power is being transferred from executive and administrative action to the judiciary. This transfer has consequences for the government's ability to promote social objectives in the sector, particularly in the extension of service to rural areas and cross subsidies . . . there are many unresolved questions about the proper role of government and the means to achieve universal service and to structure competitive markets.[13]

Once again the Chilean judiciary appear as guardians of the rights of property, charged with screening the market from the interference of elected politicians. As in the case of water, it is questionable whether Chilean judges have the necessary skills and incentives to serve the overall long run public interest in this dynamic area of the economy.

A final 'public interest' point concerns the question of foreign ownership. Even with a complete transfer of operations to the private sector, governments often reserve the right to nationalize vital infrastructure to safeguard national sovereignty. Historic examples are the UK, Sweden and Spain. 'Additionally, governments may place restrictions on the permissible level of foreign ownership of the telecommunications infrastructure, as in the US.'[14] Although this quotation refers to telecoms, the point is more general. For example, laws concerning the US merchant marine, ports and harbors, and air traffic control systems all include national security protections. Yet many privatizers in Latin America are inclined to dismiss any such provision as an archaic residue of interventionism. Foreign advisers, in particular, should be pressed to explain why deregulation should go further in Latin America than in their own countries of origin.

Another area of US law and practice which could merit the attention of Latin American privatizers concerns the question of bankruptcy. As mentioned above, one key determinant of the practical consequences of allowing free market forces greater scope is that some privatized enterprises may face liquidation. One of the most recurrent reasons why public ownership increased in Latin America over the 1930–1980 period was that governments were unwilling to allow large enterprises to be dismantled through bankruptcy and the forced disposal of their assets. Whenever this prospect loomed, the state tended to step in and take over the management and perhaps eventually the ownership of the ailing enterprise. If privatization is truly to generate a fluid and efficient market economy in Latin America, it will have to be accompanied by more frequent and much smoother processes of asset reallocation among qualified creditors. It is as well to notice that US practices in this regard are considerably more fluid than those found in Western Europe, as well as in Latin America. Thus, whereas in Europe bankruptcy is a status meant to carry great stigma (Italian bankrupts lose their passports or even their right to travel away from their city of residence), in the US bankruptcy is only considered a rather minor violation of the social contract. In Europe bankruptcy is likely to be involuntary, and the result of a decision taken by one or more creditors, whereas in the US it is almost always a voluntary choice, a decision taken by the insolvent debtor. European bankruptcy procedures have a bias toward immediate liquidation and prompt distribution to the creditors, whereas US practice favors reorganization, with a multi-year stay on creditor demands. The consequence is said to be that Europeans are less willing to take on debt, whereas Americans are more entrepreneurial. Latin American legal systems are generally so sluggish and overloaded that they would be unable to operate either of these systems reliably and on a large scale. But if privatization is to work in accordance with liberal expectations of an efficient market system, this is a further area of public policy that will have to be defined and reformed. The choice between the alternative models of bankruptcy procedure is not a simple technical issue, but raises broad issues of public interest concerning the whole model of capitalism expected to accompany privatization. There is not much evidence as yet about how Latin Americans intend to develop this aspect of their new economic model.[15]

III. ALTERNATIVE STYLES OF PRIVATIZATION (TIMING AND SEQUENCING)

When, as in this chapter, privatization is viewed as a broad-gauge process, embedded in a larger strategy (or even ideology) of market-oriented restructuring, then it becomes possible to identify a variety of alternative possible stages and trajectories. This section distinguishes between three alternative styles, each with its own specific rhythm and temporal sequence. The three styles are root-and-branch; incremental; and opportunist. The respective rhythms are intense and sustained; gradual and measured; and erratic. Actual examples are always somewhat hybrid, of course, but in Latin America the contrasts are sharp enough to illustrate these distinctions. Chile provides the prime example of a root-and-branch process; Brazil can be taken as an illustration of incrementalism; while the Venezuelan path has been highly erratic.

The Pinochet dictatorship exercised unrestricted power for over 16 years. It originated as a reaction to the socialism and statism of the preceding Allende administration. Its pro-market orientation was 'root and branch' in the sense that it aimed to systematically strengthen and guarantee the private property system which had come close to suppression. In this context 'privatization' was only one element in a broader ideological program. The regime could work to a long time-frame, across a wide array of policy areas, deploying its concentrated power to produce a holistic transformation. Nevertheless it was driven by a sense of urgency, and its activities were intense as well as sustained. The military probably have a bias in favor of emergency measures, and the propertied classes had been unified by the Allende threat. In addition, they were initiating privatization at a time when the regional and to some extent even the international climate was still against it, and their aim was not just to restore the *status quo ante*, but to consolidate an exemplary and irreversible new model of post-socialist enterprise and economic dynamism. In contrast to most other Latin American countries the Chilean administrative apparatus was more capable of implementing a coherent and integrated program of national transformation.[16]

Even with this root-and-branch objective, and the capacity to make policy in a sustained and intense manner, the privatization process in Chile was neither simple nor straightforward. Eduardo Silva distinguishes between three strongly contrasting phases which he labels 'gradualist;' 'radical,' and 'pragmatic.' We have already mentioned the gap separating ideology from reality in the case of privatized water rights, and the problems of judicial oversight in the telecoms sector. As is well known, the state-owned copper company, Codelco, was never privatized. Instead it was run in competition with new private mining investors, by state managers who knew that 10 percent of their foreign exchange earnings had become earmarked revenue allocated directly to the armed forces. In the same national security spirit, when the state electricity monopoly ENDESA was privatized in the late 1980s, the military government insisted on spinning off the Colbún-Machicura Dams as a separate state company that might provide some counterweight to private monopoly power. There were also fluctuations in policy over time. In particular, the most dogmatic phase of the Chilean program took place before the deep financial crisis of 1982. The newly privatized banks plunged into insolvency at that time, and had to be rescued by the Chilean taxpayer. Thereafter, the program was recalibrated and conducted in a more pragmatic and successful manner.

In conception, Brazilian incrementalism offers a clear contrast to Chilean maximalism, and yet as the process has gathered momentum there have been certain signs of convergence. In Brazil the preceding state interventionist economic model was identified not with Marxism and a politicized labor movement, but with statist nationalism/military rule. The model did not end in a spectacular defeat, but was eroded by a protracted crisis which still left many elements of its legacy looking viable and enjoying influential support. The post-military democratic regime was not initially much in favor of market-oriented reform. The 1988 Constitution contains many provisions that restrict domestic competition and an international economic orientation. Over the subsequent decade attitudes towards economic liberalization have become progressively more favorable, but the process of change has been stepwise and incremental.

Privatization began slowly, experienced a setback between 1992 and 1994, and has gathered momentum thereafter as large inflows of foreign private capital became available. Following the *real* crisis of January 1999, pressures to accelerate the program of market-oriented reforms are likely to intensify but so may resistance, given that the foreign appetite for Brazilian assets has weakened, and that the terms available are likely to be less attractive.

In contrast to the Chilean process, privatization in Brazil may be classified as 'measured' in the sense that each step was decided as a distinct operation, rather than derived from an overreaching commitment; that time was allowed for lobbyists to bring their preferences to bear, both for and against; and that the key decisions were subject to legislative and party political debate and oversight. In fact Brazilian democracy provides for multiple (possibly excessive) institutional veto points – legislative, judicial, electoral, administrative and state/federal.[17] Nevertheless, it needs to be emphasized that over time and through a succession of discrete decisions the Brazilian government has ended up authorizing an interlocking set of market-oriented reforms, public enterprise divestitures, foreign investment incentives, and product and capital market liberalizations, which may be cumulatively almost as transformative as the Chilean counterparts. The differences of conception, timing, and process may be greater than the variations in eventual outcome.

The erratic course of privatization in Venezuela illustrates a third possible style, with a different rhythm and probably also a different outcome. In this case the pre-existing system was a highly interventionist and politicized electoral democracy structured around the distribution of rent derived from the state ownership of a massive oil revenue. As illustrated in the telecoms discussion in the previous section, there have been some large-scale privatizations in Venezuela during the 1990s. Indeed, the administration of Carlos Andrés Pérez (1989–92) might even be described as starting out with ambitions for root-and-branch transformation on something like the Chilean model. However, it soon encountered sufficient resistance not only to block its ambitions but to bring the entire political order into question. After President Pérez was impeached, President Caldera was elected on an anti-liberal economic platform. Even so, in the wake of a massive crisis in the financial system, the pressures for a return to market-oriented reform prompted another change of course. The recent election of ex-coup leader Colonel Hugo Chávez, again on an anti-liberal platform, leaves many questions unresolved concerning the eventual direction of Venezuelan economic policy. (The next section includes some further observations on this matter.) The main comparative points to emerge from this brief reference to the Venezuelan experience are that it is possible for the logic of privatization to be blunted or even frustrated by domestic opposition; it is possible that the interests built up around an alternative model of *rentier* politics may be capable of blocking cumulative advance in a market-oriented direction, even through the consensus is purely negative, and no coherent public interest alternative is available; if the main benefits of privatization arise from the signaling it provides of a long-term commitment to market-related patterns of allocative efficiency, then erratic (and potentially reversible) divestitures of state assets may fail to deliver such reassurance, or may even transmit the opposite message.

The three styles of privatization outlined and illustrated above in no way exhaust the range of observable alternatives. For example, Menem's Argentina presents many features of the 'root-and-branch' approach associated with Chile, yet it was the product of a constitutional government, subjected to electoral constraints, and it followed on a previous administration which displayed a more Venezuelan-type instability of course. The Mexican process also contains several stages with different prevailing styles. In Uruguay incrementalism of the Brazilian type has proceeded still more slowly, because of the provision that privatization can be overturned through popular plebiscites. In Bolivia and Peru extreme hyper-inflationary crises paved the way for urgent root and branch transformations; whereas in Puerto Rico the benefits of the US dollar, the American legal system, and a generous flow of federal subsidies has meant that decisions to privatize are taken within a framework of normality, rather than under the spur of emergency conditions.

There appears to be at least as much variation between the styles of privatization encountered in post-communist Eastern Europe, if not more. The Treuhand in East Germany certainly obeyed a very different logic from that of the Hungarian Privatization Agency, or the Czech Voucher Scheme, and Romanian policies seem almost as erratic as those of Venezuela. The Ukraine offers yet another model of privatization in the presence of intense regional rivalries, and in the absence of secure property rights. In this region, as in Latin America, lopsided policy experiments are followed by sharp course corrections. For example, the Czech voucher scheme failed to provide much legal protection for minority shareholders who were therefore mistreated. Subsequently, Prague has tried to introduce US-style securities regulation.

One additional observation is pertinent here. At least in Latin America, there are considerable analogies between the various styles and rhythms of privatization identified above, and the styles and rhythms of state interventionism that preceded them. An equivalent to Chilean 'root-and-branch' privatization under dictatorship could be either Cuba after 1959 or Peru after 1968. A counterpart to the incrementalism of Brazilian privatization might be found in the progressive expansion of the Mexican public sector in the 1960s, and 1970s. The erratic course of policy recently exemplified by Venezuela resembles many earlier counterparts where state ownership was blocked or contested. Viewed from this perspective, perhaps the current upsurge of privatization initiatives in Latin America should not be viewed in too unilinear a manner. The range of privatization styles, rhythms, and eventual outcomes may prove as diverse as the preceding range of statist experiments.

We lack the historical perspective needed to reach firm conclusions about the range of eventual privatization outcomes, but these processes have now been underway for long enough to permit some provisional or 'snapshot' evaluations of the current scene.

IV. THE CONTEMPORARY SCENE: MOMENTUM AND RESISTANCE

On a narrow definition of privatization (divestiture of state assets) there clearly comes a point when not much is left to transfer to the private sector. Argentina under Menem must have already disposed of most of what can be sold, when the latest items on the list are the Post Office and the air traffic control system. With Brazil now turning to Petrobrás, and Mexico preparing its electricity generators for sale, it is foreseeable that within the next three or four years this phase of the process will be substantially complete. There are some obvious hard cases – for example, PEMEX, Codelco, and PDVSA – but these are finite in number and may eventually be reduced to residual status. The pendulum would only swing into reverse if the remaining state enterprises started growing much more rapidly than their private competitors (for example, if PDVSA or Codelco developed large low cost reserves); or if another private sector crisis delivered a new cohort of insolvent enterprises whose losses the state was willing to socialize. Only PDVSA had much potential to follow the first route, and that is currently being blocked off. As for the second alternative, the hypothesis is harder to assess, but the evidence from East Asia is that in the event of a massive private sector crisis, emerging market governments will be placed under intense pressure to sell off assets cheaply to multinational investors, or failing that to liquidate failures. Certainly the 1995 peso bail-out and the Mexican congressional debates over Fobaproa suggest that neither US nor Mexican taxpayers would be keen to socialize future private enterprise losses. From this standpoint, therefore, privatization-as-divestiture is likely to continue until exhausted, and is unlikely – at least in the next few years – to be reversed.

However, a broader definition of privatization would indicate that much more remains to be done, and that the relevant time horizon is far longer. For example, to establish and routinize effective and predictable insolvency procedures is mainly a task for the next generation. To generalize contested markets so that all managements – private as well as public – can be ejected for failure to perform would take even longer (especially in those countries where family firms continue to operate much the same as in the old days of state capitalism).

To create authoritative, professional, accountable and speedy systems of market regulation will also require much further work. In most countries judicial legislative and media oversight remains weak or incipient. If privatization is understood in these terms, then the process will take far longer, and the momentum behind it is considerably more open to question.

This brings us to the actual or potential sources of resistance. With regard to divestiture, the nationalists and statists within the political élite have generally been marginalized or bought off.[18] Trade union opposition can still be found, and may cause delays (for example, the 41-day strike against the sell-off of PRTC in Puerto Rico in 1998) but it is usually too isolated and self-interested to achieve more than that. In current conditions of high fiscal pressure the government almost always has a strong enough financial incentive to over-ride or compensate the most influential losers.[19] As international capital flows to emerging markets have contracted in the wake of the Asian, Russian and Brazilian crises, the Washington-based international financial institutions have stepped up their pressure in favor of accelerated economic reforms as a condition for financial support, although on at least one issue – the abolition of all restrictions on short-term capital movements – they have softened their stance.

Nevertheless, on a broader view of what constitutes a privatization process, and what trends are now at work in the international economy, the signs of resistance are greater than before. For example, on taking office the Chávez administration in Venezuela revoked a 38 percent rise in electricity charges authorized by the outgoing Caldera administration at the end of 1998, causing a one-third fall in the share price of Electricidad de Caracas. The telephone company CANTV fears the government may also violate the terms of the contract drawn up during the 1991 privatization, terms which (as shown above) were politically controversial. Similarly the Brazilian Minister of Justice imposed a maximum fine of 2.9 million *reais* on each of the two major telephone companies (for São Paulo and Rio) that had been privatized in July 1998, for providing inadequate services. In February 1999, during the hottest period of the summer vacation, half a million inhabitants of Buenos Aires were subjected to electricity blackouts which deprived them both of light and of water for about a week. As a result the privatized Chilean operator, Edesur, faces a fine of no less than $75 million. Proposals to privatize the Chilean ports and the post office, and the Mexican electricity generators, have become heated issues in the respective election campaigns. On a wider canvas, George Soros, in *The Crisis of Global Capitalism* (1998) states that there was only one genuine auction of state enterprises in the Russian Federation in which the treasury was not shortchanged. This concerned the state-owned telephone holding company Svyazinvest, the sale of which he describes as the 'direct cause of the internecine battle between the oligarchs' which led to the August 1998 financial crisis.[20]

This list of recent privatization mishaps in 'emerging markets' is becoming tiresome. It is by no means exhaustive. It is also far from demonstrating that market failure is so ubiquitous as to overwhelm the prospects for successful privatization in all these countries (although it may be sufficient to establish that privatization is likely to fail in at least a few of them). Perhaps the only general conclusion to be drawn is that such problems are sufficiently widespread, visible, and recurrent to elicit a substantial risk premium in world capital markets, and that a great deal of further confidence-building and institutional reform will be required before these doubts can be fully dispelled. Given the scale and complexity of the privatization and post-privatization tasks still to be undertaken, therefore, it seems almost inevitable that further resistance will be generated and uncertain whether recent reform momentum can reliably be maintained. Between 1990 and 1998, according to the ILO, privatization and deregulation have reduced the amount of good quality employment available in the major economies of Latin America. It estimates that for the region as a whole the proportion of the labor force consigned to the 'informal' sector rose from 52 percent to 59 percent over that period. This was attributable to a decline in public sector employment from 15.5 percent to 12.9 percent of the workforce, and a decline from 32.7 percent to 28.4 percent in the formal private sector. In such circumstances, and in conditions of electoral democracy, the potential and actual losers from privatization can be expected to generate some degree of resistance and even obstruction. Of course, this discussion can provide no more than a very partial indication of the balance of forces at work. To take the analysis further we would need to choose between the available theories of what drives privatization in emerging markets.

V. LOPSIDED THEORIES

This section summarizes five alternative ways to account for the region-wide upsurge in privatization initiatives, in each case checking the argument against pertinent examples. The assumption is that each approach, although one-sided, contains at least some degree of insight, but that more than one approach is needed to account for the range of experiences. In the recent period only one of these theories – the first, namely liberal universalism – has dominated the public debate and the thinking of most policy-makers. By setting this 'hegemonic' viewpoint side-by-side with other equally useful alternatives, the aim is not to refute liberal universalism, but rather to underscore its incompleteness. The preceding discussion has already indicated that a combination of several approaches may be needed to fully account for any specific national process. The five possible approaches are liberal universalism; cyclical interpretations; wave theories; catch-up theories; and structural explanations.

Liberal Universalism

As this volume attests, privatization in Argentina bears sufficient resemblance to privatization in Poland to permit a systematic comparison of the two countries. Supervising a recent doctoral dissertation on the Hungarian privatization agency, I was able to draw on analogous writings about the Mexican state bureaucracy without too great a sense of incongruity. Although this is more speculative, it is at least possible that those knowledgeable about Romania would find points of reference in the experiences of Nicaragua. More generally, then, this provides us with a *prima facie* case that the processes under study are, if not completely universal, then at least very widely distributed. Wherever liberal values, private property rights, and processes of peaceful exchange between unconstrained juridical equals are understood and appreciated, a similar logic of pro-market reform can be anticipated. This broad predisposition toward liberal universalism can be reinforced from various directions. An influential school of economic analysis regards the reduction of transaction costs as a virtually universal imperative, from which far-reaching and recurrent institutional consequences can be derived. Desires for individual autonomy and security can be posited in a similar way, as the foundations for an almost universal endorsement of standardized property rights (and fundamental human rights of a broader kind). More contingently, but equally powerfully, the logic of the contemporary international economy may be so relentless and universally present that economic agents and enterprises with the most dissimilar histories are subject to its homogenizing impact.

These are weighty considerations, and they help us to understand what might otherwise seem inexplicable – the sustained pursuit of remarkably parallel programs and policies in so many diverse and structurally distinct societies. But, of course, the analysis would be incomplete if it failed to deal with another aspect of these disparate realities, namely the fact that before 1989 (in eastern Europe) or before 1982 (in Latin America) the desire and need for, or feasibility of, wholesale privatization was perceived only by a handful of visionaries. Neither a liberal cultural heritage, nor the wish to reduce transaction costs, nor aspirations for individual self-realization, nor indeed the need to earn a living in the international marketplace, gave rise to any serious drive for the divestiture of state assets or the enhancement of economic competition. If anything the dominant tendency was towards greater state ownership and regulation. Liberal universalism was under siege.

So this theory needs some account of its prior constriction before it can explain its current success, let alone predict an unconstrained future ascendancy. This may seem unproblematic to east Europeans, for whom subjugation by the Red Army could be thought to account for everything. But Latin Americans, securely lodged in the US sphere of influence are not able to dismiss the difficulty so lightly. Even in Chile, Peru and Nicaragua, where functional equivalents of the Red Army can be conjured up, everyone knows that there was widespread popular support for increased statism before the switch to privatization. Elsewhere, the Brazilian Constitution of 1988, the Uruguayan plebiscites, and the electoral preferences of the Venezuelan voters all testify to the limits of liberal universalism. International market pressures may have intensified, but that is not enough on its own, certainly not for the indefinite future. So this theoretical position is insufficient to explain why privatization was not sought before the 1990s and so it provides unreliable assurance that privatization will continue to be favored in coming decades. It may help to underpin current policy choices, but on its own it seems thin. Other alternatives will be required to supplement it.

Cyclical Interpretations

On 2 February 1999, President Ernesto Zedillo announced his intention to reform articles 27 and 28 of the Mexican Constitution so that, with effect from December 2000 (when he expects to leave office), private domestic and foreign investors will have the right to acquire or construct new electric power stations. The justification offered for this measure was surprisingly similar to the terms on which, on 27 September 1960, his predecessor from the same party, President Adolfo López Mateos, had justified the nationalization of the electricity industry (meaning their purchase from the foreign owners through a stock market takeover). López's Secretary of Finance, Antonio Ortiz Mena, elaborated on the nationalization measure, explaining that the rapid growth of demand exceeded the likely increase of supply that the private foreign companies were willing to create through their investments, and that the country required an integrated national network, in particular capable of delivering electricity to the regions and to the countryside. Zedillo justified the opening of the electricity sector to private investment on the grounds that large new investments in modern capacity were required, and he preferred to use state resources to meet social needs. On the basis of this example one could construct a cyclical theory according to which the underlying public interest remains rather stable over time, but that at one stage it seems best served by nationalization, whereas at another the same interest seems best served by privatization. It is important to note that in this instance the Mexican authorities are not claiming that nationalization was an error, or that the resulting state enterprises were inefficient. On the contrary President Zedillo stated that the objectives pursued in 1960 had been 'very satisfactorily' fulfilled by the Comisión Federal de Electricidad.

Latin American economic history provides various other examples that would seem to confirm a cyclical interpretation. Most striking is the history of oil production in Bolivia. In the 1920s Standard Oil was brought in to provide the capital and technology needed to tap Bolivia's geological potential. In 1937 Standard Oil was expropriated, and the state-owned YPFB acquired a monopoly over these promising assets. In 1955 the monopoly was revoked, and foreign companies were again invited to do what the Bolivian state was unable to do on its own. In 1969 the Gulf Oil concession was nationalized and YPFB regained its monopoly status, at a time when hydrocarbons were becoming the country's leading economic activity. In 1997 YPFB was 'capitalized,' meaning that in effect the new multinational partners required control over the sector, in return for a commitment to bring in large amounts of new capital and technology. What this example seems to demonstrate is that throughout the century the Bolivian state has been seeking to reconcile conflicting aspects of the public interest. Privatization has been found to serve one of these public policy objectives (modern and capital intensive prospection) but at the cost of another (national control, and the formation of national expertise, in the exploitation of a key natural resource). The solution has been to alternate between policy stances. On this cyclical interpretation it remains to be seen whether the new capitalization formula will prevail for the indefinite future, or whether it too will prove exhaustible and reversible after another generation or so.

More debatable examples of a cyclical pattern would concern the privatization of state-owned banks in Argentina, Chile, Mexico and elsewhere. When these banks proceeded to engage in unsound borrowing, and thereby entered into a state of generalized insolvency, they were 'rescued' by the public authorities, who effectively nationalized the risks that the private sector had assumed. This provided an attractive one-way bet for the beneficiaries of privatization. They were effectively licensed by the state to gamble with the funds of their depositors. If they won, they kept all the proceeds, and if they lost, the taxpayer would have to assume the liabilities. So long as prevailing doctrine insists on the evils of state ownership in the financial sector, investors may be tempted to repeat this cycle indefinitely. (It is not a phenomenon confined to poorly regulated 'emerging markets,' as the US Savings and Loan débâcle of the 1980s amply demonstrated.)

Another area where this kind of long-term cycle is particularly likely concerns the pensions industry. The failings of universal state provision in Latin America require little elaboration. This has given rise to a very widespread shift towards privatized pension provision. But it is foreseeable that in at least some countries as the privatized schemes reach maturity, a large section of the elderly population will have been left in indigence. If democratic processes remain in operation, some reaction against the present fashion for personal pensions, and in favor of a restoration of universal coverage and defined benefits can readily be anticipated.

Each of these examples is rather distinct, and could provide the basis for a specific variant of cyclical theory. What they all have in common (and which distinguishes them all from the unilinear assumptions of liberal universalism) is that the conditions leading to a decision to privatize are viewed as time-limited. Once privatization has occurred a new constellation of forces and incentives emerges which is itself subject to shifts over time. Thus, in a first post-privatization phase the restoration of state ownership may seem unthinkable (it would render worthless all the adjustment costs incurred to bring about the new state of affairs). But over time those adjustments come to be seen as 'sunk costs,' and the relative merits of private vs. public ownership can again be assessed in terms of a pragmatic evaluation of the locus of the public interest. In due course that evaluation may shift against private ownership. The coalitions which support it may come to be seen as self-serving and contrary to the collective good. Then state intervention could be undertaken again. But in turn the same cyclical forces that erode the privatized sector would also come into play here too.

Although there are some good arguments in favor of the cyclical hypothesis the counter-arguments also deserve considerations. If we regard privatization as essentially no more than a component within a broader process of economic liberalization, we have to consider whether such liberalization as a whole is likely to go into reverse. Provided trade liberalization and the opening of capital markets remain intact, a bias towards privatization will be 'locked in' to economic policy. For the present it is difficult to envisage what would be needed to produce a wholesale reversal of the overall trend towards liberalization. But despite this, in particular markets and specific political conjunctures individual privatizations could fail or be repudiated. This could take the form of re-regulation rather than re-nationalization. In federal systems the center may privatize, but the states may try to reassert control.

At the most abstract level, one might hypothesize that any particular system of ownership/management of productive enterprises may become complacent and collusive with the passage of time. A drastic change in public policy can have the effect of galvanizing management into greater efforts, and subjecting long-standing systems of economic organization to critical scrutiny. The extension of state ownership in Latin America may initially have served some efficiency-enhancing purpose of this kind, just as the current wave of privatization may be doing. But what happens thereafter could be a more open question.

Wave Theories

Cyclical theories concern long-run patterns of change in a single process. Wave theories concern successive changes across a series of cases that are closely linked in time. For example, the Peruvian oil nationalization of 1968 was clearly a factor in precipitating Bolivia's action against Gulf Oil the following year, and both helped to create the climate of opinion for the Chilean copper nationalization of 1971. The privatization of British Telecom in 1984 opened the door to successive measures of the same kind in other European countries than in Latin America, and most recently in Eastern Europe. As these two examples indicate, wave theories and cyclical theories are not necessarily mutually exclusive. Both can be in operation simultaneously, and each may reinforce the other.

There are alternative variants of wave theory just as there are variants of cyclical theory. All need a precipitant cause in the first episode; a transmission mechanism from early to late instances of the process; and some way to account for the limits of the wave. The key task is to identify the initial precipitant factors adequately. Transmission may then be at least partly explained by the operation of similar causes in analogous cases, encouraged by the first demonstration that the process is feasible. The limits of the wave may then be understood either in terms of the absence of analogous conditions, disillusion with the results of previous experiences, or some deliberate reaction or blocking mechanism. (The same reasoning applies to sequences of military takeovers, or waves of democratization, or the collapse of communist regimes.)

With regard to privatization, there are three main areas we might explore in a search for initial precipitant factors. The first, as emphasized in the introduction, is fiscal crisis, or more generally economic over-reach by the public sector. In Latin America this is generally associated with the 1982 debt crisis, although it arrived earlier in some countries (Chile and Peru) and was postponed until later in others (Venezuela). Privatization typically followed, but not until after a considerable time lag. Initial steps were mostly quite timid. In general the wave did not build up into a crescendo until around the mid-1990s. So we might look to a second supplementary area. This would concern academic and intellectual debate and even fashion. During the 1980s socialist ideas lost ground in the face of challenges from reinvigorated liberal theories, and the emergence of new orthodoxies in economic analysis. The Chicago Boys in Chile were very conscious of this aspect of causation, and they aimed to prove the superiority of their ideas by applying them more quickly and wholeheartedly than elsewhere. In other countries the intellectual debate moved more slowly, and it was not uncommon for new policies to be introduced before the rationale for them had been fully internalized. Brazil is a good example of a reluctant and somewhat unbelieving convert. In Cuba the debate is still rejected, and yet some policy measures have nevertheless been adopted. To account for this disjuncture between theory and practice it is helpful to turn to a third possible area of explanation – pressures and incentives generated by the international economy. The collapse of the Soviet bloc eliminated an alternative source of resources, and increased the confidence of international investors and multinational corporations in the safety of expanded operations in the 'Third World.' The Washington-based international financial institutions (greatly empowered by the consequences of the debt crisis) became much more active in promoting market-oriented structural reform in Latin America. Again, different countries were affected differentially. Mexico (with the prospect of entry into NAFTA) was subject to particularly compelling international inducements to privatize. Ecuador was not.

This sketch of the three main types of precipitant factor should serve to illustrate the potential explanatory power of wave theories. But it is not by any means fully specified, and only scratches the surface of the issues.[21] When all three types of inducement are weak, it is more likely that the privatization will fail to take hold. In Venezuela, for example, the hope still exists that an expansion of the oil industry will overcome the fiscal crisis. Venezuelan élites have not been won over by neo-liberal theory. And the international economy may not exert the same pressures in Venezuela as in non-oil countries.

Catch-up Theories

The most celebrated 'catch-up' theory is that of Alexander Gerschenkron, whose *Economic Backwardness in Historical Perspective* (1962) argued that whereas the United Kingdom, as the first industrializing nation, required very limited state involvement in the economy, the later industrializers had to make a great collective effort of discipline to mobilize resources if they were to catch up with the leader. Hence German industrialization was more statist than that of Britain. Extending the argument to its limit, Gerschenkron suggested that it was the extreme backwardness of the Russian economy which explained the extreme statism of the Soviet system. The limitations of this theory as an account of these cases is nowadays all too apparent, but a version of this hypothesis can be adapted for use in the comparative analysis of privatization. In this context the independent variable would not be the absolute level of economic development, but rather the scale of the economic failure associated with the pre-privatization regime. The further below potential, the greater the policy effort that may be justified to induce a national economy to 'catch-up' with its neighbors, and with the standards of competitive efficiency achieved in the outside world. On this reasoning, Chile and Argentina have made greater and more sustained efforts to promote pro-market reforms (including privatization), because of the depth of their preceding systemic crises. Brazil never underwent such a severe setback, and therefore cannot muster the unity and resolve to pursue comparably drastic strategies of 'catch-up.'

This is obviously rather simplistic, but it may have some explanatory power, at least when undertaking selected and controlled comparisons. The question of case selection is of particular importance here – only after screening out irrelevant or inappropriate cases is the analysis likely to generate much leverage. Clearly, the Cuban economy is performing further below its potential than most in Latin America, but it does not follow that an exceptionally far-reaching program of privatization is to be expected there. The Uruguayan economy has long performed poorly, and underwent a period of extreme crisis at roughly the same time as Chile, but with different results. Nevertheless, at a time when Argentina, Brazil, Paraguay and Uruguay are all undertaking extensive adjustments in order to make their economies compatible within Mercosur, it is reasonable to expect that the pressures for reform in any one country will intensify if voters and consumers find that this is the only way they can 'catch-up' with the higher standards or faster improvements being enjoyed by their now more directly comparable neighbors. Similar considerations probably apply within other experiments in 'open regionalism.'

As a tentative suggestion, one might hypothesize that 'catch-up' effects may be more powerful levers of change in certain industries and sectors than in whole economies. For example, if an outdated national telephone monopoly fails to meet business demand in one country when a privatized and digitized service is boosting the efficiency of competitors in another, then the logic of 'catch-up' may induce a telecom privatization, without necessarily stimulating broader reforms. Similar considerations could apply in particular to other types of international business service, such as airlines, banking and insurance. This hypothesis leads on to a fifth and final area of theorizing.

Structural Explanations

A final set of explanations for the privatization process directs attention to the requirements of industrial structure. These differ, both between industries, and over time. At the height of the railway age, for example, the logic of a unified and coordinated transport system seemed to exclude the disciplines of competition and to maximize the potential for monopolistic exploitation. This industrial structure favoured state ownership, and in due course that was the system that came to prevail in almost all major railway systems, including Latin America and Europe (where, to be sure, the logic of war always played a part). For a variety of reasons which deserve further examination, it is currently believed that many railway systems can better serve the public interest through privatization.[22] Here we have an example of an explanation based on industrial structure, including the changing requirements of an industry in its stages of growth, maturity and decline. Something approaching the reverse pattern might make more sense for the information technology industry. In its early days it required huge investments of capital and specialist know-how with only very uncertain and long-term prospects of commercial reward. The industry therefore required the nurture of lavish public investment (and also the shelter of government-imposed controls to protect dissemination of the most promising lines of discovery). Large missile defense and space research budgets and classified communications systems in the public sector financed the development stage of the industry. But as it reached maturity the range of commercial applications multiplied in an explosive and unforeseeable manner. Secrecy and monopoly became the enemies of industrial development. Whereas the Soviet system clung to these statist arrangements, and so lost its position in the development of the industry, the Americans in particular promoted forms of private appropriation and dissemination of the technology, thus giving the USA its current ascendancy in this hugely transformative industrial sector.[23]

Undoubtedly most industries are located somewhere between these two extremes, and in any case it would be reductionist to conclude that industrial structure alone *determines* the pattern of state or private ownership/management. Nevertheless, there are some quite promising lines of enquiry here. Large domestic markets may provide better benchmarks for competition between privatized firms than small home markets which either shelter a monopoly supplier or retain no domestic supplier at all (for example, airlines). In very general terms we might distinguish between standardized mass production, involving the reliable but repetitive performance of precisely defined tasks; and interactive customized variable lines of production. The first (Fordist) could be delivered through large-scale vertically disciplined production until such firms might be candidates for public ownership (the great nationalized industries of western Europe at mid-century). The second ('flexible specialization') can only be produced through knowledge-intensive horizontally coordinated networks that can monitor and respond rapidly to shifts in customer demand, or in technological possibilities. Insofar as any economy's productive structure shifts from Fordist to flexibly specialized types of activity it could reasonably be argued that this will virtually necessitate some accompanying shift from state ownership to privatization.

VI. PARTIAL OUTCOMES

Throughout the 20th century Latin American leaders have been searching for the right form of government, and the most appropriate development strategy, to resolve the inherited deficiencies in their societies. Over the past decade an unusually wide and deep consensus has emerged that the best governmental form is democracy, and that the most appropriate developmental strategy is outward-oriented and pro-market. Privatization has gathered momentum as an integral component of this new consensus, and as a powerful (and perhaps irrevocable) means to cement the linkage between political and economic liberalization. Privatization has also been promoted with a number of both macroeconomic and sectoral objectives in mind. It is also supposed to help to 'depoliticize' the economy, and to stimulate a more entrepreneurial society. In view of this multiplicity of objectives, and the still incomplete nature of the associated reform processes, we can hardly expect to arrive at a definitive and uniform evaluation of its success. Certainly this chapter has tended to emphasize complexity, diversity, and the potential for chain-effects of results spread over time, some of which may correspond to initial intentions, while others will not. That assessment must not disguise the fact that in many cases some form of privatization (and a more general shift toward economic liberalization) was unavoidable – the previous economic model had reached an impasse. Moreover, there are at least as many examples of spectacular success as of unanticipated difficulties. Privatization has gathered momentum during the 1990s because in many cases it has been found to work surprisingly well.

This may eventually turn out to be the final verdict, and we may conclude that at the end of the 20th century Latin America did eventually settle on both a form of government and a strategy of development that could be continued, deepened, and made irreversible for the indefinite future. However, the broad-gauged, long-run, comparative perspective adopted in this chapter has drawn attention to at least three potentially substantial qualifications.

First, by comparing the current wave of privatizations with an earlier wave of nationalizations, and by highlighting cyclical, catch-up, and structural considerations, it has brought into question the dichotomous reasoning which underlies the current consensus. Instead of viewing all aspects of previous interventionist experience as misconceived, and all aspects of a current market orientation as inherently superior, it has provided a perspective through which to relativize such judgments. In particular, it leaves open the possibility that the current wave of reforms will turn out to be one more episode in the long succession of Latin American experiments in search of the right development strategy. In that event it will deliver some benefits, encounter some resistances, deteriorate over time, and in due course face a further round of experiments aimed at overcoming the (rightly or wrongly) perceived failings of the latest model.

Second, this raises the question of the potential 'reversibility' of measures which must currently be sold as irreversible (otherwise private investors will not respond appropriately). Both the sketch of the current scene in Section IV above, and the various explanations of privatization reviewed in Section V raise doubts about the irreversibility of the current property regime. Historically, external shocks – violent fluctuations in the availability of international capital inflows, combined with the openness of the markets to which Latin American trade has been oriented – have destabilized earlier sequences of market-oriented internationalism. Perhaps the international political economy has now been rendered secure against further upheavals of this kind, but that is to take a lot on trust. Were the international environment again to become more unfavorable at some point in the future, the irreversibility of the new model would depend upon the solidity of its domestic foundations. For example, the preservation of private property rights would depend substantially upon the strength of the rule of law, and the quality of the legal and justice systems in place in Latin American countries. If impunity for violating property rights were to continue, then arbitrary infringements of the property system would tend to recur. Similarly, if social inequalities were to be left untouched. Perhaps the most specific way to underscore the continuing reversibility of the privatized economy is to focus on bankruptcy procedures. There are really only three basic possibilities, even though actual outcomes may be hybrids. Either market failure leads to liquidation of the enterprise and the reassignment to other agents of the assets thus released; or it leads back to public ownership; or if the absence of bankruptcy proceedings is accompanied by a rejection of public ownership, then it leads to repeated cycles of the privatization of profits and the socialization of losses, creating 'moral hazard' each time the balance sheet is cleaned up and the assets are passed back into private ownership. Until the first option is securely established in contemporary Latin America, the privatized economy will not be fully irreversible.

Third, there is the issue of the 'public interest' under conditions of political democracy. Neither democracy nor the market are entirely secure as yet in Latin America, but let us work on the assumption that both are likely to persist and become more deeply entrenched. In that setting, defining where the public interest lies involves a complex process of debate, bargaining, and political interaction. If democracy becomes consolidated, then voters, citizens, and parties will expect to play their part in shaping that public debate. In broad terms they may be constrained by the wish or need to respect market rationality. But, as this chapter has indicated through its discussion of definitional issues (in Section II), and of the range of timing and sequencing possibilities (Section III), the market does not generate a unique static equilibrium solution to every problem of allocation and distribution. It too involves a succession of complex balancing acts. If both democracy and the market are to coexist and to interact in accordance with the public interest, a considerable degree of mutual adjustment will have to take place. This would mean not merely that a durable liberal democracy must be market-friendly, but also that a broadly privatized economy may be subject to extensive political re-regulation.

NOTES

1. Although this chapter focuses on Latin America, it contains a few cross references to post-communist Eastern Europe, and some of the lessons are perhaps of more general applicability. However, post-communist privatizations arise from very different initial conditions, so that their trajectories and consequences are unlikely to be that similar.
2. Leslie Elliott Armijo (1999), p. 23.

3. William Glade (1996a), p. 23.
4. Dieter Helm (1989a), pp. 32–3. This section concludes 'despite the apparent consistency and coherence of the theory behind the general policy approach, the programme has frequently resorted to *ad hoc* pragmatism . . . it has often been plagiarised to meet political necessity. The result is frequently a mishmash of ideas, influences and values' (p. 36).
5. Glade (1996a), p. 23. Just what kind of behavioral constraints have motivated the managers of PDVSA is not a topic closely examined by Glade, since it might undermine his overall enthusiasm for market disciplines. This case has been examined in considerable detail by Juan Carlos Boué in his 1996 Oxford D.Phil. dissertation. The Chávez administration is now attempting to curb such anti-state managerialism, but risks lurching to the opposite extreme.
6. Carl J. Bauer (1998), p. 121.
7. The Chilean case is among a series evaluated by Raquel Alfaro, Ralph Bradburd and John Brisco (1998). The Valparaíso municipal water and sewage system was privatized at the end of 1998, but within a fairly strong regulatory framework. The public sector retains a 'golden' share (to control possible takeovers), horizontal integration is forbidden and vertical integration is restricted. This set the precedent for a subsequent larger privatization of the municipal water and sewage utility in Santiago.
8. Similarly TPSA accounts for about 40 percent of capitalization on the Warsaw stock market and telecoms also head the list in the Czech Republic and Hungary.
9. Eli M. Noam (ed.) (1998), p. xv.
10. Noam (1998), p. xvi.
11. Noam (1998), p. xxiii. This provides something of an antidote to the optimism expressed by Glade concerning Argentine telecoms (Glade (1996a), pp. 17–18).
12. Noam (1998), p. xv–xvi, and xxviii. Again this judgment runs counter to the positive evaluation given by Glade, but corresponds to my own observations in Bolivia.
13. Noam (1998), p. xxvi.
14. Noam (1998), p. xv.
15. Argentina's new 1995 Insolvency Statute shifts power from the Labour Court to the Bankruptcy Court, and to committees of creditors and to the receiver. However, analysts express doubt over how they will really work. There is no new legislation elsewhere in Mercosur.
16. 'The Chilean case suggests that a well-ordered hierarchy of ministries staffed with competent personnel is key. Such a hierarchy limits and orders points of access, thus favouring policy coherence. However, extremely insulated, rigidly ideological policy-makers in contact with a narrow coalition of conglomerates may contribute to skewed reform measures and inflexible policy-making styles.' Eduardo Silva (1996), p. 9.
17. Marukh Doctor's forthcoming Oxford doctoral dissertation on the Brazilian port privatization process amply illustrates these features. The September 1999 postponement of plans to privatize Banespa (Brazil's fifth largest bank and a key asset of the state of São Paulo) could provide another eloquent case study of how state–federal relations can become entangled with tax and pension regulations to produce a procedural gridlock.
18. Although this seems a fairly solid generalization, initial reactions within the Mexican political class to President Zedillo's February 1999 proposal to privatize the Federal Electricity Commission suggest that it may not be a universal law.
19. For example in Puerto Rico the government earmarked some of the $2.1 billion proceeds from the telecom privatization to finance overdue infrastructure spending that would overcome the island's problems of water shortage, in association with General des Eaux and Thames Water.
20. The Soros consortium paid $1.9 billion in 1997 for a 25 percent stake in Svyazinvest, but this produced little discernible effect on how the company is run. It has proven unable to exert effective control over the 809 operating companies which are controlled by powerful regional bosses, such as the Mayor of Moscow.
21. Indeed, John Welch made a fair comment on a draft of this chapter at the April 1999 conference, when he referred to 'wave observations' rather than 'wave theories'.
22. To some extent this may be driven by the increased value of the real estate assets that would be released in comparison to the residual transport services still provided.

23. It would be highly speculative to suggest that later on, when this industry matures, it might become more of a candidate for state ownership, although the current Justice Department case charging Microsoft with monopolistic practices is intriguing.

REFERENCES

Alfaro, Raquel, Ralph Bradburd and John Brisco (1998), 'Reforming public monopolies: water supply', in Nancy Birdsall, Carol Graham and Richard H. Sabot (eds), *Beyond Trade-Offs: Market Reforms and Equitable Growth in Latin America*, Washington, DC: Brookings.

Armijo, Leslie Elliott (1999), 'Balance sheet or ballot box? Incentives to privatize in emerging democracies', in Philip Oxhorn and Pamela K. Starr (eds), *Markets and Democracy in Latin America: Conflict or Convergence?*, Boulder, CO: Lynne Riener.

Bauer, Carl J. (1998), *Against the Current: Privatization, Water Markets, and the State in Chile*, Boston: Kluwer Academic Publishers.

Doctor, Marukh (forthcoming), 'The politics of port reform in Brazil', (Oxford D.Phil. due for submission in early 2000).

Gershenkron, Alexander (1962), *Economic Backwardness in Historical Perspective*, Cambridge, MA: Harvard University Press.

Glade, William (1996a), 'Privatization: pictures of a process', in William Glade (ed.), *Bigger Economies, Smaller Governments: The Role of Privatization in Latin America*, Boulder, CO: Westview Press.

Glade, William (ed.) (1996b), *Bigger Economies, Smaller Governments: The Role of Privatization in Latin America*, Boulder, CO: Westview Press.

Helm, Dieter (1989a), 'The economic borders of the state', in Dieter Helm (ed.), *The Economic Borders of the State*, Oxford: Oxford University Press.

Helm, Dieter (ed.) (1989b), *The Economic Borders of the State*, Oxford: Oxford University Press.

Herrara, Alejandra (1998), 'Argentina', in Ellie M. Noam (ed.), *Telecommunications in Latin America*, Oxford University Press, ch. 11, pp. 131–56.

Noam, Eli M. (ed.) (1998), *Telecommunications in Latin America*, New York: Oxford University Press.

Oxhorn, Philip and Pamela K. Starr (eds) (1999), *Markets and Democracy in Latin America: Conflict or Convergence?*, Boulder, CO: Lynne Riener.

Silva, Eduardo (1996), *The State and Capital in Chile: Business Elites, Technocrats and Market Economics*, Boulder, CO: Westview Press.

Soros, George (1998), *The Crisis in Global Capitalism*, Boston: Little, Brown.

COMMENTS ON LAURENCE WHITEHEAD, 'PRIVATIZATION AND THE PUBLIC INTEREST: PARTIAL THEORIES, LOPSIDED OUTCOMES'

Alexander Kozhemiakin

Dr Laurence Whitehead states at the beginning of his chapter 'Privatization and the public interest' that his work is just a preliminary review of the conceptual issues surrounding the world-wide privatization trend. Despite its preliminary nature, the chapter is very thorough, replete with illustrative 'real world' examples and thought-provoking theoretical insights. In fact, the main attraction of Whitehead's piece is that it generates new questions by identifying gaps in our current thinking about privatization. Of particular importance is his putting the current enthusiasm for privatization into historical perspective, thereby highlighting the potential for reversibility of the processes which may now appear irreversible.

The most basic, foundational issue addressed by Whitehead is the very definition of the process of privatization. Like 'democracy' or 'liberalism,' 'privatization' refers to a wide variety of phenomena that are similar in some critical respects, yet that may contain important differences or variations which tend to be masked by being subsumed under a single heading. The chapter identifies three definitions of privatization. In brief, the first one is the narrowest, defining privatization as an ownership transfer. The second definition takes a broader view by adding the possibility of privatization through liquidation and 'simulated privatization,' in which state-owned enterprises are subject to the same market constraints as private firms. Finally, the third definition views privatization as a broad policy orientation with an initial pro-market theoretical foundation.

Whitehead himself prefers to use privatization as an umbrella term encompassing a large number of sub-categories in order to capture a 'prevailing pro-market internationally-oriented mood in favor of liberalization – a *zeitgeist* as much as a calculated choice'. By doing so, he asserts a link between privatization and a policy of economic liberalization (broadly defined as the 'Washington consensus') even though he stresses that in some cases the results of privatization may not be pro-competitive, because of regulatory distortions or institutional weaknesses (for example, unreformed judiciary). Yet, even if we set aside an important question of regulatory prerequisites for successful privatization – since this is ultimately an issue of implementation (as opposed to original intentions), there appear to be many cases in which the proposed link between privatization and economic liberalization is quite tenuous. Allow me to elaborate:

If we define privatization most narrowly as a transfer of ownership from the state to private hands, it would still remain a very complex phenomenon, as it can be used to achieve many disparate objectives including:

1. enhancing long-term productive efficiency of the economy;
2. signaling to domestic or international audiences a commitment to economic liberalization;
3. attracting foreign direct investment;
4. financing structural public sector reforms (for example, transformation of a social security system);
5. financing immediate fiscal gaps;
6. deliberately altering a balance of political forces in the society;
7. creating opportunities for personal gain.

While the first four objectives are consistent with a thrust of neo-liberal economic policies, the last three either contradict that thrust or bear no direct connection to the 'Washington consensus.' What if a government implements privatization primarily because the resulting proceeds allow it to continue with an otherwise unsustainable fiscal policy? The problem here is that it is difficult to know when privatization is used for 'neo-liberal purposes' and when it is merely a convenient way to finance bloated current expenditures without spurring inflation. In this regard, it has been insightful to observe how the initial lukewarm support by President Chávez's administration for privatization in Venezuela completely eroded during 1999 as oil prices (and thus Venezuela's fiscal revenues) continued to rise. Arguably, many other Latin American countries have more market-friendly Presidents. Still, how much of President Cardoso's commitment to privatization can be explained by his desire to meet goals 1 to 4 and how much of it stems from the fact that Brazil has a really big problem reaching goal 5? If one takes a cynical, yet plausible, view that the latter is much closer to the reality, then, in spite of its potential neo-liberal side-effects, a wave of privatization which has encompassed Latin America in the 1990s has not been driven by neo-liberal intentions.

It is also possible to use privatization as a tool to change a political balance in the society. Russian officials in charge of privatization explained their preference for an extremely speedy process of transfer of state productive assets into private hands by emphasizing the perceived need to quickly create a powerful class of property owners who could then defend the process against the anticipated political and bureaucratic opposition. Deliberate attempts to boost the status of the propertied class through the intense privatization program can also be detected in Chile under General Pinochet. How consistent is this goal of altering the balance of political power with economic liberalization? The answer is not clear, as it at least partially depends on whether the power structure is changed to ensure the viability of neo-liberal reforms or whether other goals, such as the survival of a certain political faction, dominate. At least in the Russian case, the process of privatization did succeed in creating a group of 'oligarchs' capable of defending their new property, but it did little to promote the societal acceptance of neo-liberal ideas. As a result, if anything, the distorted privatization experience has undermined popular support for economic liberalization.

And then, of course, there is corruption. In the absence of the proper regulatory environment (which, almost by definition, most 'emerging' economies of Latin America, Asia, Eastern Europe, Middle East and Africa lack to a varying degree), privatization creates enormous opportunities for public officials to either enrich themselves or to increase their power by handing out favors. Once again, privatization driven at least in part by these motives is not exactly what those promoting the 'Washington consensus' had in mind.

Given the wide variety of goals, not all of which are neo-liberal, that can be potentially achieved through privatization, it becomes clear why Whitehead finds that the existing theories of privatization are incomplete (his chapter discusses five different theoretical approaches). First and foremost, a good theory has to provide an answer to the question of why privatization takes place when it does. The preceding discussion suggests that there can be at least seven answers to this question and, to some extent, all of them can be simultaneously true.

12. The neo-liberal experiment in Latin America: an evaluation

Albert Fishlow

INTRODUCTION

Over the last 15 years Latin America has changed decisively. It is not only the economics, but the politics that has altered as well. Today, after primary elections in Mexico, a close presidential election in Chile, and a change of the ruling party in Argentina, democracy seems more deeply embedded than it ever has been. But the ultimate persistence of that pattern depends very substantially on whether the new capitalist model – termed by some the neo-liberal experiment – can, and will, survive.

This new style of economic development is far different from that of the past. Latin America had gained prominence previously by its application of an import substitution model in the post-war period that promised rapid and efficient industrialization. It failed to deliver that objective – Brazil and Mexico were the prominent regional exceptions – and along with that attempt came fundamental disequilibria in foreign trade and domestic expenditure that only in the 1990s are finally being resolved.

Some see in the new model a strong line of foreign influence. But although some of the changes required in the 1980s were first termed the 'Washington Consensus' by John Williamson, it is important to appreciate their strong local emphasis. Inflation was brought under control everywhere by limiting the expansion of money, but the particulars of that process varied substantially. In Argentina, it was a fixed exchange rate; in Brazil, first the anchor was the exchange rate, but that was successfully switched in 1999 to monetary and fiscal policy; in Chile, it was a much longer process of control over expenditures. In similar fashion, the nature of trade strategy has been far different. National influence has been of the essence.

Members of the 'Left' everywhere have been forced to rethink their earlier commitments to larger government expenditures and active participation in the economy. That is not to suggest their support of the current experiment. They have been quite critical of the results so far, and with good reason. Growth rates throughout the 1990s have been quite modest, and that was before the general decline in 1999. Income distribution has failed to show signs of sustained improvement, even where economic expansion has been strong, as in Chile. Exports have expanded weakly in recent years as commodity prices have headed downward. These problems are not idle ones. They help explain the change in party in several recent national elections.

There is wide agreement that the changes that have emerged thus far, although impressive, are not enough. The Inter-American Development Bank has spoken of the need for a second stage of reforms to bolster those already taken. In Brazil, the political right, symbolized by Antônio Carlos Magalhães, has gone further, insisting that income distribution should receive immediate priority over the claims of the International Monetary Fund. More drastic and elaborate political alteration has occurred in Venezuela.

Yet, if the new model is to be effective, it will have to retain as a centerpiece the three major changes in economic policy that have already been established. First, a low rate of inflation must continue as the basic objective of macroeconomic strategy. Second, the new initiative of privatization must be sustained and deepened: the state should be the regulator of economic activity rather than the manager. Third, the recent openness to trade must be extended. That means not only limited protection against imports but more active pursuit of exports higher up the ladder of comparative advantage.

Only in these circumstances will the present commitment to capitalism prove sustainable and worth the effort. Only then can one move on to the long needed social reforms that can begin to alter the present conditions of concentrated income distribution and deprivation of the chance for the many to grow as successfully as the few.

MACROECONOMIC POLICY

Stabilization has occurred over the last 15 years throughout the region. The rate of inflation in Latin America as a whole has descended to single digits, a marked contrast to the earlier average of hundreds of percent a decade ago. It has not been easy: Argentina's Austral Plan failed, and gave rise to runaway price increases before the successful commitment to the currency board. Brazil's Cruzado Plan similarly, but even more quickly, faded, giving rise to many additional efforts before the *real* was introduced in 1994. Mexico only seems to be returning to single digit price increases in 2000, many years after the major devaluation in December, 1994. Chile moved up significantly in inflation before the inauguration of a civilian, Patricio Aylwin, in 1989, requiring his Concertación government (supported by Christian Democrats and Socialists) to prove its capacity for restraint.

As clever as the successful anti-inflation strategies have been, there is no special secret that lies behind their ultimate success. Two factors are fundamental. First is the careful management of the public sector, and thereby the avoidance of sustained monetary expansion. Second is the ability to secure increasing external creditworthiness. Let me explore each of these.

Inflation comes from substantial and continuous increases in the money supply. That in turn results from significant public sector deficits that cannot be financed through external or internal debt increases. These are the first sources usually utilized in order to avoid a large increment in local money. They also quickly become unavailable as fiscal deficits mount and continue. Then one is forced to rely on the forced savings that temporarily result from public issue of money, until higher and higher rates of inflation force holdings of money to be substantially reduced and end that gain. Most calculations suggest that rates of inflation much above 10 or 15 percent are potentially unstable and carry no benefit.

In an initial period of inflation containment, the rate of exchange of the domestic currency against the dollar usually plays an essential role in guaranteeing stability. Argentina went to the extreme of setting up a currency board and a fixed exchange rate associated with it, in order to control inflation. Nothing less would work in the midst of a rampant rise in prices. But in most other cases – Brazil most recently – the exchange rate has to be replaced by domestic monetary and fiscal conservatism. Otherwise, as we have seen, the outflow of foreign reserves becomes impossible to contain.

This process of moving from the initial support of the exchange rate to domestic economic policy is central to the continuing success of the policy. It is also the most difficult part of the task. The degree of creditworthiness – measured by the interest rate differential required on external borrowing – makes a big difference. If one is required to pay interest rates with a spread of 20 or 30 points (and not basis points), as Brazil did in 1999, the task becomes much more difficult. The primary internal deficit, exclusive of interest payments, can be small, while the deficit inclusive of interest payments turns out to be very much larger. It is the latter, of course, that must be financed.

Today, one sees large interest rate differentials among countries. Asia, despite the 1997 crisis, again exhibits much lower margins than Latin America. And within Latin America, Chile currently has real interest rates of about 5 percent – despite having moved to a floating exchange rate – while Brazil has real rates above 10 percent. Even Argentina, fixed exchange rate and all, is somewhere between the two. These values provide a measure of the differential creditworthiness assessed by outside investors.

Chile has a low interest rate because of its historical record of full payment of its external debt; because of its limited public debt; because of its recent real rate of growth exceeding 6 percent over the last decade; and because of the growth and diversification of its external exports. Brazil has a much higher rate because of its historical record of inflation; its high level of public debt, including a period of temporary default; its poor growth performance in the 1980s and early 1990s; and because its level of exports in 1999 will only be a little higher than in 1996.

Nonetheless, rates in the region have come down. The end of the international turmoil beginning in December, 1994, with Mexico and ending with Brazil in January, 1999, has been a principal reason. Apparent recovery in Europe and Japan, while ironically causing rises in local rates, have also helped to reduce differentials. The question now is whether domestic rates of investment will correspondingly advance, beginning a continuing period of economic growth above the 5 percent level that is required to assure high rates of employment.

That issue is related to another. Savings rates within Latin America have been one of the great disappointments of the post-war period. Whereas in Asia these have moved to levels of 30 percent and above, Latin America continues with less than the 20 percent it had already attained in the 1950s. Chile is virtually the only exception. While frequently credited to its private social security system, now imitated in much of the region, only a limited proportion of the Chilean gain can appropriately be allocated to this source. There are many valid reasons for reform of social security in the region, including current high returns to the public sector as in Brazil, but a guaranteed high personal saving gain is not among them.

Part of the reason for the comparatively large regional differentiation within Latin America is the higher level of public savings in Asia. Here is where a significant and decisive change is possible to accelerate Latin American performance. Larger public sector savings can be accomplished through a mix of increased revenues in some countries, where public command over resources has been low, and through reduced central government expenditures in others. This is not a casual proposal. While government policy in the aggregate has been much altered by the new macroeconomics, it has not always been extended to operating ministries. There, past practices and frequent excess spending continue. Thus there is scope for economy. These savings can be made available not only for badly needed public areas such as education and health, but, more fundamentally, can also be allocated to finance private investment.

What is being advocated is no less novel than the anti-inflation programs that have begun to flower throughout the region. It is a full reversal of past practice where the private sector saved, and the public sector spent. Now the public sector will have responsibility for assuring an adequate level of saving, and it will be the obligation of the private sector to determine areas for the profitable application of capital – using market rather than government rules.

This alteration in responsibility is made the more necessary by the reality of the privatization process that has occurred in recent years. The public sector has become smaller and has much less managerial obligation. Private investment is now needed to assure effective growth of such areas as telecommunications, electric energy, petroleum, finance, steel, and so on. Some of the resources will come from abroad, but this should be a marginal rather than a major source.

To a considerable degree, domestic saving has become a crucial element for Latin America. Up to now, it has not responded positively to high domestic interest rates. Some believe saving will come automatically with resumption of growth, thereby avoiding any serious constraint. But even if a strong private response comes, it will have to be coupled with the fundamental change in the role of the public sector discussed here. Ending inflation is the consequence of more effective monetary and fiscal policy. Starting cumulative growth will be the consequence of the combination of higher levels of private investment and public saving.

PRIVATIZATION

The broad commitment to the private sector that has evolved in Latin America over the last decade has been, with the exception of the Chilean case, more a means than an end. It has occurred as a practical consequence of stabilization policy: resources were needed early in order to establish the credibility of the anti-inflation programs. They could come more quickly and reliably through sale of national resources than from increases in taxes. In the cases of Argentina, Brazil, Mexico, Peru and others, the extent of privatization has become universal, and for one fundamental reason: there was the need for continuing finance. Only later did the consequences of private ownership for productive ends make itself felt.

Chile was different. There, privatization was a political response accompanying the coup against the Marxist government of Salvador Allende; and in Chile, the process of terminating nationalization played a relatively minor role in the move to stabilization. There the concern was less the net sum received by the Treasury from privatization than the ideological statement inherent in the process. It was accomplished early, and with much less governmental profit than later instances. In this regard, the relationship with the process in Eastern Europe is worth noting: Russia's virtually complete privatization – the fruits of which soon thereafter fell into the hands of the new 'robber barons' – is ironically the most comparable case. Chile, at least in the 1980s, avoided that.

Privatization has both a macroeconomic and microeconomic logic. The resources obtained from the sale immediately served as revenue to finance current government expenditures. But this effect occurs only once. Other sources become necessary in the next period to cover outlays, or expenditures must be reduced to avoid deficits. The positive effect on productivity, on the other hand, is a continuing one. In the first instance, it reflects itself in an initial displacement of labor employed. Thereafter, it is associated with continuing gains in output from the application of new, and more advanced technology. This negative employment effect, sometimes offset by direct payments to labor, as well as the accompanying higher salaries received by workers in the state sector, explains a good bit of the opposition to privatization. Elaborate legal actions have delayed planned sales; political opposition has been organized; and news accounts have been widely disseminated of apparent corruption in organizing sales.

Telecom privatization has been notable in its technological novelty. Cell phones have become prominent in the major countries of the region, and at progressively reduced cost. Buenos Aires is predicted to become 25 percent dependent on cell phones over the next two years. In Mexico City, São Paulo, Santiago, and other large cities, usage has also grown rapidly. Such substitution promises real capital savings over the next several years, something that was not initially envisaged when sales were first undertaken. Equal efficiencies, if less dramatic in their origin, are possible in other activities ranging from steel production to local supply of water where privatization has occurred.

Spain has been particularly active as a source of demand for many of these formerly nationalized sectors. Spanish investment stands out, virtually throughout the region, in the resources committed to telecommunications, electric power and finance. The country has rapidly moved up as a competitor to the United States in foreign investment committed to the region. Moreover, linkages of investment have spanned more than a single country. One is seeing new strategic planning emerging from the sales repeated in country after country. Very much in the picture, moreover, is the competition between the United States and Europe for a special trade relationship with the countries of the Southern Cone. Spain heads up the European effort.

Privatization has thus been extensive in Latin America. Hundreds of billions of dollars have been transferred. Yet it is still too early to reach definitive conclusions about its net consequences. Initial contracts were, on the whole, favorable to the purchasers. These have usually gained the opportunity to raise their prices immediately – something difficult to accomplish under public ownership. But in return they have been compelled to accelerate their supply substantially. Telephone service throughout the hemisphere is now more reliable and available than it had been previously. So is a variety of other goods and services newly produced by private sources.

In some areas, such as privatization of toll roads, results have been less impressive. Large tolls have led to modest usage and financial problems. This is not altogether surprising. The mere fact of private ownership and management is no substitute for careful economic analysis and pricing. These newly private activities almost always fall into the category of 'social overhead capital,' widely necessary for efficient direct production. As such they inherently play a critical role in the future.

Much of the eventual evaluation will hinge upon the regulatory framework that is put together to keep track of these newly privatized activities. This is an area where much effort, and much institutional borrowing, is needed. Especially in smaller countries, some of these newly privatized sectors will have monopoly capability. It will require careful regulation to avoid replicating the past, when public control created no incentive for efficient expansion, as well as to avoid giving the foreign private interests complete command over all major decisions.

Most countries are at the very beginning of this process. As the new investments mature, they will require a public statement of principles on which they can rely in the future. The private bargaining process that was so typical of the import substitution period is an inappropriate basis for the future. Some countries additionally will have problems related to the overlapping interests of the state (or provincial) and central governments: Brazil immediately comes to mind. Other countries will face an inadequate judicial appeal process. Such issues, substantially in the background in the past, will begin to emerge in the immediate future.

Privatization means changing, not eliminating, state interest in these important sectors. Moreover, regulation will function best in a democratic setting, where open participation will help guarantee the quality of decisions. Historically, countries in the region suffered from regulated sectors that bore low prices, out of concern for indexes of inflation and adverse reaction from the urban sector. There will be temptation to repeat that experience, which in the short term seemingly extracts national benefits from foreign owners. In the opposite direction, the new owners must avoid immediate private profits at the expense of longer term gains.

It has been more than two generations since the extent of private participation has been as substantial in the region as it is currently. If anything, investment in these areas is much more likely to increase rather than diminish over the near term. The test of the new capitalism will be the ability to combine the initiative of investors with the constraint of public regulation. This will be as novel to Latin America as is the anti-inflationary thrust of macroeconomic policy. Both are integral parts of the structure that has been under development for the last several years.

OPENNESS TO TRADE AND INVESTMENT

Latin America today has a much smaller amount of trade relative to gross product in 1999 than it did in 1950. After decades of commitment to import substitution, and consequent reduced reliance on external commerce, it has now embarked on a new strategy. The international arena has been perhaps the most reliable source of growth in the post-war period. International trade has expanded at a rate just about double the rate of annual internal growth over this interval, and its variation has been smaller in recent years.

Trade has provided one of the means used by Asian countries to increase their incomes. South Korea and Taiwan have per capita levels of foreign trade that are something like three times the Latin American average. Other Southeast Asian countries, such as Thailand, Malaysia and Indonesia, have benefited from expanded commerce. Even India has begun to pay attention to the external sector.

To a considerable degree, the recent Latin American success in achieving low rates of inflation has been much dependent upon opening the economy to imports. Just as privatization was the means toward the goal of fiscal balance, so reduced tariffs and a diminution of trade barriers have equally proved essential components of stabilization. The potential price competition of foreign imports, and their actual substantial quantity rise in the first years of stabilization, provided an important means for preventing a recurrence of inflation. That is the reason for the rapid growth of United States exports to the region in the early 1990s, and explains why support for the Free Trade Area of the Americas in this country moved forward so substantially at the same time.

This dramatic rise in imports was financed primarily by increased foreign investment, both direct and that through the financial market. Exports, while gradually moving upward over the post-war period, had only managed to reach a region-wide real rate of growth of 5 percent a year in the 1980s. In the 1990s, that almost doubled, to a level of more than 9 percent, but adverse terms of trade had a negative impact on current dollar trade exchange. Exports were not sufficient to meet the task.

That rise in foreign investment unfortunately contributed to the Mexican imbalance in 1994 and the subsequent recession. One of the requirements that the region has not yet met is an ability to regulate its balance of payments successfully. A good part of the reason for the negative aggregate regional performance in 1999 was the need everywhere to restrain imports. That is something Latin America learned in the 1980s. But it is not the most effective way to deal with the problem: clearly, export growth is far more desirable. That we clearly see in the rapid Asian recovery now underway, but it is a hard lesson to learn for much of Latin America.

Mexico has differentiated itself from its neighbors during the recent period since NAFTA came into effect. Over that interval it has achieved an annual rate of increase of exports of something like 20 percent. Contrary to early expectations, the establishment of free trade with the United States and Canada meant a continuing source of external demand that helped Mexico out of its 1995 downturn, and contributed to its subsequent expansion. As a result, despite growing aggregate investment, Mexico's current account deficit is estimated to rise in 2000 to a reasonable value of little more than 3 percent.

What Mexico has been able to achieve has not been widely duplicated in the region. Chile, virtually alone, has also had a continuous growth of exports. New fruit and vegetable products have been introduced, wine and salmon have taken their place among the leaders, and paper products have shown expansion. But copper remains the principal export commodity. Perhaps the most important change for Chile has been the development of an Asian market: Today, that region receives more exports from Chile than does the United States.

For the larger countries, the performance has been much more mixed. Brazil, Argentina, Peru, and Colombia have all had difficulty sustaining their exports during the recent period. And this is in the midst of a record expansion of United States activity that had yet to cease at the end of 1999. To be sure, prices of commodities have been low, aggravating the difficulties. But the region's failure to move up the export scale has also been a problem: unlike the Asian countries, Latin America has never moved into the export of computers, consumer electronics, and similar goods that have been much in demand in recent years. Instead, it has stayed with the commodities, automobiles, machine tools, and so on, that have been the staples for the last two decades.

In the midst of the continuing discussions surrounding the Free Trade Association of the Americas, obviously complicated by the failure of the United States to approve 'fast track' procedures, the countries in the Southern Cone have moved toward a regional free trade arrangement. Mercosur, incorporating Argentina, Brazil, Paraguay and Uruguay, has grown more rapidly in its internal trade – at least until 1999 – than in exports outside the region. Associate members Chile and Bolivia have been accepted, and discussions have already begun with the Andean Pact.

But the substantial Brazilian devaluation has had the expected negative regional consequences. Brazil – whose *real* had been somewhat overvalued since 1994 – had become the largest Argentine market overall, and especially for manufactured goods. At the heart of the relationship – and also one of the most difficult issues – is the question of trade in automobiles. Argentina had the wit to except it from free trade; Brazil has been struggling since to accommodate. It is one thing to seek compromise and adjustment in order to allow production to flourish in both countries; it is another when relative national prices have suddenly changed by something like 50 percent. In other industrial areas such as textiles, shoes and steel, similar problems have evolved. They are being resolved by temporary quotas against Brazilian imports. These arrangements have been worked out in the midst of ever tenser diplomatic relations between the two countries. It is no accident that Argentina's President-elect Fernando de la Rua made his first foreign visit to Brazil, mere days after his election, and that trade was very much on the agenda.

The permanence of Mercosur and NAFTA, let alone the establishment of a potential FTAA, are dependent upon limited variation in real exchange rates. Even in the case of Mexico, what saved matters in 1995 was the differential size of the United States market, as well as the continuing growth there. That made acceptance of larger Mexican exports, and reduced imports, possible. Their size was large relative to Mexican gross national product, though modest for the United States. But Argentina and Brazil, despite a significant difference of population, are not of dissimilar aggregate income. Brazil's advantage is less than double Argentina's, compared to the ten-fold difference between the United States and Mexico.

That is the reason why Argentina's outgoing President, Carlos Menem, strongly advocated adjustment of internal debt, a sharp decline in Brazilian real income and a fixed exchange rate in January 1999, in preference to Brazil's actual choice of devaluation and a permanently floating exchange rate. He saw that this would make Argentina unable to compete. That is also why, on virtually every subsequent occasion, Argentina has emphasized the need for a fixed future exchange rate, if Mercosur is to flourish. Brazil has agreed to study this new linking of the countries of the region, but more as a political salve than a serious commitment.

It remains to be seen whether these regional alliances, or a future one, can effectively substitute for a broader commitment to exports that Latin America very much needs. For Mexico, linked ever more closely to the flourishing United States, and benefitting from growing automobile production that exceeded that of Brazil in 1999, NAFTA looks to be much more positive than some had initially speculated. In large measure that is the product of continuing United States growth, but widening trade specialization and growth in the north of Mexico have also contributed. Indeed, with reduced domestic inflation and a stronger peso, there has been much discussion in Mexico about a possible dollar link as a final way of assuring macroeconomic stability and more rapid expansion.

Certainly, the initial conditions seem to be present. Mexico has some 80 percent of its trade with the United States. An equal amount of foreign investment originates there. There is free exchange of capital across the border. Two other factors help Mexico: emigrants, while subject to formal limitations, move northward illegally in large numbers, and domestic monetary policy, set in the Bank of Mexico, is now isolated from politics as a result of legal changes.

The only real issues are two-fold: the seignorage emanating from peso issue, which would disappear with circulation of the dollar; and the question of central bank assistance in the event of crisis. Neither appears insuperable. The former can be reasonably estimated, and allowance made through an inter-governmental grant. The latter can be accommodated. What is necessary – and for the United States is certainly not simple – is the creation of a Federal Reserve District in Mexico City (and in Toronto), thereby giving the two neighboring countries participation in the existing system. That may now seem to be out of the question. But another decade of extraordinary growth in trade may change the situation.

The consequences for Mexican interest rates would be substantial. Differences from the United States 10-year bond would diminish from the 491 basis points reported in mid-November, to a margin of 100 or even less. That would clearly have very positive consequences for Mexican investment rates and long term growth prospects. Domestic macroeconomics would become irrelevant.

To some degree, successful Mexican integration into the United States market, whether or not it goes all the way to dollarization, is already a reality. For South America, the pattern of future association is much more complicated. We have already discussed the Mercosur, and some of its current problems. The Andean Pact is much affected by the political problems affecting some of its members, as well as the inherent problem of limited transportation links and modest trade levels. A likely outcome is a South American Free Trade Organization that could negotiate with NAFTA.

In the end, openness to trade for Latin America has to extend beyond inter-regional commerce. It is the broader external world that counts for almost all of the countries in the region. For them, there can be no substitute for greater reliance on imports. The region has made a commitment to reliance on market forces through its extensive privatization and its acceptance of careful monetary and fiscal policy. A major impulse to future growth can come from the further step of expanded trade. That is what the past expansion of the international market over the last 50 years, as well as the current creation of the World Trade Organization, and its extension into such areas as investment, patents and subsidies, tells us.

Freer trade is perhaps even more revolutionary for the region than controlling inflation or extending the role of the private sector. It goes against the grain of a century and more of high rates of protection and the emergence of national policy. But without the force of international competition, the capacity to proceed with the rest of the agenda becomes doubtful. In the worst case, domestic political interests will dominate, and at the cost of a return to protection of particular sectoral interests, much expenditure for industrial policy, and ultimate denial of market signals.

CONCLUSION

The capitalistic model that has been asserted here is neither neo-liberal nor foreign in its conception. It is much more likely to emerge as a Latin American contribution to the Third Way that British Prime Minister Tony Blair has sought to popularize. It is far from the vision of survival of the fittest predominant at the end of the last century.

Over the course of the last 15 years, we have seen an impressive narrowing of initial divisions in economic choice, not merely within the region, but externally as well. The countries of Western Europe, Eastern Europe, Asia, and the Middle East are all embarked on experiments granting greater power to the market, while at the same time seeking to retain cultural individuality. This is a different world than that viewed by Raúl Prebisch (Latin America's leading advocate of 'inward-directed development') in 1949.

Latin America requires much more than the threefold commitment to stable macroeconomics, private microeconomics and expanding trade stressed above. That program is just the beginning of the reforms needed. Multiple and sequential reforms are required to begin to deal with the fundamental institutional features needed. But they are likely to be easier to accomplish within a context of continuing economic expansion.

The major missing element is a vigorous commitment to expanded public education. The deficiency here with respect to Asia in average number of years of training has substantially reversed since the 1960s. Here is a great irony. Countries in the region spend substantially on education, but a large part of those resources goes to virtually free public universities of high quality but limited enrollment. A great number of students come from private secondary schools charging significant tuition; this is how students manage to pass the difficult entrance examinations. Until this issue is confronted seriously, little will happen to bring the high rates of income inequality down to reasonable proportions.

Other areas of concentration can easily be added. Better provision for health and housing come immediately to mind. So do requirements for a social safety net to ensure that unemployment is matched by minimal conditions for survival. In some countries, the question of land reform still remains. In others, now largely urban, issues persist of how to ensure an effective public sector. What is essential is that the initial priorities are not vitiated. Too much to be done easily translates into too little result. Latin America has to follow its neo-social model to its logical conclusion.

13. Institutions and property rights across time and space: lessons from Eastern Europe and Latin America[1]

Lee J. Alston

History matters.[2] This statement is intuitively appealing to scholars researching transition economies as well as to the casual observer. A large part of its appeal is its vagueness: it can mean different things to different people. Yet, to be useful to the analyst, we need to specify the myriad ways in which history determines where you can go from here. By so doing, we will be able to construct testable hypotheses about the importance of different historical factors. In this way we can help policymakers limit the extent to which 'history repeats itself.' In this chapter I will explore the possible ways history mattered and will matter in the future. In so doing, I will draw on examples from the chapters in this volume.

HISTORY BEFORE THE TRANSITION/PRIVATIZATION PROCESS

'When You Ain't Got Nothing, You Got Nothing To Lose'[3]

This quotation captures the concept of opportunity cost. A greater discontent with the past allows a leap of faith to markets. In short, societies risk little if the past was miserable. For Central Europeans the bitterness toward past 'invaders,' in particular the most recent period of Soviet control, encouraged them to adopt markets more quickly than they otherwise might have. For example, Kochanowicz argues that for Czechoslovakia, 'For all its isolationism, the experience of 1968 seemed to bury whatever sympathies existed in Czechoslovakia for Marxism–Leninism, contributing at the same time to the emergence of the civil liberties movement of Charter 77.' (Chapter 7, p. 171.)

In a similar vein for both Central Europe and much of Latin America, the dissatisfaction with authoritarian regimes encouraged a more general move to liberalism, of which markets are a part. On the economic front, the 1980s were disappointing years for Latin America and Central Europe. Compared to the West, both regions slumped. In Latin America, the eighties were known as the 'Lost Decade.' Several authors illustrate this statement. Graham argues that for most of South America:

> … authoritarian regimes have undergone liberalization or collapsed, and democratic transitions have gained the upper hand. Where the military was dominant and economic performance did not measure up to expectations, pressures grew to return power to civilian leaders. … military governments built technocratic alliances in which macroeconomic projections supported by economists in key industries and private-sector business leaders looked to the state to create the conditions for sustained economic growth, and to maintain order. …Yet in very few cases did these policies produce the economic breakthrough these technocratic alliances promised … (Chapter 8, pp. 183–4.)

Several Latin American countries have moved toward privatizing land. The rationale is a disappointment with the economic performance of communal agricultural arrangements. Hall lists Mexican, Peru and Ecuador as examples.

For Central Europe there was a noted slowdown in the eighties compared to the West. Brada in particular highlights this element:

> Another factor conditioning the popular response to economic travails of the early transition period was the performance of the East European economies in the decade of the 1980s. ... this decade was one of extremely slow growth in most of these countries; GDP growth was less than 1 percent per year as both technical progress and capacity utilization slumped. … and they kept falling further behind the advanced industrial countries in the application of new technologies. These poor dynamics of the socialist economy affected popular perceptions of transition-era economic performance in two ways. First, both policymakers and ordinary people had been aware of communist-era economic stagnation, and so they may have responded with less alarm to the post-transition downturn than they might have had if the last decade under communism had been one characterized by buoyant growth of consumption and output. Second, it is likely that the growth of the post-1993 period that characterized most transition economies represented, in fact, a significant ray of hope. (Chapter 4, pp. 79–80.)

Given the generally low performance in the 1980s across most of the formerly communist countries, it is not economic performance *per se* that matters for prompting change, but performance relative to expectations. In this light, are we to presume that those countries that embraced more dramatic reforms were disillusioned with the past regime? Kochanowicz argues that '… support for economic liberalism was also quite widespread internally, even well before the political turnabout of 1989. In a large measure, it was a product of disillusionment with earlier attempts of market socialism reforms.' (Chapter 7, p. 160.) And, do formerly high expectations lead to lower expectations about the transition and more patience in waiting for returns from the transition?

Greskovits argues this for Hungary, but for Eastern Europe as a whole, it appears that the jury is still out.

'One Does What One Knows How To Do'[4]

Differing experiences with markets in the past have shaped the differing attitudes of the respective populations and of the opinion makers (leaders) toward markets. To embrace markets whole-heartedly means to internalize the notion that markets entail mutually advantageous voluntary exchange. To those, for example, the Russians, with little or no experience with capitalism, the transition to a market economy would be fraught with difficulties. On this point it is worth quoting Chirot:

> Unfortunately for Romania, the period of rapid industrial growth lasted less than one full generation [1925–1937]. This was not enough time for many Romanians to learn the skills necessary for operating in a modern economy. Hungary and Poland began their economic modernization at least 30 to 40 years before Romania, and the Czechs earlier than that, so that by the start of the communist period, all had had about three generations of experience. ... This is what the historical legacy of differential rates of modernization really means: skills are learned, but given only a small period in which to develop them, a society may lose them relatively quickly, too. (Chapter 5, pp. 115–16.)

Similarly, Greskovits maintains, 'what separates Hungary from the less successful radical reformers is that this country did not have to start economic liberalization from ground zero. On the contrary, the Hungarian success might have been facilitated by a number of institutional and behavioral legacies of its long "market-socialist" period.' (Chapter 6, p. 128.)

Though most countries in Latin America have always viewed markets with some suspicion, all have had private markets for most of their history. For this reason, there was less of a transition issue than for the formerly communist countries. Many countries that embraced state intervention in the 1970s and 1980s on the ideological grounds that markets advantaged the élite and foreign capitalists (dependency theory) swung back to favoring the market during the lost decade of the 1980s.

Equity also Matters

The ability to privatize and the support for privatization depends on the perceived legitimacy of privatization. For both Latin America and the formerly communist countries, the previous regimes were seen as favoring the élite. This seems to have been more the case in Central Europe than in Russia or some of the other Eastern European countries, for example Romania. In the formerly communist countries, the party hierarchy was perceived as enjoying advantages, whereas for those Latin American countries that underwent hyperinflation in the 1980s the poor suffered disproportionately. In both situations public opinion regarding the legitimacy of policy and the perceived distribution of the gains affected the pace of the move to markets. A relatively equal income distribution may help societies weather the storm of transition. Greskovits argues that this was the case for Hungary, '... the absence of extreme income inequality and of poverty of a Third World type ... may have contributed to weakening the threat of violent political mass actions.' (Chapter 6, p. 132.)

Ethnic/Religious/Political Fragmentation

Fragmentation may occur across many lines; ethnic, religious, political or class. In the face of significant fragmentation, institutional change is difficult to achieve. Some of the fragmentation in the formerly communist countries has deep historical roots. Before the break-up of communism, fragmentation was kept in check by a coercive state, but the process has recently recrudesced in a number of countries, most dramatically in the successor states of Yugoslavia. In the absence of a sense of trust, it is difficult to provide the credibility necessary for institutional change, and without a credible commitment to change, private capital will not flow in. Ethnic fragmentation accounts for many countries' willingness to cut their ties with Russia while within Russia, political fragmentation *inter alia* has made it impossible to adhere to the rule of law. For most of South America fragmentation is less of an issue, though some countries, for example, Brazil, face significant regional cleavages based on disparate economic interests. Meanwhile, religious beliefs are more diverse in Eastern Europe than in Latin America. Interestingly, in the view of one researcher, the recent track record suggests that, in Eastern Europe, Catholicism is associated with greater ease of transition than is Orthodoxy, for example, as the cases of Poland and Slovenia seem to indicate.[5]

LOOKING INTO THE CRYSTAL BALL

What can the recent transition/privatization process tell us about the future? After ten years of transition are there any lessons we can learn? Has the wave of privatization in Latin America washed ashore? Is there an undercurrent to the wave of privatization? Much would be gained by having answers to these questions, but I am not so bold as to suggest I know what they are. Nevertheless, at the risk of stating the obvious, there are some signals as to what lies ahead. In particular I will focus on the extent to which the reform movement will be sustained, maintained or rolled back.

Have Reforms been Perceived as Fair?

Perceptions of fairness by the public at large constitute an important determinant of public policy in the countries discussed in this volume. People care about both their levels of income and their income relative to others. In a similar vein, the gains or losses associated with privatization have both a direct income effect on citizens, as well as an income effect relative to other citizens. The greater the sense that the costs and benefits of privatization are shared widely, the greater the likelihood that the process is viewed as legitimate and as such will be maintained. Here the track record across our countries is mixed. In Hungary, Greskovits argues that democratization allowed a peaceful channeling of grievances that kept the lid on mass protest movements. In addition the government targeted those most politically potent who might have been harmed by the transition. As such, the transition included pension, wage and social benefit increases. Kochanowicz argues that Poland's transition also involved recognition and compensation to some of the groups harmed by the transition: 'a slow process of dismantling the socialist welfare state, as well as hidden subsidies to inefficient state enterprises, which allowed them to keep workers on the payroll, might also have reduced social tensions – albeit at a certain cost in economic efficiency.' (Chapter 7, p. 167.) This contrasts sharply with the case of Russia and other countries that formerly made up the Soviet Union. Goldman maintains that the perception of privatization is that it enriched a few while disadvantaging many. The social indicators of crime and declining life expectancy are in accord with this view. To a lesser degree, the situation in Romania and Bulgaria is one where the transition is perceived as bringing costs to the majority of the population. Chirot states that

> ... as far as the Romanian population is concerned, needless to say, the comparative statistics are meaningless when the brutal fact remains that life is getting harder, not easier, and there is no prospect in sight for immediate relief. Surely this will test the population's will to stick with liberalizing economic reforms and a liberal political regime. (Chapter 5, p. 113.)

The perceptions of fairness from privatization are also varied across Latin America. Those countries that moved slower, for example, Brazil have had a greater political consensus around the reforms than countries which embarked on liberalization based more on the personalities of its leaders, for example, Menem in Argentina or Fujimori in Peru.[6] In the future, I would expect a greater threat of reversal in countries where the initial imposition was less democratically imposed.[7] When times get tough and unemployment increases, as in Argentina recently, public opinion can turn quickly, and the reforms can be reversed.

Institutional Change within an Institutional Context

Reforms were put in place through a variety of political mechanisms from executive decrees to more democratic systems involving checks and balances. In the latter the process entails more 'veto' points, meaning that the reforms are more difficult to reverse. There is considerable variation across the countries studied in this volume. In Latin America, Brazil has the most veto points in its privatization process. Whitehead describes the process as 'incrementalism:'

> In contrast to the Chilean process, privatization in Brazil may be classified as 'measured' in the sense that each step was decided as a distinct operation, rather than derived from an overreacting commitment; that time was allowed for lobbyists to bring their preferences to bear, both for and against; and that the key decisions were subject to legislative and party political debate and oversight. In fact Brazilian democracy provides for multiple (possibly excessive) institutional veto points – legislative, judicial, electoral, administrative and state/federal.[8] (Chapter 11, p. 273.)

Other countries in Latin America give almost free rein to the executive office. These are referred to as strong presidential systems. Perhaps the best example is Peru and the reforms put in place by President Alberto Fujimori.[9] Much of the privatization in Peru resulted from executive decrees, supported by public opinion. Given the fickleness of public opinion, there is little institutional backstop should conditions in Peru deteriorate, for example, if unemployment increases dramatically. Under such conditions I would expect a reversal.

There is a third model of privatization efforts in South America. It might be called populist politics within a working judicial and/or legislative system. Argentina under President Carlos Menem fits this category. Menem was able to push through much privatization based on his popularity that derived from the (initially) successful convertibility plan. Now that the luster of the convertibility plan has worn off and unemployment has increased, the prospect for arresting or reversing state liberalization seems likely.

Lastly, there are some Latin American countries, for example, Venezuela, which appear to cycle from embracing liberalization to state intervention. Such countries lack the veto points to give stability to institutional change. This cycling appears common in Latin America.[10]

For the formerly communist countries the privatization or transition process has generally been framed as one of 'big bang' or 'gradualism.' This misses an important element; namely whether there was an institutional backdrop to provide credible commitment to the changes. For Russia, there never has been an overwhelming consensus in favor of dismantling the role of state in economic affairs. As such the reformers had to garner support by increasing the gains to those with veto power – the managers of state enterprises. Goldman illustrates the early weak constituency in favor of mass privatization: 'Chubais' first goal

... was to create as large a block of supporters for privatization, and as quickly as possible. One way was to allow factory directors and their workers to gain easy access to a controlling share of their enterprise's stock; in effect to make them stake-holders.' (Chapter 9, p. 212.) This might not have been so injurious to the Russian economy if there were limits to the control of the assets of privatized companies. Unfortunately, this was not the case and asset stripping has been all too common.

For most of the Central European countries privatization occurred within a democratic process, making the changes less reversible. Poland, Hungary and the Czech Republic fit this mold. In all three cases there was a 'game plan' to the changes that helped solidify and legitimate the transition process. This was not true of most countries in Eastern Europe, for example, Bulgaria and Romania, where changes have been of the 'stop and go' variety.

Winners, Losers and Political Power

The privatization process creates winners and losers, sometimes intentionally and sometimes unintentionally. For example, did anyone forecast the rise of the Russian oligarchs? Despite the questionable legitimacy of the distribution of the gains or losses associated with privatization, what is important for institutional change is whether those affected have the political clout to maintain, sustain or roll back privatization. In the former communist countries, there have been notable scandals in the process of privatization. In Russia the oligarchs have amassed fortunes in the absence of a rule of law. Because of their wealth, many have political influence. The question to ask is: now that they are rich, do they stand to gain by moving toward a rule of law that would legitimate and solidify their gains?

Russia is hardly the only case in the former Soviet bloc with a less than stellar record of economic performance in the post-communist era. For most of the Baltic nations and the Asiatic CIS countries, plus Armenia, Bulgaria, Bylorussia, Georgia, Moldova, and Romania, the social costs associated with privatization or attempts at privatization have been large, and the number of winners relatively few. Though there is an urban intellectual élite that pushes for privatization, it is constrained by the weight of public opinion. Under such conditions nationalism may emerge as means of deflecting the wrath of a public dissatisfied with the palpable costs that privatization entails. Yet in Central Europe, it is highly unlikely that change will be reversed. Here the question is: at what pace will future reforms occur? The Czechs are pushing forward with privatization of their banks, and the form this will take is influenced by the public's perception that the gains from earlier privatizations have redounded to the few. The front-running Poles have set in motion a virtuous circle, but the farm sector – which never succumbed to collectivization – may block reforms that are needed in the rural areas. In the rest of East Central Europe the rural sector is not so politically potent.

For much of Latin America, especially where inequality of wealth is particularly high, the distribution of gains and losses matters because it affects public opinion. To the extent that public opinion influences political outcomes, the distribution of the benefits and costs matters a lot. For example, the privatization of utilities in Latin America, despite bringing gains to consumers, has been perceived as disproportionately benefiting the purchasers. Such perceptions may influence the shape of future privatizations. For example, will they take the form of concessions, sales with regulatory boards, or price controls? In some instances there have been rollbacks, as Whitehead notes:

> … on taking office the Chávez administration in Venezuela revoked a 38 percent rise in electricity charges authorized by the outgoing Caldera administration at the end of 1998, causing a one-third fall in the share price of Electricidad de Caracas. ... Similarly the Brazilian Minister of Justice imposed a maximum fine of 2.9 million *reais* on each of the two major telephone companies (for São Paulo and Rio) that had been privatized in July 1998, for providing inadequate services. In February 1999 … half a million inhabitants of Buenos Aires were subjected to electricity blackouts which deprived them both of light and of water for about a week. As a result the privatized Chilean operator, Edesur, faces a fine of no less than $75 million. Proposals to privatize the Chilean ports and the post office, and the Mexican electricity generators, have become heated issues in the respective election campaigns. (Chapter 11, p. 276.)

The Latin American honeymoon with privatization may be over as far as public opinion is concerned, but this does not portend a full-scale divorce.

The Outside World: Financial Markets, Trade Agreements, IMF and World Bank

Once banks have been privatized and competition allowed, world financial markets will discipline attempts at renationalization. Of course, this does not preclude some nationalist parties from espousing a return to the old system, but it makes it less likely that any attempts will be successful. The lure of foreign exchange will constrain governments in taking over financial intermediation. This does not mean that governments will not interfere in financial markets, but only that interference comes at a cost.

Trade agreements or economic unions give those with the political will, but lacking the political power, some ammunition to sustain economic reforms in general. This rings most true for those countries who have a reasonable chance in the short term to enter a desirable trading bloc, for example Poland, Hungary, the Czech Republic, Slovenia and some of the Baltic nations. The rallying cry is: 'we must do *x*, if we are to enter the European Union.' For most of the other countries in the region, they are so far from meeting the necessary criteria for entering the EU, that the hope of joining will not determine the fate of economic reform.

In Latin America, trade agreements have not been much of a constraint on behavior, with the exceptions of NAFTA and MERCOSUR. Paradoxically, these two agreements have had opposite effects: For Mexico, being a member of NAFTA has encouraged liberalization, but for Argentina, because of the straitjacket of the convertibility plan, being a member in MERCOSUR has caused some economic pain since the devaluation of the *real* in January, 1999.

Despite recent criticism, in particular that concerning the IMF's handling of the Russian crisis, the IMF and the World Bank will continue to be players in the privatization game. It is clear that some economies are 'too big to fail,' and both institutions have and will continue to devote considerable resources toward economic reform (the World Bank) or preventing economic collapse (the IMF) – Russia and Brazil come quickly to mind. But both will also continue to influence the fate of smaller economies. Note the term 'influence,' rather than 'determine.' The two Washington-based institutions can mitigate the budget constraints that countries face, but they cannot force a country to do something that it does not have the political desire to do. Individual governments have too much private information and agenda control for this to be the norm. Anyone questioning this has only to look at the use of World Bank and IMF resources in most of Africa.

Crises

One of the wild cards in the future of privatization and economic reform is crisis. Crises can be either political or financial. The 1990s witnessed three financial crises that have had worldwide impact: the Mexican, Asian and Russian crises. One thing is certain in times of crisis: governments must do something or at least act is if they are doing something.[11] Whether government action in response to crisis augurs well for economic reform is not clear. For example, in the wake of the Mexican crisis, Argentina privatized its provincial banks, while Malaysia imposed capital controls following the Asian crisis.

Like history, politics matters, and political crises will have unforeseen effects. In some countries, charismatic leaders have or have had considerable agenda control, for example, Fujimori in Peru, Menem in Argentina, or Cardoso in Brazil. What happens when the luster fades from the leader? It depends how much a policy was tied solely to a particular leader and how much it was undergirded by checks and balances. Peru, with fewer checks and balances than Brazil, is more subject to political shock. In other countries, though politics may be less controlled by a single person, certain individuals are in pivotal positions and clearly matter a lot. Yeltsin was certainly such a pivotal player, and it remains to be seen how stable the regime will be without his presence.

In the early stages of privatization in the Czech Republic, Vaclav Klaus was an instrumental force behind privatization. Since the scandals leading to Klaus' departure, no one has stepped in with the same power or authority. The list could go on, but the point is that political crises are more likely to affect those countries where there is less of a stable political equilibrium, and where checks and balances in policy are absent. Russia typifies one end of the spectrum, with neither a stable equilibrium nor checks and balances. Brazil typifies the other end of the spectrum, where some reforms, for example, controlling pension payouts, though needed, are difficult for the Cardoso administration to push through congress. Here the problem seems to be the excess of checks and balances in the Brazilian federal system adopted in 1988.

WHAT HAVE WE LEARNED FROM THE PRIVATIZATION PROCESS?

The main lessons are: (1) there is no political blueprint for successful economic reform; (2) reform is not costless; and (3) economic reform means more than privatization. We do have a blueprint for economic reform itself: secure property rights along with transparent and stable institutions promote economic success. But how to achieve economic reform politically remains elusive. Reform is never costless, and many of those adversely affected are in a position to block or impede change. All political systems have institutional rigidities that often prevent movement toward policies where aggregate potential gains outweigh aggregate potential losses. Several factors prevent the winners from buying out the losers: (1) informational problems abound, and the public at large is often not aware of the costs associated with inefficient policies; (2) there are severe collective action problems associated with making political side-payments; (3) there is not a well-functioning market for making political side-payments, nor would we necessarily want one.[12]

Privatization is easy, compared to establishing the proper institutional framework within which markets prosper. The rule of law involving both a respect for the law and an honest judiciary is not developed overnight, nor are the informal norms that are a large part of doing business in the western world. This in part explains the patterns demonstrated by Good and Bulmer-Thomas in this volume: within each region the relative economic performance of countries in Central and Eastern Europe and Latin America differs little from that of a century ago. Does this tell us that nothing can be done, that the die was cast in the distant past? I do not think so, but it does suggest a large element of path dependence.

What can we learn from the recent as well as the longer-term track record? My conjecture is that we can learn most about turning some countries around by examining carefully those countries that seem to be outliers from a century ago. In South America, the notable relative success story for the 20th century is Brazil, while in Central Europe, Poland takes the laurels relative to a century ago. As Good argues, it is difficult to speculate on the counterfactual growth rates (that is, in the absence of communism), for most of East Central Europe, given the history of political instability in the region.

This chapter has been long on speculation and conjecture, and short on the development of testable hypotheses concerning the role of history in determining the course of the future. Nevertheless, my goal has been to begin the process. I hope that others will join me in testing how history matters.

NOTES

1. For comments, I thank Joseph Love. For research assistance, I thank Andrés Gallo.
2. Kochanowicz uses the same phrase in Chapter 7.
3. Bob Dylan, whom I quote, may not concur with the following.
4. Jonathan Hughes used this phrase to describe why the colonies for the most part adopted the institutions of England. See Hughes (1976), p. 122.
5. See Larry Neal (1999).
6. For Brazil one notable exception has been in the case of land. See Hall (Chapter 10, pp. 232–58, in this volume) as well as Alston, Libecap and Mueller (1999).
7. Here an exception is Chile. Though General Pinochet instituted changes under a military dictatorship, the courts maintained their integrity on economic issues, a fact which may help to explain civil society's acceptance of the reforms after the dictatorship ended in 1990.
8. The recent judicial veto of pension reform is a good example of the multitude of ways legislation can be side-tracked.
9. See Tavera (1999).
10. See Whitehead (Chapter 11, pp. 262–89) for a lengthy discussion of this issue.
11. Yeltsin's government, for example, often seemed to be 'acting as if' it were doing something.
12. For an elaboration of these issues, see Alston (1999).

REFERENCES

Alston, Lee J. (1998), 'A Framework for understanding the new institutional economics', Paper presented at the First Annual Regional Conference of the New Institutional Economics, São Paulo, Brazil, August.

Alston, Lee J., Gary D. Libecap and Bernardo Mueller (1999), *Titles, Conflict and Land Use: The Development of Property Rights and Land Reform on the Brazilian Amazon Frontier*, Ann Arbor: University of Michigan Press.

Hughes, J.R.T. (1976), *Social Control in the Colonial Economy*, Charlottesville: University Press of Virginia.

Neal, Larry (1999), 'A shocking view of economic history', Presidential address to the Economic History Association, Baltimore, Maryland, October 9.

Távera, José (1999), 'An institutional analysis of reforming the state: the case of Peru', PhD. Dissertation, University of Illinois, Department of Economics.

GENERAL COMMENTS: LIBERALIZATION IN LATIN AMERICA: THE REGIONAL DIMENSION

Geoffrey J.D. Hewings

In international parlance, the term 'regional integration' is most often applied to groups of nations; however, in the field of regional science, attention is focused on space usually defined as subsets of national economies. As nations liberalize their economies, attention needs to be directed to the potential for the exacerbation of already serious differences in levels of welfare across regions within these countries; the regional dimension of liberalization is often forgotten in the enthusiastic embrace of a new paradigm for development.

Renewed interest in economic geography and its links with international trade theory have suggested that, increasingly, the appropriate unit of analysis may no longer prove to be the nation, but rather its constituent regions. Liberalization is fostering a greater variety of spatial interactions between regions in one country and those in another. This process has created interesting opportunities and tensions that need to be explored. For example, trade expansion, *inter alia*, will enable exploitation of scale economies since liberalization will expand the market reach, but it is not altogether clear in which country these scale opportunities will be realized. In some cases, regions enjoying some form of competitive advantage may be able to expand their market share at the expense of less competitive regions in other countries. The tensions arise, often within one country, when liberalization can lead to differential gains/losses to different regions. As a result, it is not clear whether the liberalization programs will be welfare-enhancing in the sense of reducing disparities between regions or even between individuals. Further, there are complex interregional feedback effects to consider. In a three-region analysis of tariff reduction in Brazil,[1] all regions (North, Northeast and Center-South) gained in absolute welfare terms, but the share of national GDP accounted for by the Center-South increased. This occurred as a result of the significant interregional trade flows from the Center-South that are necessary to support production in the North and Northeast; but the flows are asymmetrical, with the Center-South far less dependent on the other two regions than vice versa. Countries with a strong regional policy orientation may find that the rules of international membership of WTO may conflict with national policies to address regional competitive disadvantages.

In addition, some of the enthusiasm for liberalization must be tempered with the realities of the spatial structure of economies undergoing this transformation. For example, when the European Union and NAFTA were formed, scholars developed computable general equilibrium models to assess the expected impacts; when MERCOSUL was formed, a similar process took place in Brazil. In Europe and North America, with sophisticated, efficient transportation systems, little direct attention was paid to problems of bottlenecks, delays, inefficiencies and so forth in moving goods and services across more spatially extensive markets. However, some major issues were overlooked in the MERCOSUL case; for example, it was estimated that at one time almost 75 percent of highway trade between Argentina and Brazil used but one bridge with considerable delays and a concomitant increase in transportation costs.

Hence, liberalization's extension into the transportation and general infrastructure arenas may be just as important as the opening of product and service markets. In many cases, such as Brazil, the federal and state governments are ill-equipped financially to address the short- to medium-term transportation infrastructure needs. Yet without significant improvements in interregional connectivity, many of the anticipated gains from liberalization may not be realized. In addition, there is the additional problem of institutional management and commitment; a recent case in the state of Minas Gerais highlights the problems: under the previous state government, a significant portion of the electric utility, CEMIG, was privatized; the newly elected governor vowed to open the whole process up to negotiation once more. Such an action sent chills through international investors, whose concerns about their long-term equity will probably induce considerable caution in the evaluation of future opportunities. In such an environment, it becomes more difficult to attract and sustain much-needed international investment, especially at a time when the state's fiscal position was such that it probably could not afford to purchase back the privatized portion of the utility.

In summary, the geography of liberalization needs to move across a spectrum of spaces – from the international level, to the interregional level within countries, down to the level of urban areas. There is no guarantee that all gains from liberalization will be positive on all spatial scales, and the potential disruptions created – both positive and negative – need to be considered. It is a challenge that makes analysis of the process even more interesting.

Note

1. See Eduardo A. Haddad and Geoffrey J.D. Hewings (forthcoming).

Reference

Haddad, Eduardo A. and Geoffrey J.D. Hewings (2000), *Trade and Regional Development: International and Interregional Competitiveness in Brazil*, Aldershot, UK: Ashgate.

Index